## The Jossey-Bass Nonprofit & Public Management Series also includes:

# CONDUCTING A SUCCESSFUL CAPITAL CAMPAIGN

The New, Revised, and Expanded Edition of the Leading Guide to Planning and Implementing a Capital Campaign

SECOND EDITION

Kent E. Dove

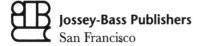

**Jossey-Bass Publishers**
San Francisco

Jossey-Bass books and products are available through most bookstores. To contact Jossey-Bass directly, call (888) 378-2537, fax to (800) 605-2665, or visit our website at www.josseybass.com.

Substantial discounts on bulk quantities of Jossey-Bass books are available to corporations, professional associations, and other organizations. For details and discount information, contact the special sales department at Jossey-Bass.

**Library of Congress Cataloging-in-Publication Data**

Dove, Kent E., date.
    Conducting a successful capital campaign / Kent E. Dove. — 2nd ed.
      p. cm.    (The Jossey-Bass nonprofit and public management
series)
    "The new, revised, and expanded edition of the leading guide to
planning and implementing a capital campaign."
    Includes bibliographical references and index.
    ISBN 0-7879-4989-2 (acid-free paper)
    1. Fund raising—United States. 2. Nonprofit
organizations—United States—Finance. I. Title. II. Series.
    HG177.5.U6 D68 2000
    658.15'224—dc21                    99-6681
                                          CIP

*HB Printing*  10 9 8 7 6 5 4 3 2 1                      SECOND EDITION

# CONTENTS

This book is dedicated to the memory of my parents;
to my wife, Sandy, my friend and strength;
and to our children, Jason and Kerrye,
the pride and joy of our lives.

# PREFACE

In the late 1980s, when I was writing the first edition of *Conducting a Successful Capital Campaign*, I never imagined the response. It was a book that came about by accident; I had never intended to write a book at all.

That changed, however, after a lunch with Lynn Luckow, then an editor at Jossey-Bass and now its president and CEO, and Rod Kirsch, a member of the campaign staff at Berkeley and a longtime friend of Lynn's who is now the vice president for development and alumni relations at Penn State University. We met at midday at the Faculty Club on the campus of the University of California–Berkeley. By the time lunch was over, Lynn had convinced me not only that I was the person to write the book—mind you, I had no outline, no chapters developed, not a word on paper—but also that there was a large audience waiting and eager to read it. I had seen little hope for sales, beyond the usual small group of family members supportive of anything one does; but Lynn was right.

Writing a second edition of the book is something else I thought I would never do. Principles don't change, I reasoned; it's hardly fair to offer readers little more than a rehashed version of something they already have. For two or three years, however, Rod and Lynn have been telling me that it was time to update the book, and so have some of my other friends. The last straw came during a visit to Vancouver in July of 1998, during lunch with my friend and colleague Marilyn Wright and her husband, Charles (a noted Canadian physician). Marilyn, like Rod and Lynn, is someone who knows me too well, and whose suggestions and advice

I find hard to ignore. She too urged me to update the book, but it was Charles who sealed the decision by pointing out that if I didn't do it, I would be "obsolete." Perhaps I am, but I'm unwilling to accept that verdict without a rebuttal. So—for Rod, Lynn, Marilyn, Charles, and others who encouraged this project—here is the second edition of *Conducting a Successful Capital Campaign*.

This volume is an attempt to assemble, in one source, the primary ideas and techniques central to all modern capital campaigns. As such, it sets forth, in systematic fashion, the principles that govern any successful campaign. A small regional historical museum in Virginia conducting a campaign for $1 million must take the same considerations into account as a major midwestern state university attempting to raise $150 million. Therefore, rather than concentrate on the differences among capital campaigns (of which there are assuredly many), this book focuses on their similarities (of which there are even more).

Today's typical educational, arts-related, religious, community, or healthcare organization is considering, conducting, or concluding a capital campaign, and yet many nonprofit organizations are inadequately prepared to plan, initiate, and manage such campaigns successfully. This situation is complicated even further by the large number of inexperienced professionals who hold demanding, high-level positions within these organizations. For example, the National Society of Fund Raising Executives, or NSFRE (1995), indicates that 35.2 percent of the professionals in fundraising have entered the field within the past six years. Likewise, the Council for Advancement and Support of Education (CASE) estimates that roughly one-third of the professionals with whom it is affiliated have had three or fewer years of professional development.

## Audience

Given these facts, who should read this book? It can be used as a review and guide for seasoned practitioners; as an introduction to the principles of campaigning for newcomers, volunteers, and professionals without campaign experience; and as a source for philanthropic agencies that are in the process of assessing the caliber of the programs they are asked to fund. As such, it was written for executives and staff of a wide range of nonprofit organizations: chief executive officers, chief development officers, governing boards, development staff members, key volunteers, and funding agency personnel who desire a fundamental understanding of capital campaigns. The principles discussed throughout the book are equally relevant to arts-related, religious, educational, community, environmental, and healthcare organizations that are either contemplating or conducting capital campaigns.

It is a real challenge to present an effective approach to capital campaigns that is both universal in its application and valuable in specific situations; perhaps this is one reason why so few books on this subject have aimed for such a broad readership. Nevertheless, to judge from my experience as a practitioner, consultant, and lecturer—and from detailed conversations with respected and experienced campaign professionals from all the "third sector" walks of life—I am confident that the principles that govern campaigns are equally applicable to organizations both large and small, and to campaigns that are both local and national in scope.

This book takes account of the fact that many organizations with capital needs, and with the desire to launch capital campaigns, have very small staffs. One-person offices are common; sometimes fundraising is only one aspect of a staff member's responsibilities; many grassroots organizations have no professional development staff members at all. For example, an NSFRE membership survey (1995) found that 31 percent of its members work by themselves, and another third work with three or fewer colleagues. It is possible to conduct a successful campaign under these conditions, but the organization will need to improvise. In many cases, a dedicated volunteer or team of volunteers has conducted a successful campaign in an organization that has no paid development staff at all. In other instances, a member of the administrative staff has carried out the task. Improvising works best, however, when the basic precepts and principles of successful campaigning are followed.

## Overview of the Contents

The chapters in this book are organized around the fundamental issues and challenges that must be met if a capital campaign is to achieve success. Chapter One sets forth the global considerations one must take into account when contemplating a campaign. I identify the ten prerequisites for a successful campaign, which largely form the basis for the remainder of the book. Chapter One also reviews a number of secondary factors that affect the size of the campaign goal and the timing of the campaign.

Thorough preparation sets the pace for the campaign and ultimately determines its result. An organization must assess how ready it is, in the eyes of its external constituencies and those inside the organization, to campaign. Chapter Two discusses the steps that the organization should take early in the campaign process.

The human element of campaigns is emphasized throughout this book, particularly in Chapter Three, which looks at the layperson who leads and the staff member who serves. The success or failure of most campaigns is ultimately attributed to the effectiveness of the members of the governing board, the chief executive officer, and the chief development officer. Their respective roles are reviewed here.

A dedicated volunteer force, in addition to campaign leadership, is essential to accomplishing the goals of most capital campaigns. Chapter Four establishes the procedures for mobilizing volunteers.

Chapter Five examines the single most definitive document in any campaign: the case statement. This chapter describes the characteristics of the case statement, how it is organized, who should write it, and how it should be used in conducting market surveys, enlisting volunteers, and soliciting major gifts.

Chapter Six details one of the most fundamental components of the campaign: the gifts chart. It explains the formula for creating a gifts chart and, more important, the chart's efficacy in raising donors' sights, determining the adequacy of a prospect pool, relating required campaign gift levels to named gift opportunities, and keeping track of the campaign's progress.

There are probably as many different campaign structures as there are campaigns. Chapter Seven lists seven factors that influence the amount of detail a campaign structure requires. The chapter goes on to describe the special campaign functions that have to be implemented by various committees, and it stresses the particular importance of the major gifts committee. Before an organization starts campaigning, it should select an appropriate strategy for soliciting gifts, and Chapter Seven also defines and presents the advantages and disadvantages of various asking strategies. The campaign should also establish, at the very start, a criterion for the gifts that it will report as part of the campaign total over the course of the campaign. As an illustration, Chapter Seven includes an accounting criterion for one campaign.

Chapter Eight, along with Chapter Nine, describes the multistep process for obtaining the major gifts that are crucial to a campaign's success. Obtaining major gifts demands not just a strategy but also thorough research and—in addition to the accurate evaluation, careful management, and systematic cultivation of prospects—skilled soliciting techniques.

Chapter Ten, new to this edition, written by Rodney P. Kirsch, of Penn State, and Martin W. Shell, associate dean for external relations at the Stanford Law School, asks and answers several questions: Who makes lead gifts? What compels such acts of philanthropy? How do lead gifts come to pass? What, if anything, do lead gift donors have in common? Even more important, what environmental conditions influence such gifts?

Chapter Eleven reviews the many operational aspects of the campaign. Discussed in this chapter are the campaign's timetable and budget, the acknowledging and reporting of gifts, donor stewardship, and the selection and use of professional campaign counsel.

Chapter Twelve, by William V. West, a former senior management consultant with Andersen Consulting, former manager of information consulting at Ernst & Young, and currently executive director of Alumni and Foundation Information Systems at Indiana University, is also new in this edition. The technological explosion surrounds us all; this chapter helps define and determine technological needs and discusses how to select technology vendors, the best technologies to use in particular situations, and using the benefits of technology to the best advantage in fundraising.

Several pieces of campaign literature in addition to those discussed in Chapter Five should be developed. These materials and their desired features are described in Chapter Thirteen.

Achieving financial success on schedule is the ultimate goal of all campaigns. Chapter Fourteen discusses how to conclude the campaign successfully and take care of such post-campaign matters as recognizing donors and volunteers, writing final reports, and auditing the campaign's productivity.

Chapter Fifteen contains a look at emerging fundraising trends and at what people conducting campaigns may experience in the twenty-first century. The chapter ends with a brief discussion devoted to the pros and cons of capital campaigns and to the importance that every organization should place on creating and sustaining a continuous lifetime giving program in the years to come.

The book concludes with a section devoted to resources: a sampling of literature taken from several campaigns. The resources are included not only to illustrate the outcomes of processes described in this text but also to enable readers to easily develop the support materials needed for any campaign effort.

There is a growing body of literature about fundraising, and much of what is being written is extremely well done. I hope that others will continue to add to our knowledge about fundraising in general and capital campaigns in particular, and that this book will prove useful to those who do choose to continue. If after reading this book you feel better acquainted with the principles and practices that guide campaigns, then the effort that went into first writing it and now updating it will have been well spent.

*August 1999*                                                        Kent E. Dove
*Bloomington, Indiana*

# ACKNOWLEDGMENTS

Space limitations prevent me from thanking again by name all those who contributed to the first edition of this book. They should all rest assured, however, that I remain deeply grateful to them for their insights and thoughtfulness, and for the help they gave me in writing the previous edition. But there are some people not mentioned in the first edition whom I wish to acknowledge and thank now.

Over the past decade I have done much work in western Canada. One of my assignments was the World of Opportunity campaign at the University of British Columbia (UBC), a campaign that raised $262 million—a record Canadian total, which stood for a decade. (The University of Toronto is now engaged in a campaign that will substantially raise the bar again in Canada.) UBC's success was no accident: what a leadership team! President David Strangway; his chief development officer, Peter Ufford; the campaign's chief operating officer, Ron Dumochelle; and their campaign chair, Bob Wyman—here, arguably, was the best team ever assembled in Canada, and one that goes on the short list of the best leadership teams ever assembled anywhere. Another exceptional fundraiser I worked with in Vancouver is Marilyn Wright, with whom I shared a wonderful campaign experience in service to the British Columbia Institute of Technology. Peter, Ron, and Marilyn are role models for all of us who call ourselves fundraisers; there are no better professionals anywhere.

Three people—Ann E. Kaplan, editor of *Giving USA;* Jan Alfieri, senior coordinator of the National Society of Fund Raising Executives' Fund Raising

Resource Center; and Vicky Martin, manager of research at the Indiana University Foundation—did a great deal to facilitate research on this book. Every time I called looking for something, I had it in hand within a day or two.

Some of my friends and colleagues here at the Indiana University Foundation must be mentioned, too. Curtis R. Simic, president of the foundation, has been a friend for over 30 years. One of the true professionals in our field, Curt encouraged me to rewrite this book and opened the door to allow my use of many internal campaign documents, some never published before; these will be found in this edition's greatly enhanced resources section in Part Two. Kathy Wilson, director of development services at the Indiana University Foundation, and Bill West greatly assisted me in updating the research coverage in Chapter Eight and explaining to me in terms I could understand the use of technology in twenty-first-century fundraising. Lori White, my executive assistant, prepared the manuscript, a task not made easy by my many handwritten notes.

I am most grateful to the many individuals and organizations granting me permission to quote from their work or to use it as illustration. Their contributions have been invaluable.

During the last decade I spent a little more time in hospitals than I had planned. I owe a great debt of gratitude to four physicians—to Thomas O. Clanton of Houston and to Martin Milgrom, Richard J. Hamburger, and Daniel E. Lehman, all of Indianapolis—who did an exceptional job of trying to maintain my health and, when that didn't work, of fixing the problems. Special thanks, also, to the CAPD nurses at the Indiana University Hospital and Outpatient Clinic (now Clarion Health)—Patty, Rita, Connie, Kathy, Kathy, Sandy, and Theresa. I'm fine now, thanks to their care.

Finally, I want to thank all the good people at Jossey-Bass who once again got me through this process. My editor, Dorothy Hearst, asked good questions and gave wise counsel. Xenia Lisanevich, my production editor, took a rough manuscript and turned it into a sparkling gem. Until now I did not believe that one could indeed make a silk purse out of a sow's ear, but Xenia proved it can be done. And of course there's Lynn Luckow: even though he no longer edits books, he now runs the whole show; he remains freshly interested in this book, and his support and encouragement have never wavered.

Two years ago, at Suzanne Thorin's home (she's dean of university libraries at Indiana University), we asked Lynn to chair our library committee for the Indiana University–Bloomington endowment campaign, and he asked me to seriously consider rewriting this book. Lynn, we both got what we wanted; thank you for saying yes to your alma mater.

—K.E.D.

# THE AUTHOR

KENT E. DOVE received his B.S. degree in education from Indiana University in 1968 and his credential as a certified fundraising executive (CFRE) from the National Society of Fund Raising Executives in 1985. After nearly four years of service as Indiana University's executive director of capital campaigns, he was named vice president for development at the Indiana University Foundation in 1997. Before accepting his present position, Dove held various educational fundraising management positions at Rice University, the University of California–Berkeley, Drake University, the University of Alabama, Northwestern University, the University of Tennessee Center for the Health Sciences, and West Virginia University.

Dove's involvement in capital campaigns spans nearly thirty years, during which he has been associated with campaigns throughout the United States and also in Canada. As a practitioner, he has participated in the staffing and management of nine successful major campaigns and has provided various consulting services to nearly fifty more. He has also served as a consultant to numerous third-sector institutions.

From June 1989 to December 1993 he operated Kent E. Dove & Associates, a small firm designed and organized to offer highly personal, specialized attention to a select client base. His areas of interest are assessment of institutional development programs, institutional planning, market surveys, management and supervision of capital campaigns, staff and board training, and management of nonprofit organizations.

Dove has served three terms on the Educational Fund Raising Committee of the Council for Advancement and Support of Education (CASE) and one term on the board of directors of the National Society of Fund Raising Executives. In 1986 he received the CASE Steuben Glass Apple Award for Outstanding Teaching.

# PLANNING AND IMPLEMENTING YOUR CAPITAL CAMPAIGN

## TABLES, FIGURES, AND EXHIBITS IN PART ONE

# CHAPTER ONE

# THE KEY COMPONENTS
# OF A CAPITAL CAMPAIGN

A capital campaign is an organized, intensive fundraising effort on the part of a third-sector institution or organization to secure extraordinary gifts and pledges for a specific purpose or purposes (such as building construction, renovation, equipment acquisition, or endowment funds) during a specified period. The nature of campaigns, like the nature of society itself, is in continuous transition; for example, new campaign models are emerging, and campaign goals are beginning to include operating as well as endowment components. Indeed, the period since World War II has shown that one of the most permanent features of our environment is change, and it appears that change will move at an even faster pace in the future than it has in the past. Milton (1660) said it best: "The ship of the Commonwealth is always under sail."

Although we will certainly do things differently in the future from the way we have done them in the past, it is equally certain that the significant essential features characterizing capital campaigns will endure. This book is about the abiding principles that define and provide the context for a successful capital campaign or ongoing major gifts program; it is not about exceptions to the rules, even though there are many exceptions; certainly, few principles in campaigning are immutable. The nature of a campaign is as complex and challenging as human nature itself because each campaign essentially and fundamentally deals with people and with their motivations, needs, desires, aspirations, and hopes even more than it deals with formulas, organizational charts, and timetables. But a check of the record, over time and through all types of philanthropic and charitable organizations, shows beyond any doubt that those who abide by these principles win more often, win more convincingly, and usually win not only the day but also the future.

Those who occasionally win by other methods almost always are lucky, and some would rather be lucky than good. (And, for goodness' sake, take and enjoy all the luck available: everyone does; there is nothing wrong with being lucky.) But successful campaigns organized and managed "by the rules" generally enjoy their fair share of luck, too, and it is better to be good than to be lucky. Those who are good—those who operate their campaigns within a prescribed structure—will make their own luck as they go along; opportunities will be met by preparation. The others will have to wait for luck to come along, but it may not come at a strategic time during a campaign, or it may not come often enough to bring the campaign victory. And winning is important; especially when the case is truly compelling, winning is often essential.

This book is about the means used to reach an end. Do not be misled, however. The ultimate objective is not simply to raise money, and the means is never people just "giving away" financial resources. Successful campaigns seek and secure investments in a better society, a higher quality of life, and an enriched culture, and they showcase humankind at its best, expressing love and hope and caring for others who have greater needs. There is clearly an evangelical aspect of fundraising, one that motivates most professionals, volunteers, and donors. Never lose sight of that fact. If it is forgotten, society will lose a central thread binding the fabric of philanthropy and charity as they are known today, and as they ought to be known. The effects of a loss like that would be incalculable.

Philanthropy and charity are as old as humankind itself. Fundraising, however and particularly the capital campaign as it will be practiced in the twenty-first century, is a modern phenomenon. If we trace the roots of giving in American society, as well as the development of the fundraising function, we find several benchmark periods. In 1641, for example, Harvard College sponsored the first systematic effort to raise funds for higher education when it sent a trio of preachers to England on a begging mission to raise funds (Chewning, 1984, p. 16). Once in England, these fundraisers found they needed a fundraising brochure and relayed the need back to Harvard. In response to this request came *New England's First Fruits*, largely written in Massachusetts but printed in London in 1643. It was the first of countless public relations pamphlets and brochures. To take another example, the first attempt to stage a community chest–type fund drive was undertaken in 1829 by Matthew Carey in Philadelphia. The net result of this federated fundraising effort, America's first, was a total of $276.50 given by 137 subscribers. This effort contained, in embryo, the elements of modern fundraising:

the paid solicitor, the advance promotion, the classified prospect list, and the federated drive. As another example, major gift fundraising became an established practice through both the rise of industrialization and the new willingness of major donors to give to third-sector institutions. Thus, during the late nineteenth and early twentieth centuries, such capitalists as Andrew Carnegie and John D. Rockefeller began underwriting libraries, museums, research projects, and even entire universities. Fundraising and public relations firms (for instance, the John Price Jones Corporation) were established to assist nonprofit organizations that did not have the staff or expertise to conduct these efforts on their own. Finally, early in this century, one of the first successful major campaigns was directed by Charles Sumner Ward and his colleague Lyman L. Pierce, campaign directors for the YMCA; over the course of three decades, Ward's fundraising techniques raised more than half a billion dollars for that organization. His efforts became the foundation on which today's capital campaigns are still built, earning him recognition as a master campaigner, and his strategies were copied by many other successful fundraisers.

It is impossible to understate the importance of a capital campaign to any institution at critical moments in its history. Throughout this century, the capital campaign has been the one public undertaking that exposes the hopes and aspirations of an institution to critical market segments, which ultimately are asked to invest the time, energy, and financial support crucial to the institution's quality and even, at times, its survival. The role of campaigns in the future of institutions is becoming ever more important, as is the impact of campaigns on institutions' future development. Several factors are principally responsible for this situation:

- Institutional budgets are tightening and becoming more strained.
- The size of enrollments/patient loads/service markets is leveling off or declining (most noteworthy in this respect are the decreases in hospital patient-care loads and average days per stay).
- Competition for contributions is dramatically increasing.
- Public grant programs are being reduced or eliminated as a part of the current federal administration's strategy.
- The donor public is becoming both more pressed and more discriminating as resources are becoming more scarce.
- Fixed operating costs are escalating ever more rapidly, especially in programs whose budgets are personnel-heavy.

Given these factors, capital campaigns are becoming a standard feature of virtually every size and type of third-sector institution.

Modern capital campaigns can be grouped into three categories according to the size of their fundraising goals: less than $25 million, $25 million to $100 million, or more than $100 million. By far the largest number of campaigns will involve goals of less than $100 million. Campaigns in the $100,000–to–$1 million range, if they are true capital campaigns, will be less numerous in the future than in the past, simply because few true "capital" needs can be met by campaigns with goals in this range: even modest construction projects these days often require more than $1 million. The number of campaigns in the $25 million–to–$100 million range is significant and growing. In virtually every major population center in North America, there is at least one campaign with a goal in this range under way today, and the list of colleges and universities with announced campaign goals in this range is too long to enumerate.

What is even more surprising is the number of announced campaigns with goals of $100 million or more: forty-three in higher education alone in the summer of 1987, according to a telephone survey conducted by the *Chronicle of Higher Education* ("Fact-File," 1987). And the next size barrier was broken in February 1987, with the announcement of Stanford University's campaign and its goal of more than $1 billion. Almost a decade later, in a similar update, the *Chronicle of Higher Education* reported on 142 colleges and universities conducting campaigns; 39 of the 142 had goals in excess of $100 million, 7 had goals in excess of $1 billion, and in 1994 Harvard became the first to pass $2 billion when it announced a $2.1 billion effort ("Fund-Raising Campaigns of 142 U.S. Colleges and Universities," 1996). The most recent update appears in the *NonProfit Times* ("The Billion Dollar Club," 1998), which reports on 18 colleges and universities currently engaged in campaigns with goals of $1 billion or more; another university will soon announce a similar campaign, and two more institutions are considering announcing campaigns in the range of more than $1 billion. Moreover, Columbia University, by extending the $1.15 billion campaign it announced in 1990, has joined Harvard as the second university in the $2 billion club, with a goal of $2.2 billion.

But higher education is not alone when it comes to conducting capital campaigns with significant goals. The *Chronicle of Philanthropy* contains a regular feature, Campaign Update, that tracks campaigns across all sectors; consider the diversity of the campaigns now under way across the United States in support of a wide variety of organizations and needs (the following goals are mentioned in the issues of May 7, June 18, and August 13, 1998):

- Arkansas Arts Center: $18 million for endowment and capital needs
- Newberry Library (Illinois): $20 million to support its collections and maintain free admission
- Jesuit High School (Oregon): $55 million for endowment and capital needs

- Homeward Bound (Arizona): $7.1 million to construct and endow a transitional housing facility
- Cleveland Orchestra (Ohio): $100 million for endowment, capital needs, and general operation
- Boys and Girls Clubs (western Pennsylvania): $7 million to upgrade eight branches and a camping facility
- Center for Enriched Living (Illinois): $4 million for capital needs
- Chicago Symphony Orchestra (Illinois): $105 million for a new concert hall and administrative facility
- North Shore Country Day School (Illinois): $6.9 million for endowment and capital needs
- Wisconsin Conservatory of Music: $4.9 million to renovate its facility
- YMCA of Metropolitan Dallas (Texas): $21.5 million to build eight new facilities and improve fifteen existing ones
- Jack S. Blanton Museum of Art (Texas): $42 million for endowment and capital needs
- Missouri Historical Society: $16.7 million to renovate the Jefferson Memorial Building and upgrade Forest Park
- Neuberger Museum of Art (New York): $10 million for endowment and capital needs
- Opera Omaha (Nebraska): $ 1 million for endowment
- Planned Parenthood (New York): $25 million for endowment, capital needs, and program support
- Southwestern Baptist Theological Seminary (Texas): $30 million for endowment and capital needs

It must be remembered, however, that the basic ground rules for success are the same for every campaign, whether the goal is $100,000 or $100 million. History is convincingly clear on this point. It is these basic ground rules that must be the focus of anyone who plans and implements a campaign.

## Ten Prerequisites of Success

Before a campaign is formally undertaken and publicly announced, precampaign work (sometimes even pre-precampaign work) is necessary. First and foremost in any capital campaign effort is the need for commitment on the part of the governing board, the administration, and the volunteer leaders. A decision must also be made that the effort will be one of teamwork; no campaign, if it is to be successful, can be undertaken by staff alone or by external professionals alone. To be successful, a campaign must be characterized by the following ten prerequisite elements:

1. Commitments of time and support from all key participants (the governing board, the chief executive officer, prospective major donors, key volunteer leaders, the professional fundraising staff, and the institutional family)
2. A clear organizational self-image and a strategic plan for organizational growth and improvement
3. Fundraising objectives based on important and legitimate institutional plans, goals, budgets, and needs
4. A written document that makes a compelling case for supporting the campaign (larger, more complex campaigns will need additional support materials)
5. An assessment of the institutional development program and a market survey addressing internal and external preparedness
6. Enlistment and education of volunteer leaders
7. Ability and readiness of major donors to give substantial lead gifts before any public announcement of the campaign
8. Competent staff and, perhaps, external professional counsel
9. Adequate, even liberal, funds for expenses
10. Consideration of other factors (as described in the following section), which, rather than determining whether the campaign should be undertaken, tend to determine the size of its goal and its timing, in terms of both length and starting date

## Other Factors

As an organization plans its campaign, factors such as the ones discussed here will undoubtedly need to be considered from time to time. Although an institution that finds itself less than well prepared to meet these contingencies need not abandon its plans, it may have to slow its pace or postpone its campaign until it has acquired the necessary strength, or until the situation has changed to the point where the campaign can proceed. Failure to consider these factors and contingencies can place the campaign at risk and may predestine its failure.

### Age of the Organization

Older organizations tend to be better established than younger ones. They have longer track records of service and past success; they often have better-defined, older constituencies, and their support bases are often more developed. As a university president once asked, "Do you remember the last time a college one hundred years old or older was closed?"

## Caliber of the Constituency

Research on patterns of charitable giving by Americans suggests that, on the whole, heads of households contribute more than others. Contribution amounts are generally correlated with wage earners' income levels, occupations, employment status, educational levels, and ages (The Gallup Organization, 1982). Many of these conclusions are confirmed by another important piece of research commissioned by the Rockefeller Brothers Fund and conducted by Yankelovich, Skelley and White, Inc. (White, 1986). According to this survey, major influences on giving include income level, life expectancy, age, religious involvement, and marital status. Older, more prosperous individuals, especially the religious, give proportionately more. Organizations do better when their constituencies are older, wealthier, better educated, and more skilled. The most recent research published by INDEPENDENT SECTOR (1996) continues to confirm these earlier findings, which have all reached essentially the same conclusions. The evidence is all around, as can be seen in any community.

## Range of the Institution's Giving Program

The most productive fundraising programs characteristically include four key functional elements:

1. An annual giving program
2. A planned giving program
3. A major gifts program
4. A prospect research program

An organization that lacks any of these programs, or that has failed to fully develop them, tends to be less prepared for campaign activity than an organization that already has them in effective operation. As a result, the organization that lacks them may have to accept lower campaign goals. Pickett (1984) has demonstrated this point convincingly in his sampling of institutions of higher education.

## Size and Geographical Distribution of the Constituency

The individual demographic factors mentioned earlier are certainly the most important determinants of the ability of a constituency to support a capital campaign. It is also generally true, however, that organizations with larger constituencies tend to have a better base from which to work. (This will not always be the case, of course: an organization that provides services for indigent or low-income groups may well have a very large client list but few major gift prospects within this constituency who are able and willing to give at the levels required to support a capital campaign.)

The geographical distribution of the constituency is another factor to be considered in determining the preparedness for a campaign and the size of goal that is realistic. Less time and money and fewer staff are needed to organize and manage a campaign in a small geographical area, such as a city or one section of a city, than to conduct one over a wider area, which presents more complex organizational problems. The national campaigns, especially those being conducted by large educational institutions, such as Harvard University, demonstrate this principle.

## Previous Fundraising Success

Realism is necessary in determining a capital campaign's goals or, indeed, whether an institution is even ready to enter into a capital campaign. How long ago was the last one conducted? For how much? Was it successful? Past performance as well as current trends in giving must be analyzed. An institution annually raising $500,000 is unlikely to be prepared to mount a successful campaign for $30 million.

There is no ironclad prescription for using recent and current giving totals to project a capital campaign's goals, but a random review of several successful recent campaigns suggests that organizations normally set goals that range from four to six times the current amount of total annual development income. A major consulting firm proposes that the cumulative total of gifts for the previous five years represents a good starting target in determining a campaign goal; therefore, an organization that has raised $20 million in five years will probably end up with a "new money" campaign goal of $15–$25 million. If the comprehensive campaign model described later in this chapter is used, however, one must be especially careful about employing such rules of thumb in determining a goal; it is too simplistic to use mathematical assumptions alone in making projections. It must also be remembered that part of the comprehensive goal is ongoing annual support, and the amount of this support should not be included in the capital component of the total goal.

## Quality of the Program and Impact of Its Services

In determining campaign preparedness and goals, two extremely important variables to be considered are the quality of the services being provided and the impact that these services have on the constituency or community being served. Institutions that provide higher-quality programs and a broader range of services tend to have greater access to a wider segment of the philanthropic market. High-quality organizations (such as the Mayo Clinic, Boys Town, the Girl Scouts of America, the better YMCAs and YWCAs around the country, and the "best" churches and synagogues in a community) are more competitive in the most competitive environments, reaching known philanthropists, foundations, and corporations. These funding sources must always choose among numerous organizations requesting donations, and among the organizations meeting their giving criteria, they most often select those that demonstrate the highest qualifications.

## Location of the Organization

Organizations in urban areas tend to have a better climate in which to seek significant contributions than organizations in rural areas. Residents of larger cities, and of geographical areas in which individual wealth and corporate and foundation headquarters are concentrated, tend to be more experienced and sophisticated with regard to campaigns and more generous in their support of them. Communities with United Way campaigns also tend to be more receptive to and supportive of capital campaigns.

There are regional differences as well, both in the United States and in Canada. In the United States, organized fundraising by nonprofit organizations is generally more mature and sophisticated and involves more realistic expectations on the East Coast than in the Midwest or on the West Coast, and the same contrast holds between eastern Canada and western Canada, although there are specific exceptions in both countries. There are other factors to be considered, too. In the United States, there is a noteworthy concentration of foundation wealth on the island of Manhattan, and a significant portion of the support provided by these foundations tends to go to East Coast institutions. Texas has a number of large foundations, many of which restrict their giving to organizations in that state. In North Dakota, South Dakota, and Alabama, however, with fewer large foundations and corporate headquarters, there is much less charitable giving. The concentration of population and/or wealth, and the institution's proximity to it, are often important variables. Nevertheless, every community has a power structure, and any organization that is planning a campaign can maximize its potential by effectively involving these key community leaders.

## Human Factors

Human emotion and motivation are factors that should never be underestimated. Three factors transcend all others in motivating people to give: urgency, importance, and relevance.

An earthquake hits Central America and destroys a hospital; a tornado rips through the Midwest and flattens a church: there is an urgent need, and people respond to it immediately. Never mind that the organization affected may not have an organized fundraising operation or the essential elements of capital fundraising; donors will react to an urgent situation, and the decision to give is often spontaneous (Panas, 1984).

Importance is the second strong motivator. If something is important enough to people, they will see that it gets done. For example, if a community decides that a YMCA/YWCA building is important to it, or that a program to shelter and feed the homeless and hungry should be at the top of its agenda, this importance alone can transcend other factors in getting the job done. Again, never mind that the organization falls short in critical ways; even if the prospective donor does not feel the urgency of the situation or does not deem it personally relevant, the prospective donor's support can be and will be generated if the need is perceived as being important, and particularly if it is perceived as being important to peers and colleagues whose esteem the prospective donor values.

The third factor is relevance. People respond to things that are personally relevant, often on a totally emotional basis. Individuals give emotionally, not cerebrally (Panas, 1984).

## State of the Economy

Later in this book, concrete evidence shows that, over time, giving is relatively unaffected by the economy. But tell that to a nonprofit organization in Michigan when the automobile industry is suffering a downturn, or to those involved today in campaigns related to British Columbia's forestry and mining industries. The state of the economy matters more psychologically than financially. Nevertheless, organizations generally tend to tread lightly in economic downturns and are always hoping to launch and conduct their campaigns in strong economic circumstances.

## Competing and Conflicting Campaigns

The timing of other campaigns and fundraising drives is another consideration. In the face of competing and conflicting capital fundraising efforts, an institution may decide to alter its own time frame, or it may choose to proceed more cautiously because the leaders it desires to attract are already committed to other efforts or because other efforts have already overextended its constituency's ability to give.

## Trends in the Nonprofit Sector

Certain areas of the nonprofit sector seem to enjoy continuing and enduring support. Sometimes, however, there are attitudinal or mood changes directed toward a sector or within the nonprofit sector.

There are also new and emerging causes, and there are causes whose time is past. As an example of the first case, the HIV/AIDS epidemic has given rise to an entirely new cause in the past fifteen years. As an example of the second, when Dr. Jonas Salk invented the polio vaccine, the March of Dimes was faced with going out of business or reinventing itself; it chose to do the latter. And with the success of the new protease inhibitors, certain HIV/AIDS-oriented ancillary organizations are now facing the same choice.

In addition, entire new sectors are emerging. In *Giving USA 1986* (American Association of Fund-Raising Counsel Trust for Philanthropy, 1986), six sectors were identified: religion; education; health; human services; arts, culture, and humanities; and public/social benefit. In *Giving USA 1998* (American Association of Fund-Raising Counsel Trust for Philanthropy, 1998), two new sectors are included: environment/wildlife and international affairs.

## Unfavorable Publicity

Unfavorable publicity can crush a campaign before it begins, and it can even have a dramatic effect on a campaign already in progress. If the publicity is going to be short-lived, wait until the storm passes. If it is of a more long-term variety, plans may need to be altered, delayed, or abandoned in keeping with the nature of the negative publicity.

## Local Issues

Only you know what may be happening in your own backyard to affect no one else but you. Again, in keeping with the nature of the situation, actions and plans may have to be adjusted.

## Challenge Gifts and Matching Gifts

Never underestimate the power of a challenge gift; North Americans love the "buy one, get one free" concept, and the ability to leverage a gift is an irresistible temptation for many. Obviously, a 1:1 match—every dollar that the donor gives is matched by another dollar—is more appealing than a 1:2 challenge (a dollar is given for every \$2 contributed by the other donor), but even if the match is diluted by a factor of 2, it can still be very helpful. Challenges presenting a less than 1:2 incentive usually see their influence fall off significantly, and a richer challenge (2:1) greatly adds to the match's attractiveness:

- A magnificent \$50 million challenge grant was among the forty largest gifts in U.S. history ever made to an institution of higher education by an individual ("Drake University Receives \$50 Million Gift from Dwight Opperman," 1997). Opperman's was an especially rich match, with \$10 million provided in a 2:1

ratio for gifts to Drake's Law School, of which he is a graduate; the remaining
$40 million will serve as a challenge to all other alumni and friends on a 3:1 basis.

- In a two-year period, through the power of a matching gifts program, Indiana
  University more than tripled the number of endowed faculty positions that had
  been created in the university's first 175 years.
- The state of Florida sponsors the Major Gifts Trust Fund, which matches gifts
  of $100,000 and above for academic endowments at state colleges and uni-
  versities on a progressive scale ranging from 1:2 at $100,000 up to 1:1 at
  $2,000,000 and above. The state also sponsors the Facilities Enhancement
  Challenge Grant Program, which requires a specific legislative appropriation
  of the matching funds for a specific project. According to Paul A. Robell (personal communication, Sept. 7, 1998), "Because of the great success of the program, the Major Gifts Trust Fund runs behind and donors' gifts are placed in
  a queue waiting for funding from the following legislative session. The University of Florida Foundation, Inc., has received well over $50 million from the
  Major Gifts Trust Fund and well over $30 million from the facilities program."

Any institution that can develop a matching gifts program will enhance its
fundraising potential and will help to ensure the success of its capital campaign.

## Forms of Capital Campaigns

Although the general principles of capital campaigns tend to be universally applicable to any type of organization, there are different campaign models. Four
rather distinctive forms are found today:

1. The historical capital campaign
2. The comprehensive campaign
3. The single-purpose campaign
4. The continuing major gifts program

### Historical Capital Campaign

The historical capital campaign is a fundraising effort designed to secure gifts of
capital assets to meet the capital needs of an organization, to build buildings, and,
in some instances, to build the endowment. It is characterized by a highly motivated volunteer group working in a tightly organized and managed manner to
meet a specific overall capital goal with one or more objectives during a specific
period, usually three years or less. The volunteers make every reasonable effort to

see all constituents and special friends on a face-to-face basis because the campaign is viewed as a once-in-a-lifetime program: historical capital campaigns typically are spaced many years, even decades, apart, and they usually occur only once during the donor population's giving life. They are often superimposed on the ongoing development effort. In some instances, other fundraising efforts, especially annual campaigns, are suspended or downplayed during historical capital campaigns. It is common to create a separate campaign office, budget, and staff for the sole purpose of supporting this type of effort.

The historical capital campaign is still used in a variety of situations—a church building an addition, a YMCA/YWCA constructing a swimming facility, a Scout organization creating a summer camp—but at least three important changes in campaigning have made the historical model less fashionable today (and have led, increasingly, to the use of the comprehensive campaign and the single-purpose campaign):

1. A historical capital campaign seeks gifts of capital assets to meet the capital needs of the institution. Today's capital campaigns are often designed to meet other needs, however; today, more and more, gifts are being made in all forms, including capital.
2. An institution conducting a historical capital campaign runs the risk of restricting or damaging its other established, ongoing giving programs, a risk that fewer and fewer institutions are willing or able to take.
3. The historical capital campaign attempts to reach all constituents and friends of the institution on a one-to-one, face-to-face basis. For many of North America's third-sector institutions, given the number of constituents, the constituents' geographical distribution when these organizations serve wide areas, and the frequency today of these organizations' other, ongoing campaign efforts, sheer economics—the cost of fundraising—simply precludes this kind of activity, financially if not logistically.

## Comprehensive Campaign

The comprehensive campaign is a major development program with specific goals and timetables. It almost always includes, under one umbrella, its current operations, one-time goals, and endowment objectives. It generally lasts for three to five years, although some campaigns are longer, and some are conducted in phases. Gifts and pledges of all kinds, including annual as well as planned and deferred gifts, are often sought and counted in the campaign total. In many instances, there is less dependence on volunteers, and there may be increased involvement of administrators and staff, not only as cultivators but also as solicitors, who concentrate on maximizing the gifts of major prospects through intense personal solicitation, often approaching both special and general prospects by telephone or direct mail. This type of campaign is related to the total development program and often encompasses other ongoing giving programs. The comprehensive campaign model is especially attractive to larger, more complex organizations that want to keep the total fundraising effort under one umbrella or want to create a more substantial total goal than the "new money" goal might otherwise be.

## Single-Purpose Campaign

The single-purpose campaign raises money for an individual building, an endowment fund, or any other isolated objective. It is often targeted at one particular special-interest constituency, and it generally is not undertaken as part of the entire development effort, although it is related to that effort.

Generally speaking, regardless of an institution's size or complexity, it is best to conduct a single, unified campaign. In larger, administratively complex organizations, however, which use the single-purpose campaign almost exclusively, a single, unified campaign is not always possible or, sometimes, even desirable. Indeed, many institutions today are continually moving into and out of single-purpose campaigns—and, occasionally, into two or three or more at the same time.

It is becoming more and more common for this form of campaign activity to lead the institution to employ a full-time professional fundraiser, sometimes with a staff, whose responsibility is major and special gifts, and who carries a corresponding title.

## Continuing Major Gifts Program

A continuing major gifts program, designed to be proactive in gaining financial support for a planned future, is administered by a professional staff. In this model, the major gifts program is integrated into a planned, ongoing development program.

Institutional leaders, realizing that there is a limit to the number of times extraordinary fundraising efforts can produce quick and effective solutions to today's problems, are accepting two premises: (1) that strategic organizational planning will become an accepted, even required, practice in all nonprofit organizations, and (2) that this type of planning will eventually lead to better management practices and better managers for the institutions using it, and for their development programs. Where strategic planning is used, development programs become multi-year efforts designed in supportive concert with institutional strategies. This approach results in perpetual campaigning to satisfy capital and other needs through a coordinated, ongoing fundraising effort, with major "subcampaigns" harmoniously integrated into the ongoing program. These "subcampaigns" are thus far less obvious as extraordinary fundraising efforts than is the case when the other models are used.

This is not to suggest that institutions using the strategic planning method will not, from time to time, continue to engage in intensive, time-specific "capital campaigns" with defined goals. They will. Apart from the sheer volume of dollars that can be raised when a heightened sense of urgency and importance is created, and apart from the psychological and motivational strategies that can maximize giving in the excitement of a campaign, sometimes an institution simply wants to bring to itself the special attention that a campaign provides. What is different in the future-oriented strategic planning environment is that those institutions that campaign will do so because they choose to do so, not because they have no other plausible alternative. Therefore, announced capital campaigns, as they historically have been known, will probably become less frequent; when undertaken, however, they will, curiously, have many of the traditional characteristics of the campaigns that Charles Sumner Ward organized eighty years ago.

The selection of the campaign model to be used in a particular situation will be influenced by a number of factors:

- The commitment to and quality of strategic institutional planning
- The development program's current level of maturity and sophistication
- The development staff's experience and ability
- The availability of leadership for the campaign
- The impressiveness of the case to be made
- The potential of the major donor prospects
- The range and scope of the anticipated campaign effort

There is no one correct model for all institutions or all situations. In fact, to best serve a particular situation, there may be opportunities to incorporate features of more than one of the models.

# CHAPTER TWO

# PREPARING FOR A CAMPAIGN

## Three Essential Steps and an Important Check

This chapter discusses three essential aspects of the early stages of campaign planning:

1. Strategic institutional planning and its impact on the campaign
2. The purpose and organization of the market survey
3. The use of a development program assessment to determine institutional preparedness

The chapter also discusses a newly developed index for gauging institutional preparedness.

## Strategic Planning

The first requirements for any capital campaign are a clear image of the institution, and a plan for its growth and improvement so that it can better fulfill its purpose. What is needed, in other words, is a strategic plan. Strategic planning is an approach that asks most institutions to be more intentional and more organized than they have been in the past.

Everywhere today, board members and local leaders are asking questions about the future of their third-sector institutions. They want to know the aims and goals. They are interested in assessing the development programs of the organizations that they are asked to support. Any development program presupposes, of course, that the institution knows what it is going to develop; no amount of public relations can substitute for an institution's having a reason for being. But an institution without a strategic plan is at the mercy of pressure groups. It is in danger of being manipulated by an influential individual's whim, a board member's pet project, or uninformed community opinion.

It is the business of all nonprofit institutions to do strategic planning, but many institutions have neglected—or avoided—the self-analysis and planning that would define aims and set goals. Without a strategy based on knowledge of the philanthropic marketplace, however, they will have only random ideas, without a guiding purpose. Lord (1996, pp. 32–35) puts it this way:

> As the Roman philosopher Seneca said, "When a man does not know what harbor he is making for, no wind is the right one." Or, as Yogi Berra put it more recently, "You've got to be very careful if you don't know where you are going, because you might not get there." Many forces outside individual institutions are trying to legislate how they ought to be doing their jobs. So an institution has to have a plan for its future, particularly when it is preparing to embark on a fundraising campaign, if for no other reason [than] because people deserve to know how the institution intends to use the money—and what kind of benefits are expected. What makes planning even more valuable is the opportunity it presents for involvement. If an institution's leaders are on the ball they will use the planning process to get people involved in mapping an organization's future —especially those people who have the power to bring about that future. Authentic involvement in a planning process promotes a sense of ownership among prospective donors and volunteers. People are simply motivated to work for and invest in the realization of plans they themselves have helped to develop.
>
> The act of planning also focuses and clarifies thinking. This is another way in which the process itself is more important than the resulting document. Furthermore, with regard to fundraising, planning makes an institution look good. Most donors don't want to know all the details—but they do want to be assured that an organization knows its future and sees a path for getting there. They want to know that not-for-profit organizations are using the skills of the business world, and that they are treating the eleemosynary enterprise in an intentional, organized, and strategic manner. Any institution will make an excellent impression if it can tell those it is trying to attract, either as volunteers or as potential donors, that it has conducted surveys among the people it serves, designed a strategic plan, and produced a financial plan for the next three to five years or more.

This kind of planning is exactly what one philanthropist wanted when he asked a hospital trustee: "What's your mission? And I don't mean that formal stuff, either. What are you doing? What does your five year plan look like? What services are you going to add? To abandon?" More and more prospects are asking these tough questions. Too many organizations still have no answers, or only the vaguest ones. The sharp organizations, those that are attracting big money, are ready with their plans. Corporations, foundations, and wealthy individuals, after all, are only asking that not-for-profits follow the same discipline that they—the prospects—have been practicing for years. Let's be clear, what's being talked about isn't the kind of "long-range planning" many organizations already do, but real strategic planning. The difference is important.

Bryson (1995) defines strategic planning as a disciplined effort to produce fundamental decisions and actions that shape and guide what an organization is, what it does, and why it does it. To deliver the best results, strategic planning requires broad yet effective gathering of information, development and exploration of strategic alternatives, and an emphasis on the future implications of present decisions. Strategic planning can help facilitate communication and participation, accommodate divergent interests and values, foster wise and reasonably analytical decision making, and promote successful implementation. In short, strategic planning at its best can prompt in organizations the kind of imagination—and commitment—that the psychotherapist and theologian Thomas Moore (cited in Bryson, 1995, pp. 4–5) thinks are necessary to deal with individuals' life conundrums. Bryson adds that strategic planning is clearly no panacea; it is simply a set of concepts, procedures, and tools designed to help leaders, managers, and planners think and act strategically. Strategic *planning* is not a substitute for strategic *thinking* and *acting*, Bryson says; only caring, committed people can think and act strategically. Used thoughtlessly, strategic planning can actually drive out precisely the kind of strategic thought and action it is supposed to promote. Nor is strategic planning a substitute for leadership: when it comes to using strategic planning to enhance organizational performance, there simply is no substitute for leadership. At least some key decision makers and process champions must be committed to the strategic planning process, or any attempts to use it are bound to fail (Bryson, 1995, p. 9). (See Resource A, "Sample Strategic Plan.")

## Conducting a Market Survey

In order for an institution's board to establish monetary and programmatic goals for its capital campaign, the institution needs to conduct both internal and external evaluations of its programs. Whenever it is possible to do so, of course, the institution should bring its goals under one umbrella and thus unify the campaign; this makes sense in terms of both organizing the fundraising volunteers and ensuring institutional cohesion.

To determine the goals for a successful capital campaign, an inventory of needs and a determination of priorities are imperative. There is a great deal of difference between an institutional needs list and an institutional "wants" list. It is absolutely essential that the "wants" list be carefully pared down to a substantiated, documented needs list.

The needs list is initially generated in house. It evolves from the planning process, to determine all the important needs that might be met with private funding. Then the needs must be ranked in order of their priority.

Institutional planners should always be cognizant of the importance of identifying goals that appeal to their constituents. This is not to say that legitimate institutional needs should be dramatically altered or abandoned if they lack appeal for constituents (although these needs may require special educational programs for the constituents before a campaign can move forward). This does mean, however, that items of little or no interest to the constituents generally should not appear as major components of a campaign goal. How much constituent appeal a particular campaign component has can best be determined through a selective surveying (that is, a market survey) of the key constituents. In other words, a market survey is a test of an institution's philanthropic potential.

It is generally recommended that the institution, before conducting a market survey, undertake an assessment of its development program, to measure the institutional level of internal preparedness (see the following section, "Conducting a Development Program Assessment"). The institution must also have the following essential elements in place:

- An institutional plan that anticipates funding needs
- A financial plan for approved projects and programs
- Support from board members, in the form of advocacy and gifts
- A sales and production staff
- A comprehensive program for financial development
- Prospects capable of providing the expected support
- A strong case for substantial support

These essentials of fundraising are the threads that run through the fabric of all capital campaigns.

The market survey itself has a number of objectives:

- To provide an accurate assessment of the factors that may affect the campaign
- To investigate and evaluate external opportunities for the institution to mount and successfully accomplish a large-scale major gifts campaign

- To determine, on the basis of reactions to the case statement (see Chapter Five), attitudes toward the institutional priorities and the campaign goal and, as warranted, to suggest changes in the priorities, the campaign goal, or both
- To educate potential major donors and campaign leaders
- To identify and evaluate the people best suited to providing leadership for workers or for major donors to the campaign
- To afford the institution an analysis of all the information that has been gathered

No two sets of market survey questions should look exactly alike. Any survey will ask a certain set of standard, basic questions, but each will also ask specific questions focused on the distinctive needs of the institution for which it is being conducted. As important as asking the correct questions correctly is listening to the answers, accurately recording them, and, as necessary, asking appropriate follow-up questions, which should include questions that may not belong to the questionnaire proper.

The questions should be written in such a manner as to be objective and neutral. The best and most valid questionnaires are even taken to market research or opinion survey groups, or to individuals with this type of expertise, to be validated before use. The matrix of questions must also be designed to check and cross-check certain key points, issues, and attitudes that the institution is particularly interested in investigating. It takes trained professionals to ensure this kind of cross-checking. (See Resource C, "Sample Market Survey Materials.")

Market surveys must be conducted by individuals whom the respondents consider to be "honest brokers." If respondents perceive that an interviewer is carrying institutional baggage or an institutional agenda, their answers may be less than complete and may severely limit or even invalidate the survey's conclusions and recommendations. An institution that proceeds on the basis of limited or invalid survey findings is at serious risk. To be certain that your market survey is conducted properly, use a valid survey instrument and have your survey conducted by objective, qualified professionals.

A market survey generally takes from thirty to ninety days to complete. The size of the survey population, as well as the geographical area to be covered in the face-to-face interview process, will determine the time needed. For example, it takes longer to conduct ninety interviews for the Canadian Diabetes Association or the Canadian National Institute for the Blind, whose areas range from Halifax, Nova Scotia, to Victoria, British Columbia, than it does to conduct thirty-five interviews for the YWCA of Calgary, all of which can be completed within the Calgary city limits.

Regardless of the organization's size, the fact is that a correctly and carefully drawn sample of thirty to thirty-five respondents is adequate to provide the knowledge needed for completing the market survey. Smaller organizations, if they are knowledgeable or well guided in this process, can often complete their surveys in twenty to twenty-five interviews, but many opt to do more so as to include more people, whether or not these interviews add to the survey's outcome. Larger organizations often do more interviews simply as a result of their need to be inclusive of the various leadership groups that they do not want to offend by exclusion.

For a market survey consisting of fifty to seventy face-to-face interviews, one to five days of consultation are required for completing the following tasks:

- Developing the design of the survey
- Assembling and evaluating the list of prospects to be interviewed
- Drafting and reviewing the interview contact letter and needs statement
- Developing interview strategies
- Drafting the interview questionnaire
- Assembling and mailing any ancillary marketing materials that may be required

All market surveys must be based first and foremost on face-to-face interviews with a carefully selected respondent pool; there is no substitute. The interviews used in a market survey should be conducted with a cross section of board members, community leaders, service users, alumni and friends of the institution, and other key constituents. The people to be interviewed are selected on the basis of their close relationships to the institution, their familiarity with the persons and situations pertinent to fundraising, their potential as donors, and their ability to influence others to work and to give.

Sophisticated organizations are increasingly supplementing face-to-face interviews with additional input gathered through phone interviews and direct-mail surveys. These two supplementary approaches permit the institution to gain further validation of the survey's statistical results and, more important, to expand the universe of individuals who are brought into the "inner circle" early in the process of planning and preparing the campaign. Ultimately, the size of the sample and the nature of the data-collection techniques that are used will be determined by the size and complexity of the institution's constituency and by the design and goal of the campaign.

Once there is a properly constructed questionnaire, the market survey is ready to begin. It is now important to ensure that the survey sample is correctly drawn from among the institution's constituencies. Again, people experienced in conducting market surveys should be involved in this process.

For a sample of fifty to seventy people interviewed over a wide area, the interview portion of the study generally requires three to five weeks. The initial list of major constituents should be supplemented by basic profile information on each interview candidate. In order for the appropriate number of interviews to be conducted, the list of names should be about twice as large as the sample that is actually needed.

Every prospective respondent receives an initial contact letter and a brief case statement describing the funding needs of the organization. These letters are followed up by telephone calls to each individual, and survey interviews are scheduled. Interviews that must be kept confidential are conducted by professional counsel or by institutional staff under the direction of counsel. A significant but smaller number of interviews can be conducted with selected administrators and staff, although this group is not included in all cases.

Every effort must be made to conduct the interviews objectively. It is important that each person interviewed be assured that the conversation will be held in strict confidence, if that is the respondent's wish. The privileged information thus obtained becomes invaluable in the process of evaluating the potential for a successful capital campaign.

In general, the value of face-to-face interviews does not rest solely on the apparent facts that have been obtained. It must be remembered that, in some instances, what appear to be facts are merely subjective observations. As the interview process continues, however, those conducting the interviews are in a unique position to check and cross-check the reliability of various opinions and to assess the perceptiveness of each person interviewed. It usually becomes clear which responses should be given greater weight, and those responses are emphasized in the market survey report.

Normally, each face-to-face interview takes from thirty minutes to an hour to complete. Focus groups, telephone interviews, and direct-mail questionnaires are increasingly being used to supplement and further validate the traditional face-to-face interview, but each of these methods entails its own limitations, and none should not supplant the traditional interview as the principal technique.

It is extremely important for the organization to understand that a market survey used to determine the feasibility of a campaign should not deal at length with the presentation of a campaign plan or timetable. These items should be covered in detail after the market survey has been accepted formally by the organization's board.

After the interviews have been conducted, an additional six to ten days are usually required for evaluation and analysis of the results. This process involves three tasks that absolutely require experienced, skilled professionals:

1. Accurately weighting the responses (some respondents and responses are more important than others)
2. Correctly analyzing and interpreting the data
3. Translating the data into a report that achieves acceptance, inspires confidence, and creates a plan for action or points the institution toward such a plan

These three tasks cannot be left to guesstimation, but very few institutions have individuals on staff who can perform them all without assistance. Even if an institution does have such people, it still may be advisable to involve outsiders, thereby eliminating potential concerns about objectivity.

In an organization that is not conducting a development program assessment or making use of ongoing consultation, the modern survey will check the following internal systems:

- Individual, foundation, and corporate records
- Quality and range of information maintained
- Ongoing efforts to expand and update prospect files and other donor records
- The gift processing system and financial record-keeping procedures
- Other data-processing support services (for example, daily and monthly tracking of prospects, donors, and corporate and foundation proposals)
- Quarterly and annual gift progress and management reports
- Word-processing support services that facilitate the development program (for example, correspondence, proposal preparation, other text and manuscript services)
- Basic techniques of donor research and prospect rating by internal staff

Finally, one to two days should be reserved for presentation of the survey to the administration and the board.

The market survey should provide an accurate, perceptive assessment of the constituents' views of the institution, as well as information about how aware and supportive they are of the needs that the institution is putting forward. The survey should also supply information about the correct timing of a capital campaign, about whether the right leadership is available for it, and—undoubtedly most important from a financial standpoint—about whether sufficient money can be raised to undertake the campaign. Beyond these, there are other significant benefits that a market survey provides:

- Its value in terms of public relations
- The opportunity for constituent leaders to review the institution
- The opportunity for the institution to have a positive impact on business and civic leaders by including them in the survey sample
- The valuable information about development that is gleaned from the interviews
- Other information from the interviews that is helpful not only in formulating the campaign plan but also in doing comprehensive institutional planning

Properly done, a market survey can minimize the cost and maximize the success of the campaign. Moreover, it is very often the first public step taken to cultivate key support for the campaign, especially among those constituents who are close to but not directly included in the institution's immediate family.

Institutions today are increasingly deciding in advance that they will campaign and then using the market survey both to inform potential volunteer leaders and major donors that a campaign is being planned and to gain the benefit of outside expertise in establishing a strategy for the fundraising effort. The purpose of the market survey is different in these instances; accordingly, its presentation will have a different focus. The organization must understand whether it seeks a true feasibility study or is already committed to a campaign (unless counsel can dissuade it on the basis of the findings of the market survey) and is using the market survey fundamentally as an educational technique to advance its efforts. It must communicate its situation to counsel before the market survey is undertaken so that counsel can appropriately structure its efforts and reports to the organization.

One organizational feature that is emerging today is the creation of a market survey committee. The purposes of such a committee are to develop among its members a sense of direct involvement and active leadership during the early, key planning stages of the campaign and to provide knowledge and background information about significant campaign issues. Members of the market survey committee typically are asked to perform the following tasks:

- Review a draft list of those to be interviewed, and make recommendations
- As necessary, facilitate access for the consultant to those whose views are being surveyed
- Meet with the consultant to review and comment on the detailed design of the survey instrument
- Review and comment on both the draft and final versions of the market survey report

The members of the market survey committee will include its chair, high-level representatives of the major constituency groups that the campaign will target, representatives of the board, and, perhaps, the individual who will be asked to serve as general chair of the campaign. The committee functions best when there are no more than ten members; in most cases, five to seven members will be the optimum number.

Dedicated volunteer leaders are also essential to a campaign's success. Because their connection with the campaign eventually leads them to make investments of time, energy, and resources, a few wise institutions today are also involving key prospects as volunteers at this very early stage; many more institutions will adopt this approach as it becomes more widely known.

Market surveys are like produce: they do not remain fresh for long. Therefore, the timing of a survey is important. It is conducted only after other prerequisites (planning, setting priorities among needs, completing an assessment of the development program that supports the campaign's moving forward) have been satisfied. The results of a survey, once received, are generally valid for six to nine months and may remain valid for up to one year. If the institution, for whatever reason, does not launch its campaign within a year, the survey probably should be at least partially updated and perhaps even redone.

## Conducting a Development Program Assessment

For a capital campaign to be successful, it must be well organized and well managed, both internally and externally. Too often, institutions devote most of their time and attention to external preparedness while doing little or nothing to address the internal conditions, both within the institution as a whole and within the development office itself, that can enhance or handicap a campaign. It is unfortunate, in these situations, that so much is done to raise significant sums of money when the institution is not internally prepared to handle the effort and, as a result, forfeits many of the effort's lasting benefits.

One of the first requirements for internal preparedness is to make all the organization's internal constituents aware of the campaign and help them feel that they have an active part to play in it. Key administrators should be consulted or informed about all proposals for fundraising activities that are related to their specific areas. At the same time, key institutional personnel should be actively involved in providing the kind of information that will lead to the eliciting of large campaign gifts. It is advisable to conduct an internal program assessment even before the capital campaign is undertaken.

What exactly is an institutional development program assessment? It is a formal, comprehensive evaluation of an institution's development program and of the institution's relationship to the people in the areas it touches. The assessment is conducted by a facilitator (an experienced, qualified fundraising professional) or a consultant who gathers both objective and subjective data by observing and interviewing as well as by reviewing institutional literature and written reports. This information is then analyzed to produce an assessment of the institution's fundraising program.

An assessment conducted in advance of a capital campaign can do the following things:

- Establish the facts (as opposed to feelings or perceptions) about the institution's development program
- Suggest, at this critical early point, new and better ways of doing things

- Justify the role of the development program and its budget, both to the institutional leaders and to the development staff
- Involve managers and volunteer leaders in the development program, and encourage their help and support

In addition, an assessment conducted in a timely fashion before the capital campaign can help those at the top of the institution—senior managers and board members—gain a clearer understanding of what the development officers and the program do, how they do it, why they do it, and the results that can be expected. This comprehensive overview can encourage the kind of synergy between top managers, key volunteers, and development professionals that is essential to making the capital campaign a success.

How is this comprehensive overview developed? It is best accomplished on the basis of asking and answering at least these twenty fundamental questions:

1. Do you have a reason for being (that is, a mission statement)?
2. Do you have a strategic plan spelling out your purpose and direction for the next five to ten years?
3. In your plan, have you determined the placement and importance of development?
4. Do you have a formal procedure for devising institutional priorities?
5. Have you made an analysis of the programs and projects with the greatest potential for attracting private funding?
6. Have you made a commitment to a comprehensive development program designed to attract annual, special, major, capital, planned, and deferred gifts?
7. Do you take a coordinated approach to communications, volunteer services, public relations, publications, and development?
8. Do you provide adequate funding (including salaries and benefits) for employees to conduct a coordinated, comprehensive, productive development program?
9. Do you insist on having an up-to-date organization chart and job descriptions for each discrete fundraising activity, as well as regular performance evaluations for all professional employees?
10. Do you regularly monitor the progress and results of development activity, provide feedback to the staff, and document achievements to the development program's constituents?
11. Do you insist on adequate financial controls, to ensure donors' confidence and the institution's credibility?
12. Do you maintain adequate, up-to-date donor and gift records?

13. Are special attention and consideration for your major donors and prospective donors made mandatory by your fundraising program's system of rating, cultivating, and soliciting prospects?
14. Are your chief executive officer and your development staff actively involved in the cultivation and solicitation process?
15. Do you properly and promptly acknowledge the receipt of all gifts, incorporating meaningful personal touches?
16. Do you encourage key volunteers to participate actively in the fundraising process by providing them with information (through news reports, educational materials, a public relations program) and helping them make efficient use of their time and effective use of their talents?
17. Do you use a comprehensive array of techniques to keep your various constituencies informed and involved?
18. Do you have a plan for interpreting the fundraising process to the institution's family, whose cooperation and understanding are essential?
19. Do you periodically use consultants for the experience and objectivity they can provide?
20. In terms of the scope and effectiveness of your fundraising efforts, do you periodically compare yourself with peer institutions (while realizing the inherent limitations of such comparisons)?

In order for these questions to be answered, it will be necessary for at least the following materials and data to be reviewed:

- Any marketing or promotional material about the institution
- The institution's statement of mission and purpose
- Résumés (including salaries) of all professional personnel working in the area of advancement (that is, in development and community relations)
- Organization charts for the institution as a whole and specifically for the advancement area
- Job descriptions of professional personnel in the advancement area
- The organization's budget (by division) and advancement budget (line item)
- The organization's planning document, and the year's plan of activity for the advancement effort (if a written plan exists), giving details about goals, objectives, and the annual advancement calendar
- Any management indicators for monitoring the progress of the institution's current efforts
- Any mechanisms, if they exist, for monitoring programs in the development area
- Current standards, if any exist, for measurement and evaluation of the development area

- The personnel evaluation system, if any, as it is currently implemented in the development area
- Any instruments for market research, as well as any data (formal or informal) produced by these instruments that the organization may have used in the past thirty-six months
- A five-year history of giving to the organization, itemized by source and by purpose, as well as an indication, in terms of a ratio of expenditures, of the gifts received in each of the five years
- Comparisons of annual achievement to projections for each program or project and with respect to overall organizational goals
- Samples of proposals prepared for individuals, corporations, foundations, and organizations
- Samples of the written development publications and fundraising pieces used in the past year
- Any accreditation reports or other, similar reports received in the last three to five years, with a primary focus on any sections or comments directed at the advancement effort
- Histories of all board members and, as applicable, their corporate giving histories

Many people representing the institution's various constituencies should also be involved in providing the answers to the questions that are posed. The facilitator of the development program assessment should interview board members, the chief executive officer, senior managers, the chief development officer, the professional development staff, representatives of the secretarial and clerical staff, other key individuals within the institution, important volunteers and lay leaders, and, perhaps, influential and affluent community members. The facilitator should make every effort to conduct these interviews objectively and should assure each person interviewed that the conversation will be confidential. This interview process should go on until the facilitator is certain that enough information is available to provide a complete report to the institution. Finally, the facilitator should supplement these interviews with personal observations about such factors as space allocation, the visual impact of publications, and so on. The report of the development program assessment, which should be presented in writing, will often be supplemented by an oral report to the board and the chief executive officer.

For the purposes of preparing for a capital campaign, it is best that this assessment be conducted by an external facilitator of some kind, whether that means an individual, a team of individuals, or a professional consultant with expertise in this area. The advantages of using an independent facilitator are that he or she brings special expertise and experience not generally found among institutional personnel and that he or she is free of the biases often found in organizations. It is important to conduct this assessment of the development program at the right point before the capital campaign begins. The stakes are so high that the institution cannot run the risk of having the job done any less professionally, less objectively, or less competently than it can be done.

## The Dove Preparedness Index

Another tool that has been developed and introduced in the past decade is the Dove Preparedness Index (DPI). It is not essential that a DPI review be done, but institutions are now beginning to use this tool during campaign preparation as a way of evaluating the current state of preparedness.

The DPI can be used at a variety of strategic points leading up to the formal launch of a campaign. It can be administered internally or facilitated by an independent third party. Having a facilitator work with the organization is recommended if the institution's background in campaigns is weak or nonexistent, or if the institution lacks confidence that it has the knowledge, understanding, or ability to determine numerical values correctly and objectively.

The DPI individually considers the ten essential prerequisites discussed in Chapter One. Each is scored on a scale of 1 to 10, with 1 representing the lowest score and 10 the highest score. Three of these ten prerequisites are considered to be key (the "key three," italicized in the example that concludes this chapter). If the overall score on all ten prerequisites is 75 or higher, and if the score on the "key three" is 25–30, then the institution is very well positioned to go forward with its campaign. If the overall score is 60–75, or if the "key three" score is 20–25, then the institution is in a gray area—close, but probably not quite ready. If the overall score is lower than 60, or if the "key three" score is below 20, then there is still work to do. Here is the DPI for a hypothetical organization:

- Commitments of time and support from all key participants (9)
- A clear organizational self-image and a strategic plan for organizational growth and improvement (8)
- Fundraising objectives based on important and legitimate institutional plans, goals, budgets, and needs (8)
- *A written document that makes a compelling case for supporting the campaign* (3)
- An assessment of the institutional development program and a market survey addressing internal and external preparedness (8)
- *Enlistment and education of leaders* (1)
- *Ability and readiness of major donors to give substantial lead gifts* (5)

- Competent staff and, perhaps, external professional counsel (5)
- Adequate, even liberal, funds for expenses (6)
- Consideration of other factors (age of the organization, caliber of the constituency, range of the institution's giving program, size and geographical distribution of the constituency, previous fundraising success, quality of the program and impact of its services, location of the organization, human factors, state of the economy, competing and conflicting campaigns, trends in the nonprofit sector, unfavorable publicity, local issues) (5)

In this hypothetical case, the DPI was 58 and the "key three" score 9. This organization is not yet ready to proceed.

What needs attention? Certainly, the case needs development; the matter of leadership needs to be addressed, and the major donor pool has to be expanded. Raising these "key three" scores alone to the level of 8–9 each would position the institution to go forward. Moreover, the cultivation process must be expedited, and it appears that the proposed budget is inadequate. There are some issues around staffing, and "other factors" were noted that either are causing concern or require some attention.

Let it not be forgotten: today's preparation is tomorrow's performance. Use all these tools—strategic planning, a market survey, development program assessment, and the DPI—carefully, thoughtfully, and thoroughly, and use them all very well.

# CHAPTER THREE

# DEFINING ROLES OF LEADERS AND VOLUNTEERS IN THE CAMPAIGN

A good fundraising program has two kinds of leadership—the layman who leads and the staff member who manages and serves. The better each is and the better they work together, the better the results will be. Leadership in itself, let it never be forgotten, is always the key factor in successful fundraising, whatever the cause, whatever the goal, and whatever the scope of the campaign" (Seymour, 1966, p. 179).

The chair of the governing board, the general chair of the campaign, and the chief executive officer of the institution have the principal roles in a capital campaign, especially in the early phases. They are responsible for setting the pace and establishing the right mood for the campaign. They also have to be confident that the planning stage is completed correctly and precisely, and that all the tools necessary for a successful campaign are present, especially a market survey, a case statement, and a comprehensive campaign plan. The success or failure of most campaigns is ultimately attributable to these individuals.

In recent years, the dramatic increase in fundraising competition has had a significant impact on the enlistment of top volunteers. Today there are more large, important campaigns and relatively fewer qualified, interested individuals to fill key leadership roles. Experienced volunteers now ask tough questions before they commit themselves to a project. Responsibility for enlisting and motivating these top volunteers falls to the chief executive officer, the professional staff, and key members of the board. It is they who must be prepared to win, convincingly, the commitment of top volunteer leaders.

## Campaign Leaders

The selection of leaders is of the utmost importance in a campaign. Top leaders should be excited and exciting, and leadership should come primarily from within. Among its board members, its service users, its advisory groups, and its other "institutional family" constituents, any institution should be able to find the bulk of the leadership it will need during a campaign.

The power structure of a community may be a supplemental source of leadership. Community leaders fall into four main groups:

1. Those who have inherited both wealth and its tradition of public service
2. The newly rich and newly powerful (the Horatio Algers of the modern world)
3. The top professional managers of key corporations
4. Respected and admired men and women of the community

An absence of leadership at this level is an early warning sign that the institution is not yet adequately prepared to undertake a campaign.

For a campaign to be successful, its top leaders, whether they come from within the institution or from the community at large, must make a commitment of time, effort, and dollars. The top leadership group should consist of respected individuals who have the following characteristics:

- Immediate name recognition with the groups served by the institution
- A strong identification with the institution
- A history of association and active involvement with the institution
- A substantial record of major gifts to the institution
- The ability and willingness to be forceful, dynamic leaders
- Connections with colleagues and friends who are also leaders and who represent the institution's various constituencies

An organization chart and job descriptions should be prepared for the leadership group and should clearly describe specific responsibilities, as well as the amounts of time that will be required (this figure will include time spent in meetings). Recruitment should begin at the top and work down, so that these volunteers recruit the people who will be working for them.

## The Role of the Campaign Chair

The campaign chair generally has the following duties:

- Serving as the campaign's chief executive officer
- Enlisting chairs for the principal functioning units of the campaign organization
- Cultivating and soliciting a limited number of appropriate prospects
- Assuming specific responsibility for personal and corporate commitments from members of the campaign steering committee and from all the principal operating chairs
- Serving as chair of the campaign steering committee and presiding over its meetings
- Making day-to-day decisions regarding the problems of the campaign, in consultation with the chief executive officer, the chief development officer, and others at the institution when important considerations arise
- Acting as campaign spokesperson for all news stories, campaign publications, special events, and other functions

The general campaign chair is the chief operating officer of the capital campaign. Therefore, the best that an organization has to offer may be barely good enough; no one is too big or too important to be asked to take this leadership post. The person who accepts it will be the key to the campaign and, more often than not, the measure of its success. The general campaign chair should have the following characteristics:

- Demonstrated capabilities
- Influence, affluence, and the willingness to use them on behalf of the institution
- Dedication to seeing that the job is done on schedule
- Ability to command respect without demanding it
- A personality and character to which others will readily respond (people give to and work for people, not for causes)
- Intimate knowledge of the institution and the full scope of its program
- Persistence that compels others to follow suit
- Accessibility
- Willingness to follow the campaign plan and procedures and to accept direction
- Willingness to devote sufficient time to leadership
- Awareness that the early phases of planning and recruiting may require a considerable amount of his or her time

- Determination to overcome obstacles and invalid excuses
- Willingness and ability, at the start of the campaign, to make a personal pledge that is generous, thoughtful, and proportionate (in the event that the chair represents a corporation, a significant commitment from the company should set an example of leadership for other business and industry prospects)

## The Role of the Governing Board

The members of a governing board, according to Stuhr (1977, p. 46), have four main functions:

1. To define the concept of the institution, set institutional goals, and approve plans for reaching them
2. To approve top administrative officers and motivate them (rather than just rubber-stamp administrative recommendations), give affirmative support to administrators, and lend administrative support to board leaders
3. To audit and assess the performance of the institution in all its parts, as well as the work of its top executives in the pursuit of established goals
4. To take appropriate action on the board's assessments of what must be done to reach institutional goals, and to build a more effective institution

To carry out these four functions effectively, a board is often asked, first, to make decisions that lead the institution into a capital campaign and, later, to act effectively within the campaign structure. In a capital campaign, individual board members' help is needed in a number of areas:

- Setting goals
- Encouraging the staff
- Formulating plans
- Identifying, cultivating, and soliciting major gift prospects
- Readily accepting major posts in the campaign (the community expects the institution's lay leaders to accept the key jobs)
- Taking on sufficient dollar goals for themselves to launch the campaign

Leadership from the governing board, according to Broce (1979), is the single most critical factor in the success of a campaign and even in whether an institution should conduct a capital campaign. Without board members' visible and unanimous commitment, it will be difficult if not impossible to motivate others to participate. And it is the governing board members, independent of others, who eventually must commit themselves to seeing that a stated goal is reached because they themselves have unanimously determined that it will be reached.

J. Jay Gerber (cited in Stuhr, 1977) reinforces Stuhr's points, stating that leadership from the top—in recruiting workers, cultivating prospects, soliciting support, and giving—is absolutely crucial to a successful capital campaign. Additional people will be needed as volunteer leaders, workers, and givers, but Gerber emphasizes that what governing board leaders give cannot be matched by any other group. More than anything else, the role of the governing board's members is to establish a policy framework within which the institution will operate, and to set an example for others. Where the capital campaign is concerned, the board member sets an example for others by doing the following:

- Taking a place in the volunteer organization and becoming a worker
- Early in the campaign, making gifts that are generous and appropriate to his or her means
- Being informed and enthusiastic about the campaign and the institution
- Working to bring other volunteers into the program
- Communicating with others in the constituency about the institution and the campaign

The governing board as a whole must be significantly involved in the campaign from the start, according to Livingston (1984). For example, the board's executive committee, its finance committee, and its development committee must be informed about and supportive of the project. Because much of the money to be raised through the campaign will come through the efforts of board members, it is mandatory to get their approval to raise money, and it is imperative that they be sold not only on the project but also on the institution. The more enthusiastic they are about the institution's leaders and the institution itself, the more effective they will be in raising money.

As a part of its overall responsibility, the board should review the timing of the campaign. How does it relate to prior drives? What have similar institutions recently done, begun doing, or announced? Has anything happened recently to affect the institution and make this a particularly propitious or unpropitious time?

Another area of the board's responsibility, not generally considered part of the campaign but nevertheless very significant, is investment of the funds as they are received. The board's investment committee should determine in advance the amounts expected and should formulate an investment plan. If the funds will be needed relatively soon, some kind of short-term investment is probably called for; if the funds are earmarked for endowment, longer-term debt or equity may be considered. The most important thing is to put the donations to work.

The plan for a major campaign is ordinarily developed by an institution's administration. Administrators are involved daily and are probably more aware of needs than outside board members are. This is not to say that there will never be occasions when the board suggests a campaign; the initial step, however, is usually taken by the chief executive officer of the institution in discussing a need with the chair of the governing board. This discussion will probably be followed by another with the board's executive committee. After preliminary approval has been granted, the staff generally will be asked to prepare, for formal submission to the board's executive committee, a detailed report of the specific need, as well as of the costs and benefits involved. After the need has been reviewed and approved, perhaps with input from the board's finance and development committees, the concept is submitted to the full board for approval. If the board approves, a capital campaign is usually referred to the board's development committee, for planning and overall supervision of its implementation.

The development committee and the development staff are the likely organizers of any capital campaign. The board's role in this area is first of all to ensure that the campaign is properly planned. It should look at the organization and structure; the people involved; the individuals, corporations, and foundations being solicited and how they will be solicited; how much they will be asked for; the timing of efforts; and the marketing aids being used.

Next, having approved the concept and the plan, the board members themselves should be asked to give. (First, however, they should be thoroughly cultivated and involved; see Chapter Four.) Their involvement in planning, both for the institution and for the campaign, is extremely important because involvement begets investment: the institution should evaluate both the potential and the probable giving ability of each board member and should also ask key board members to help rate fellow members. As a part of the involvement and cultivation process, board members should be shown the first draft of the case statement. Their active reactions to it should be sought, as should their involvement in formulating the final draft. It is important that the institution not take board members for granted, and that they be cultivated at the highest level.

Before board members are solicited, the possibility of a formula for board members' giving should be considered—a certain percentage of net worth or of annual income, for example. A policy should also be formulated for counting deferred and planned gifts from board members and others; this method may help board members enhance their participation in the campaign. The degree to which a board member's giving might be a leverage factor in setting the total goal should be considered as well: "If the board gives $1 million, we would have a chance of raising $4 to $5 million." Most important, a key group of board members should be involved in resolving these matters and establishing the goal for the board's giving. Once this goal has been established and the board has been fully involved and properly cultivated, it is time to solicit gifts from board members.

Remember, the single greatest mistake made in fundraising generally, and in capital campaigns specifically, is *not asking for the gift*. Early in the campaign, the institution must ask its board members to give and thus serve as an example to others (potential donors in the local community, major donor prospects, service users, and friends of the institution). But each solicitation should be carefully planned; no board member should ever give before having been asked to do so, because when board members' gifts (as well as gifts from others) are offered in advance, they are generally much smaller than if they had been properly solicited.

The solicitors should be carefully chosen, and each needs to have made a personal financial commitment first. Members of the board should be solicited by the chief executive officer or by other board members. Team solicitation, preferably with two callers on each prospect, is the most successful method. In making a solicitation, it is important to know the board member's areas of interest and relate them to the campaign: the biggest gifts will be generated when board members are asked to provide support in their areas of personal interest. It is also extremely important to note that capital gifts are not to be made in place of annual gifts. Careful consideration should be given to the method of asking (the separate ask, the double ask, or the triple ask; see Chapter Seven) before board members or others are approached.

In successful campaigns, contributions from board members and from the foundations and firms they control can range from 20 percent to more than 50 percent of the total goal. There are exceptions, of course, but there must always be a core or nucleus group ready to provide this kind of financial leadership, and it most often includes strong participation on the part of the governing board. In a capital campaign, 100 percent participation from the board is a powerful signal to other donors that the institution has vitality, vigor, and the confidence and enthusiasm of its governing board, who should know the institution better than anyone.

Once board members have given, their role becomes that of solicitors. Every board member should be responsible for some part of the campaign. It is not necessary that the campaign chair be a board member; ideally, however, all members of the board should be in leadership positions and should have groups of nonboard solicitors working for them and with them. This arrangement makes the board's involvement better known and demonstrates the board's backing of the program. It also provides the nonboard solicitors with people who are knowledgeable about the institution and who can answer their questions and accompany them on calls.

Board members should be used to identify potential solicitors, such as people with past, present, or future involvement with the institution. Board members, presumably, have useful contacts in the community, and so they should, as solicitors, use those contacts to bring in people who could be significant givers. They should ensure that enough of the right people are involved to get the job done in an organized manner, and that the people brought in also have enough contacts to be useful solicitors or significant contributors themselves.

Several such people should also be numbered among the institution's board. Board members should be asked to make important fundraising calls; their participation will add to the significance of these calls. They need not be involved with all the calls, however: being a board member is a part-time responsibility, and most board members probably have other, full-time positions; they cannot afford to spend a great deal of time making calls, and so the calls that board members will make should be carefully selected. Board members are most helpful in calling on people they know or on people of similar standing in the community or the corporate world. If an institution's board includes the chief executive officer of a significant corporation, the institution should use that person to make calls on other chief executive officers.

Legon (1997) concludes that board members who are effective fundraisers share the following characteristics:

- A natural relationship with or commitment to the institution
- Willingness to contribute
- Willingness to use the appropriate method of asking and thus persuade others to give
- Enough interest in the institution to ask tough questions and ensure that staff members carry out their administrative responsibilities
- A sense of passion about the institution and its mission, and a willingness to become advocates on its behalf
- Thorough knowledge of the institution, including its past and present, its traditions and values, and the likely direction of its future

In summary, then, these are the responsibilities of the board in a campaign:

- To review the need for the campaign
- To help structure the organization and timing of the campaign
- To suggest people as solicitors and potential donors
- To set giving levels for prospects
- To ensure proper research on prospects
- To review all printed material that will be used in presentations
- To make early, lead gifts commensurate with its members' ability to give
- To be volunteer solicitors in the campaign
- To follow up on and cultivate other major donor prospects, as appropriate
- To ensure that there are proper investment plans for the funds

Today, both in the United States and in Canada, there are many public, multicampus universities as well as large national organizations with headquarters at one location and geographically scattered affiliates or branches. A prevalent arrangement in such institutions is to have the fundraising program assisted by a foundation, a development council, or an advisory board that has focused responsibility for fundraising but does not have broader responsibility for governance and oversight. Under this arrangement, the institution's fundraising staff faces a special set of challenges in working with the volunteers provided by such foundations, councils, or advisory boards.

An advisory board or development council of this type is different from an institutional governing board. First, this type of group, because it has focused responsibility for raising money—indeed, that is its primary if not only purpose—should consist almost totally of influential, affluent individuals. (A governing board is necessarily attentive to issues of representation and must appoint members who reflect the diversity of the organization; this kind of group need not do so.) Second, because of its highly focused responsibility, this group's members are often not in a position to make institutional policy, set priorities, direct investments, or directly shape the future of the institution. Therefore, the challenge for the institution's development staff and top administrators is to involve this group in a meaningful way so that the members' inability to directly chart the organization's direction does not defeat their enthusiasm, desire, and singular ability to help.

To further this purpose, it is imperative that the institution's governing board make itself accessible to this group. For example, one or two members of the governing board should serve in the group and ask its members for advice, listening carefully and thoughtfully to what they have to say. The group's members should be substantially and deeply involved in the processes of planning the campaign, setting priorities, and making the case for giving. If they are to seek—and give—substantial investments, they must feel included and important.

## The Role of the Chief Executive Officer

An institution's chief executive officer and its senior management determine the personality of the institution; they give it life and vitality. It is increasingly clear that chief executive officers are also central to the success of today's capital campaigns. Graves (cited in Stuhr, 1977, p. 72) says that the chief executive officer's role in a capital campaign can be described by four functions.

> The chief executive officer must personify the character and the goals of the institution being led. Every constituency of the institution expects this of the chief executive officer. Successful results from development efforts depend on

the chief executive officer's ability to exemplify the character and lifestyle, the hopes and aspirations of all those who comprise the institution at any given moment. Benefactors are becoming more discriminating in their selection of institutions to support. They want to know what the institution is trying to accomplish and how it expects to achieve its objectives. Therefore, any institution needs an easily recognizable image, one [that] is unusually appealing. It is the chief executive officer who must know the institution thoroughly.

Second, the chief executive officer must communicate these goals to the institution's constituent body. The chief executive officer must understand how the institution's constituents perceive its character and goals and must provide them with the synthesis, a structure within which [the volunteers and the chief executive officer can] carry out their representations. People respond most generously to institutions whose representatives exude clarity, solidarity, and confidence respecting their missions and the means for their pursuit.

Third, a chief executive officer must create a strong development staff. Chief executive officers need to find chief development officers with whom they can share their public relations and fundraising programs in an environment of complete confidence. These two should complement each other in administrative skills and working styles. Together, the chief executive officer and chief development officer must build and keep a strong staff, people who are creative in the production of institutional publications and . . . sensitive and talented in public relations activities, people who can find those who can be interested in supporting the institution and who can help the chief executive officer and their chief development officer cultivate this interest and consummate gifts.

Finally, the chief executive officer must be primarily responsible for fundraising. How the chief executive officer accomplishes this mission depends greatly upon individual personality and style of operation. No matter what other valuable contributions a chief executive officer makes to the quality of the individual institution being served, this person will have failed if the institution's financial needs are not provided for. This does not mean the chief executive officer cannot get a lot of help from others. In fact, the job cannot be done without it. If a chief executive officer has a good development staff, keeps the board informed and properly involved, . . . [and] has the cooperation of key staff members and just a little bit of luck, success in the everlasting quest for funds will be possible. But it falls to the chief executive officer to have money on the mind most of the time, not as an obsession, but in service of the institution's mission.

With the help of the board, the chief executive officer must see that the organization has plans that are specific enough to identify its needs. The plans must be institutionwide. The chief executive officer should participate in the planning process but not make the plans. The plans should include items that the development staff can clearly articulate and passionately believe in. These become the basis of any capital campaign. If the institution is worth supporting, the plans will have something exciting to sell.

Nobles, speaking to a development workshop in 1976, had this to say (cited in Stuhr, 1977, pp. 73–74):

There is no way that a chief executive officer of any organization can sidestep leadership in fundraising. In the areas of making solicitation calls, cultivating major gift prospects, and contacting foundations and corporations, the leadership of the chief executive officer is particularly important. But this individual's time must be conserved and well spent and [his or her] specific involvement tailored to play to personal strengths.

The chief executive officer must be prepared to manage the function as well as to lead it. This may well mean delegating responsibility and authority as well as exercising [them]. It is vital in the stimulation of volunteers to assist with these endeavors, but not necessary to directly become personally involved with everyone and every step of the process. The relationship of the chief executive officer to donors, but especially to major donors, should be personal and individual to the extent it can be. The chief executive officer is called on to represent the total institution to the best of [his or her] ability. A managed program involving strategic contact with, and continued interest in, those persons and organizations . . . best able to support an institution is the major basis for any large gift and represents the mode of operation for the chief executive officer not only during the capital campaign but also over a longer period of time. The staff and volunteers should assist the chief executive officer in this process, and the chief executive officer must not only let them assist but also delegate appropriate responsibility and authority to enable them to assist effectively.

The chief executive officer's enthusiasm, knowledge of [the institution's] direction, sensitivity to the climate of the institution and to the donor's particular interest in it, and strong articulation of [and belief in its mission] will provide the subject matter for any number of presentations during the campaign. Patience and perseverance in building through innumerable small steps . . . the interest of someone only peripherally interested in the institution [and] an alertness to every opportunity to speak for the institution—these are the characteristics that must be consciously built into the job of the chief executive officer during the campaign.

Indeed, the essential role of the chief executive officer in the development of private support is to be the energizing, vitalizing central force that will provide an institution with an enduring future. In this entire area of leadership, however, it cannot be forgotten that financial resources never take the place of ideas, convictions, and diligence in the making of a great institution.

In summary, the chief executive officer is to play the following roles:

- Lead the institutional planning process and advocate for the plan
- Open doors for the campaign to key constituents and prospects
- Build bridges of understanding and acceptance with all key constituencies
- Remove roadblocks that might impede or imperil the campaign's success, and overcome the objections of key prospective donors should they arise
- Be involved in the closing of gifts
- Express appreciation and gratitude to donors and workers for their involvement

## The Role of the Chief Development Officer

In any capital campaign, the institution's chief development officer will be the catalytic force—an educator, manager, researcher, communicator, facilitator, leader, guide, and stimulator. The principal purpose of the chief development officer in a capital campaign is to obtain understanding and support for the total program. This professional should hold a rank equal to that of other administrative officers and should report directly to the chief executive officer. He or she must be an effective manager of staff and should provide support for the chief executive officer, the governing board, and key volunteers, ensuring that calls on prospects are actually made, not just planned and talked about. The role of the development staff is often in the background, not in the limelight. That belongs to the volunteers and the donors on the one hand and to the institution's chief executive officer on the other. More than anything else, the role of the chief development officer is to give structure and direction to any capital campaign effort.

How is this done? Every manager is different, and each has an individual style (moreover, no single management style is always best in all situations). Nevertheless, it can be said that most of today's professional development staff and volunteers believe that the following characteristics can be attributed to the manager of a successful capital campaign:

- Less orientation toward authority, and more orientation toward the provision of good working conditions
- Helpfulness in solving problems and accomplishing goals
- Capacity to keep out of the way and, to the degree possible, permit people to manage their own work

- Ability to provide a climate where staff members can gain confidence in each other, where goals are felt to be understandable and meaningful, and where everyone can participate successfully

The management function is important to the overall production of the entire staff and all volunteers. The campaign manager should have two primary goals: to be a contributor through his or her actual involvement in the campaign, and to provide leadership and guidance for both the staff and the volunteers. Actually, the manager's function today is considered to be more coordination of effort than actual fundraising. The roles are interdependent. Because most staff members and volunteers will agree that the campaign manager leads through demonstration, this individual should possess considerable knowledge of the profession, better than average skills, and an ability to employ successful techniques in making a contribution to the campaign.

The campaign manager works in a group environment where all functions are highly interdependent and interrelated. Therefore, this individual must take advantage of the diverse talents of the group members, staff and volunteers alike. Rather than working through others in the traditional sense of assigning tasks to subordinates, he or she should have the ability to work with peers, associates, and even superiors to get the job done. This desired ability, of course, places a premium on good and flexible personal qualities. The campaign manager, while building the overall approach on the best practices of traditional management, should augment this approach with new directions, techniques, and attitudes.

The campaign manager's role should be built on the recognition that a great deal of the organization's planning, organizing, directing, and controlling can and will be accomplished by others who are also managers, if only of their own time and effort. In other words, the campaign manager should provide the necessary climate to facilitate the best work of all subordinates, whether staff or volunteers.

A successful campaign manager generally serves the following functions:

- Recognizes the needs of staff and volunteers
- Delegates authority or responsibility (or both)
- Solicits and cultivates donor prospects
- Involves staff and volunteers, as appropriate, in decision making at every level
- Provides meaningful support, direction, and leadership
- Recognizes the challenge of changing times and human motivations
- Provides adequate feedback and recognition of achievement

Chapter Eleven provides a more detailed description of this role in a capital campaign.

# CHAPTER FOUR

# RECRUITING, EDUCATING, AND MOTIVATING VOLUNTEERS

The selection of volunteer leaders is perhaps the most crucial of all the decisions to be made. All volunteers are not equal; some are of the utmost importance to the success of a campaign, whereas others have lesser abilities.

Volunteers are people who offer themselves to perform services of their own free will, and there is no substitute for the influence that a volunteer leader can have on certain prospective donors. In many cases, the influence of the institution's staff is negligible compared to that of the right volunteer. Always remember, however, that all volunteers can do something, but only a few can do a lot. And since the success of any capital campaign usually depends on what a handful of donors do, it becomes critically important to the success of the campaign that the right volunteer leaders be enlisted, the term *right* meaning that they have the ability to influence the people who will make or break the success of the undertaking.

Every volunteer will do something, within reason, to help the institution, but volunteers usually do nothing to help unless they are asked to do something specific. It is not the number of meetings attended that determines the volunteer's power. Some volunteers are of great importance because of the one principal contact they can make with the top-flight prospect. It is the responsibility of the staff to be certain that the best assignments go to volunteers who have demonstrated records of performance, or who have the best credentials, and that other volunteers are brought along, through training, to higher levels of performance. Always make assignments on a peer-to-peer basis (for example, chief executive officer to chief executive officer) or on a peer-down basis (for example, chief executive officer to vice president), and always be certain that the top volunteers are assigned to the top potential donors.

Almost every institution has access to top volunteer leaders, although some institutions do not believe it. (If an institution truly does not have such access, it probably cannot mount a successful campaign.) The top volunteer leaders are characterized by certain recognizable traits:

- They are respected in the community.
- They are visible.
- They are able to influence others.
- They are success-oriented.
- They are involved in causes outside their work.
- They are able to attract other top leaders.
- They are self-assured and comfortable in most settings.

In looking for volunteers who are willing to work for the institution, first look to the organization's own family of constituents. If it is a college or a university, then its alumni, the parents of its alumni or current students, and its friends constitute the closest family members. For many community service organizations, those closest would include the individuals who use the services of the organization and their families. Other places to find volunteers include the corporate community, churches (if the institution is a church-related organization), other volunteer organizations, and groups of local citizens.

## Recruiting Volunteers

Any organization wants the most capable, the most visible, and the most committed people out front. The people who fill such roles usually are found among the prominent members of the organization's constituency or community. They are immediately recognizable, not only for what they do for particular institutions but also for what they do in the professional, civic, or political arenas. Ask busy people to do the job. The secret in using the time of busy people is to have them do what is crucial to the project, but no more; the next level of volunteers can do what is at the next level of critical importance.

Recruitment of volunteers is a shared task and is usually done most successfully from the top down. The campaign chair should be recruited by the top people in the organization. Before recruiting the chair for a capital campaign, the institution should have searched for the right person, figured out what it wants from that person, and, as an enlistment aid, prepared the institution's case statement. Having done all these things, the institution should not send in a low-level manager to ask for the commitment. Send top guns—the chief executive officer and the board chair.

In recruiting the next level of volunteers—cochairs and the campaign "cabinet"—the campaign chair reviews the pool of potential draftees with the staff and then participates in the recruitment visits. The campaign chair should do the actual asking but should be accompanied by the chief executive officer and the board chair. Some feel that the chief executive officer and the board chair need not be involved, but that belief is erroneous. The last thing an organization wants to do is convey to its newly committed campaign chair that he or she must do the job all alone. The organization must convey the sense of a well-built, well-staffed, rolling bandwagon. The development staff can assist the division chairs (the "cabinet") in the recruiting that they do. This process continues all the way down through the organization until, ultimately, volunteers are recruiting other volunteers without staff assistance.

The recruitment process is also a key part of the training and motivation process. No clear-thinking volunteer will accept a responsible assignment without asking a lot of pertinent questions. The institution must anticipate such questions and organize accordingly. Inform, but do not propagandize. Explain problems. The objective is to inform volunteers fully about the project and the campaign objectives and to give them confidence that they can do their assigned tasks successfully and with enjoyment. In fact, enjoyment is one of the greatest motivators, and it is the staff's responsibility to make volunteering a satisfying experience. According to Kughn (1982), the best way to do this is to choose the right people for the right tasks and thereby ensure success.

Because the kinds of people sought for the top jobs are known in the community, it is not difficult to learn a great deal about them, and it behooves the organization to learn as much as it can. The more an institution knows about these top leaders, the better prepared it will be when the time comes to ask them for their help in achieving its goals. Hale (1980) provides a partial checklist for ensuring a successful first encounter in the recruitment of a key leader:

- Relying on the case statement, point out in some detail the importance of the campaign to the institution in general, those who will benefit from the services of the organization, and those who will come later. Stress the philosophical side of the case. People respond to ideas first, mechanics second.
- Meet personally with the prospective volunteer leader at a place and time most conducive to an unhurried discussion.
- Make it clear what the job is that is being offered.

- Assure the prospective volunteer that the institution will provide all of the backup needed to conduct a successful campaign.
- Assure the prospective volunteer that the top leadership of the institution on the board and among the institution's friends will be willing to help.
- Clarify the amount of time needed to do the job.
- Describe the goals and how they were set. Let the prospective volunteer see that they are obtainable.
- Answer all questions fully.
- [After providing the] institutional [background, describe aspects] of the program that the institution thinks will be most meaningful to the candidate.
- Decide before the meeting who among those calling on the person will actually ask the person to take a volunteer assignment in the campaign. Try to work out ahead of time how the prospective volunteer will be approached.

## Working with Volunteers

The organization's staff serves behind the scenes in a supporting relationship to the top volunteer leaders. In working with these volunteers, the staff function should be carried out with a passion for anonymity. Staff members should coordinate and stimulate. They should furnish technical know-how, supply mechanical and clerical support, furnish resource information, and keep records. Finally, staff members help to motivate and energize the volunteers, but at the center of the activity—in the spotlight—are the volunteers themselves.

Dunlop (1981) recommends that the staff be guided by the following principles:

1. Before the first meeting with a volunteer leader, it is well for the staff to find out certain things about him or her (birth date and birthplace, religious affiliation, business background, family status, location of home, directorships, political affiliations, clubs, honors, awards). Some might question the value of taking the time for such details, and some of the benefits are obscure; attention to these details is worthwhile, however, if only to avoid embarrassment.

2. At the initial meeting with the volunteer leader, first impressions are important. The staff member should try to appear presentable, considerate, reliable, well organized, and knowledgeable. To be presentable, avoid appearing too different. People feel more comfortable around people who seem similar to themselves. Individual manner, speech, and dress will affect how volunteers feel about staff.

3. To show consideration, begin the first meeting with the volunteer leader by asking how much time he or she has to spend at this meeting. Respect the time limit the volunteer suggests, of course, and use a watch, if necessary. Doing so

shows that the staff recognizes the demands on the volunteer's time and values the time given.

4. To appear well organized, make open use of an agenda. Give the volunteer leader the original, and work from a copy. Let the volunteer see that items are checked off as they are covered. Doing this reinforces a sense of accomplishment and refocuses attention on the agenda items still to be discussed.

5. To build confidence in the staff's reliability, take notes openly. Doing so stresses the significance attached to the thoughts and ideas being discussed.

6. To show that the staff is well organized and plans ahead, consult the volunteer leader about the stationery to be used in his or her work for the institution. Some volunteers may permit the use of their own business stationery, but others will not. Some volunteers have several other pieces of stationery from which to choose. The staff should understand the criteria for the use of each piece. Also ask whether the volunteer's secretary can provide samples of the volunteer's writing style, as a guide for drafting letters and other material. If the staff will be preparing printed materials to go out over the volunteer's signature, ask for three or four sample signatures in black ink, and have a pen with black ink and paper ready for the volunteer, of course, when this favor is asked. Ask whether the staff may consult the volunteer's secretary for the salutation to be used in writing to the key people with whom the volunteer will be dealing on behalf of the campaign. By giving attention to these details, staff members demonstrate to the volunteer the forethought that they have given to all aspects of the volunteer's work.

7. An additional show of consideration comes in asking the volunteer leader about the best times for the staff to call, and about when he or she would like to avoid being interrupted.

8. To give a sense of urgency to the work that the staff plans to do with the volunteer leader, set the time and place of the next meeting. Doing so suggests a general time frame for the accomplishment of tasks even if specific deadlines have not been set.

9. In routine contact with the volunteer leader, be prompt. The emphasis on promptness should go beyond being on time for appointments. It is a matter of faithfully delivering whatever has been promised, when it was promised (whether that means a report, the draft of a letter, an opinion, or a staff member for a meeting). Courtesy also requires that staff members not keep the volunteer waiting on the phone. If an organizational secretary places calls for staff members, never keep the volunteer leader waiting for the staff member to come on the line: think of how discourteous it seems when a call interrupts a volunteer's work and then keeps him or her waiting.

10. Document the work accomplished at each meeting with the volunteer leader. Put each key decision, strategy, or plan in writing, and then invite the vol-

unteer to make additions or corrections. This practice not only makes sure that there is mutual understanding of decisions but also provides a timely reminder and reference for the work being done.

11. A volunteer leader's suggestion should never be rejected at the time when it is offered, no matter how unworthy it may seem. If no merit can be found in the volunteer's idea, simply say that it is something the staff would like to consider further, or that the idea is new and there is a need to consult others about it. Then hope that at least some worthwhile element can be found in the idea. This delayed response not only allows the volunteer to save face but also gives everyone more time to consider the suggestion.

12. Never delegate the proofreading of material that will bear a volunteer leader's signature. It is the staff's responsibility to make sure the copy is perfect. When it is perfect, submit it to the volunteer "for your consideration or approval," not "for your signature." No matter how many drafts have been gone through, always be graceful about giving the volunteer an opportunity to make additional changes. Remember that when a volunteer has been asked to sign something, it becomes his or her work, and he or she has the final say in its preparation.

13. Be candid with the volunteer leader. Sometimes staff members are tempted to offer optimistic encouragement rather than candor. It may be acceptable to project optimism in publicly announcing or discussing the campaign's progress, but not in talking with a volunteer campaign leader.

14. Staff behavior shows an attitude; keep it on the professional side. The objective of staff relationships with the volunteer leader is not to become his or her bosom buddy. As Seymour (1966) has said, "A party may be a party to a layman, but remember a party is a business meeting to you."

15. Do not be an expert. No one likes the person who is right all the time, and a know-it-all attitude defeats the very relationship that the staff is trying to build with the volunteer campaign leader.

## Educating Volunteers

The adage "easier said than done" certainly applies to educating volunteers. Orientation is necessary, and so are meetings. The campaign needs the power and stimulus that result when people come together to consider and attack a problem. In order to have a successful training session or meeting, however, the staff needs to take the following steps:

- Provide plenty of advance notice to the volunteers
- Draw up a well-planned agenda, with a copy for everyone, and mail it in advance

- Give the meeting a purpose
- Envision a result of the meeting (decisions made, actions taken)
- Make sure that the minutes of the meeting summarize what is to be done as a result of the meeting
- Put someone in charge of the meeting who will start on time, keep the meeting on track, and end on time

Volunteers expect professionalism from staff members. The staff must provide good training and the tools to complete the campaign successfully. As professionals, they must do their work in a businesslike manner and in a businesslike atmosphere, with well-prepared materials and a comprehensive training program. It is the ultimate objective of the institution to have the volunteers catch fire with enthusiasm. A carefully planned volunteer training session can help to do this, and carefully planned meetings can keep fanning the flame. Among the points to be covered at any orientation session are the following:

- A clear explanation of each person's role in the campaign (a chart will help)
- The points in the case statement that have caused the campaign to take on philosophical meaning
- Information and effective tools for each person to complete the assignment
- Questions, with complete answers
- Instructions for the volunteers (what they are to do, with whom, when, where, and why)
- Careful selection, rating, and assignment of prospects
- Guidelines on preparing for a successful call
- Clear instructions on what to do and what not to do on a call
- Instructions on what to do after a call
- Where to phone if there is a problem
- How to handle objections
- The importance of large gifts

A number of other elements may be included, as appropriate:

- A tour of the institution's facilities
- Presentation of architectural designs and floor plans, if a renovated or new building is a goal of the campaign
- Role playing of a solicitation call on a prospective major donor
- Presentation of any audiovisual aids that have been prepared to make the case or assist the volunteers
- A timeline for making solicitations

- Appropriate remarks from the board chair, the chief executive officer, and the campaign chair
- Introduction of the staff members and the assignment that each one will have during the campaign

The quality of the orientation session depends on the person in charge, those in attendance, expectations before the meeting, the planning that has gone into the meeting, where the meeting is held, how the room is arranged, the program, and the enthusiasm of the leaders.

During the volunteer training session, the explanation of the campaign plan, the campaign timetable, and the campaign objectives should be the shared responsibility of the institution's chief executive officer, the top campaign leader (usually the campaign chair), and the chief development officer. If the chief development officer is also serving as campaign director, it is especially important that the volunteers recognize this fact so that they will know this person as their contact within the organization. During the training session, the campaign director should be the one to explain the mechanics of the campaign and the materials in the workers' kit. (See Resource D, "Sample Volunteer Kit.") This is important not only because the professional knows the materials best but also because it demonstrates the competence of the director and builds confidence that the program is well conceived and carefully planned.

There are many kinds of volunteer training sessions, including workshops. For a nationwide campaign, the institution needs to recruit campaign leaders far in advance, usually six to ten months before the campaign begins, so that it can be certain of getting the workshop included in the busy schedules of its key volunteers. Once at the workshop, the volunteers will have ample opportunity to meet key institutional personnel and, ideally, some of the beneficiaries of the institution's services, as well as to hear firsthand about the institution and its objectives.

Bringing campaign leaders to the institution or to a local resort for a one- or two-day workshop requires a tremendous investment. Nevertheless, a meeting at a resort, or at any off-site location, means that there can be no distractions by phone calls or other intrusions. Those volunteers who have come back to the area from a long distance may be returning for the first time in many years. That can be inspirational and should help prepare them further for their leadership work; they can also see who else is involved, and this alone can be rewarding. Even a local or limited-area campaign should also bring volunteer leaders on site, of course, but the logistics are not as difficult.

The volunteers should feel equipped to answer the major questions that will be asked by prospective donors, and the staff must prepare all the explanatory materials that will enable each volunteer to be a complete advocate of the program.

These materials will be found in the volunteer worker's kit, a staff responsibility, which contains the following elements:

- The case statement
- Campaign objectives
- A description of the campaign plan
- Information about how to give noncash gifts
- Pledge cards
- Rating instructions
- Information about the range of gifts needed
- Report forms and envelopes

The kit will also include other supporting materials. Chief among them is a volunteers' guide. This type of guide can be prepared in many different forms and formats, but it should always stress the following points to each volunteer:

- Know the case. Be able to present it concisely and with enthusiasm.
- Make your own gift. It gives you a psychological boost and helps you ask others.
- Be positive; never be apologetic. Assume that the prospect is going to give. Remember, you are asking not for yourself but for an institution worthy of support.
- Make personal calls only. See prospects on a face-to-face basis; do not use telephone calls or letters except to arrange or confirm meetings. (If volunteers will not do this for the organization, then it will be better not to use their services.)
- Keep your sights high, and emphasize that this is a capital campaign. Ask the prospective donor to consider the amount suggested on the rating card.
- Go back to see the prospect again, as necessary. It is best not to leave the pledge card to be returned later. If the prospective donor wants to consider making a gift, tell him or her that you will return at a specified time. Decisions for major gifts take time; therefore, be prepared to make a number of visits if you need to.
- Obtain multiple-year (usually three- to five-year) pledges. Most donors can give more if they can spread the payments over a period of years. Some donors, however, will not pledge for more than a year but will make a gift. If that is the situation, ask whether the institution can seek a renewal of the gift each year of the campaign period. Many donors are receptive to this approach.
- Get the job done—do not procrastinate. Take the best prospects first. Success will build your confidence. Report gifts promptly so that others will see your success and so that the institution will be able to announce progress toward its campaign goals.

At this point, it is also necessary to discuss what can be done about hesitant or reluctant solicitors, and what staff members can do to help:

1. Recommend that volunteers make their own gifts first. It is a fact that the volunteer's commitment is a source of psychological strength in asking another to make a commitment.
2. Suggest that volunteers team up to make calls on their prospects, so that one volunteer can bolster another. The team approach should be used anyway for most major prospects; therefore, suggest this approach to unsure or reluctant volunteers.
3. For some volunteers, asking for the gift is the most difficult part of the personal call. Give them phrasing that helps take the sting out of the request. For example, the prospective donor cannot be offended if the volunteer asks, "Would you consider giving [the rating amount] over the next three years to help [name of organization] reach the goal?" The solicitor is asking for consideration of a request, not telling the donor what to do. This approach makes the appeal, but not in a hard-sell, aggressive way.

## Servicing Volunteers

It is an axiom of any capital campaign that no institution can hire enough development staff to do the job of fundraising alone. Volunteers are invaluable in research (the basic element of all fundraising), and they are absolutely indispensable in cultivating prospects and selling the program. Therefore, according to Kughn (1982), servicing volunteers is vital: it is not often that they provide their own steam, try to solve the problems that crop up, or motivate themselves.

The key to effectiveness in using volunteers is to assign them tasks that they can and want to do in the campaign. Those tasks must also be important. Thus volunteers should have assignments consistent with their interests, as well as with their abilities. Before giving a volunteer an assignment, it is necessary to ask, "Is success possible for this volunteer?"

The organization has the right to expect certain things from volunteers. In addition to taking specific assignments, volunteers should take responsibility for the following areas of communication:

- Informing the staff if something occurs that has affected their ability or willingness to do the job
- Promptly reporting all progress concerning their prospects

- Never overstepping or exceeding the scope of their assignments without first clearing the changes with the staff
- Letting the staff know if conflicting interests arise that could put the institution at a disadvantage
- Checking with the staff before departing from agreed-on plans

The staff must always remember that most volunteers agree to serve on boards or committees in the hope that they can be of constructive help. Typically, volunteers look to the institution and ask it to show them how they can best serve. They assume that the institution will be wise enough to give them tasks that are within their experience and capabilities, and that are important to the institution's goal. They expect to be used wisely and successfully.

It has often been repeated that an institution receives important sums by having important people ask important prospects for the support of important projects. Give volunteers the time, attention, and service they require and deserve. That kind of servicing will pay great dividends.

# CHAPTER FIVE

# BUILDING AND STATING THE CASE FOR THE CAMPAIGN

Campaigns are built on the institution's case statement. This chapter defines what a case statement is, how it is organized, how it is used, and how it is presented to an institution's constituencies.

Seymour (1966, pp. 42–43) writes of the case statement, "This is the one definitive piece of the whole campaign. It tells all that needs to be told, answers all the important questions, reviews the arguments for support, explains the proposed plan for raising the money and shows how gifts may be made, and who the people are who vouch for the project, and who will give it leadership and direction."

The absence of an effective case, or of someone able to formulate it properly, can mean that its preparation will consume precious time, when time is at a premium: at the beginning of a campaign effort. Seasoned campaign directors know that the preparation of a case statement is often the first—and can be the most formidable—challenge in any campaign effort. The case statement is one of the initial key management requirements for successful institutional development of a campaign.

Experience has shown that a sophisticated and carefully developed case, and the active involvement of key governing board members, other top volunteer leaders, and major potential donors, are the most critical elements affecting an institution's ability to receive financial support. These elements—together with institutional planning, documented research and evaluation of the constituency,

the enlistment of leaders, the organizing of volunteers, the existence of a qualified staff, and an adequate budget—represent a basic step in the direction of winning greater philanthropic support.

Pendel (1981) believes that the case statement must be a motivational document—
that is, it must be persuasive, not merely an essay of either institutional glorification
or expression of the institution's need for survival. The case statement must accomplish the following things:

- Serve to justify and explain the institution, its program and needs, so as to lead
  to advocacy and actual support.
- Attempt to win the reader with the nature of the vision [that] characterizes the
  leadership of the institution and to reassure the reader of the wisdom and responsible nature of its management.
- Characterize the organization so that it is distinctive in the eyes of the reader
  (this does not necessarily mean unique).
- Be positive, forward looking, and confident, with all the facts and projections
  reasonable, clear, vital, and accurate.
- Carefully set forth the fundraising plans in terms of policy, priority, and enduring benefits. (The following questions must be anticipated from the reader:
  Why this institution? Why now? Why me? How?) The case must be clear and
  concise, even though it may, in fact, be lengthy.
- Be a substantial plan for the future, not a burdensome revisiting of the past, no
  matter how honored or glorious. . . . In a real sense, it is a prospectus. It invites
  investment.

A case is a reasoned argument for an organization to receive the support it
can demonstrate it needs in order to continue living and flourishing as an essential
community resource. Only after the institution has isolated, defined, and researched its target market (its donor market, its service market, and its client base)
is it ready to develop its case. The institution's case, then, poses the institution's
mission, goals, plans, and programs in terms of the role these play or can play in
the life of the larger society. The "case" must be the institution. It aims, above all,
to be persuasive—to motivate the reader to respond.

The case statement should contain a view of the organization and a brief history. This document is not a fully developed essay on the philosophy of the organization; rather, it is a statement about the perspective that the organization takes
on the issues being addressed by the immediate campaign. It is almost never type-
set. Its appearance is most effective when it has the format of a loose-leaf binder
of typewritten, photocopied pages—obviously a draft document meant to be reviewed and revised, a working document that is kept on a word processor and is

updated periodically to remain immediately relevant. Distribution should be limited to board members and others who are interested enough in the organization to take the time to read it, and who have the interest and ability to act on its recommendations and requests. Where good planning is being done, the case statement and the institution's planning document are companion pieces.

## Organization of the Case Statement

The organization of a case statement can take many forms, and there seems to be no one formula for success. (See Resource E, "Sample Case Statement," and Resource F, "Sample Case Statement with Companion Pieces.") Nevertheless, certain essential elements are always included, and a good case statement does the following things:

- Describes the organization's mission in terms of the human and social issues that are of central concern to the organization
- States the organization's objectives in specific, quantifiable terms
- Describes a set of tasks or strategies for reaching the objectives within a given period of time
- Reports on the facilities, staff assignments, and budget required to carry out the tasks and strategies, which will include control procedures for continuing evaluation
- Identifies those who will benefit from the services offered by the organization
- Puts forth the reasons why anyone should make a contribution to support the organization, and thus the cause that it serves
- Stresses the strengths of the organization (avoid the trap of publicizing weaknesses or needs; emphasize the positive by selling strengths, successes, and opportunities, demonstrating the potential of the institution, and showing how it can become even better, and therefore more valuable, if it is supported)

In addition to these essential elements, the case statement should include the following kinds of information about the service area or environment in which the organization functions:

- An analysis of its market or service area, examining any significant changes that have occurred and the anticipated organizational impact of these changes (for example, a university's case statement may include a comparison of the institution's endowment with the endowments of other, similar universities; a healthcare facility's statement may compare that facility's patient/physician load per square foot with the same statistics at comparable facilities)

- Demographic and psychographic data in addition to socioeconomic indices
- An outline of the institution's immediate, short-range, and long-range plans, and a description of its expected future capabilities
- A list of its current and anticipated long-range needs, as well as annual, special, capital, and endowment requirements, all drawn from the institutional plan
- A list of the organization's personnel, including the curricula vitae of key staff and members of the governing board
- An analysis of the organization's recent gift history
- The financial history of the organization, including recent financial statements and audits
- A general history of the organization

To be complete, a good case statement will also include messages of endorsement and commitment from top leaders, a detailed plan for using the resources sought (and a compelling rationale for their provision), a budget detailing the gift opportunities, and a list of those who will lead the campaign and of those who have managerial responsibility for the institution.

## Outline of a Case Statement

In collecting, organizing, and presenting the written case—the printed document that grows out of the original case and is shared publicly—it is best to have an experienced professional do the writing and to use highly qualified designers and printers. If such people are not immediately available, they should be sought out. There are professional firms that specialize in preparing case statements for public distribution and consumption, as well as highly talented individuals who work independently.

Preparation of the case statement provides an important opportunity for involving institutional insiders, prospective volunteer leaders and major donors, and the organization's power structure; in fact, the case cannot be properly developed without the benefit of their insights and perspectives. Research in the institutional files, personal interviews to gather pertinent data, and keen observation are all tools of the statement writer.

Thompson and other members of the firm Frantzreb, Pray, Ferner and Thompson (1978) have drafted the following typical outline of a case statement for working purposes. The institutional staff can use this outline as a checklist in pulling together material pertinent to the case:

*Preface or Summary* (This section should express the essence of the case in one or two pages and state overall goals to be achieved.)

I. *Institutional Mission*

   A. Role in society

   B. Philosophy of purpose

   C. Mission, goals, and program

   D. Salient factors in its history—heritage and distinctions that have endured

   E. Factors that appeal to

      1. Service users (a collective term used to describe those who receive services/benefits from a third-sector organization including students, patients, members, clients, recipients, etc.) and their families

      2. Institutional family

      3. Governing board members and volunteers

      4. Friends and community

      5. Past donors

      6. Potential leadership and financial resources

II. *Record of Accomplishment*

   A. Service growth—regular and special programs

   B. Service users—meeting their needs

   C. Institutional family

      1. Nature and quality

      2. Role in teaching, research, policy, preservation, collection, services

   D. Service users/constituents

      1. Further education/services

      2. Careers/specialty goals

      3. Civic leadership

   E. Community service

   F. Improvements in environment and physical facilities

   G. Financial growth

      1. Annual operations

      2. Capital—current and endowment

      3. Methods used to finance accomplishments

   H. Philanthropic support—distinctive gifts and bequests

   I. Where the institution stands today

III. *Directions for the Future*

   A. Distinctions that must continue to endure

   B. New directions

   C. Objectives, curriculum, programs, services

   D. Service users

         1. Number to be served

         2. Nature of constituency

         3. Qualifications

    E. Institutional and administrative projected requirements

    F. Governance projected requirements

    G. Financial policies

         1. For tuition, fees, charges

         2. For investment management

         3. For business management

         4. For private gifts and grants

         5. For public support

    H. Physical facilities

         1. Campus/environment

         2. Buildings

         3. Equipment

IV. *Urgent and Continuing Development Objectives*

    A. Priorities and costs

         1. Endowment for

             a. Service users

             b. Professional staff/faculty, physicians, curators

             c. Library/equipment restoration

             d. Laboratories/service units

             e. Operation of buildings

             f. Facility maintenance

         2. New buildings

         3. Redevelopment of present facilities

         4. Property acquisition

         5. Debt reduction

    B. Master plan

V. *Plan of Action to Accomplish Future Objectives*

    A. Goals

    B. Programs

         1. Support current operations

         2. Support capital expansion

         3. Support special programs or projects

         4. Role of estate planning

    C. Organization

    D. Timing

    E. Resources

        1. Constituent sources

        2. Range of gifts needed—gift table

        3. Opportunities for memorials and tributes

        4. Methods of giving, including planned gifts and deferred giving

  VI. *The Institution's Sponsorship*

    A. Membership of the governing board

    B. Membership of the development groups

    C. Church/government sponsorship

## Uses of the Case Statement

Pendel (1981) identifies six ways in which the case statement is most profitably used:

1. It is used by the institutional family as an internal document to resolve, sharpen, and focus planning and policies into a written statement that interprets the institution to others.
2. An abbreviated form of the statement should be used in testing the market (that is, as a market survey).
3. The statement serves to rally present leaders around the policy, planning, and sales story. It is the expression of the institutional policy and of the plans that have been agreed on by the governing board and that are being aggressively promoted by the professional development staff and by other, volunteer groups.
4. The statement serves as a vital campaigning tool for the campaign leaders. It is easier to enlist new members for the governing board and top volunteers when there is a statement that argues the case for stability and security as well as for leadership and gift support. Communicating the case will also enhance the ability to recruit high-quality staff and administrators.
5. The statement serves as a supporting tool in the solicitation of large annual, capital, and special gifts through tailored appeals to selected prospects who have considerable gift potential.
6. It serves as a basic reference guide for proposed publications and communications of various kinds that will be distributed to the institution's various constituencies.

A thorough, honest case statement will transform apathy toward the institution into a sense of mission that prompts people to act. The case statement, properly prepared, can challenge the entire institution to provide greater service and engenders enthusiastic support for this direction.

## Presenting the Case Statement

Although the traditional case statement is sufficient for most campaigns—a building drive to provide a shelter for the homeless, or a neonatal care unit for a hospital—many modern campaigns, especially for complex and large institutions, present the case through multiple publications. A series of documents can be more understandable, attractive, and effective in educating and persuading than a single piece. There is no standard way of dividing the case into components, but it is not unusual, particularly for a public institution (such as a tax-assisted college or university), to present the case in the following segments:

- A "historical piece" that indicates a long-established tradition of private support for the public good, if the institution has such a tradition of philanthropy (if it does not, a more general argument, based on a solid rationale, can still be made and is often required to persuade certain potential leaders and givers)
- A financial case that delineates the economic benefits derived from the institution by the community, highlights the role of private support in the budget, and encourages the investment of private dollars in the campaign
- A traditional program brochure that makes the arguments for the immediate campaign
- A companion piece that outlines gift opportunities and ways of giving

In complex organizations, such as large universities, museums, medical centers, and hospitals, it is not unusual to find several separate objectives within the overall campaign goal. In these situations, separate case statements are often prepared to support each of the major campaign objectives, and individual pieces may also be prepared for each unit of the organization that has a major objective within the overall campaign goal (see Resource F).

## The Case-Stating Process

According to Curtis R. Simic (personal communication, 1985), the case-stating process is "the process of making 'insiders' out of 'outsiders.'" The case statement will continue to be the centerpiece in the presentation of capital campaigns; in future campaigns, however, and particularly in larger, more complex campaigns, as well as those in which specific issues demand extraordinary attention, the case statement will be only one part of the overall case-stating process. As Simic argues, in support of this larger process, volunteers' and prospective donors' acceptance of a campaign often depends on frequent and repeated reinforcement. Therefore, the case-stating process usually involves a series of presentations—oral, written, and audiovisual—to introduce the campaign to all the organization's constituencies.

Those asked to provide leadership, both as workers and as givers, must be fully informed about the campaign and its objectives. These vitally important constituents must also accept the premise of the campaign, understand its logic and its persuasion, and be moved to act on its behalf. What is most often required is a series of events, often repetitious, rather than a single presentation to any one group of key constituents. A single presentation will neither teach people everything they need to know nor permit key individuals to ask all the questions they need to ask in order to be knowledgeable, to fully satisfy themselves about the urgency, importance, and relevance of the campaign, and to fully invest themselves in it.

Individuals who have the strongest ties to or involvement with an institution are at the center of the institution's orbit. They are the ones most likely to read and react to the case statement. Prospects more distant from the center represent diminishing interest, and so a program brochure and a question-and-answer pamphlet are often more appropriate publications to be used with these prospects.

By implication, then, the institution should prepare a program brochure and a pamphlet in addition to the case statement. Many institutions consider a program brochure to be a case statement. Unfortunately, it is not; rather, it is often a shortcut that has been taken because the institution has neither the will nor the ability to prepare a proper case statement. Even when there is a well-stated case, however, a program brochure is still a necessity, although it does not and cannot replace the case statement. The principal differences between a case statement and a program brochure lie in length, the use of typographical features, the quality of the printing, and the scope of distribution. The brochure should be attractive, but not too elaborate or overwhelmingly expensive. It is often best to deliver this type of document by hand. If it is mailed, it should be accompanied by a personal note. The format should be flexible, particularly in a comprehensive campaign encompassing several objectives.

The pamphlet—usually with four or six panels, and consisting of questions and answers—focuses directly and concisely on the major objectives and issues of the campaign. This piece is designed for those who currently are not close to the organization or to the campaign, and who will not give their attention, at least initially, to lengthy, detailed arguments for support. It is designed to be carried easily by a volunteer or a prospect and to be read in two minutes or less. It can either be mailed or presented in person and is designed for very wide distribution.

# CHAPTER SIX

# CONSTRUCTING AND USING THE MAJOR GIFTS CHART

A standards-of-giving chart, or gifts table, is the concrete mathematical demonstration of the essential importance of major gifts to a successful capital campaign. Important to volunteers and donors alike, it can and should serve several functions throughout the course of the capital campaign:

- It indicates the number and size of the various gifts that will be needed if the institution is to reach its goal.
- It serves as a reality test, especially with the board and the major donors from whom leadership gifts are expected.
- It is a vital part of the market survey used to determine the feasibility of the projected goal.
- Once firmly established, the gifts table defines the goals that must be met in order for the campaign to succeed. (It is also to be hoped that the gifts table will raise the sights of prospective donors.)
- It establishes specific guidelines for volunteers to use in patterns of gift solicitation.
- It is an essential management tool, providing the purest and truest indicator of progress to date in any given campaign.
- It is a valuable evaluation tool after the campaign.

## Constructing a Gifts Table

Certain mathematical assumptions are followed in arranging a gifts table. The 80/20 rule says that 80 percent of the money will come from 20 percent of the donors. This is a common rule of thumb, although many campaigns, in very recent years, have seen 90 percent of the money come from 10 percent of the donors, and in at least one case 99 percent of the money came from 1 percent of the donors. In his book on fundraising principles, Seymour (1966, p. 32) states the rule of thirds. This rule, succinctly put, says that the top ten gifts in any campaign will represent 33 percent of the goal, the next hundred will represent another third of the goal, and all the rest of the gifts will represent the final third of the campaign goal. All these equations, when plotted on the gifts table, generally work out mathematically to about the same kind of representation (except, of course, when 99 percent of the dollars come from 1 percent of the donors). Tables 6.1 through 6.5 present typical gift charts for a $2 million campaign, a $4 million campaign, a $6 million campaign, a $25 million campaign, and a $60 million campaign, respectively.

A traditional gifts table is constructed as follows: The lead major gift—the single largest gift needed—is calculated to be 10 percent of the campaign goal.

### TABLE 6.1. STANDARDS OF GIVING NECESSARY FOR SUCCESS IN A $2 MILLION CAMPAIGN.

| Gift Type | Gift Range | Number of Gifts | Total |
|-----------|-----------|-----------------|-------|
| Major gifts | $400,000 | 1 | $400,000 |
| | 250,000 | 1 | 250,000 |
| | 150,000 | 1 | 150,000 |
| | 100,000 | 2 | 200,000 |
| | 50,000 | 2 | 100,000 |
| Special gifts | 25,000 | 10 | 250,000 |
| | 10,000 | 15 | 150,000 |
| | 5,000 | 25 | 125,000 |
| General gifts | less than 5,000 | all others | 375,000 |
| | | | $2,000,000 |

## TABLE 6.2. STANDARDS OF GIVING NECESSARY FOR SUCCESS IN A $4 MILLION CAMPAIGN.

| Gift Type | Gift Range | Number of Gifts | Total |
|---|---|---|---|
| Major gifts | $500,000 | 1 | $500,000 |
| | 300,000 | 1 | 300,000 |
| | 200,000 | 2 | 400,000 |
| | 150,000 | 3 | 500,000 |
| | 100,000 | 5 | 500,000 |
| Special gifts | 50,000 | 10 | 600,000 |
| | 25,000 | 14 | 400,000 |
| | 10,000 | 25 | 375,000 |
| General gifts | less than 10,000 | all others | 425,000 |
| | | | $4,000,000 |

## TABLE 6.3. STANDARDS OF GIVING NECESSARY FOR SUCCESS IN A $6 MILLION CAMPAIGN.

| Gift Type | Gift Range | Number of Gifts | Total |
|---|---|---|---|
| Major gifts | $750,000 | 1 | $750,000 |
| | 500,000 | 1 | 500,000 |
| | 300,000 | 3 | 850,000 |
| | 200,000 | 4 | 800,000 |
| | 150,000 | 4 | 700,000 |
| | 100,000 | 6 | 600,000 |
| Special gifts | 50,000 | 10 | 600,000 |
| | 25,000 | 14 | 400,000 |
| | 10,000 | 25 | 375,000 |
| General gifts | less than 10,000 | all others | 425,000 |
| | | | $6,000,000 |

### TABLE 6.4. STANDARDS OF GIVING NECESSARY FOR SUCCESS IN A $25 MILLION CAMPAIGN.

| Gift Type | Gift Range | Number of Gifts | Total |
|---|---|---|---|
| Major gifts | $2,500,000 | 1 | $2,500,000 |
| | 1,000,000 | 4 | 4,000,000 |
| | 500,000 | 6 | 3,000,000 |
| | 250,000 | 10 | 2,500,000 |
| | 150,000 | 12 | 1,800,000 |
| | 100,000 | 30 | 3,000,000 |
| Special gifts | 50,000 | 50 | 2,500,000 |
| | 25,000 | 60 | 1,500,000 |
| General gifts | 10,000 | 135 | 1,350,000 |
| | less than 5,000 | all others | 2,850,000 |
| | | | $25,000,000 |

### TABLE 6.5. STANDARDS OF GIVING NECESSARY FOR SUCCESS IN A $60 MILLION CAMPAIGN.

| Gift Type | Gift Range | Number of Gifts | Total |
|---|---|---|---|
| Major gifts | $6,000,000 | 1 | $6,000,000 |
| | 5,000,000 | 1 | 5,000,000 |
| | 2,500,000 | 3 | 7,500,000 |
| | 1,000,000 | 6 | 6,000,000 |
| | 750,000 | 8 | 6,000,000 |
| | 500,000 | 10 | 5,000,000 |
| | 250,000 | 12 | 3,000,000 |
| | 100,000 | 20 | 2,000,000 |
| Special gifts | 50,000 | 50 | 2,500,000 |
| | 25,000 | 100 | 2,500,000 |
| General gifts | less than 25,000 | all others | 14,500,000 |
| | | | $60,000,000 |

Thus, in a $1 million campaign, the lead major gift needed to predict the campaign's success is $100,000. Then, each successively smaller gift needed is half the amount of the previous one, and the number of donors needed is doubled, as illustrated by Table 6.6.

Of course, this simplistic approach does not always produce an appropriate gifts chart; one reason is that, in the majority of campaigns with goals of less than $25 million, there is a clear trend toward fewer and fewer major gifts accounting for more and more of the total goal. For example, reports from recent campaigns suggest that at times as few as four to six gifts, and often no more than ten to fifteen, account for 50 to 70 percent of the total goal in successful campaigns within this goal range, and gifts tables are now being designed to reflect this trend (see Tables 6.1, 6.2, and 6.3). The trend is evident in larger campaigns, too. Table 6.7 shows that 35 percent of the goal in a $51 million campaign was provided by just twelve gifts, and Table 6.8 shows 48 percent of a $25 million goal coming from only eleven gifts. Moreover, in very large campaigns (those with goals of more than $100 million), the projected amount of the lead major gift is sometimes set at less than 10 percent of the total goal (see Tables 6.9 and 6.10). In this situation, however, the percentage of the overall goal expected to be met by major gifts is not reduced; rather, the portion of the goal that is expected to come from other major gifts is increased, to compensate for the smaller lead major gift that is expected.

A standards-of-giving table is a sobering thing, and rightly so. It says, in effect, that without gifts on the order indicated, the entire effort has little if any chance for success. In the mood of urgency created by this awareness, campaign leaders are better prepared to offer specific suggestions to prospective donors, and

### TABLE 6.6. ILLUSTRATION OF A MATHEMATICALLY DEVELOPED TRADITIONAL GIFTS TABLE—$1 MILLION GOAL.

| Gift Type | Gift Range | Number of Gifts | Number of Prospects Needed | Total |
|---|---|---|---|---|
| Major gifts | $100,000 | 1 | 4 | $100,000 |
| | 50,000 | 2 | 8 | 100,000 |
| | 25,000 | 4 | 16 | 100,000 |
| Special gifts | 12,500 | 8 | 24 | 100,000 |
| | 6,250 | 16 | 48 | 100,000 |
| | 3,125 | 32 | 96 | 100,000 |
| | 1,560 | 64 | 128 | 80,000 |
| General gifts | less than 1,500 | many | many | 320,000 |
| | | | | $1,000,000 |

### TABLE 6.7. MAJOR GIFTS CHART OF A CAMPAIGN WITH A GOAL OF $51 MILLION.

| Gift Range | Number of Gifts Required | Number of Gifts Received | Amount Required | Amount Received | Percentage of Goal |
|---|---|---|---|---|---|
| $1,000,000 | 10 | 12 | $14,000,000 | $19,200,000 | 35 |
| 500,000 | 12 | 14 | 7,000,000 | 9,000,000 | 16 |
| 100,000 | 80 | 82 | 10,500,000 | 15,100,000 | 28 |
| 50,000 | 75 | 64 | 5,000,000 | 4,100,000 | 7 |
| | | | $36,500,000 | $47,400,000 | 86 |

### TABLE 6.8. A CAMPAIGN THAT SUCCEEDED WITHOUT ITS LEAD MAJOR GIFT.

| Gift Type | Gift Range | Donors Needed | Donors Committed | Total Gifts Requested | Total Gifts Received |
|---|---|---|---|---|---|
| Major gifts | $2,500,000 | 1 | 0 | $2,500,000 | $ 0 |
| | 1,000,000 | 4 | 7 | 4,000,000 | 9,536,107.51 |
| | 500,000 | 4 | 4 | 2,000,000 | 2,500,000.00 |
| | 250,000 | 6 | 6 | 1,500,000 | 1,513,000.00 |
| | 150,000 | 10 | 10 | 1,500,000 | 1,934,520.10 |
| Special gifts | 100,000 | 23 | 12 | 2,300,000 | 1,319,890.00 |
| | 50,000 | 42 | 15 | 2,100,000 | 897,783.80 |
| | 25,000 | 54 | 35 | 1,350,000 | 1,031,990.37 |
| | 10,000 | 135 | 58 | 1,350,000 | 709,192.52 |
| | | 279 | 147 | $18,600,000 | $19,442,484.30 |

### TABLE 6.9. GIFTS NEEDED TO RAISE $270 MILLION.

| Gift Amount | Number of Gifts Needed | Total |
|---|---|---|
| $20,000,000 | 2 | $40,000,000 |
| 15,000,000 | 2 | 30,000,000 |
| 10,000,000 | 3 | 30,000,000 |
| 5,000,000 | 6 | 30,000,000 |
| 2,500,000 | 10 | 25,000,000 |
| 1,000,000 | 20 | 20,000,000 |
| 750,000 | 30 | 22,500,000 |
| 500,000 | 40 | 20,000,000 |
| 250,000 | 75 | 18,750,000 |
| 100,000 | 100 | 10,000,000 |
| less than 100,000 | many | 23,750,000 |
| | | $270,000,000 |

**TABLE 6.10. STANDARDS OF GIVING
NECESSARY FOR SUCCESS IN A $1 BILLION CAMPAIGN.**

| Gift Range | Number of Gifts | Total |
|---|---|---|
| $10,000,000+ | 7 | $125,000,000 |
| 5,000,000+ | 20 | 175,000,000 |
| 2,500,000+ | 30 | 100,000,000 |
| 1,000,000+ | 125 | 150,000,000 |
| 100,000+ | 1,000 | 230,000,000 |
| 25,000+ | 2,000 | 100,000,000 |
| All other gifts | 200,000+ | 120,000,000 |
| | | $1,000,000,000 |

volunteers are better able to base each approach on the specific standards of giving needed to ensure the campaign's success. Inevitably, goal setting and gifts tables are interrelated, certainly to the extent that one of the important ingredients in setting a campaign goal has to be a realistic assessment of what the potential is for big gifts (Addison L. Winship II, personal communication, 1986).

The mathematical development of the gifts table should take account of known information about major gift possibilities. For instance, if a campaign goal of $25 million is contemplated, and if it is felt that a single gift of $10 million is a virtual certainty, then a gifts table should be established that includes a gift of $10 million, even if the circulation of the table is limited until the gift is actually received. This practice falls outside the guidelines provided by the mathematical principles and other standard assumptions that normally guide the construction of such a table, but in these circumstances it is reasonable. It demonstrates sound logic and common sense if it is properly used as a sight-raising technique, or as a technique for securing that single potential donor, who ultimately may make this magnificent gift. Be certain of the gift, however, before circulating the table publicly: if the gift fails to materialize, such a skewed gifts table obviously will create a problem for the campaign from the beginning.

Known gift needs should also be taken into account. For example, one institution, in a recent campaign, included in its goal forty endowments to partially fund professorial positions. The gifts table (see Table 6.9) was designed with the knowledge of this need and reflected it. If a $10 million building has three floors, and if each floor can be named for a $2.5 million gift, then show three $2.5 million giving opportunities available in the gifts table. If there is a need for fifteen endowed scholarships at $100,000 per scholarship, then show at least fifteen $100,000 gift opportunities. It is a sign of poor planning, and a source of possible embarrassment, to have a list of named and memorial gift opportunities that is not in concert with the gifts table.

## The Gifts Table as an Essential Management Tool

During the market survey, the gifts table is used to show survey respondents the size and number of the gifts that will be needed to ensure the campaign's success at the dollar level that the survey is testing. Indeed, one of the most vital pieces of information that any market survey provides is the respondents' assessments of the tested goal's feasibility in relation to the gifts table. Thus, used as part of the market survey, the gifts table is one of the strongest indicators of whether a goal has been set at a level that is too high, too low, or appropriate. Often, as one result of a market survey, the campaign goal must be decreased, and the gifts table for the campaign itself must be correspondingly adjusted.

After the gifts table has been designed, it is important for the institution to do solid prospecting. It is a generally accepted rule of thumb that an institution must have at least four legitimate gift prospects for each major gift required (see Table 6.6). As the institution moves down the gifts table, fewer prospects are required for each gift—three prospects for each special gift, and two for each general gift—because a prospect who is in the upper gift ranges, but who does not give a gift as large as anticipated, may give a smaller gift, thereby contributing to the goal set for a lower category on the gifts chart, even before the campaign phase corresponding to that category is undertaken.

Once the campaign commences, the gifts table becomes an essential management tool. It is not uncommon to hear a campaign director report, "We have 80 percent of the goal in hand and ten months to go in the campaign." On the surface, this may appear to be a favorable report. Nevertheless, if the lead major gift—the top gift on the chart—has yet to be received, and if there is little or no probability that it will be received, then the report is far less encouraging than it might be if in fact all the gifts at the high end of the range had been secured and the campaign needs only to conclude the general gifts phase. Volunteers and staff should use the gifts table as a "scorecard" during the campaign.

Table 6.7 illustrates how a gifts table can be used to indicate the number of gifts required in a range, as well as those received to date. It is a far more accurate indicator of progress in a campaign than any other representation. The actual campaign from which this example is taken exceeded its goal of $51 million by nearly $4 million, and 86 percent of the total funds were received from fewer than 3 percent of the donors. As the table indicates, the amount received in all the top major gifts ranges exceeded the requirements that had been projected at the beginning of the campaign. This gifts chart confirms a trend now obvious in many capital campaigns: a greater proportion of funds received is coming through major gifts at the high end of the range in successful campaigns.

In addition to the campaign illustrated in Table 6.7, at least two other very recent indicators confirm this trend. One indicator was reported by Addison L. Winship II (personal communication, March 1986), who shared his experience of supervising a campaign at Dartmouth College. The review of the gifts table strongly suggested that a successful campaign would be expected to raise between 45 and 50 percent of its goal in gifts of $1 million or more. Winship surveyed six other large university campaigns with goals of more than $100 million. His evaluation of these campaigns showed that 74 percent of the total gifts to these six campaigns had come in amounts of $100,000 or more. The second indicator was noted by Anderson (1986), who reported the same findings from a survey of campaigns with goals ranging from $300,000 to $300 million. In the campaigns he surveyed, consistently 75 percent of the campaign goal was received in gifts of $10,000 or more. He also reported that the overall mean value of the top ten gifts in these campaigns came to around 45 percent of the campaign total. This pattern was fairly consistent for all campaigns covered in this analysis, and the Winship survey of larger campaigns showed only a slightly different pattern. The trend in all campaigns is clear and consistent.

For institutions now using the model of the comprehensive campaign, it is almost always true that from 95 to 99 percent of the goal will come from 1 to 2 percent of the donors because this campaign model counts all donors and gifts, including annual gifts. In these situations, there is a need for a new, more relevant way of instructing institutions about what is realistically needed to achieve goals. A review of a number of comprehensive campaigns conducted over the past quarter-century suggests that a new standard should be established: In campaigns with goals under $100 million, 80 percent (or more) of the total goal will come through the top 50 (or fewer) gifts; in campaigns with goals between $100 million and $500 million, 80 percent (or more) of the total goal will come through the top 200 (or fewer) gifts; in campaigns with goals of between $500 million and $1 billion, 80 percent (or more) of the goal will come through the top 400 (or fewer) gifts; and in campaigns with goals of $1 billion and above, 80 percent (or more) of the total goal will come through the top 750 (or fewer) gifts. Therefore, if your organization does not have a pool of ready and able lead and major gifts prospects that can produce these numbers, then prospect identification, education, and cultivation remain to be done.

Can a campaign succeed without receiving the lead major gift that has been established on the gifts table? Yes, it can. Table 6.8 provides an example of an actual campaign that succeeded without receiving its projected lead major gift. But a campaign probably cannot succeed unless the total of the major gifts received equals or exceeds the amount represented by the percentage of the total goal that is expected to come from major gifts. Tables 6.7 and 6.8 show the results of two actual campaigns that more than met their goals for major gifts. With success at the major gifts level, even if the lead major gift is not received, a campaign can succeed; without success at this level, a campaign is almost certainly doomed to failure.

## An Unworkable Gifts Chart

One of the most common fallacies regarding gift ranges and distribution patterns is the notion that a campaign can succeed if everyone in the constituency gives the same amount. For the purpose of illustration, this theory suggests that a campaign with a prospect universe of one thousand possible donors can achieve a $1 million goal by having each prospect give $1,000. It never works. Why? This type of approach is not fair or equitable to donors. Wealth is not distributed democratically in this society. If all are asked to make gifts that are "generous within their own means," each donor will not be expected to give the same amount; much will be expected of a few, and many more will be expected to do as much as they can. Not only will everyone not give the same amount to any given campaign, many will choose to give nothing at all. In addition, this approach limits the amount asked from those who could give more, and donors seldom give more than they are asked to give.

## The Gifts Table as an Evaluation Tool

The gifts table can be a helpful evaluation tool after the campaign is completed. Table 6.8, from a recent campaign, illustrates the growing trend toward an emphasis on major gifts and the weakening of support in the traditional "special gifts" range. The same trend is in evidence in the campaign depicted in Table 6.7, and this phenomenon is being reported by other campaign directors across the country. The trend may be appearing because the middle class has less disposable discretionary income available today. Indeed, some research suggests that the middle class is shrinking, and that if some in this group are moving up the economic ladder, more are falling back down (Rose, 1986).

For example, a study done for the American Association of Fund-Raising Counsel Trust for Philanthropy by the Gallup Organization (1987) compares individual giving in 1986 and 1987. It shows that 42 percent gave more in 1986 than in 1985, that 57 percent of those who gave more said they had done so because they had more to give, and that 28 percent of those who gave less said they had done so because they had less to give.

Likewise, INDEPENDENT SECTOR (1996) has found that the total percentage of households reporting charitable contributions was lower in 1995 (68.5 percent) than in 1987 (71.1 percent), but that the percentage of income from contributing households increased between 1987 and 1995, from 1.9 percent to 2.2 percent, and that average household giving had therefore increased because of higher levels of giving from a narrower base of supporters. Of the households surveyed for this study (a sample including households that gave nothing), the average household reported 1995 contributions equal to 1.7 percent of its annual household income—the same as in 1993. (Similarly, the American Association of Fund-Raising Counsel Trust for Philanthropy, 1997, estimates that the average percentage of household income contributed from all households in 1995 was 1.9 percent.) Further, according to INDEPENDENT SECTOR (1996), the average household gift, after adjustment for inflation, increased by 2 percent between 1993 and 1995, whereas giving from contributing households only (that is, from a sample excluding those households that gave nothing) increased almost 10 percent after adjustment for inflation.

Other studies, notably one by Schervisch and Havens (1995), find that percentage of household income contributed increases with household wealth, and that the question of whether a household contributes at all is strongly related to its wealth. Moreover, almost all households where net worth is more than $50 million contribute, and contributions from those households represent, on the average, 18 percent of income (p. 101). INDEPENDENT SECTOR (1996) also indicates that income is a determinant of the decision to make contributions, and that households with higher incomes give to charity more frequently than do lower-income households. More recent evidence for this point is provided by the University of Michigan, which in 1997 raised $1,415,162,693, or 141.5 percent of its goal, in a campaign with a goal of $1 billion. Roy E. Muir writes:

> Our experience in the Campaign for Michigan demonstrated once again the absolute essential importance of a leadership gift program in a comprehensive campaign. We received 55 percent of the total from gifts of $1 million and above. In fact, we received 27 percent of the total from donors of $5 million and above. I believe that most of the true campaign "increment"—that which would not have been raised if we had not mounted the campaign—came from donors of $1 million and above.
>
> One major goal for Michigan's campaign was the $350 million sought for endowment. This was a significant change in the giving patterns and habits of

our donors—most whom had not given to endowment in the past. Virtually all of the $377 million raised for endowment came from gifts of $1 million and above—certainly it came from gifts of $100,000 and above [personal communication, 1998].

All of this information, taken collectively, suggests that major gifts at the high end of the gifts chart will be more and more important to the success of any campaign. This suggestion is a strong argument for concentrating efforts at the high end; the implication is that institutions with an interest in entering into a campaign must have prospects able and willing to give at the major gifts level if the institution is to have any real hope of success, whether the campaign goal is $250,000, $2.5 million, $25 million, $250 million, or $2.5 billion.

# CHAPTER SEVEN

# ESTABLISHING THE CAMPAIGN STRUCTURE AND SOLICITATION PROCESS

The responsibility of professionally staffing a campaign falls primarily to the chief development officer, the campaign director, and the development staff. The chief development officer should bear primary responsibility for preparing a comprehensive campaign plan, organizational chart, and campaign schedule before the campaign is launched. (See Resource H, "Sample Campaign Plan.") These elements should include a leadership recruitment system and schedule and a public information plan and schedule covering media, printed materials, typescript materials, and audiovisual materials. The development staff should see that provisions are made for production of a prospect list as well as for an evaluation system for all campaign prospects; this system should include evaluation committees for larger gift prospects and formulas for giving for smaller gift prospects. There must also be a campaign budget and a system for controlling expenses, a system for recruiting volunteer workers, informational meetings for those recruited, and training workshops for volunteers and leaders.

It is important that the development staff establish a progress reporting/control system for prospects. It should include a system for assigning prospect pledge cards, a system for assigning workers and tracking their activity, a schedule for report meetings, mailings of progress reports, and a prospect reassignment system with a redistribution system for pledge cards. Systems for tabulating gifts and auditing the campaign should be well thought out and planned for in advance; they should include posting of the section listing and the master listing, as well as the auditing of all cash and pledges. Steps should also be set forth to address organizational issues, volunteer recruitment and training, public announcement of the campaign, subsequent report meetings, and the follow-up and cleanup necessary to the success of area campaigns. There should also be systems for acknowledging gifts, collecting pledges, and conducting the final follow-up.

It is important for the campaign director to work effectively with the volunteer organization and the top levels of institutional administration, but this officer must also make sure that the entire institutional community is aware of the campaign and feels that it has an active part to play. Key administrators should be consulted on or informed of all proposals and fundraising activities related to their specific areas. At the same time, key institutional personnel should be actively involved in the cultivation and solicitation process.

## Campaign Organization

An organization chart for a typical capital campaign will generally resemble that shown in Figure 7.1. Organization charts can and do take many forms. Nevertheless, every campaign's organizational pattern should incorporate at least the structural features shown in the figure; this is the basic pattern from which other, more complex patterns are developed.

The exact structure of any campaign organization will have the following determinants:

- The method chosen for the campaign
- The "ask" method chosen
- The extent to which the organization intends to rely on a "rifle shot" approach versus a "shotgun" approach (the latter requires a more extensive volunteer structure)
- The size and diversity of the institutional constituency
- Whether the campaign is a community campaign or a wide-area campaign
- The extent to which the campaign will rely on volunteers to do solicitation
- The mix of face-to-face, telephone, and direct-mail solicitation that will be incorporated into the campaign structure

A chair and members for each committee should be enlisted according to the following pattern: the chair of the board and the chief executive officer should enlist the general campaign chair in a personal visit; and the general campaign chair, the chair of the board, and the chief executive officer, working as a team or, as applicable, in pairs, should enlist members of the campaign's executive committee

## FIGURE 7.1. CAPITAL CAMPAIGN ORGANIZATION CHART.

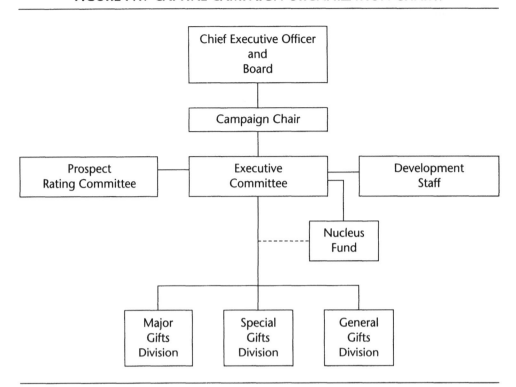

(these appeals, too, should be made in person). Enlistment should be as official and dignified as possible. Each volunteer should be given a job description, with definite assignments and specification of the results that will be expected within a definite period. Professionals find that sharing the results of the market survey and/or a preliminary version of the case statement is often very helpful in selling top prospective leaders on the campaign; doing so makes the prospective leaders feel that they are in on the ground floor—and they are.

Volunteer enlistment is a top-down process. Once the board chair and the chief executive officer have enlisted the campaign chair, and once the three of them have enlisted the key campaign leaders, all the members of the volunteer structure in turn should be expected and required to enlist the individuals who will work with them throughout the campaign. In every case, even at the level of special and general gifts, it is best for leaders to be enlisted through personal visits.

The success of any campaign depends on an overall volunteer organization designed to facilitate rather than restrict the effective solicitation of prospects. Organizational concepts must be realistic and practical. Overorganization can be cumbersome and stifling. The best organizational structure permits efficient flow of communication and easy performance of functions by everyone involved. The size of a volunteer organization is dictated by the scope of the campaign, the size of the constituency, and geographical requirements. The effective rule of thumb regarding volunteer solicitors and prospects is that there should be one prospect per volunteer at the major gifts level; two to three prospects per volunteer at the special gifts level; and five prospects per volunteer at the general gifts level. Often, the pattern followed is three to five major gifts prospects per volunteer, four to seven special gifts prospects per volunteer, and, occasionally, ten or more prospects per volunteer for solicitation of general gifts. This pattern is less effective because busy people are being asked to do more; nevertheless, it is reality for many organizations.

## Committee Responsibilities

Any campaign structure requires a number of committees, or at least one committee functioning in a number of ways. A typical campaign includes a policy committee, an executive committee, and committees on prospect evaluation, major gifts, special gifts, general gifts, and public relations (the role of public relations is discussed in Chapter Thirteen). According to the campaign model and structure chosen, there also may be a need for an institutional family campaign committee, a community campaign committee, a corporate campaign committee, and a foundation campaign committee.

The development committee of the governing board generally functions as the policy committee. It determines the general policies of the program and sets the goals. It approves the organizational pattern, staffing and budget requirements, and proposed timetable. It also sets guidelines under which memorial gifts or named gift opportunities may be established and determines guidelines for gift acknowledgment and donor recognition. The top development officer staffs this committee. Its recommendations are presented for approval to the full governing board.

The executive committee provides general direction and active management of the program. It coordinates the activities of volunteers and sets the operating schedule. The executive committee generally includes the chairs of the several campaign operating committees, advisory groups, and top administrators. The chief executive of the institution and the chair of the board should be ex officio members. This committee, too, is served administratively by the top development officer. This committee normally reports to the chief development officer and/or the chief executive officer.

The prospect evaluation committee should be active early in the program, measuring both interest and financial capability. It evaluates what the prospects can give (not what they will give) in terms of both effort and contributions. Confidentiality and anonymity are absolutely essential to this committee. The research staff of the development office is assigned to this committee.

The major gifts committee has the critical task of evaluating, cultivating, and soliciting the institution's most important prospects. Because 80 percent or more of the campaign goal will probably come from a very small number of lead and major donors, it is important that the most affluent and influential group possible be enlisted to serve on this committee. The members of this committee must be the best volunteers who can call on the best prospects at the appropriate time to secure maximum investments. Committee members are often assigned only one or two prospects to work with at a time. This group constitutes one of the most important task forces in the campaign organization. It is the responsibility of this team, under the direction of its chair, to persuade its members to take appropriate assignments and to keep them in steady and productive pursuit of their prospects. Because this committee is so important, the selection of its chair should be carefully considered. Generally, the chair should be a resident of the community in which the campaign is taking a place (or, in the case of a wide-area campaign, be able to commute readily to the organization's location), be capable of making a major gift, be active in the business or social community, and be someone with considerable influence who is not afraid to ask for major gifts. In brief, the tasks of the major gifts chair are as follows:

- To put together a strong committee willing to seek gifts in the major gifts range
- To work closely with the campaign chair in all matters affecting the committee's responsibility
- To make a personal gift that is generous within his or her own means
- To ask for certain major gifts personally
- To hold regular meetings of the committee in which its members can screen and rate new prospects, take additional assignments, and report on progress
- To follow up periodically with members of the committee and make regular, timely reports to the committee on the progress of the campaign
- To see that members of the committee are fully informed about the campaign and that each member has made a personal commitment in accordance with his or her ability
- To work with the other committee chairs to identify and develop other individual leadership gifts throughout the campaign structure

The special gifts committee deals with substantial gifts just below the major gifts level. The duties of committee members are similar to those of members of the major gifts committee. The ratio of one worker to two to four prospects is commonly used. Liaison may be provided by development staff other than the top development officer.

General gifts solicitation is generally the cleanup phase and in most modern campaigns is targeted to the general constituency of the institution. Personal solicitation is encouraged, but telephone solicitation and direct-mail solicitation are often used. For personal solicitation, one worker to five prospects is the generally accepted ratio. Telephone solicitation, second in effectiveness to direct-mail solicitation, is growing increasingly popular; mail techniques are the least effective of the three. Some campaigns have recently reported success with combination phone and mail programs.

# The Solicitation Process

As repeatedly demonstrated through many years of fundraising experience, personal solicitation is both the most economical and the most effective form of campaign solicitation. Telephone solicitation is an extension of the personal visit but usually is not nearly as effective. Phone-mail solicitation, which should be used for prospects the institution cannot reach personally, is an increasingly effective method, although some believe that overuse is already causing it to lose some of its effectiveness. The principal purpose of a broad mail campaign is to elicit new interest and to cultivate those who may give more later. If mail must be used for individual solicitation, pave the way by telephone where feasible.

But how, exactly, does an institution go about structuring its gift solicitation and determining the scope of solicitation for its particular campaign? Evans (1978, 1979) outlines three distinct approaches to asking that gifts be considered: the "separate ask," the "double ask," and the "triple ask."

## The Separate Ask

With the separate ask, donors are solicited at two separate times, once for an extended commitment to a capital gift and once each year for annual giving. There are three advantages to this approach:

1. Two separate solicitations clarify the difference between capital giving and annual giving.
2. Worker training may be made easier because those who volunteer to solicit capital funds need only inform the donor that the capital fund is distinct from annual giving, and that donors will be asked at a different time to consider annual support.

3. A special solicitation may lend annual giving more emphasis because it will not appear subordinate to the capital campaign.

A separate ask also presents problems:

1. Donors may resent a second request that comes only a few months after they have made a major commitment to a capital campaign.
2. More volunteers may be required if the annual fund solicitation is to involve more than direct mail.
3. If solicitations come at separate times, some donors may merely shift their annual giving to the capital campaign, declining later on to support the annual fund and thus not increasing their total contributions.

Although this approach can be used with any of the types of campaigns described in Chapter One, it is not particularly well suited to the comprehensive campaign, because the institution that has chosen the comprehensive model has done so to create harmony and unity within its total program, and this approach creates division.

## The Double Ask

Among institutions that have continuing capital programs and reasonably satisfying experience in annual campaigns, the double ask—soliciting the donor for the capital gift and the annual gift at the same time—is a popular method of coordinating the annual and capital campaigns. People who are not ready to be solicited for capital gifts continue to be solicited for annual gifts; those who are ready are asked for both. The advantages of the double ask are as follows:

- If capital funds are solicited personally (and, with major donors, they must be), this system automatically provides for face-to-face solicitation of the annual gift as well
- This system provides an efficient use of volunteers because the volunteer for capital solicitation will handle annual giving at the same time
- It reduces "harassment" of the donor by providing for a single approach during the year
- It keeps the concept of annual giving alive while also bringing attention to the capital campaign

The double ask also presents some problems, however. Donors may not appreciate the distinction between the types of gifts and may simply say, "I'll make a gift to the institution, and you divide it up as you want." It may also make worker training more difficult—the more forms of solicitation a worker must present, the greater the potential for confusion.

There are two forms that the double ask can take. The first is the *multiple-year capital, one-year annual* form. Here, the donor is asked to make a pledge to the capital campaign, to be paid over a period of years, and at the same time is asked to make a contribution to the current annual fund, with a reminder that another solicitation for annual giving will occur each year while the capital pledge is being paid. The second is the *multiple-year capital, multiple-year annual* form. Here, the donor is asked to make a pledge to contribute over the next three to five years, allocating a portion to capital giving and a portion to annual giving. The disadvantage of this approach is that it limits the possibilities of presenting the case to the donor annually, if the donor has made a commitment to both the capital and the annual funds.

### The Triple Ask

With the triple ask, not only are the capital and annual gifts solicited at the same time, but a planned gift commitment is also sought. The advantages and disadvantages of the triple ask are similar to those of the double ask. This is a very sophisticated form of ask, requiring both an extremely well planned approach by staff and volunteers and a prospective donor who is extremely knowledgeable. It is to be used selectively and sparingly—only where the situation warrants it.

## Scope of Solicitation

Having considered the ways in which the annual fund and the capital campaign can be combined, Evans (1978, 1979) suggests that an organization must consider the scope of each solicitation—that is, will the organization solicit everybody for everything, or will it limit solicitation of certain prospects to capital gifts and solicit others only for annual gifts? Once an organization has decided to continue annual giving in some form while conducting a capital campaign (and this is almost always the case), the traditional practice has been to solicit all constituents for both gifts. The advantages are obvious: everyone is given ample opportunity to participate in the several elements of the total development program; and the organization, by going to the entire constituency with the capital funds campaign, may have the opportunity to discover a few major donors not previously known to it. There are also problems with this approach, however. Maximum solicitation of constituents requires maximum commitment of staff and volunteers (as noted in Chapter One, it may be impossible for an institution with limited numbers of staff and able volunteers to approach its entire constituency), and soliciting everyone for everything is expensive—indeed, it may not be cost-effective.

Each time a solicitation moves to a larger number of prospects, the sights of the donors drop. When ten donors give a total of $10 million, the level at which people are contributing is perfectly clear. When five thousand givers contribute a total of $500,000, the level of giving is equally clear but less impressive, and the sights of major donors may be reduced. When it is known that everyone will be asked to provide the capital funds required, the burden is lifted from the handful with potential for major support, and they may wait for the masses to provide the funds needed. This puts the institution at peril because the masses, without lead and major gift support, will never provide all the funds needed.

A new concept is now emerging in capital fund solicitation: for capital gifts, solicit only those with capital potential; for annual giving, ask all others. To make use of this concept, an organization must identify the people capable of making significant multiple-year capital gifts and solicit them for that purpose; all other constituents will be solicited only for annual giving because the organization has made the judgment that they do not have capital potential at present. The advantages of this type of approach are twofold. First, it allows the organization to focus staff time and its best volunteers on the top major prospects. Once an organization moves a campaign to larger and larger numbers, it dilutes staff time and volunteer attention; by focusing only on major donors for major gifts, the organization can more effectively use the "rifle shot" approach. Second, this approach makes the annual fund an integral part of the overall objectives; it requires a total development goal that includes annual giving, and its inclusion permits annual donors to feel that they are part of the program.

There are four problems with this type of approach:

1. Major donors may resent the fact that only a small number are being asked for capital gifts.
2. The masses may feel they have no role in "laying the bricks" if their gifts go only for current operations. (It is possible to overcome this feeling by emphasizing the total development program, and especially by highlighting the relative merits of sustaining the ongoing program while the capital drive is in progress.)
3. If only selected capital prospects will be approached for capital giving, the organization must continue a never-ending search for new major donors, and this will require a strong annual giving program as a means of identifying capital donors.
4. Unless the masses clearly understand their vital importance in meeting the overall objectives, they may develop the habit of letting the big donors do it all. The large number of annual donors should not come to believe that an institution is dependent on only a handful of people.

Once the institution has decided whether to drop the annual fund or integrate it into the campaign effort, whether to exercise the separate, double, or triple ask, and whether to solicit select constituents for capital gifts or everyone for every purpose, the next important task is to coordinate this package with the planned or deferred giving program. Again, options are open to the institution. One is to exclude planned giving—any charitable life income trusts, annuities, or promised bequests—from the campaign results (if a donor died, however, such funds might come to the institution during the campaign). A second option is to count everything, even a future bequest from a four-year-old. A balance somewhere in between is suggested, and a approach is proposed at the end of this chapter.

In planning for a major development program, it is reasonable to include in the goal an expectation for income trusts, annuities, and other irrevocable commitments. This approach allows the institution to talk to potential donors about irrevocable gifts with retained life interest. A donor may be more apt to make a decision if he or she knows that establishing a life income trust will make him or her a participant in the campaign.

Bequests are a bit more difficult. On the one hand, it is certainly unwise (and perhaps even dishonest) to include in an institution's campaign results a potential bequest from a very young person. On the other hand, it may be unwise to completely exclude a future bequest from a donor who is advanced in years and is willing, for the satisfaction of participating in the total development program, to add a codicil to his or her will for a major gift.

Institutions should think about what is both fair and a good incentive for fundraising and then set up clear guidelines in advance. For example, an institution may decide to include all estate notes from people over sixty-five and all promises of bequests from those seventy and older. In any event, the institution should make its decision before it sets its goal. It certainly would be unwise if a goal reflected only direct needs for the cash that will be required in the near future, but the institution then counted toward that goal all promises of bequests, some of which might not materialize for many years. It is extremely important to exercise good judgment in a campaign where bricks and mortar are a major issue. It is imperative not only that an institution receive commitments to build the structure under consideration but also that a cash flow be established to pay for construction and reduce debt in a timely and equitable fashion. The use of planned gifts to meet payment schedules for construction is a highly risky business.

A final consideration is not only what to count but also, for the purposes of accounting and recording, how to value gifts, especially noncash gifts. In the educational sector, the guidelines provided in the *CASE Management Reporting Standards* (Council for Advancement and Support of Education, 1996b) are becoming an accepted approach to resolving this issue. These guidelines can be obtained from CASE, 1307 New York Avenue NW, Suite 1000, Washington, D.C. 20005–4701. The following organizations endorse the *CASE Campaign Standards: Management and Reporting Standards for Educational Fund-Raising Campaigns* (Council for Advancement and Support of Education, 1996a, p. 91):

American Association of Colleges of Nursing

American Association of Community Colleges

American Association of Fund-Raising Counsel

American Council on Education

American Prospect Research Association

Association of Community College Trustees

Association for Healthcare Philanthropy

Canadian Council for the Advancement of Education

College Board, Council of Graduate Schools

Council of Independent Colleges

Hispanic Association of Colleges and Universities

Lilly Endowment, Inc.

National Association of College and University Business Officers

National Association of Independent Colleges and Universities

National Association of Independent Schools

National Association of State Universities and Land-Grant Colleges

National Council for Resource Development

National University Continuing Education Association

Any organization can look to these guidelines as a model approach, realizing that different circumstances may suggest the need to modify the standards to make them applicable and useful.

The Association of Governing Boards of Universities and Colleges, while supporting the CASE standards, urges institutions to go even further, especially in the area of reporting deferred gifts in capital campaign totals. A 1996 statement from that organization said, "The Board of Directors of the Association of Governing Boards [AGB] of Universities and Colleges commends CASE for developing the *CASE Campaign Standards*. AGB endorses the standards except for those provisions addressing testamentary bequests and deferred gifts. AGB urges institutions to count bequests only when actually realized. With regard to deferred gifts, AGB urges that campaign totals be based on present value only" (Council for Advancement and Support of Education, 1996a, p. 92). The point is well taken, but there will be understandable initial reluctance on the part of institutions to take this further step, for three primary reasons.

First, over the short haul, changing to these standards will create a series of practical "public relations" problems as it relates to donors. Donors accustomed to being given credit and public recognition for the face value of deferred gifts will now be "credited" for smaller gifts. As an illustration, consider the gift of a

$100,000 life insurance policy from a fifty-year-old donor. Under current standards, the donor is credited and recognized as a $100,000 donor; in terms of the policy's present value, however, the donor's credited gift will be appreciably less. Will this kind of adjustment dampen donors' enthusiasm? And, to use another life insurance policy as an example, what is the public relations effect if two campaign cochairs each want to give a $100,000 life insurance policy—two "equal" gifts—but one is fifty years old and the other is fifty-eight? In terms of the gifts' present value, the two cochairs will be credited with "unequal" gift amounts. Again, will this have a harmful effect?

Second, North Americans are intensely competitive; we keep score. This is a far less compelling consideration than the first one, but it is nevertheless real. Therefore, which institutions, particularly among those that insist on comparing themselves to others in their sectors, will be the first to step forward and institute these new standards? What type of commitment to the new standards will it take for an institution to tell a potential donor, one who has multiple philanthropic interests, that his $100,000 life insurance policy will be credited at its present value, when other institutions are still crediting it at face value?

Third, it is axiomatic that campaign goals are constantly going higher. When these new standards are implemented, however, it is clearly possible—in fact, it is likely—that campaign goals, at least for a while, will actually be lower than they are now. What impact, if any, will this development have on the energy and commitment of volunteers who are asked to lead these campaigns with seemingly smaller goals? Will it limit the vision of the donors who are asked to support these campaigns, causing them to lower their own sights? It should not matter, but will it? Campaign goals are not (or at least should not be) established to set records; rather, they should be established to meet legitimate institutional priorities that are consistent with the institution's mission and with its current and future needs.

The further transition that AGB encourages should occur, and governing boards should take the lead in supporting this movement. It is fiscally responsible and intellectually honest to do so. Movement in this direction will take time, however, and it needs to be phased in. One possible way to do that (and some organizations have already done so) is to begin reporting gifts in terms of both face value and present value. This practice can lead to a transition process, as seamless as possible, toward the point where it becomes acceptable for goal reporting to be based on present value alone.

With these observations and caveats in mind, an institution might consider the guidelines shown in Table 7.1 (which come from an actual campaign) as a basis for consideration and discussion. It is important to establish such guidelines at the beginning of a campaign, when they can be considered (and perhaps adopted) in a calm, rational way, without influence from the pressures that often exist when an institution is midstream in its campaign and pressing to achieve success.

## TABLE 7.1 CAMPAIGN ACCOUNTING GUIDELINES.

| Type of Gift | Public Value | Internal Value | What Will Count | What Will Not Count |
|---|---|---|---|---|
| Cash | Full amount | Full amount | | |
| Securities | Fair market value of securities on date of transfer | Fair market value of securities on date of transfer | | |
| Real estate | Appraised value at time of gift | Appraised value at time of gift | Real estate received during the campaign | |
| Personal property | Appraised value at time of gift | Appraised value at time of gift | Personal property received during the campaign | |
| Pledges | Full amount | Full amount | Signed pledge card or letter from donor<br>Pledges fulfilled within five-year period | Verbal pledges |
| Bequest expectancies | Face value | Discount based on donor's age | Copy of will or excerpt from will<br>Donor society enrollment<br>Signed gift agreement<br>Letter of intent from donor<br>Letter from donor's attorney or financial adviser | Contact report<br>Contingencies<br>Donor under sixty-five years old |

| | | | | |
|---|---|---|---|---|
| Realized bequests | Full amount | Full amount | Monies actually received from an estate or trust distribution | Gifts that were counted in prior campaigns as bequest expectancies |
| Charitable gift annuities | Face value | Value of charitable remainder interest | Annuity agreement in place | |
| Charitable lead trusts | Face value of annual income received during the campaign and discounted value of annual income after the campaign | Amount of annual income | Copy of trust agreement | |
| Pooled income fund | Full value of contribution to the fund | Discount based on donor's age | Contributions to pooled income fund | |
| Charitable remainder trusts | Face amount | Value of charitable remainder interest | Trust agreement in place Copy of trust agreement (or excerpt) if an outside trust | |
| Retirement plan assets | Face amount | Discount based on donor's age | Signed gift agreement Letter of intent from donor | |
| Insurance | Face value | Discount based on donor's age | Organization as owner of the policy Fully paid-up policy | |

*Note:* In general, the following will not count: gifts or pledges counted in previous campaigns, investment earnings on gifts, and governmental funds.

# CHAPTER EIGHT

# IDENTIFYING, RESEARCHING, AND RATING CAMPAIGN DONORS

There is no way to overemphasize the importance of major gifts to the success of a capital campaign. But major gifts do not just happen; someone makes them happen as a result of a well-thought-out plan. To obtain major gifts, an organization must involve itself in the process of identifying, cultivating, and soliciting major donors. This chapter, together with Chapter Nine, discusses the steps involved in successfully generating major gifts.

## Defining Major Gifts

What exactly is a major gift? In campaigns with goals ranging from $5 million to $50 million, a major gift is generally defined as any gift of $100,000 or more, a special gift as any gift of $10,000 to $99,999.99, and a general gift as any gift of less than $10,000. In campaigns with goals of more than $50 million or less than $5 million, the definitions may be different. A lead gift is a gift that serves to establish a trend for giving by others believed to be capable of making gifts at the same level. It is possible to secure lead gifts in the major, special, and general divisions of the gifts table. A nucleus gift is a gift received at the earliest stages of the campaign—usually a major and/or lead gift, and most often given by an institutional "insider" (a board member or previous major donor). Nucleus gifts collectively provide a nucleus fund to create a giving momentum to launch the campaign.

## Characteristics of Major Donors

Major donors have strong values and deep beliefs, according to Campbell (1985). They believe in people and have great respect for knowledge. They often desire to provide opportunities they did not themselves have, to help the less fortunate, to improve the quality of life, to solve problems in society, and to preserve and perpetuate values of humankind, especially those that they hold dearest. Major gift donors usually are quite religious, have a deep belief in the free enterprise system, and are generally conservative. They already know someone in or something about the institution they will be asked to support. Someone has already made an impression on them. They have come to believe in someone, or something, the institution represents—the chief executive officer, a member of the board, a volunteer, a professional staff member, or some part of what the institution stands for. They have values that are comparable with the institution's, and they are probably regular donors to the institution or to one that is similar.

They view giving as an investment, and through their investments they desire to solve a problem or issue and find ways to express themselves (self-actualization). They also expect to see and understand the "return" on their investments. They will not seek but will accept (in fact, they expect) recognition. They may want to honor or memorialize someone else rather than themselves, although many will in fact honor themselves. They have the resources to make a major gift. In some instances, these resources may not be liquid at the moment. Their spouses and families are usually involved in the gift decision. Major donors tend to stay with programs and activities that have been of interest to them over a long period. Those who will give major gifts to an institution in the future generally have given to it in the past.

Price and File (1994), aiming to quantify the traits that motivate high-income people to make charitable contributions, studied more than eight hundred individuals and developed seven basic profiles. The general perspective on philanthropy embodied in each profile suggests a specific and unique approach to fundraising for different kinds of nonprofit organizations.

## Identifying Prospects

A prospect is any individual, foundation, corporation, or organization that has the potential to give and is likely to do so. In cases where potential exists but probability does not, it is mandatory for the institution to move these prospects through what G. T. Smith (personal conversation) describes as "the cultivation cycle." The cultivation of potentially large donors is a systematic and continuing effort to develop a power structure, either actual or potential, for an institution. It involves five steps:

1. Identification
2. Information
3. Interest
4. Involvement
5. Investment

In nearly every instance, the final four steps constitute a continuing cycle of learning additional information about potential donors, heightening their interest through the dissemination of information (via personal contact and mailings), encouraging a meaningful involvement (such as volunteer service or active participation), and, ultimately, receiving significant financial investment. Involvement is the highest level of cultivation in that it requires that the prospect be brought into active contact with the organization through service on a committee, membership on the board, or some other, equally important, way.

## Effective Research

Prospect research is a process whereby the staff evaluates the organization's constituency to identify individuals, foundations, and corporations capable of making substantial commitment to the capital campaign. In this way, effective solicitation strategies can be designed. Research has the following objectives:

1. To identify people and their relationships with other people
2. To determine people's interest in, associations with, and gifts to the institution
3. To discover facts about the ownership, control, influence, and wealth of people, corporations, and foundations
4. To reduce great quantities of information to readable, understandable, concise reports pertinent to the current campaign

To meet these objectives, the professional staff must correlate, control, and interpret data in order to carry out the following five tasks:

1. To develop a strategy for action
2. To determine appropriate projects to which the prospect can be assigned
3. To identify the prospect with the right groups

4. To assign the right people to cultivate the prospect
5. To establish a time schedule for implementation of the cultivation and solicitation program

The best prospects for major gifts to any organization are those who are committed to the organization and have already given. Many will already have accepted leadership positions in the organization. Prospect research involves both basic and sophisticated processes. Whittaker (1983) outlines the basic information that must be gathered:

- Name, nickname
- Home address(es)
- Business title, address, and phone number
- Telephone, fax, and cell phone number(s), and e-mail address(es)
- Date and place of birth
- Education (secondary and higher, along with academic major)
- Job history
- Marital status
- Spouse's name
- Spouse's education and business
- Number, names, and ages of children
- Family connections to the organization
- Family connections to other organizations
- Honors and achievements
- Clubs and organizations
- Political affiliation
- Religious affiliation
- Personal interests
- Estimated net worth
- Net salary
- Stock holdings
- Directorships
- Family foundations
- Favorite charities
- Gift record
- Names of secretaries
- Name of attorney
- Name of banker
- Names of close friends

It is also important to keep a record of the prospect's contacts with the organization. These may include the following:

- Last visit to the organization
- Date, place, and purpose of last contact with the organization
- Results of that contact
- Next steps to be taken
- Staff assignment
- Volunteer assignment

Among the sources of this information are institutional records (including the records kept in the development office, in the chief executive officer's office, and in the alumni/public relations office), institutional publications, and institutional staff members. Other especially good sources of information are board members, service users, and friends who can provide information from their own personal knowledge. The following printed and published materials are excellent sources of information:

Local, regional, and national newspapers

*Who's Who in America*, and its separate editions on women, government, finance, industry, the East, the West, the South, and business

Magazines such as *Forbes, Fortune, Business Week,* and others

Clipping services

Proxy statements

*Standard & Poor's (S&P), Dun & Bradstreet, Moody's,* and *Taft Corporate Directory*

State directories of corporations and executives

Chambers of commerce

Corporate annual reports

Foundation annual reports, directories, and grant indexes

*Taft Information System and Monitor*

State foundation directories

*Chronicle of Higher Education*

*Chronicle of Philanthropy*

*Philanthropic Digest*

*Foundation Directory*

According to Kathy K. Wilson (personal communication, 1998), the Internet, on-line services, and the CD-ROM medium have reduced the number of printed and published materials that research offices purchase and review. Because of the expense of on-line and CD-ROM products, it is advisable for smaller operations to work with local librarians in formulating search strategies for on-line services and, perhaps, to share the expense of CD-ROM products. One useful tool is the Lexis/Nexis database, which is available on CD-ROM or can be found on the World Wide Web (if your institution has Internet access and has purchased membership in Lexis/Nexis). Another CD-ROM that is used extensively is the *Biography and Genealogy Master Index;* the microfiche version is called *Biobase.* The Lexis/Nexis database offers four general headings (several more specialized sites are offered under three of the four):

1. General news topics (major newspapers, regional sources, major trade journals)
2. Company news (major newspapers, regional sources, major trade journals)
3. Company financial information (Hoovers Online, Companies Online, U.S. private company reports, company intelligence, S&P corporate descriptions)
4. Biographical information

A very good on-line source for individual, corporate, or foundation research is Dialog. This, too, can be accessed via the World Wide Web (www.dialog.com) and allows a researcher to browse more than 450 databases from more than 200 different information providers. A few of the favorites here are *Marquis Who's Who,* a biography master index, SEC [Securities and Exchange Commission] Online, *INVEST/NET Insider Trading Monitor,* the *Wall Street Journal,* ABI/Inform, Business Dateline, Foundation Directory, and journals of the American Management Association.

One of the best ways to stay informed and ask questions is through PRSPCT-L (prspct-l@bucknell.edu), an electronic discussion list that gives people who conduct research a way to share advice through electronic mail. Another resource for individual and corporate research is the on-line *Internet Prospector.* This combination Web site and monthly newsletter has a People section for searching individuals, with articles and links to other sites. One of *Internet Prospector's* best-known features, especially for beginners, is David Lamb's Prospect Research Page, which includes an annotated list of links to companies, people, foundations, commercial information providers, search engines, and more.

Another tool for identifying prospects is the demographic screening service. Although screening is not new, such services have become more sophisticated with the use of computer-based methods. According to Barth (1998), screening companies often use a combination of tools to provide data. One such tool is geodemographic screening, or your matching constituents against the characteristics of their neighborhoods and against models of consumer behavior in order to rate their probable interests, lifestyles, and philanthropic giving trends. Another tool is asset screening, which compares publicly reported stock holdings and property ownership to the names in your database. Predictive modeling helps you segment your database into different categories by matching your addresses to census and market research data; these results may help target your prospects for annual, major, and planned gifts. Lifestyle clustering assigns households to socioeconomic categories. Regardless of the type of demographic service you use, these data should enhance, not replace, your own. Because these kinds of screening often increase the workloads of research staff by asking them to validate or negate the ratings for particular prospects, it is a good idea, before contracting with a screening vendor, to ask some questions: What would be the purpose of our using this service? What do we want to achieve? How will the results be processed? How much data can we process internally?

Once research is completed, the development staff should review the results to determine whether all the needed information is there and whether the prospect belongs in the prospect pool. Prospects who do not belong should be deleted from the list early in the review process, and their names should be given to the annual giving staff. The next step is an in-house financial rating of the prospects. This rating includes prospects' *potential* to give (what they would give if the institution were their number-one philanthropic cause and they wanted to make the biggest gifts of their lives) and a *probable* gift size (the gifts they could pledge over the next eighteen months, without much solicitation, and that would be payable over the next three to five years). For an individual, figure the potential gift as 3 to 5 percent of total assets outside personal real estate and life insurance. To determine the probable gift, look at the prospect's giving history (including the largest previous gift), other obligations, financial health, type of investments and rate of return, family obligations (parents, children), attitude toward giving, ties (if any) to the institution, and "conspicuous consumption" (the visible signs of wealth—private schools, estates, vacation homes, and so forth).

For corporations and foundations, look at obligations to other nonprofit organizations, and, most important, closely study current interests and funding trends. In determining how much to ask for, think of the organization as also representing sources of other income. Corporations may have five or six channels of potential funding (corporate contributions, corporate foundations, matching gifts programs, research and development, marketing, advertising, and the discretionary budget of the executive office).

Once the potential and probable gift sizes have been determined, it is time to evolve a strategy. Look at the nature of the prospect's asset base. Is it liquid? Is it in stock? Define how the institution wants the prospect to give. Are there tax considerations? What are the prospect's possible interests in the institution, and how are those interests tied in to its priorities? Who is the best person to make the first contact, and who is the best to make the solicitation? Determine the next move: whether to get more information, visit the prospect, invite the prospect to attend some function, and so on.

According to Wilson (personal communication, 1998), research on corporate prospects needs to address four vital questions:

1. How financially healthy is the business?
2. What are its current products, and what are its interests in your institution?
3. What existing relationships could be used for moving this prospect to the next step of cultivation or solicitation?
4. How has the corporation supported your institution in the past, and why would it want to give support again?

The following basic information should be gathered on each corporate prospect:

- Full name and correct address
- Corporate assets
- Type of business
- Names of corporate officers and directors
- Names of officers of any existing corporate foundation
- The corporation's sales volume
- The corporation's previous giving record
- The corporation's decision-making process
- The corporation's gifts to other institutions (more difficult to determine if there is no corporate foundation)
- The corporation's connections with the institution (if yours is an educational institution, names of alumni employed by the corporation; if a hospital, names of patients the corporation employs; and so forth)
- History of the corporation's dealings with your institution
- The corporation's local subsidiaries, and the names of their officers
- Information about the corporate gift committee (names, connections, and kindred interests)

Corporate financial analyses are available on the World Wide Web, particularly via Dialog, Lexis/Nexis, Dun & Bradstreet, and CDA/INVESTNET, as well as on CD-ROM and in such print-based sources such as *The Directory of Corporate*

*Affiliations* (the CD-ROM version is *Corporate Affiliations Plus*), the *Million Dollar Directory, Standard & Poor's,* and the Moody series of industrial manuals. The Dun & Bradstreet on-line database is one of several that provide information on public and private companies. One of the best places to gather information on public companies (and on some private companies) is the EDGAR Database of Corporate Information at http://www.sec.gov/edgarhp.htm (the acronym stands for "electronic data gathering analysis and retrieval"), which offers free access to SEC documents that have been filed electronically by public corporations.

From the standpoint of corporate and foundation relations, it is equally important to learn something about company products, research and development, and future marketing plans. An annual report can supply some of this information. Other possible sources are the institution's office of sponsored research (if it has one), which may be aware of research and development interests within the corporation. Philanthropic publications such as *Taft Corporate Giving Watch* and *Philanthropic Digest* list corporate contributions, which can be reviewed for trends in grants for research and development. In addition, several databases list awards of government contracts. Finally, newspapers and journals can provide a glimpse of the future. Articles in such magazines as *Fortune* and *Forbes* may provide a vision of the direction in which the corporate prospect is moving. Local newspapers are an equally valuable resource.

Working with the appropriate in-house staff, the institution needs to expand on the basic questions about relationships with corporate prospects. If yours is an educational institution, for instance, how many alumni are employed by the corporation? Do any members of your institution's staff serve on the corporation's advisory board or science advisory panel? Does the corporation in any way rely on your institution for services? What about funding history? Has funding come from the corporation or from the corporate foundation? Enlightened corporate self-interest is the basis of these relationships, and so it is important to understand these components in planning a campaign approach. Except for a few national corporations and corporate foundations, and the local corporate community, this category of prospects has become more specialized in recent years. Most do not give outside the areas where they have plants, programs, or people. Very often, "quid pro quo" considerations (stockholder concerns, for example) determine the granting policies of national corporations.

Corporations tend to support campaigns in areas where they have plant operations, and particularly headquarters. Corporations will also support campaigns if they have subsidiaries in the service area of an institution. Besides major corporations, other sources for support of a campaign include local independent businesses, vendors, and businesses that are owned by or that employ people who are affiliated with the institution, whatever their geographical locations. In dealing with any prospect, but especially a corporate or foundation prospect, a campaign should never extend its boundaries beyond the circle represented by its volunteer leaders. This is a cardinal rule, but one that is often broken in campaigns.

Billian (1985) says that foundations are the easiest of the three types of prospects to research in that they usually have specific funding interests that are known or that can easily be determined by potential applicants. For the most part, these interests are dictated by policy and by the foundation's granting history. The information sought about a foundation is basically the same type of information as that sought about a corporation, and it will include the following elements:

- The full, correct name of the foundation
- The foundation's precise street address and phone number
- Names of the officers or directors of the foundation, and their professional connections
- A brief historical sketch of the foundation (when it was created, by whom, and for what purposes)
- The foundation's current assets
- Amount of the foundation's recent grants, by year and by individual recipient
- The foundation's decision-making process
- The foundation's pattern of giving (to what kinds of institutions and for what programs, with specific examples)
- Your institution's best contact with the foundation (the person to visit or send a proposal to)
- The foundation's connections with your institution
- History of your institution's contacts with the foundation
- A copy of a recent PF 990 tax form for the foundation, with a listing of income and grants made (copies of this form are available through the Associates Program of the Foundation Center, a fee-based service through which materials can be requested via e-mail, fax, or the U.S. Postal Service)
- The foundation's giving guidelines (available through the Associates Program of the Foundation Center) and statements of interest published by the foundation
- The foundation's most recent annual report (also available through the Associates Program of the Foundation Center)

In addition to the Associates Program of the Foundation Center, there exist several other excellent sources of such information. Four of the most widely used comprehensive references are *Prospector's Choice* and *FC Search* (both on CD-ROM), the *Foundation Directory*, and the Taft products. These sources, along with the Associates Program of the Foundation Center, provide information about foundations' financial assets, interests, giving focus, grants to other institutions, and requirements for submitting proposals. One valuable component of these references is their indexing of information according to foundations' giving interests. Many of these materials are also available on Dialog.

There are several sources of information about where a corporate or foundation prospect has contributed in the past. A few of the more popular sources are the *Directory of Corporate & Foundation Givers* (Taft), *Corporate Foundation Profiles* (The Foundation Center), *Corporate 500* (Public Management Institute), *National Directory of Corporate Giving* (The Foundation Center), *Directory of International Corporate Giving* (Taft), *Corporate & Foundation Grants* (Taft), *Chronicle of Philanthropy, Corporate Philanthropy Report,* and *Corporate Giving Watch.*

The best foundation prospects for a campaign are those that are geographically nearby; the likelihood of investment is much greater when the foundation is in the institution's local area, state, or region. A foundation is also more likely to support a campaign if its philosophy is similar to the institution's. It is important that there be a match between the organization's interests and the foundation's. If individuals associated with the foundation are directly or indirectly affiliated with the institution, and especially if they are on the institution's board, the chances are enhanced that it will receive favorable consideration. Any review of foundations requires a systematic study of all sources to locate those foundations that might have matching interests.

Remember to talk to members of the institutional board and others close to the institution to see whether they can help to establish links with the foundation. It is extremely important in a capital campaign that the effort to secure gifts from foundations be focused on those foundations that are most likely to support the institution. In many instances, the great majority of foundations will not be interested in a particular program. Again, it makes no sense to pursue nonprospects.

One of the best places to start as a beginner in research is to join the Association of Professional Researchers for Advancement (APRA). An increasing amount of information can now found via the Internet, and APRA members can share the most helpful sites, as well as helpful tips for more effective on-line searching.

# Rating Prospects

Once effective research has been done and prospects have been identified, the next step is to evaluate the prospects. Prospect rating is often done by staff, but it also must be done by volunteers in order to validate the staff effort. The purpose of external prospect rating is to accurately determine an individual's *ability* to give. The evaluator should not be concerned with what the individual *may* give, or even with whether he or she *will* give; further research subsequent to the evaluation, as well as future cultivation and solicitation activities, will address these questions.

During any rating session conducted by or with volunteer evaluators, the sole criterion should be what a donor *can* do, given his or her personal circumstances. Staff members should not participate in this evaluation other than to explain the purpose of the session, keep the session moving, and clarify and answer questions about form and procedure. Four rating-session procedures are commonly used:

1. In *group discussion*, evaluators engage in roundtable discussion until they agree on a rating. A group leader should conduct this session. A professional staff member should be present to record observations but should not make any comments that could influence the ratings. This is the best method of evaluation, but its success depends on the group leader's ability to initiate discussion and on the group's willingness to participate openly and forthrightly, as well as on the evaluators' ability to make informed ratings.

2. In *group/individual ratings*, each member of the group is given a rating book and works individually, without discussion, to rate the prospects and offer appropriate written comments. A professional staff member collects the evaluations at the end of the rating session and tabulates the information after the meeting. The major disadvantage here is lack of exchange of ideas or information within the group. The advantage is that the confidentiality of this method may lead the evaluators to provide higher evaluations as well as more pointed and more useful comments. The success of this kind of session often depends on getting someone who is well known and well connected to serve as host or hostess.

3. In the *individual/one-to-one* approach, a professional staff member meets individually with volunteer evaluators and verbally goes through the prospect list, recording pertinent comments on the evaluation form. The advantage of this process is that the evaluator can feel complete assurance of confidentiality: no one else will hear the comments or know the evaluator's personal feelings about the prospect. The disadvantage is that the validity of the evaluation is limited to the extent of the evaluator's knowledge: there are no second or third opinions. Moreover, the evaluator may not know a number of the prospects well enough to rate them, and so it will be necessary to hold additional rating sessions with other evaluators.

4. In the *individual/solitary* approach, evaluators are given a list of prospects and rating instructions and are left on their own. The evaluation book is either picked up or mailed back by a mutually agreed-on date. This procedure should be used only in special circumstances. Its advantage is that it gives the evaluator time to reflect on and consider the ratings and comments; properly used, this procedure generally leads to very thoughtful, thorough evaluations. Its disadvantage is that individuals often put off doing the evaluations and thereby stall the process.

No matter which procedure is used, the evaluations should be done by knowl-edgeable individuals. Secondhand and hearsay information is of little or no value; speculation is just that. The best evaluators tend to be bankers, lawyers, invest-ment counselors, financial planners, insurance executives, the socially prominent, and those actively involved in organized philanthropy in communities with orga-nized efforts. Evaluation of individual prospects should continue until an adequate database is established. For each prospect, many institutions acquire at least three evaluations, preferably all within a fairly narrow range (say, $10,000, $15,000, and $12,000), before assuming that the prospect's rating has been validated.

## Estimating an Individual's Giving Potential

When giving potential is being considered, any information known to the evalu-ator about an individual's financial circumstances should play a part. Factors to be considered in assessing potential include accumulated or inherited wealth, stocks and bonds, real and personal property, full or part ownership in business enterprises, access to family or other corporations, foundations or trusts, and an-nual income level.

There are no absolute rules to suggest how much an individual may be ca-pable of giving on the basis of accumulated assets and income, but a useful frame-work for making decisions is shown in Table 8.1. These guidelines are suggestions and should be used only as a starting point to help focus institutional thinking about an individual's potential to make charitable gifts. Remember, the institution is rating potential to give, not inclination to do so; measurements of inclination

### TABLE 8.1. CAMPAIGN GIFT RATING TABLE.

| Income Level | Assets Accumulated | Gift Rating |
|---|---|---|
| $2,500,000 or more | $250,000,000 or more | $60,000,000 or higher |
| 2,500,000 or more | 150,000,000–250,000,000 | 40,000,000–60,000,000 |
| 2,500,000 or more | 100,000,000–150,000,000 | 25,000,000–40,000,000 |
| 2,500,000 or more | 50,000,000–100,000,000 | 10,000,000–25,000,000 |
| 2,500,000 or more | 25,000,000–50,000,000 | 5,000,000–10,000,000 |
| 2,500,000 or less | 20,000,000–25,000,000 | 2,500,000–5,000,000 |
| 2,000,000 or less | 10,000,000–20,000,000 | 1,000,000–2,500,000 |
| 1,000,000 or less | 7,500,000–10,000,000 | 500,000–1,000,000 |
| 500,000–1,000,000 | 5,000,000–7,500,000 | 250,000–500,000 |
| 100,000–500,000 | 2,500,000–5,000,000 | 100,000–250,000 |
| 100,000–250,000 | 1,000,000–2,500,000 | 50,000–100,000 |
| less than 100,000 | less than 1,000,000 | 10,000–25,000 |

tend to be less precise and more subjective. Factors to be considered include the prospect's level of interest as well as his or her number of years of giving to the organization, involvement with the organization, and cumulative previous giving.

These evaluation sessions have a twofold goal:

1. To uncover fresh information about important prospects (first priority) and about all other prospects (second priority)
2. To promote the cultivation and involvement of the volunteer evaluators who participate in the process

Other benefits may also accrue. For example, these sessions are often a valuable tool in staff training. They are a way of identifying suitable solicitors, they can raise the sights of volunteers who eventually will become donors, and they provide an opportunity to educate participants about the campaign.

## Keeping Evaluation Sessions Manageable

It is extremely important to keep evaluation sessions manageable from the standpoint of the volunteers. It can be counterproductive if too many prospects are expected to be evaluated in one sitting. No evaluation session should be scheduled to last more than one and a half hours. How many prospects can be rated in ninety minutes? The answer depends on the rating method being used, the level of the prospects being evaluated, and the ability of the evaluators. Some evaluators, working alone, can rate as many as 500 prospects in one session, whereas a group discussion may cover only 100 to 150 prospects. If evaluators are asked to rate too many prospects, or if the session is too long, the level of concentration will drop off toward the end. Therefore, it is generally recommended that all prospect lists be kept as short as possible.

## Storing the Information

Information from the rating sessions should be returned to the organization's research department, where it can be entered and the following elements can be recorded and tracked:

- The name of each prospect who has been rated
- The individual who rated the prospect
- The level at which the prospect was rated

- Whether the rater can help in the cultivation/solicitation process, with more information, and so forth
- Other comments made by the rater

The ratings are then entered into the prospects' records and into the system.

Because the rating sessions are confidential, raters' names and comments are not shared except on a need-to-know basis with those development officers who are working most closely with the prospects. The research department can then take the top-rated prospects and either start conducting additional research or forward their names to their assigned development officers for validation of the ratings.

# CHAPTER NINE

# CULTIVATING AND SOLICITING MAJOR GIFT PROSPECTS

Once prospects have been identified, researched, and evaluated, the organization must begin to cultivate them. Cultivation is a continuous process. It often takes several steps, and anywhere from a few months to several years, to obtain a major gift. On average, campaign directors indicate that it now takes twenty-four to thirty months to successfully cultivate and negotiate major gifts.

## Guidance System for Soliciting Major Donors

Bringing in major gifts is a matter of hard work, imagination, and good taste. Certainly, major gifts occasionally come from unexpected sources, but usually many cultivation contacts by staff and/or volunteers are necessary to bring prospects to the point of making major gifts. Therefore, the pursuit of the extraordinary gift should be a well-planned, properly funded, adequately staffed part of any campaign effort.

Prospect management is a systematic approach to identifying and tracking major gift prospects. Prospect management systems, whether they use large and complex databases, straightforward word processing, or manual systems, both rely on and encourage careful planning and follow-through. By recording vital information on major gift candidates and donors, an institution may know at any given time who its best prospects are and where it stands in relation to them.

According to Baxter (1987):

The concept of prospect management is a relatively recent trend in development, made possible by the widespread use of technology in fundraising. Data-processing technology, which has revolutionized gift processing, acknowledgment, and record keeping, will play now an important role in shaping development activities on the front end—long before solicitation occurs.

Prospect management enables an institution to focus attention on the individuals and organizations that hold the most promise for major gifts. These top-tier prospects are generally a small percentage of an institution's database, but they account for the greatest proportion of gifts. Whether the threshold for a major gift at an institution is $500 or $50,000, the prospects with the potential to give that or a greater amount are candidates for prospect management.

All institutions with sound fundraising programs—no matter what their level of automation—practice some sort of prospect management with their major contributors and prospects. However, computer applications in prospect management allow an institution to record and track a greater level of detail on major prospects than is possible in any manual system, and they are safer than relying on the information that staff and volunteers carry around in their heads.

A well-designed and -maintained prospect management system can improve major gift fundraising and help an organization to measure the effectiveness of its development program. It can provide detail on a single prospect, select all prospects with a common trait, or give an overall view of a campaign's progress. The objectives of most tracking systems are to manage effectively cultivation and solicitation processes that are highly individualized; to identify and quantify measures of progress in the cultivation and solicitation process; to maintain momentum over long periods of time; to provide information that will educate, motivate, and reward volunteers and staff involved in the major gifts effort; to focus attention on top prospects; to facilitate regular reporting to volunteers and staff; and to develop a written history of prospect cultivation that will provide an institutional memory of communications with major supporters.

There are a number of tracking systems available today, ranging from manual [types] to those using word processing or spreadsheets through very sophisticated systems using state-of-the-art computer hardware and software. The criteria for selecting a tracking system include size of major prospect pool, size of development staff, complexity of fundraising program, existing computer capability, and budget. Systems developed for prospect management need not be complex, but they should accommodate all of the data needed for identifying, assigning, and tracking major prospects.

When planning for a prospect management system, an institution should consider its information needs, the size of its file, and its hardware and software. If the system is already in place in the office—both computer (hardware) and programs (software)—this will have an effect on the data and number of records that can be tracked. Ideally, the first two considerations—needs and size—should determine the kind of equipment selected. A number of systems are on the market that have been developed expressly for prospect management. If one of these meets an institution's specifications for data, file size, and system cost, it will save developing a system from scratch.

It may also be possible to use an existing system for prospect management and tracking. If an institution's system is flexible, a means of flagging major prospects and the addition of a few fields may be all that is needed. However, it is not always feasible for institutions with very large master databases to add the prospect management feature, since it focuses on such a small percentage of the file. Since it is a system tailored to an institution, the most important consideration is to provide the information that is essential to its development program. This will vary from institution to institution and may mean simply an alphabetical list of major prospects and a few details about them, something that can be managed easily on a word-processing system. If, on the other hand, it is important to be able to select prospects by geographic region, by staff or volunteer assignment, by rating, gift target or a combination of elements, a more complex system will be required.

In setting up a system, an institution should plan for the kinds of routine reports needed as well as for the data it will need to call up at any given moment. Plan for growth, and, if possible, select a system that is flexible enough to allow for modifications and newly identified information needs. Include all important data fields, but do not clutter the system with unnecessary data. Remember, the more fields in the system, the more maintenance required. An elaborate system that has outdated information or empty data fields is almost worse than no system at all.

To ensure that the prospect management system is a useful tool, Baxter (1987) emphasizes that information must constantly be relayed to the person or department responsible for data entry and system maintenance. This means documenting all contact between the institution and prospects and forwarding the information to the system, submitting any additions or deletions, and keeping the system manager apprised of changes in a prospect's status. Regular reports from the system can identify any information gaps or highlight errors.

Baxter (1987) suggests the following list of possible data elements as a guide in setting up a prospect management system. Please note that these are suggestions rather than hard-and-fast requirements, because each institution has unique characteristics that influence system design.

| Data Element | Comments |
|---|---|
| Identification | If possible, should be consistent with master file ID number. |
| Name | Prefix (title), last, first, middle, suffix. |
| Address, phone | Can allow for home, business, second home, and so on, but must keep in sync with master file. |
| Title | Business or professional position. |
| Salutation | Needed where prospect management system has word-processing capabilities. |
| Geographic region | Useful for institutions with constituents spread out over a large area, where location determines staff assignment, and for planning cultivation/solicitation trips and visits. |
| Source | Indicates type of prospect (alumnus, trustee, parent, corporation, foundation, and so on). |
| Wealth code | For those institutions whose lists have been screened by an outside vendor. |
| Class/degree | For educational institutions. |
| Gift rating | Prospect's capacity to give: usually a range of figures. |
| Interest rating | Prospect's involvement with the institution (readiness for solicitation). |
| Status | Where prospect is in solicitation cycle (cultivation, solicitation, stewardship, and so on). |
| Giving areas | The project, campaign, or type of gift the prospect is targeted for or given clearance for (can be multiple occurrences). |
| Staff | Staff member assigned to manage the prospect. |
| Volunteer | Nonstaff volunteer assigned to prospect. |
| Moves | Contact between institution and prospect, generally a date and brief description of the contact. Systems can be designed to accommodate numerous entries, to record last contact and next move, or [to have] comment fields that summarize past activity and future plans. |

| | |
|---|---|
| Solicitation | Request date, amount, purpose, solicitor (if other than volunteer); response date, amount, purpose. |
| Connections | Other ties to institution: spouse, family, classmates, business associates, and so on. |
| Identifiers | Institutional codes that identify special populations (sometimes called list or select codes). |
| Tickler | Date for staff or volunteer to conduct follow-up. |
| Comments | Free-form text to flag special circumstances or provide additional information. |

Whatever the choice of data elements, and whatever the system's configuration, fields should be set up to allow for swift and easy information searches.

The prospect management system is an integral part of a comprehensive approach to pursuing the extraordinary gift. It should be designed to ensure that an institution's best prospects are identified, cultivated, and solicited according to a master plan, and that all activities are monitored. Used conscientiously, it can measurably help those who have responsibility for the success of major campaigns. Five subsystems are usually found in a prospect management system for major donors: a rating system, a priority system, an approach system, an accountability system, and a report system.

## Rating System

Step one in a program to obtain extraordinary gifts is identifying priority prospects. This system places a great deal of importance on the research function. Research and rating go hand in hand, and a solid records and research system is the foundation of any fundraising program. If not already in place, a research capability that will yield prospect ratings must be developed. The end result of a rating process should be not one but two rating codes: the prospect's giving capacity, and the prospect's interest in the organization. A prospect's giving capacity is a collective "best judgment" (after a review of all the pertinent rating and file information about the prospect) of how much the prospect could contribute to the organization over three to five years, if so inclined. The interest rating is a collective judgment of the prospect's interest in and concern for the organization. This rating is based on personal information, the prospect's giving record, and file information on hand. Table 9.1 shows the numerical rating codes that might be used in a typical system.

## TABLE 9.1. PROSPECT RATING CODES.

| Giving Capacity Code | Estimated Giving Capacity | Interest Code | Description |
|---|---|---|---|
| 1 | $2,500–4,999 | 1 | Not involved, no record of interest |
| 2 | 5,000–9,999 | | |
| 3 | 10,000–24,999 | 2 | Minimal interest, occasional donor, attends meetings infrequently, and so on |
| 4 | 25,000–49,999 | 3 | Moderately active or formerly very active |
| 5 | 50,000–99,999 | 4 | Very active, major donor, club member, committee person |
| 6 | 100,000–249,999 | 5 | Member of governing board, other boards, or executive groups |
| 7 | 250,000–499,999 | | |
| 8 | 500,000–999,999 | | |
| 9 | 1,000,000 or more | | |

## Priority System

By adding the two numerical ratings (capacity and interest), an institution can determine each prospect's priority rating. The higher the rating, the higher the prospect's priority. The higher the prospect's priority, the more cultivation moves (structured contacts designed to bring a prospect closer to making a major gift) an institution will want to make on the prospect in a given period (usually a calendar year).

As a guide to determining how much cultivation a prospect gets, it is recommended that the institution use a cultivation quotient—the sum of the two numerical ratings, multiplied by two. This quotient represents the minimum number of cultivation moves an institution should hope to make on a prospect each year. For example, one prospect is rated 3/1 (that is, a capacity rating of 3, and an interest rating of 1); another is rated 1/3; therefore, both have cultivation quotients of 8. At the moment, the first is a rather unlikely prospect for a $10,000 gift; the other one is a fairly likely prospect for a $2,500 gift. Their cultivation quotients tell the organization to plan for eight cultivation moves on each of these prospects in a year. But the institution may have to decide which prospect will get its attention first: with the first prospect, a longer cultivation period may result in a larger gift; with the second, a smaller gift can be more readily realized.

Cultivation quotients are flexible guidelines. Staff and volunteers should have the authority to make more or fewer than the recommended number of contacts, as circumstances may dictate. Another important point is that ratings—and therefore cultivation quotients—can change during the year. To return to the previous example, in the opinion of the institution the person rated 3/1 has a gift potential of $10,000 to $24,999 but has not demonstrated much past interest in the organization. Nevertheless, a staff member or volunteer who calls on the prospect discovers that the prospect has become much more interested. This discovery changes the prospect's interest rating to 3, and this change in turn increases the cultivation quotient to 12. Therefore, four additional contacts will be called for over a year.

It must be clearly understood that, ordinarily, the campaign's top leaders should be assigned to cultivate and solicit those with the both the greatest capacity to give and the greatest interest. It is equally important that the entire campaign stay focused throughout on the best donor prospects. Little time should be given to prospects rated 1/1, but what about prospects rated 9/1 or 8/2? Should time be spent on them? Yes—but it must be a measured amount of time, and the effort should be disciplined. It usually takes a series of steps to move a prospect from the point of clearly not being interested, or of having little interest, to the point where he or she serves on the institution's governing board. This kind of cultivation is not accomplished in one leap. Hence, even though great ability to give exists, the proclivity to give needs to be developed, and that often takes more time than is available in a limited-term, movement-intensive campaign. Leave some time for the long shots, and give some effort to their cultivation, but reserve the bulk of the effort for prospects with major gift potential who are already more involved.

## Accountability System

Each major gift prospect should be assigned to a member of the staff whose duty it is to see that a personalized campaign is waged to get the best gift possible. Each staff member becomes an account executive and acts as a catalyst, providing the initiative and the strategy. The institution should attempt to assign most prospects to one or more volunteers for cultivation and solicitation, and it should strive to give its volunteers the feeling that they are responsible for their prospects. Every two to four weeks, staff should report on gift prospect assignments. The reports should list all prospects (individuals, foundations, and corporations) for whom the staff person is responsible, the volunteer or volunteers assisting with each prospect, the number of cultivation and/or solicitation contacts that the campaign's master plan indicates should be made with each prospect during the year, and the number of contacts made to date. By reviewing these reports, staff members will readily see which prospects need attention and can plan accordingly.

## Approach System

Types of contact include phone calls, letters, and personal visits by staff, by the chief executive officer, or by volunteers; attendance by prospects at institutional functions and leadership retreats; involvement in key issues and programs; publications; firsthand briefings and information on important events; and recognition events. In most systems, contacts are weighted according to significance, importance, and impact. A typical weighted system looks like this:

| *Cultivation Contact* | *Contact Points* |
|---|---|
| Letter from a staff member | 1 |
| Phone call from a staff member | 2 |
| Letter from a volunteer | 2 |
| Invitation to a major event | 3 |
| Phone call from a volunteer | 3 |
| Phone call from chief executive officer | 3 |
| Visit by a staff member | 4 |
| Letter from chief executive officer | 4 |
| Attendance at an institutional activity (off-site) | 4 |
| Visit by a volunteer | 5 |
| Attendance at an institutional event (on-site) | 5 |
| Firsthand information about important events | 6 |
| Meeting with the chief executive officer | 7 |
| Personal recognition | 7 |
| Leadership retreat | 7 |

## Report System

Follow-through is absolutely necessary in making contacts with major donor prospects. There is no substitute for persistence and patience. A useful management technique is to require staff members to identify their top ten prospects. During regular staff meetings, each staff member assigned to these prospects should report on what is being done to move them closer to making major gifts, on who has the initiative, and on what is the next step. Then, at the next staff meeting, each staff member should report any progress or difficulty in carrying out cultivation plans and should discuss the next sequence of steps to be taken. A call report should also be filed after every phone call or visit.

With its five subsystems, the guidance system for soliciting major donors is a control mechanism that ensures big gift prospects are rated, given priorities, assigned to staff members and volunteers, cultivated and solicited according to a master plan, and reported on. The system should be designed to help get results, not to stimulate "scoring points" for that sole purpose. It should encourage well-thought-out, appropriate strategic moves that the institution feels will bring its prospects closer to making major gifts. No one knows for sure how many contacts it will take to bring a prospect to the point of making a gift (the average is generally thought to be seven to ten), but the institution has to use something, such as cultivation quotients, as a guide. It is appropriate to rely on this guidance system as a tool for bringing human factors into play because, after all, human factors are the most important elements in getting the prospect ready to give.

Prospect tracking and management help an organization monitor its involvement with major prospects. Once someone is identified as a prospect, it is imperative that the institution involve that person in its life. Involvement precedes and often begets investment, and investment is the end game in the capital campaign.

## Soliciting Major Gifts

Securing major gifts is both the natural and the hoped-for result of the cultivation process. Cultivation begins when the prospective donor first hears about a particular institution. It reaches its highest point when the donor asks, "How much will it cost?" Because tangible results are not usually obtained in a few weeks or months, cultivation demands a sensitive balance of patience and persistence.

Philanthropy is the act of expressing love for others, and so major gifts are much more than money contributed to meet an institution's needs. They represent a person's opportunity for investment, and they are based on his or her commitment. Solicitation is the delicate presentation of an opportunity to invest material assets in a way that brings intangible rewards and a sense of fulfillment. Solicitation is not begging; it is a high form of seeking investments.

One advantage of the capital drive is that it necessitates asking for major gifts within a definite time frame. An institution occasionally can jump immediately from identifying a project to asking for an investment, but this approach is not often successful. Nevertheless, more gifts have probably been lost through waiting for the perfect time than through asking too soon. *It is better to act, even imperfectly, than to wait forever for the perfect time.* Some factors to consider in timing are length of cultivation, date of the prospect's last major gift, his or her age and health, and the urgency of the project for which funds are sought.

## Preparing to Make the Major Gift Call

Each negotiation is a campaign in itself, according to Campbell (1985). Do the necessary homework. Know the prospect—his or her needs, wants, hopes, and ambitions. Get all the help available. Find out who the prospect's family members, friends, and advisers are and which people at the institution the prospect knows and respects. Meet with those people and learn all they can tell you about the prospect. Identify at least two possible projects that correspond to the prospect's interests. Document the need for each project and the benefits that will accrue if it is funded. Prepare a presentation—flip chart, proposal, or letter—to take to the meeting with a prospect, and perhaps leave it with the prospect. Bring prospects to the institution regularly. Candidly discuss opportunities, issues, and problems. Ask for their counsel and advice. Follow up, report back, and show appreciation whenever it is possible to do so.

Select solicitors who have made major gifts themselves. Teams of solicitors, most commonly two or three people, usually work better on major gift calls. Develop a strategy for the major gift prospects, and review this strategy with these solicitors. If necessary, give them a script, and rehearse it with them until they have internalized it.

Use the phone, or see the prospect in person, and ask for time to talk about the institution's capital campaign. Confirm this appointment in writing. It may be useful to send the prospect some easy-to-read information about the institution's plans along with the confirmation letter. Select the meeting site where the prospect will be most comfortable. Avoid noisy, congested sites. Reconfirm the meeting by phone beforehand.

Large gifts from individuals do sometimes result from personal conversations alone, without the aid of formal written presentations, but usually only when a donor is very closely identified and involved with the institution. Even then, a follow-up presentation in writing often helps firm up the appeal. A written statement may be anything from a letter to a highly individualized—and usually quite extensive—published document. Ordinarily, however, a typewritten proposal with a cover letter is adequate. The length of the proposal may vary from one page to many, with extensive supporting appendixes. Usually, however, a statement of three to ten pages in length is all that is necessary. The written proposal should cover at least these four items:

1. Statement of the opportunity or need
2. Proposed action for meeting the need or fulfilling the opportunity
3. Financial data, including information about costs, other funds available, and the amount being requested
4. A summary statement of the benefits that the donor will derive from the gift

Asking for large gifts should never be a hit-or-miss proposition, nor should such solicitations be made in casual conversations. It is a serious mission that requires preparation and planning before visits, an understanding of the techniques to be employed during visits, and the willingness to follow up after visits.

## Making the Visit

During a visit, allow an initial period for conversation on topics of mutual interest, and then introduce the reason for the visit. Present the background that has led to the occasion of this presentation. Do not let the conversation become a monologue; allow ample opportunity for the prospective donor to participate. Ask questions. Listen carefully to everything that is said. Finally, ask for the prospect's participation, and be clear about how much the institution is hoping to receive.

Be aware of body language—dress, actions, eye contact. First impressions are important. Consider objections and criticisms as opportunities for discussion and indications of interest. Deal with them as such, but never enter into an argument with a prospect.

Take ample time in a solicitation. Arouse interest to the point where the prospect asks, "How much do you want?" Remember, people give to help people. Sell the institution's programs and concepts, not the costs. Logic, emotion, and enthusiasm are the best motivators. Tax advantages seldom play a part in major gift decisions. They are most often a secondary benefit.

*Ask for the gift!* Keep the sights up, and be specific about the amount. If you can, cite some other lead gifts in the major gifts range. It is not uncommon to ask for two to four times what it is thought a prospect will give, and there is no known case of a volunteer (or a staff member) being shot for asking for too much. A large request, if it is within the giving ability of the prospective donor, is usually flattering.

Should the donor's "no" become evident, listen carefully to the reasons. Find out what must be done before a gift can be secured. Then leave the meeting without "closing," and plan a strategy for the next visit. Gifts that are made in haste, or that are made by an unconvinced donor, tend to be minimal. Clearly establish the next move, including a date for a possible follow-up meeting. It is better not to leave the pledge card with the prospect (although some solicitors do this, and some prospects insist on it): if the pledge card is left with the prospect, the solicitor loses a primary reason to follow up, and it is possible that the prospect will either "file" it or make a minimal gift.

In discussing a major gift with a prospect, emphasize that the gift can be made not only as an outright gift but also in the form of securities and other property, and that a gift can return a lifetime income if the donor so desires. In most capital campaigns, unless they are solely for construction purposes, bequests are generally welcomed, too.

During many solicitations, the prospect will raise objections. Some objections are subliminal. For instance, some elderly donors who are alone or lonely will object to closing, not because they have an objection to the case or reservations about investing, but because they fear that after a gift decision is announced, the institution will cease giving them the attention inherent in cultivation and solicitation. Most objections are more straightforward, however: "This is a bad time for us financially. All our assets are currently illiquid" or "I do not agree with your chief executive officer's priorities."

Whatever the objection, hear it out completely. In discussing the objection with the prospect, restate it, and make sure it is understood in context. Explore ways that the objection could be overcome. Never let the objection lead into an argument, however, and do not make the objection bigger than it is. Respond to it with facts, and never make excuses. If the objection is weak, deal with it as quickly as possible, and move on. It is perfectly legitimate to compromise on objections if in fact they will not be a hindrance to reaching the major goal.

Determine whether the prospect will donate if the objection can be overcome. If so, do what reasonably can be done to remove it. Always remember that objections are really questions, and that the prospect's investment in the project will help overcome the objections. Remembering this fact will help in converting objections into reasons for giving. If an objection cannot be overcome, then move along to another prospect; do not waste time on prospects who for whatever reason are absolutely not going to give.

After the visit, write a short note of thanks for the prospect's time and interest. As appropriate, draft a further note of thanks from the chief executive officer and perhaps from the board chair. Prepare a complete summary report on the visit, with particular attention to new information on the potential donor's special interests, background, and idiosyncrasies. Be sure to include at least the following information:

- Name of company, foundation, or individual visited, date visited, and place of meeting
- If a foundation or corporation, names and positions of people visited

- Who went on the visit
- The purpose of the visit
- What points were highlighted or conveyed during the visit, and whether this was done successfully
- As much detail as possible about what happened at the meeting (what comments were made by whom, and responses to those comments)
- Whether any materials were distributed during the meeting and, if so, what they were, whether there are copies in the development office's research files, and whether there is any pre- or postmeeting correspondence that others should have copies of
- What concerns (if any) were voiced by the prospect, and what positive comments were made
- Whether a request for funding or assistance was made and, if so, specific details
- Whether additional action or follow-up is needed and, if so, what types, by when, and by whom
- Whether other people should be alerted to the fact that this visit was made and, if so, who they are
- As appropriate, thoughts and recommendations on the best strategies or approaches for cultivating and soliciting the prospect

## Errors to Avoid in Solicitation

The Public Management Institute (Conrad, 1978) has identified the fourteen most common major errors that are made in soliciting a major gift:

1. Not asking for the gift
2. Not asking for a large enough gift
3. Not listening—talking too much
4. Not asking questions
5. Talking about the organization and its approach rather than about the benefits to its clients
6. Not being flexible, and not having alternatives to offer the prospect
7. Not knowing enough about the prospect before the solicitation
8. Forgetting to summarize before moving on
9. Not having prearranged signals between solicitation team members
10. Asking for the gift too soon
11. Speaking rather than remaining silent after asking for the gift
12. Settling on the first offer that a prospect suggests, even if it is lower than expected
13. Not cultivating the donor before soliciting
14. Not sending out trained solicitors

Study this list. These mistakes are all avoidable with the right preparation, approach, and presentation to the prospect.

Being asked to contribute has a powerful and positive effect on giving. In 1993, fully 84.1 percent of the households surveyed by INDEPENDENT SECTOR were asked to contribute, and 76.9 percent of those that were asked did so; by contrast, only 38.1 percent of the remaining households—those that were not asked—contributed anything, and this pattern has been observed consistently over the four surveys that INDEPENDENT SECTOR has conducted since 1987. Moreover, in 1993 respondents reported on how specific kinds of asking might affect their giving frequency. Being asked to give by someone the respondent knows well or being asked by clergy are the most significant factors that lead to higher giving levels; other methods of solicitation are not as effective, although some nevertheless do elicit giving. This finding strongly suggests the need to determine the type of contacts to be made, by whom, and how frequently.

Obtaining major gifts is a process—a cycle—open to everyone. Most of all, everyone must give this activity top priority in day-to-day and week-to-week efforts. Nothing must be allowed to divert attention from the greatest source of support for an institution: major donors.

## Acknowledgment and Recognition

Once a donor has made a significant gift, cultivation can move to a new and higher level. A sincere expression of gratitude can show the human quality of an institution. It goes without saying that every gift should be acknowledged when it is received; the donor is expecting acknowledgment. If in fact the gift has played a part in strengthening the institution, then the real opportunity to give thanks will come in six months or a year, when the effect of the gift is more fully known. In the interim period, keep in close contact with the donor, and never fail to follow up and provide the information that will tell the donor what the full positive effect of the gift has been.

Whether or not people say they want to be recognized, the plain fact is that 99 percent of all people love recognition. Because recognition is often a major motivation for giving, the campaign structure must provide a means of recognizing major donors. Opportunities should be established at the beginning of the campaign, with policy guidelines for naming facilities, providing endowments, and engaging in the many other kinds of activity that people will want to support in a comprehensive campaign. Institutions are encouraged to hold events to dedicate buildings, open offices or wings, announce the establishment of endowments, and recognize program support, and to engage in other such ceremonial activities, as appropriate. The placing of plaques in buildings is always appropriate, as is the giving of distinguished service awards.

It is important that the right people thank those who have given. In each case, an individual determination of who should do the acknowledging should be made. There should also be continuing recognition for major donors. If they are properly handled in the recognition process, they are likely to make even greater major gifts in the future.

Most of this discussion about major gifts has centered on individual donor prospects, and about 90 percent of the money given to all campaigns does come from individuals rather than from foundations or corporations. But the process of identifying, cultivating, and soliciting major gift prospects can and should be used effectively for corporations and foundations, too, so long as it is remembered that foundations do not give support to buildings, nor do corporations make investments in programs—*people give to people*. In every instance where a corporate or foundation gift has been made, it is because a representative of the institution has asked a representative of the corporation or foundation to make a gift. When all is said and done, securing major gifts is a relatively simple task: finding the right person to ask the right prospect for the right gift in the right form for the right reason at the right time.

# CHAPTER TEN

# BUILDING LASTING RELATIONSHIPS AND DEVELOPING LEAD GIFTS

Rodney P. Kirsch
Martin W. Shell

In 1997, a total of $143.46 billion was contributed to American charities. The great majority of this amount, 89 cents of each dollar, came from living individuals or through bequests. The American Association of Fund-Raising Counsel Trust for Philanthropy (1998) lists nearly 350 gifts of $1 million or more from individuals to every part of the nonprofit sector—religion, education, healthcare, human services, the arts, the environment, and more. Most of these gifts came as lead gifts to capital campaigns. This chapter focuses on the conditions needed to bring about lead investments from individuals and on ways of positioning and using the positive dynamics created by such magnificent investments. And these major acts of philanthropy are indeed investments. They result from deep and meaningful relationships that span the course of time, and they are as much "given" as "solicited." In this respect, they represent the convergence of factors that go well beyond the mechanics of soliciting large gifts during campaigns (see Chapter Nine). But there are also some cautions and considerations to be raised about how fundraisers work to achieve lead gifts in the context of a campaign, considerations that take account of the many personal complexities in donors' lives.

The American Association of Fund-Raising Counsel Trust for Philanthropy (1997) reports that there are now more than 600,000 501(c)(3) organizations registered as charities with the Internal Revenue Service. The great majority of these will not see their donors listed in the *Forbes* annual roster of largest gifts. This is not terribly important. What matters is that your organization certainly can achieve success with lead gifts, a success to be measured less by your past achievements in this area than by the extraordinary potential that you have to bring about change in the community you serve.

## Shared Purpose and Passion

A lead gift typically grows out of a close association between a donor and an organization, an association based on a shared and deeply held vision, belief, or value. At first blush, this suggests that attention be paid to creating persuasive case statements and program brochures. But these standard campaign vehicles are merely initial and, at best, superficial instruments for inspiring lead gifts. Each nonprofit organization should consider the constituencies it serves, the mission it holds dear, and the values it expresses when engaging individuals in the lead gift process. The organization's ability to articulate these important dimensions of its existence is essential to fostering an environment for lead gift possibilities.

Experienced development professionals know, both from surveys and from personal anecdotal evidence, that major philanthropy at its very core is primarily an emotion-based enterprise. This is particularly true where lead gifts are concerned. Many individuals, often without much forethought, write modest checks every day for "good causes." But lead gifts—the kind that transform an organization—are usually tied to deeply held beliefs in the purpose of a nonprofit and are given with passion. The donor does expect accountability after the gift is made, and surely the tax implications are thoroughly examined during the decision-making stage. Nevertheless, the impulse to consult a financial adviser, or concern over the measurable outcomes of a lead gift, will stem from the donor's strong convictions about the purpose and the work of the organization. This kind of passion cannot be evoked by brochures or annual reports, which, from the donor's perspective, tend over time to make organizations seem more similar than different. Instead, a donor's passion for an organization's purpose comes from his or her genuine involvement in the life of the organization. Therefore, the heart of the matter is the development of meaningful, personal relationships with prospects and donors.

The most successful organizations find myriad ways of bringing individual donors inside, where they can help shape policy, test their values and interests against the organization's, fully understand the organization's mission, appreciate the organization's impact, and, ultimately, discover the right channels for expressing, through philanthropy, their passion for the organization's work. Involvement of this type does indeed beget significant investment, and organizations have the ability to choose just how and to whom they wish to extend this special level of involvement. It should be done with the understanding that practical considerations (time constraints, governing structures, budgetary limitations, program activities) allow for only a precious few individuals to see the organization in this special way. Therefore, those few should be carefully chosen. They will discover lead donors for your organization, make lead gifts themselves, or both.

## Mature, Ongoing Relationships

Lead gifts from total strangers are wonderful but exceedingly rare. (How many times have you personally been named beneficiary of a will drawn up by someone unknown to you?) Lead gifts come almost invariably from individuals who have known an organization for a long time.

Endeavor daily to develop ever-deepening relationships with key stakeholders. The process of genuine engagement with volunteers is one that must be extended to a broader circle of interested parties. This is a process of selection, one whereby the donor selects the organization and the organization selects the donor for a long-term and even, one hopes, lifetime relationship. Nevertheless, one of the most critical errors made in securing lead gifts is failing to look beyond the immediate campaign to the lifetime value of a donor's relationship with the organization. The concept of a lifelong relationship, like the attitude of valuing lifetime friendships with donors, is central to creating an environment for lead gifts. Thinking, in a long-term context, about relationships with volunteers, donors, and other stakeholders brings several fundamental ideas into focus.

First, quality is more important than quantity. Creating a positive climate for lead giving, in and beyond the context of the campaign, is hardly a mass-production, assembly-line process; indeed, according to an unpublished Federal Reserve technical paper analyzed by the *Left Business Observer* in 1997 and cited by United Auto Workers (1997), the richest 0.5 percent of the population owned 27 to 28 percent of the wealth in America in 1995. Organizations are best advised to focus their time on and build mature relationships with individuals who can ultimately make the kinds of high-impact gifts that this chapter describes. This need not be a cold, calculating activity; rather, the organization's role is to serve as a catalyst in these relationships, and facilitating them is a process that is both consuming and rewarding—time-intensive, but worthy of the organization's investment. It is more essential than ever to focus attention on building high-quality relationships with fewer individuals instead of seeking many relationships that never go beyond the superficial level. (If you do not believe this, reread Chapter Six.)

Second, multiple relationships inside the organization add value. The best volunteers and the most generous donors are those who extend their involvement in multiple ways. Over time, they may serve on different committees, contribute to different organizational programs, and form numerous relationships, whether with the chief executive officer or with clients served by the organization. For example, several years ago one institution discovered that a prospective donor had directed, over time, gifts of modest size to nearly twenty separate purposes within the organization. Needless to say, this donor had established multiple interests and many personal relationships at different levels, and these relationships contributed to a broad understanding of the organization's mission, as well as to the impact that the organization had on its constituency. When the time came for a multimillion dollar lead investment in a single program, it was clear that this donor's many relationships had played a role in his continuing interest in the organization, as well as in his willingness to make a transformational gift—which he did, at the level of more than $20 million. In any organization, large or small, the focus should be on managing and, as appropriate, even creating multiple relationships inside the organization. Too often, however, the organization's first instinct is to direct prospects to the "priority" program rather than allowing them to explore their own interests. Organizations should encourage rather than restrict multiple contacts and connections.

Third, past donors are most likely to be future investors. Treat them well. There is nothing more fundamental than remembering to remember past and current donors. The typical nonprofit organization, however, if it were to candidly examine where it places its priorities, would probably discover that it is much busier looking for the next big prospect than stewarding the last major donor. One college president, for example, complained that his staff relied too heavily on the "*Casablanca* method" of fundraising—"rounding up the usual suspects," as he put it—instead of broadening the base of donors. Every organization surely must find new friends in order to stay vibrant and keep moving forward, but an environment conducive to lead gifts evolves from careful stewardship of relationships with past and current donors. The challenge for those in the nonprofit sector is to focus as much energy on stewardship as on solicitation, thus creating an appropriately balanced environment for continuous lead giving.

## The Act of Asking

In April 1998, Joan and Sanford Weill announced a gift of $100 million to name Cornell University's Medical Center. Mr. Weill, asked how he and his wife had decided to make this gift, pointed to Cornell's president and medical dean and said, "They asked" (Arenson, 1998). The circumstances surrounding this gift are private, of course, but it can be surmised that the decision was not quite so simple.

And yet Mr. Weill's brief, spontaneous answer is poignant. It teaches, once again, the age-old lesson of fundraising at any level: the single biggest mistake in major gift fundraising is failing to ask for the gift; therefore, asking for the gift is the most important thing to do.

This seems obvious, but asking cannot be taken for granted. How many lead gifts have never materialized for your organization because the request was not made, even though all the other factors were in place? How many lead gifts went to "another organization" because that certain nonprofit group made a request, and yours did not? How many gifts never reached their maximum potential because the basis of your strategy was insufficient thought and too little homework?

Our intention in this chapter is not to list the elements of a successful solicitation call or to provide stock answers to the typical objections encountered in such meetings. Rather, it is to underscore the significance of actively, directly, and aggressively seeking philanthropic investments of the highest possible magnitude. If the proper steps are taken to develop an environment and culture conducive to lead giving, then the achievement of significant gift commitments will naturally follow.

Exploring donors' values, fostering mature relationships, engaging volunteers in meaningful ways, personally involving the organization's top leader—all these activities play a part in getting a donor ready to say yes to a direct proposal, or to respond to a vision by asking, "How much will it take?" None of this can happen, of course, without your organization's firm commitment to sustained, focused contact with volunteers and donors.

All lead gift solicitations are unique. Each prospect represents a minicampaign requiring specialized attention, creative approaches, and a solicitation grounded in the right strategy. The solicitation of lead gifts is nothing more than choosing the right volunteer to ask the right prospect for the right amount for the right purpose at the right time and in the right form. But decisions about how to get these elements right are not made in a vacuum. They evolve from high-quality interactions with volunteers, past and current donors, and prospective donors. Establishing lead gift solicitation strategies requires a significant investment of time on behalf of the organization. The process is labor-intensive and very personalized, and the devotion of ample budgetary resources is essential. Budgetary investments leading to enhanced direct contact with prospects will create the most favorable conditions for lead giving.

In the act of asking, one more element deserves emphatic mention: challenge the donor, in terms of both the amount and the purpose of the gift. Stay within the bounds of reason and good professional judgment, of course, but do challenge the donor's competitive spirit by asking the donor to stretch, not just financially but also intellectually and emotionally. The most emotionally and intellectually committed lead gift prospects will expect nonprofit organizations to present them with concepts that respond to their own strong impulses to transform organizations through philanthropy.

# The Act of Listening

It is the responsibility of the advancement officer—the staff member in charge of development and community relations— to put these cultivation "mechanics" in place. Doing so requires an often underemployed skill: listening.

"Advancement listening," a term not normally found in books on listening skills, requires fundraising professionals and institutional leaders to develop a very keen sense of what a donor is and is not saying. For example, consider one extremely committed donor. The institution's relationship with this donor had followed the classic development track (initial identification of the donor, a visit from the development officer, a strong relationship with the chief executive officer). The donor was now a member of the institution's board. Throughout the evolution of this relationship, the donor's giving had increased. When the chief executive officer began to talk about an investment at the lead gift level, the need to grow the institution's endowment was stressed. Every time the subject was raised, however, the donor listened intently but kept turning the conversation to a specific building project that was also on the drawing board. The building was important—it would be needed within five years—but it was not the institution's highest priority. After repeated conversations, however, the advancement officer and the chief executive officer decided that they should listen to the donor. This act of "advancement listening" netted a $2 million building gift—the donor's single largest gift ever, by a factor of ten, with tremendous potential for more. Thus the organization chose, in this case, to subordinate a higher priority to an opportunity for matching a donor's interest with another worthy but less immediate project. This decision will probably net the institution millions of additional gift dollars in the years ahead, and the next lead gift from this donor is likely to be for endowment purposes.

Not every act of "active listening" ends so positively, however. Sometimes an institution must retreat from a gift discussion because the donor's wishes are incompatible with the institution's needs. Such cases are examples of the unique relationship between donors and institutions: donors make tremendous investments in organizations, but they do not run them. The chief executive officer and the institution's governing body determine which gifts can be accepted, and for what purposes; they set the priorities. It is vital for any institution, regardless of its financial condition, to maintain its integrity with respect to the gifts that it does and does not accept. Fortunate is the institution that is not financially dependent on its next lead gift!

# Stewardship

Turning away gift support is a rarity at most institutions; a much larger challenge is proper stewardship of the gifts that are accepted.

There are several concepts about stewardship. The original concept predates the Bible, but it is codified in biblical language—that all possessions belong to God, and that humanity is responsible for managing those resources while on earth. In feudal Europe, a steward was the person who ran the manor house, particularly the financial aspects of the estate. The "green" movement of the past few decades also uses the concept, emphasizing the need to be "stewards" of the earth's natural resources. An underlying element in each context is high moral quality and responsible management. A proper steward is one who is morally responsible and trustworthy.

"Stewarding" donors may not be thought of as a moral obligation, but it is an important concept. Donors have chosen to invest in your institution. They give time, energy, resources, and talents. As the "steward of the manor," the organization has a responsibility to use those gifts wisely and to properly account for those uses. Donors place high trust in institutions, and so institutions should be systematic about telling donors how their money is used. There should be immediate response to inquiries about how gifts and other assets are managed. Good stewardship also requires communication with donors when institutional needs change, and when those changes affect donors' gifts.

There are some extremely practical reasons for being a good steward. No reasonable person would continue sending money to a financial institution that failed to report regularly on the investment. If you want your most committed stakeholders to remain committed, be forthright and regular in reporting on the rich dividends that their gifts are paying at your institution.

Good stewardship leads quite naturally to stronger existing relationships and to the development of new ones with the organization. Donors are investors, and they are interested in seeing a return on their investments. The stewardship requirement for lead gift prospects and donors goes far beyond sending an annual report on endowment performance or having the organization's chief executive officer pay an annual visit. Good stewardship is a personal process that is carefully managed. It aims not simply to maintain a donor's satisfaction but to increase his satisfaction to the point where he asks, "What more can I do?" Good stewardship is not just the end of the solicitation cycle; it is the beginning of a new and higher level of a donor's involvement.

## Positioning Lead Gifts in a Campaign Context

In the 1980s, when capital campaign goals exceeded the billion-dollar mark, some speculated that campaigns could not sustain themselves at such rarefied heights. In the 1990s, with the record-breaking bull market and the growth of worldwide wealth, we have to wonder whether there is any ceiling at all to campaign goals.

Campaigns will remain part of the fundraising landscape for one simple reason: they work; they raise money. And lead gifts have never been more important to campaigns. Transformational gifts represent huge percentages of campaign totals. Capital campaigns' goals continue growing at a feverish pace because lead gifts are escalating exponentially.

Do donors really care about goals? Do campaigns provide an excuse to ask for unprecedented gifts? Twenty years ago, donors may not have cared as much about the details of capital campaigns. Today, however, they often care deeply about whether their gifts are made in the context of a campaign. Why is this so?

The decision to make a campaign gift does not always reflect a donor's desire to be included in a mass appeal for funds. Rather, it reflects the evolutionary role of campaigns and the programs that those campaigns seek to fund. It also reflects donors' increased sophistication. A successful capital campaign today is a direct outgrowth of the institution's strategic planning process. Institutional needs are not simply brought to the chief executive officer's desk and converted into a campaign brochure. The needs, goals, ambitions, and mission of the institution should be debated, discussed, and determined. The campaign is an outgrowth of the institution's strategic thinking. Lead gift donors increasingly want to know that their gifts will be used for specific, strategic purposes. For example, in February 1998 the University of Pennsylvania's law school announced the largest outright gift ever to a law school for construction and endowment purposes, and in May 1998 the Wharton School at the University of Pennsylvania announced the largest single gift ever to a business school in the United States (it was an unrestricted gift). In both cases, the donors were key volunteers who had taken a hand in shaping institutional directions and ambitions.

Involving key volunteers and donors in strategic planning is also vital to a campaign's success. Committed outsiders bring a real-world perspective to the planning process. Such donors become much more committed to the process, and they have a greater investment in its successful outcome when they have been consulted.

Donors actually cultivate themselves through this process by becoming much more familiar with the strengths and needs of the institution. This is not to suggest that the planning process should be turned over to donors and volunteers, however; institutional representatives ultimately must develop and implement a strategic plan, but the involvement of key constituents will make finding resources much easier when it is time to fund the strategic initiatives. Donors do care about campaigns when the case for support has been clearly developed and can be backed by strategic analysis.

Capital campaigns provide a framework that makes securing lead gifts much easier. Campaigns set deadlines, benchmarks, and goals. Deadlines make decision making more efficient, and donors will be more efficient with their gift decisions when deadlines are set. The deadline concept is often further refined in campaigns, too. Most campaigns do not go public until a certain percent of the goal has been committed—usually between 40 and 60 percent—and lead gifts represent the bulk of the money raised during this quiet phase. Asking lead donors to make their gift commitments early, before the campaign goes public, creates another deadline that can encourage gift decisions. Skillful campaign leaders often set several minideadlines as a way to benchmark progress and help "close" gifts.

Campaigns also provide a bandwagon effect, and campaign-conditioned donors often expect to play a part in it. Some donors will not make a gift decision unless they know it will be part of a larger institutional fundraising effort; as one donor said a few years ago, "I don't want to be a lone wolf." Donors at the lead gift level want their gifts to be counted among other large contributions. Campaigns provide a way for that to happen, and this "rising tide" encourages others to join. Donors also want to associate themselves with successful organizations, and successful campaigns provide that association.

Campaigns also offer a formal structure for recognizing philanthropy. Campaigns provide opportunities for regular stewardship and public relations–related events (donor recognition dinners, news releases, periodic campaign updates), and the campaign format increases the visibility of a donor's gift while also providing a larger audience for it. Gift announcements let institutions reinforce the campaign's overarching goals and highlight how the donor's investment supports the institutional mission. Donor recognition undergirds the stewardship process because it provides another way to thank the donor for the gift. It also encourages others to get on the bandwagon.

Not every donor prefers this kind of recognition, however. That was the situation recently when an institution received a very large gift—a record breaker—but both the gift and the donor's identity had to remain unknown; the donor did not want to make headlines with his act of philanthropy. This attitude is uncommon—even refreshing, given our world of hype and advertising—but the opportunity to take full advantage of peer-to-peer, leveraged, sight-raising philanthropy is lost in such a situation.

Some major donors also give for reasons other than simple altruism. Ego gratification is often a very important consideration. A major donor may want regional and national publicity for a commitment. The donor may want peers and other volunteer leaders in the organization to know of his generosity and may also want his family and social set to be aware of the gift. Often major donors, highly successful in their business and professional lives, have developed a strong competitive spirit, and the same drive often motivates them to make major gifts and feel challenged to make even larger commitments. Lead gifts may become a vehicle through which these highly competitive, successful individuals, whose egos are often equally well developed, can make a statement to the business and philanthropic worlds.

Donors like these can and should be exacting about the publicity they receive for their gifts. Organizations cannot guarantee media coverage of gift announcements, of course. Some donors expect it, however, and capital campaigns often help in this arena. Campaigns provide a context for, and a message complementary to, a gift announcement; the campaign messages give the media something else to report in addition to the donor's gift and how it will be used. Campaign publications can be used, too. They are no substitute for prominent news coverage, but they do ensure that the message is delivered to the audience that you choose, and at the time that you set.

An important consideration in announcing lead gifts is the staging, sequencing, and pacing of these announcements around campaign events and meetings. This strategy can have a strong motivational impact on both internal and external audiences. For example, asking a donor couple to personally announce their gift to peers has a tremendous emotional effect on those who have not yet given. These personal testimonies and the life stories behind them can be exemplary in raising the standard for the next cycle of campaign gifts.

A final word about press releases on gifts: keep the donor well informed. It is vital to stay in touch with the donor throughout the gift decision process, but it is equally important to keep the donor informed about announcement strategies. It is better to err on the side of giving the donor too many opportunities to change a news release or the circumstances surrounding an announcement. Putting up with some inconvenience is far preferable to angering a donor who feels insufficiently consulted about the publicity surrounding a lead gift that is, after all, an extremely personal matter.

## Other Considerations

In addition to working with a donor or a donor couple, organizations often work with a donor's associates. This group may include spouses, significant others, children, other heirs, administrative staff, and financial and legal advisers. These individuals can play a crucial role in the gift decision process and in the subsequent stewardship activity; they may be either advocates or adversaries in the giving process. The best rule is to involve them as early as possible: the organization benefits if its representatives know when to involve people associated with the donor.

Family and heirs present special issues in the negotiation of major gifts. They often have a personal stake in the donor's commitment and believe that they have a vested interest in the process. It is up to the institution—and sometimes the donor—to demonstrate that the gift decision is in the donor's best interest. Often, by using creative vehicles for planned giving, an institution can help to design a strategy that benefits the donor, his or her heirs, and the institution itself.

Negotiating such gift arrangements may involve the donor's financial and legal counsel, and institutional representatives often validate the donor's intended gift for these advisers. This is especially true when an adviser is looking for reasons to stop the donor from making the gift. Institutional representatives should have a working knowledge of the financial and tax implications of charitable gifts or should have ready access to people who do. Most donors make lead gifts for reasons other than the tax and estate benefits, but the tax laws do provide real opportunities for people with an interest in making charitable contributions. Never has this been so true as in today's financial markets, where millions of new fortunes—and potential new major donors—have been created with the dramatic increase in the value of equity markets.

Today, gifts of appreciated securities are becoming the currency of choice for major donors, and institutional staff must be well versed in the nuances of stock gifts. Sometimes a donor will make a gift decision when a stock reaches a specific value, or the donor may time a gift in conjunction with a capital event (such as the takeover of a company, or an initial public offering). Gifts of stock in a donor's publicly traded corporation can also create special challenges and opportunities. For example, high-profile executives or board members who use corporate stock as their gift vehicle often worry about a possible adverse market reaction to their liquidation of stock for gift purposes. Some corporate insiders will not make significant stock gifts because they fear that the market will misinterpret their intent to give away securities. In work with donors and their advisers, each circumstance requires flexibility and creativity.

Most people are living longer than their parents did and will be much more active later in life. Therefore, another consideration for most donors is the maintenance of a certain standard of living. Longer life expectancy also holds the possibility of costs associated with long-term care for the donor, the donor's spouse, or both, and this possibility can create tremendous pressure on donors to hold on to resources that otherwise might be given. Despite the old fundraising saw that "no one protects the donor's wallet like the donor," concerns about longer life expectancy are real and must be treated with respect and honesty. The ethics of our profession require us to maintain a fiduciary relationship with donors, especially older ones, and we must work with all major donors to craft gift arrangements that benefit both them and our organizations.

# CHAPTER ELEVEN

# MANAGING CAMPAIGN LOGISTICS AND DAY-TO-DAY OPERATIONS

This chapter addresses essential campaign operational matters, including the schedule for the campaign, the campaign budget, gift reporting, and the use of professional counsel. Once a campaign organizational chart (described in Chapter Seven) has been established, the next step is to develop the campaign timetable.

## Typical Timetable

Campaigns have been known to be organized and conducted in very short periods of time. For example, a campaign in Memphis took five months from start to finish, and another, in New Castle, Indiana, took only three. But it is more typical for a campaign to require between six and eighteen months of preparation and then two or three years, sometimes longer, for the active phase.

A capital campaign is an undertaking of great complexity. An organization's constituencies must be fully informed, prospective donors must be identified and classified in terms of their giving potential, and prospects must be carefully assigned for solicitation. Various committees must launch their solicitation activities at appropriate intervals. Finally, report meetings and the inevitable follow-up activities must be carried out in the closing weeks of each of the separate phases. All these activities must be scheduled with careful regard for each volunteer's time.

It is sound campaign practice to seek the biggest gifts first; therefore, early moves have uncommon significance, and premature action can be dangerous. The following simplified outline of activities shows the timing of solicitation during a three-year "public phase" campaign. This calendar illustrates the principles of working from the top down. It also shows that the larger the gift, the longer the donor may need to consider it before making the decision to give.

1. First Phase: Before the Public Announcement (12–15 months)
   - Complete the institution's strategic plan
   - Organize development and campaign office
   - Retain counsel (as necessary)
   - Draft plan and timetable
   - Draft preliminary case statement
   - Conduct market survey
   - Enlist campaign chair
   - Enlist other key campaign committee members
   - Review campaign plan with committee
   - Build prospect lists
   - Identify, research, evaluate, and cultivate primary major prospective donors for early approach (lead gifts)
   - Develop basic print-based and audiovisual materials
   - Seek lead gifts
   - Enlist and educate major gifts committee(s)
   - Solicit members for campaign committee
   - Begin enlisting and educating special gifts committee(s)
   - Enlist general committee chair
   - Publicly announce campaign (major event)
   - *End first phase:* deadline for 50 percent of campaign dollar objective (no public announcement unless a minimum of 30 percent of goal has been met)
2. Second Phase: Major/Special Gifts (18–24 months)
   - Continue adding names to lists of major and special gift donors
   - As necessary, continue prospective donor contact
   - Continue major gifts solicitation
   - Solicit members for special gifts committee
   - Launch special gifts committee solicitations
   - Continue distribution of campaign information to news media
   - Enlist, organize, and train general campaign leaders
   - *End second phase:* deadline for 80 percent of campaign dollar objective
3. Third Phase: General Gifts, Cleanup (12–18 months)
   - Formally launch general gifts solicitation
   - Continue solicitation by major and special gifts committees
   - Continue distribution of campaign information to news media

- Launch final campaign thrust, followed by final report meeting for top volunteers
- Victory event
- *End third phase:* deadline for 100 percent of campaign dollar objective

The capital campaign is, of course, a collection of individual campaigns, each with its own leaders and timing. The time schedule, once established, must be respected. In some instances, a general campaign will need to be supplemented by area or regional campaigns. The following calendar is typical for an area campaign (the time required will vary according to the area, the number of prospects to be solicited, and the size of the gifts to be solicited).

*First Week*

1. Chair and staff representative(s) meet to
   - Determine number of campaign workers needed to solicit prospects on the basis of completed prospect evaluation
   - Select names of prospective division leaders
   - Set up campaign calendar, including dates of all organizational meetings, the solicitation committee meeting, the announcement event, and the report and planning meetings
   - Determine and tentatively engage places for solicitation committee meeting and announcement event
   - Discuss arrangements for processing the necessary letters to be mailed over the chair's signature
2. Chair begins enlistment of division leaders

*Second Week*

1. Chair, division leaders, and staff representative(s) meet to review the campaign program and begin enlistment of other volunteer workers
2. Chair's invitation to the announcement event is mailed to those on the guest list
3. Division leaders begin enlistment of team members

*Third Week*

1. Letter announcing date of solicitation committee meeting is mailed to campaign workers as they are enlisted
2. Announcement of chair's appointment is released to appropriate news media
3. Area campaign goal is set

*Fourth Week*

1. Chair calls division leaders to check on progress in enlisting team members
2. Letters announcing date of solicitation committee meeting continue to be mailed

*Fifth Week*

1. Campaign solicitation committee meets; training and information session is held; workers are assigned prospects
2. Workers call assigned prospects to remind them of the announcement event

*Sixth Week*

1. Announcement event
2. One day later, brochure and chair's letters are mailed to all constituents in the area who are not scheduled for personal solicitation
3. Solicitation of campaigners begins on the day following the reception (chair solicits division leaders, division leaders solicit team members)
4. Solicitation of all prospects begins
5. After announcement event, weekly progress reports are mailed to all solicitors through a campaign newsletter prepared by area chair and staff representative

*Seventh Week*

First report meeting held

*Eighth Week*

Second report meeting held

*Ninth Week*

Third report meeting held

*Tenth Week*

Fourth report meeting held

*Eleventh Week*

1. Fifth report meeting held, as necessary
2. Final check made on outstanding pledge cards
3. Chair sends letter of appreciation to all campaign workers
4. Victory celebration held with workers at final report meeting as goal is achieved

## Acknowledging and Reporting Gifts

From the beginning of the campaign, all gifts should be promptly acknowledged, and each donor should be properly thanked. Each donor should receive a personal letter of appreciation from the institution, as well as an official gift receipt. Think about the thank-you letter, too: try to make it more than a thank-you. Make it personal, informative, and meaty. Tell the donor about what is happening, about the amount raised, about progress on the building project, about the amount of endowment money, and so forth. This is one of the details that need to be thought about in advance. Who will sign the letters? At what minimum level will institutional administrators and campaign leaders sign? $100? $500? $1,000? More? Does the plan call for the institution to ask each volunteer to thank each donor and send the institution a copy of the thank-you letter? (It should.) For larger gifts, the chief executive officer should certainly provide a personal acknowledgment. The key volunteer working on the solicitation may also choose to communicate with the donor, as may the chair of the board and the chair of the campaign. Gifts are made individually, and their acknowledgment should be considered individually. If more than one acknowledgment is to be sent, the staff should make certain that the acknowledgments are not redundant but that they complement and reinforce each other.

Acknowledging gifts will be a time-consuming task. Therefore, to enable prompt preparation of the letters, there may be a need for additional secretarial staff or word-processing capability. This is an important detail: long delays in acknowledging and thanking donors for gifts are unprofessional and make a bad impression. Be certain that everyone—donors and volunteers—is thanked as quickly as possible.

Another major consideration is reporting gifts, both internally and to volunteers and the public. As part of campaign planning, the institution must build internal recording and reporting systems that will enable it to handle gifts correctly and with dispatch. These systems must be able to compile the gift data to formulate reports showing the number, sources, and amounts of the gifts received and, more important, the purposes for which the gifts were received. This is essential, not only for practical reasons (such as reporting periodically to campaign leaders and workers) but also for internal audit controls. The staff must be able to report daily where the campaign stands; the staff will certainly be asked for such information almost daily.

The staff should also consider preparing a weekly or monthly campaign report to be mailed to all volunteers and to others important to the success of the campaign. Formats of such reports vary widely and can be determined by individual institutions. In some campaigns, a monthly report is all that is required. It helps in keeping the focus on the campaign and can be used to build fires under those volunteers who are not performing up to expectations. Each volunteer leader should review the division's or team's effort at each report session. The bandwagon effect is important in a campaign.

According to the campaign's organizational structure, the staff may want to be able to report in a number of ways—by division, by team, by area, by class, by source, by amount, by fund, or by all these criteria. (See Resource I, "Sample Monthly Financial Report.") Certainly, a breakdown of this nature will be desirable in the institution's final report of the campaign, so why not plan it in advance and have this capacity during the campaign? Most institutions now use computers, and so this is a simple task if it is programmed carefully. If an institution still uses a manual system, multipart copies can do the trick.

## Stewardship

An essential component of any follow-through program is the thoughtful, systematic organization of a stewardship effort. Stewardship effectively begins even before the first gift is received—when the board establishes policies regarding the acceptance, handling, management, and investment of gifts. Once a gift is received, stewardship encompasses a variety of activities, including recognition, appreciation, and reporting. It also, obviously, includes the wise and prudent financial management of the investment. It is the ongoing process whereby an institution continues contact with a donor to establish the basis for the next gift while exercising proper care of and giving appropriate recognition for gifts already made.

Some individuals and many corporations and foundations will not pledge for a period of years but will give initially and will renew each year after that. This category of donors should be flagged, and the donors should be asked to consider another gift near the anniversary date of the last gift. Even a single-year donor who has not promised to continue giving should be asked on the anniversary of the previous gift; this practice has also proved productive in many campaigns.

## Saving the Victory

If victory on schedule should elude an institution, it is important to do two things, according to Picton (1982). First, be candid. Announce the results to date, and indicate that all gifts have not been received. Continue in a quiet, determined way to push for a successful conclusion as soon as possible. Second, have all leaders call or visit every key prospect in their divisions or on their teams, to ask that the prospects keep the campaign in mind until the work is finished, and offer assistance to particular leaders or staff members. For example, if certain volunteers have not been effective, perhaps some reassignment of prospects is called for. It does not take long for a campaign to die, so push harder than ever. This is where the campaign leaders must be aggressive. Here again, review the status of the major prospects, and look for new approaches if they are needed. Have the campaign "cabinet" consider going back to key prospects for a second gift; rarely does the initial gift tap out a donor.

## Campaign Budget

What does it cost to run a professionally managed campaign? Obviously, there is no single answer. Several factors influence the cost of campaign fundraising:

- The proportion of institutional resources already committed to the ongoing development program
- The size of the goal (certain fixed costs that are common to all campaigns—preparation of a case statement, the use of professional counsel, a major public announcement event, a victory celebration—are more easily amortized in large campaign budgets than in small ones)
- The type of campaign model
- The asking method chosen that has been chosen
- The scope of the campaign (that is, whether it is a local or a wide-area campaign)

Very simply, campaign budgets can vary significantly. Information from recent efforts suggests that costs in large campaigns can be kept as low as 2 or 3 percent of the campaign goal. For the purposes of planning, however, most institutions should assume that it will cost between 10 and 12 percent of the campaign goal to conduct the campaign, especially if the goal is under $10 million or if the institution lacks appropriate fundraising infrastructure in the beginning. For a large segment of the institutions contemplating capital campaigns, a guideline of 4 percent is applicable. Into this group falls the institution that has a well-developed fundraising program (that is, a program with annual giving, special gifts, major gifts, planned giving efforts, and a research function) and an adequately funded operating budget, with a campaign goal in the range of $25 million to $250 million. This incremental amount of 4 percent of the goal is in addition to the established operating budget. Several variables must be considered before a final figure is arrived at, but two fundamental points are of primary importance.

First, it takes ample funding to ensure the success of a campaign, and too much attention is focused on fundraising costs. With so much at stake, it is foolhardy to be too restrictive of campaign expenses; to fixate on costs is to adopt the perspective that the glass is half empty. It does matter how much is spent, but isn't the real issue how much is realized? No matter how cost-effective an effort is, it is always possible to argue that even more costs could be squeezed out of the budget if only the campaign managers looked harder. But it is time to change the dialogue, establish a new paradigm, focus on returns—and an investment in a campaign, wisely made, will yield very high returns. *It costs money to raise money.* Is a 1,000 percent return on investment acceptable? How about 2,500 percent? What board member, volunteer, institutional employee, or donor would not be pleased with a 2,500 percent return? That's a 4 percent cost.

Second, all the campaign's needs should be considered and included at the outset. Most campaign budgets have lines for the items shown in Exhibit 11.1.

A final important consideration regarding budget is to establish an internal procedure that provides for constant monitoring and scrutiny of budget expenditures. (See Exhibit 11.2.)

In addition to the costs of campaigning, there is the little-discussed loss called "shrinkage"—that is, losses resulting from unpaid pledges. Normal shrinkage is usually 1 to 3 percent of the amount raised. The job of the professional staff member is to ensure that it stays as low as possible.

Some losses are uncontrollable, as in the case of a donor's death or the failure of the donor's business. Some, however, are caused by inadequate pledge reminder and billing systems. The amount of income that short-term investments can earn these days makes it imperative for an organization to collect its pledges on schedule—earlier, if possible. An organization that does not have a responsive system enabling it to bill accurately and on schedule may be headed for collection difficulty. The institution must check this system and, before the campaign is begun, make any necessary corrections. A status report on the campaign and information about what is being done with the funds can be included with the billing statement. This practice can help payments flow and is sound cultivation for later gifts.

## Creating and Using Report Forms

Before the campaign begins, the institution should create the various printed forms and computer programs needed to record, retain, retrieve, and reproduce the information associated with the wide variety of campaign tasks. There are two types of basic reports for which the professional staff is responsible: financial reports, and reports on people (volunteers and prospects). The number and sophistication

## EXHIBIT 11.1. LEADSHEET: ENDOWMENT CAMPAIGN.

| | | | | |
|---|---|---|---|---|
| | BUDGET LEAD SHEET | | | |
| DEPARTMENT: | Endowment Campaign for Indiana University, Bloomington | | | |
| LOCATION: | | | | |
| BUDGET MANAGER: | | | | |
| | | | | |
| Object | | 1998 | 3/31/98 | 1999 |
| Code | Description | Budget | Actual | Requested |
| | | | | |
| 80005 | Admin. Salaries (Net Reimb.) | | | |
| 70005 | IU Faculty & Staff Comp. & FB | | | |
| 80005 | Clerical Salaries | | | |
| 80010 | Contract Salaries | | | |
| 80015 | Overtime Wages | | | |
| 80020 | Wages Paid to Hourly Emp. | | | |
| 80025 | Temporary Services | | | |
| 88000 | Salary—Allow for Attrition Alloc. | | | |
| | | | | |
| | Total Salaries | | | |
| | | | | |
| 80165 | Fringe Benefits | | | |
| | | | | |
| | Total Personnel | | | |
| | | | | |
| 80200 | Job Training | | | |
| 80202 | Employee Recruitment | | | |
| 80205 | Employee Recog. & Goodwill | | | |
| 80210 | Organizational Funct. | | | |
| 80215 | Sundries | | | |
| 81000 | Travel | | | |
| 81005 | Representation | | | |
| 81006 | Represent. Activities & Events | | | |
| 81010 | Business Meetings | | | |
| 81012 | Out-of-Town Board Meetings | | | |
| 81020 | Advertising & Promo | | | |

## EXHIBIT 11.1.  LEADSHEET: ENDOWMENT CAMPAIGN, Cont'd.

| | BUDGET LEAD SHEET | | | |
|---|---|---|---|---|
| DEPARTMENT: | Endowment Campaign for Indiana University, Bloomington | | | |
| LOCATION: | | | | |
| BUDGET MANAGER: | | | | |
| | | | | |
| Object | | 1998 | 3/31/98 | 1999 |
| Code | Description | Budget | Actual | Requested |
| | | | | |
| 81025 | Membership Dues | | | |
| 81030 | Art Exhibition Expenses | | | |
| 81035 | Artists' Expenses | | | |
| 82000 | General Office Supplies | | | |
| 82005 | Kitchen Supplies | | | |
| 82007 | Food Service Expense | | | |
| 82010 | Printed Brochures | | | |
| 82015 | Newspapers & Magazines | | | |
| 82025 | Professional Publications | | | |
| 82030 | Art Production | | | |
| 82035 | Framing Supplies | | | |
| 82050 | Photocopying & Microfilming | | | |
| 82100 | Business Reply Postage | | | |
| 82103 | Bulk Mail Postage | | | |
| 82104 | Bulk Mail Postage (Contract) | | | |
| 82105 | Metered Postage | | | |
| 82110 | Postage Stamps | | | |
| 82115 | Shipping & Express Charges | | | |
| 82120 | Shipping Supplies | | | |
| 83000 | Bldg. Maintenance Contract | | | |
| 83005 | Bldg. Rental Expense | | | |
| 83010 | Bldg. Repair & Maint. | | | |
| 83015 | Bldg. Operating Supplies | | | |
| 83020 | Utilities | | | |
| 83025 | Real Estate Taxes | | | |
| 83030 | Property Insurance | | | |

## EXHIBIT 11.1. LEADSHEET: ENDOWMENT CAMPAIGN, Cont'd.

| | BUDGET LEAD SHEET | | | |
|---|---|---|---|---|
| DEPARTMENT: | Endowment Campaign for Indiana University, Bloomington | | | |
| LOCATION: | | | | |
| BUDGET MANAGER: | | | | |
| | | | | |
| Object | | 1998 | 3/31/98 | 1999 |
| Code | Description | Budget | Actual | Requested |
| | | | | |
| 83120 | Non-Depr. Furnishings | | | |
| 83200 | Computer Repair & Maint. | | | |
| 83205 | Computer Access Expense | | | |
| 83210 | Computer Insurance | | | |
| 83212 | Printer Supplies | | | |
| 83215 | Non-Depr. Computer Equip. | | | |
| 83300 | Computer Software Maint. Fee | | | |
| 83310 | Non-Depr. Computer Software | | | |
| 83400 | Telephone Expense | | | |
| 83410 | Fax Charges | | | |
| 83500 | Copier Lease | | | |
| 83505 | Copier Repairs & Maint. | | | |
| 83600 | Vehicle Gas and Oil | | | |
| 83605 | Vehicle Repairs & Maint. | | | |
| 83610 | Vehicle Insurance | | | |
| 83615 | Vehicle License & Tax | | | |
| 83620 | Non-Depr. Vehicle Parts | | | |
| 83625 | Other Vehicle Expense | | | |
| 83800 | Other Equip. Repair & Maint. | | | |
| 83805 | Other Equip. Rental Expense | | | |
| 83810 | Other Equip. Insurance | | | |
| 83815 | Non-Depreciable Equipment | | | |
| 84000 | Legal Fees | | | |
| 84001 | Non-Budgeted Legal | | | |
| 84005 | Audit, Tax, & Accting. Fees | | | |
| 84010 | Consulting Fees | | | |

## EXHIBIT 11.1. LEADSHEET: ENDOWMENT CAMPAIGN, Cont'd.

| | BUDGET LEAD SHEET | | | |
|---|---|---|---|---|
| DEPARTMENT: | Endowment Campaign for Indiana University, Bloomington | | | |
| LOCATION: | | | | |
| BUDGET MANAGER: | | | | |
| | | | | |
| Object | | 1998 | 3/31/98 | 1999 |
| Code | Description | Budget | Actual | Requested |
| | | | | |
| 84011 | Reimb. of Consulting Fees (Contract) | | | |
| 84015 | Professional Fees | | | |
| 84020 | Miscellaneous Services | | | |
| 84050 | Bank Service Fees | | | |
| 84055 | Merchant Credit Card Fees | | | |
| 84060 | Filing Fees | | | |
| 84070 | Service Bureau Fees | | | |
| 84080 | Service Bureau Conversion | | | |
| 85000 | D & O Liability Insurance | | | |
| 85005 | Blanket Bond Insurance | | | |
| 86005 | Loss from Damage/Theft | | | |
| 89000 | Miscellaneous Expense | | | |
| 89020 | Allowance for Doubtful Accounts | | | |
| | | | | |
| | Total Program | | | |
| | | | | |
| 90010 | Cap. Exp.—Building Improvements | | | |
| 90020 | Cap. Exp.—Furniture & Fixtures | | | |
| 90030 | Cap. Exp.—Computer Hardware | | | |
| 90040 | Cap. Exp.—Computer Software | | | |
| 90050 | Cap. Exp.—Vehicles | | | |
| 90080 | Cap. Exp.—Other Equipment | | | |
| 90090 | Cap. Exp.—Artwork | | | |
| | | | | |
| | Total Capital | | | |
| | Total Budget | | | |

# EXHIBIT 11.2. CAPITAL CAMPAIGN BUDGET REPORT.

Indiana University Foundation
Endowment Campaign for IU, Bloomington—Location 570/571
Expenses to date as of 8/31/98

| Line No. | Description | FY '96 Actual | FY '97 Actual | FY '98 Actual | To Date Actual 8/31/98 | '99 Budget | '00 Budget | '01 Budget | To Date Budget | Total Budget | Amount Remaining | Percent Variance |
|---|---|---|---|---|---|---|---|---|---|---|---|---|
| 1 | Salaries (net of allowance) | | | | | | | | | | | |
| 2 | Overtime Wages | | | | | | | | | | | |
| 3 | Fringe Benefits | | | | | | | | | | | |
| 4 | Total Personnel | | | | | | | | | | | |
| 5 | Training & Recruiting | | | | | | | | | | | |
| 6 | Travel | | | | | | | | | | | |
| 7 | Representation | | | | | | | | | | | |
| 8 | Supplies | | | | | | | | | | | |
| 9 | Printing | | | | | | | | | | | |
| 10 | Postage & Shipping | | | | | | | | | | | |
| 11 | Telephone | | | | | | | | | | | |
| 12 | Copier Maintenance & Supplies | | | | | | | | | | | |
| 13 | Building Repair & Maintenance | | | | | | | | | | | |
| 14 | Vehicle Repair & Maintenance | | | | | | | | | | | |
| 15 | Computer Repair & Maintenance | | | | | | | | | | | |
| 16 | Other Equipment & Furnishings | | | | | | | | | | | |
| 17 | Legal Fees | | | | | | | | | | | |
| 18 | Professional and Other Fees | | | | | | | | | | | |
| 19 | Insurance | | | | | | | | | | | |
| 20 | Miscellaneous | | | | | | | | | | | |
| 21 | Total Program | | | | | | | | | | | |
| 22 | Capital Expenditures | | | | | | | | | | | |
| 23 | Total Expenditures | | | | | | | | | | | |

of the financial reports will vary according to the size and complexity of the campaign. (See Resource I, "Sample Monthly Financial Report.") In an established development office, of course, a great number of operating procedures will probably already be in place, particularly those pertaining to fiduciary matters but also those pertaining to the wider scope of the office's activities. Two examples of the kinds of forms routinely generated in support of a capital campaign are included here. Exhibit 11.3 shows a sample weekly campaign progress report. A typical prospect status summary is shown in Exhibit 11.4. For both types of form, information can be maintained and conveyed via hard copy or computerized procedures.

The institution interested in studying a complete library of the variety of materials and tables used in a typical campaign can consult *The Campaign Manuals* (Builta, 1984a, 1984b), a two-volume scrapbook of a particular campaign. The first volume, *The Campaign,* includes, in chronological order, the most important communications between campaign headquarters and volunteers. The second volume, *Steps and Procedures,* deals directly with record-keeping systems and contains an index to simplify the location of particular forms or sets of instructions.

## EXHIBIT 11.3. CAMPAIGN PROGRESS REPORT.

*Week ending* _____

I. Campaign goal                                                    $
II. New gifts and pledges
III. Total previous gifts and pledges

    Grand total gifts and pledges

IV. Amount needed to reach goal
V. Recent campaign activities

VI. Appointments scheduled

| Donor Category | Campaign Goal | Received to Date | Balance Needed |
|---|---|---|---|
| Board | $ | $ | $ |
| Individuals | | | |
| Corporations | | | |
| Foundations | | | |
| Other | | | |
| TOTALS | | | |

EXHIBIT 11.4. PROPOSED STATUS SUMMARY.

| Major Prospects | Researched | Prospect | Assigned to Staff | Possible Volunteer(s) | Assigned to Volunteer | Meeting Held | Letter and/or Proposal Submitted | Gift/Pledge Made; Seek More | Refused; Try Again | Adequate Gift/Pledge Made | Firm Refusal | Comments |
|---|---|---|---|---|---|---|---|---|---|---|---|---|
| | | | | | | | | | | | | |
| | | | | | | | | | | | | |
| | | | | | | | | | | | | |
| | | | | | | | | | | | | |
| | | | | | | | | | | | | |
| | | | | | | | | | | | | |
| | | | | | | | | | | | | |
| | | | | | | | | | | | | |
| | | | | | | | | | | | | |
| | | | | | | | | | | | | |
| | | | | | | | | | | | | |
| | | | | | | | | | | | | |
| | | | | | | | | | | | | |
| | | | | | | | | | | | | |
| | | | | | | | | | | | | |
| | | | | | | | | | | | | |

# Outside Professional Counsel

A successful capital campaign will generally adhere to the principles stated in this book. Nevertheless, the simple memorization of these principles will not guarantee a successful campaign. Success is more likely when the mechanics are supplemented by human experience, insight, strategies, sensitivity, and judgments of the kind that transcend the prescriptions of any written document. These added ingredients are often provided by outside professional counsel.

An institution with a sizable and experienced fundraising staff may decide to proceed without aid from outside counsel, but the majority of institutions find such aid both advisable and necessary. Outside counsel is most often employed when the organization feels that it must supplement its staff's ability to handle a campaign or feels that it needs expert advice, or when the development office feels that it needs objective advice.

In considering the use of outside counsel, it is important to understand that the role of professional counsel is not to raise money but rather to help the institution raise it. The use of professional counsel does not relieve the institution's board and administration of their responsibilities for the success of the campaign. In most cases, professional counsel is used to supplement in-house capabilities. Professional counsel enables people to draw on a breadth and depth of experience not generally possessed by a single institution. It is usually retained for one or more of the following purposes:

- To conduct a program assessment in advance of the campaign
- To conduct a market survey
- To prepare the campaign case and other case-stating materials
- To provide full-time (resident) campaign management
- To provide part-time (periodic) counseling

In the latter two categories, a significant shift occurred in the 1990s. Fifteen years ago, consultants predominantly provided campaign management to their clients through resident counsel. Today, given the growth in the number of institutions with previous campaign experience, as well as the dramatically larger population of professional staff with previous campaign experience and stronger day-to-day management abilities, consultants are increasingly being used to provide strategic direction, advice, and vision, offered through periodic visits and off-site consultation.

Because consultants now generally serve more a strategic than an operational function, it may be time for institutions to consider the minimum standards on which they must insist before engaging outside professional counsel. Inexperienced consultants, or those who for some other reason have no track record, should not be engaged to manage or offer counsel to campaigns at an institution that finds itself in need of outside counsel: the institution is itself inexperienced and uncertain in this arena, and consultants who have no more (and sometimes less) experience and knowledge than their clients will be of limited use, at best. There are currently no licensing requirements or credentialing programs for consultants, nor are those being advocated here. At the minimum, however, institutions may want to ask whether a potential consultant meets the requirements of the National Society of Fund Raising Executives (NSFRE) for being (or has already been designated) a certified fundraising executive (CFRE).

Another change occurring in the consulting field is the emergence of firms, partnerships, and sole proprietorships that primarily serve geographically defined territories. This development is in contrast to the existence of the well-established, recognized national firms that work across wide areas. Given the growth in the number of consultants who work in relatively confined areas, there is a corresponding growth in the potential for conflict of interest when it comes to the confidentiality of proprietary information belonging to a single organization. It may be tempting to hire a consultant who already knows your service area well because of his or her previous assignments in the same market—and, to be sure, there is much local knowledge that can be shared legitimately between and among consultants and multiple clients. But there is also a large body of knowledge and a great amount of information that should not be shared or exchanged under any circumstances without the prior written consent of the organization. Beware the potential consultant who offers to share confidential and proprietary information obtained in service to another organization. The temptation to acquire this information may seem irresistible, but do resist: How would you feel if it were your information being passed along without your knowledge or consent?

The American Association of Fund-Raising Counsel (AAFRC) has promulgated strict standards for membership and professional conduct, and most of the leading professional firms subscribe to them. Nevertheless, there are consulting firms that are not members of AAFRC. Other professional organizations, such as the Council for Advancement and Support of Education (CASE), NSFRE, the Association for Healthcare Philanthropy, and the Association of Governing Boards of Universities and Colleges, can provide leads on firms and individual consultants who are not AAFRC members but who do have records of reputable service. Also available are individual freelance consultants, senior advancement officers from all third-sector areas, retired chief executive officers, vice presidents and other institutional administrators, and other specialists in specific fields and disciplines that may be applicable to an institution's campaign needs.

An organization should always try to engage an individual or a consulting firm with the experience, background, and particular talent to provide the assistance that is needed. It is important to check with past clients and others who know the firm or the individual. Ask whether the consultant is familiar with institutions like yours or has undertaken comparable assignments. Determine whether the individual or firm is respected in the profession and delivers the promised performance and results on time.

In selecting outside counsel, an institution should not only check references but also make certain to meet the person or persons with whom it will be working. In larger firms, the person who meets with the institution's board and administrators before counsel is engaged often is not the person who will be working actively on the institutional account.

Gibson (1983), outlining the advantages and disadvantages of using outside counsel, cites the following advantages:

- Consultants can provide an objective viewpoint to the institution, and they often have more credibility with the chief executive officer and board members. Therefore, consultants can be tougher in circumstances where toughness is called for, and they can take the heat when they have to.
- Consultants also bring credibility because they can call on a broad range of experience and can share this experience with the institution.
- Consultants are paid fees high enough to motivate the chief executive officer and the board to work with them effectively and efficiently.
- Consultants can apply the brakes to ensure that enough time is being spent on cultivation and solicitation of the critical top 10 percent of prospects while keeping an eye on the entire campaign—anticipating needs, prodding to get things done, giving support to the staff, and suggesting the systems and strategies to be used.
- Consultants also offer a sounding board to experienced development directors who have no other knowledgeable people close at hand.

Gibson lists the following disadvantages, among others:

- In the goal-setting process, outside consultants may be too cautious because they want to ensure feasible goals for their clients.
- The best person in the consulting firm—the one who is a match with the institution's needs and chemistry—may not be available at the right time. The consultant actually assigned to the institution may prove incompatible and difficult to work with, and the firm may find it difficult to provide an appropriate substitute to serve the institution's needs in the time available. When a consulting firm is used, there is also the possibility of excessive disparity between the firm's top representative and the day-to-day contact person provided by the firm.

- Because the consultant's function is to show the institution how to raise money, but not necessarily to raise money for the institution, the consultant may be able to provide good strategic counsel but limited operational help—and many campaigns need operational assistance as much as they need strategic guidance.
- If consultants are used on a full-time, in-house basis, much information may not be captured in the files at the end of the campaign and may leave when the consultant leaves.
- The use of consultants may mean a missed opportunity to train institutional staff.
- The use of consultants can be costly even though it may in fact be very cost-effective.

Almost every institution that undertakes an ambitious campaign concludes that outside counsel can be of value. In fact, almost all major institutions that have conducted successful capital campaigns over the past quarter-century have used outside counsel in one way or another. How to use outside counsel and when to do so are individual questions to be asked and answered by each institution as it considers its campaign.

## The Critical Difference

Most senior fundraisers see the conducting of a capital campaign as both a science and an art. The science—the methodology and the mechanics—is generally what is learned first, and this is what is applied by the less experienced professionals. Often, however, it is the ability to transcend scientific application and mechanical knowledge that distinguishes a successful campaign director (and, indeed, a successful capital campaign). The ability to go beyond what is commonly known and universally applied, to bring a special human touch, a liberal measure of common sense, and an insightful, experienced perspective to a campaign, is of vital importance. Unfortunately, these values cannot be learned entirely through reading, nor can they practically be taught in the classroom. They generally develop as a result of experience in the natural environment of the marketplace. This point must be stressed to anyone who is interested in working in a capital campaign. It simply is not enough to understand and apply the science of fundraising; the process must be lifted above science and brought to the level of art. Analysis of successful development programs and successful capital campaigns over a long period, and throughout a variety of organizations, makes it clear that the ability to move to a higher level—a level of uncommon human understanding and motivation—is the signature of almost every successful campaign.

# CHAPTER TWELVE

# TECHNOLOGY IN FUNDRAISING

## William V. West

This chapter is about the single most important support factor in fundraising: technology. Like fundraising literature, technology will not in and of itself raise money. Without technology, however, it is difficult if not impossible today to raise money effectively, efficiently, and economically. This chapter addresses the use of technology in fundraising generally, and not in capital campaigns specifically, because the uses of technology in fundraising are universal; technology is not used differently to support a campaign. Therefore, the applications and processes discussed in this chapter pertain to the whole spectrum of your organization's fundraising programs, although you will sometimes want to design programs for tracking the specific data and details of a campaign (by contrast with more generic uses of technology to support other fundraising activities).

## Selecting an Information System

One of the most important aspects of an effective fundraising organization is an effective information system (I/S) to support it. In an ideal world, the I/S should be as transparent to the fundraising process as the telephone. It has to be available and easy to use, and it has to contain the information you need.

There are two fundamental components of establishing a system that is efficient and effective: selecting the right system for your environment and selecting the right people to install and support that system. The 80/20 rule is an important consideration in selecting the right computer system. This rule states that 80 percent of users just want access to data (and want it now); they need to be able to see the data and produce, quickly and easily, reports that support their business. Only 20 percent will actually use the detailed functionality of any system. Remembering the 80/20 rule is fundamental in choosing the right system. Failure to do so will have two consequences. The first is that the system will contain only those features that support its most sophisticated users (the 20 percent). The second is that your organization's systems staff will then have the expensive task of building in the features that will support the remaining 80 percent of the users.

The selection of a development I/S starts with the composition of the team that will make the selection. This team should strike a balance between the 20 percent of users who enter data and the 80 percent who use the data. Its members should include representatives of the following groups:

- Front-line development officers
- Development administrators
- Research analysts
- Data and gift processors
- Technical support staff
- High-level directors
- Lower-level staff (those who actually use the I/S in the course of doing their work)

No one who lacks a thorough understanding of the detailed processes in his or her functional area should be on the selection team.

In the I/S selection process, leadership is critical. The keys to selecting the right leader are *accountability* and *involvement*. The success of the organization depends on the selection of the right system—or, to put this another way, selection of the wrong system can quickly lead to the failure of the organization. Therefore, the leader of the I/S selection team is accountable not only for the success of the system but also for the success of the organization. The leader must also be heavily involved at every step of the selection process; a leader who simply shows up for project meetings and does not understand the system's details cannot be effective. The leader should not be from the organization's technology department, however. It is best if the leader is from the development office or the executive office. The organization's development function should take ownership of the selection process—but with the technology function serving as a strong partner because the selection of a system that really impresses the development office but is impossible to support or enhance will lead to failure just as quickly as the selection of a system that uses "fresh" technology but does not satisfy development's needs.

Definition of the system's functional requirements—what the system needs to do—is an important step. The requirements must include a definition of the organization's core processes. These are the essential functions that the organization requires in order to conduct its business. The only thing more important than carefully defining the system's requirements is making sure that the system has flexibility, in terms of both its software and your own environment. It is often easier to change a process or a report than it is to change a system. Rarely will you find a new system that can still produce, in the same format, every report that you have used in the past. The focus should be on the marriage between your functional needs and the system's capabilities. If that focus is achieved, then the system should be flexible enough for you to enhance its functionality as changes occur in the organizational environment.

There is an explosion of new technologies, with new products coming to market virtually every week. In their eagerness and excitement, some vendors will make exaggerated claims, impossible promises, and empty guarantees. Guard against vendors like these, and make intelligent decisions that address your current and future needs. But how do you do this in a quicksand marketplace? Three techniques work very well:

1. Attend meetings of a user group. (If your vendor does not sponsor a user group, then you are already talking to the wrong vendor.) Attend the sessions that deal with the technical and functional aspects of the I/S that you are considering. Talk to individuals from institutions that are equivalent to yours in size. This step is vital: some of the systems now on the market work beautifully in small institutions but fail in larger ones, and vice versa. Assess the types of staff people making presentations at user meetings. Ask yourself what type of staff you have and what type you can afford. Talk with users from development, information systems, accounting, and other departments. Take the opportunity to get the total picture and identify potential weaknesses.

2. Meet with current users of the I/S that you are considering. Go to these customers' sites—and make sure that you have adequate travel funds in the selection project's budget (a few $300 plane tickets now could save you hundreds of thousands of dollars later). A site visit gives you a chance to see the I/S in action, talk to its users and support staff, learn about the customer's conversion/installation process (never visit a site that has not yet gone live), and assess the customer's satisfaction. It is best to make such a visit without the vendor: most customers are willing to be open, but not when the vendor is there. Do not allow the vendor to select the customers you will visit, and make sure that those you visit are selected from a full list of the vendor's current customers. Be sure to bring along representatives from each of the major functional areas that will be using the system.

3. Test the system by installing it at your site. A true pilot installation ("true" meaning that you are not committed to buying the system) will tell you very quickly how easy or hard the system will be to support and use. Pilot tests are not cheap. They take system resources and time. But if you think you are ready to make a selection, then a pilot test will either confirm your decision or warn you of impending danger. (It will also quickly identify any phantom functionality that may have appeared in the vendor's demo.) Buy a small server, install the system, configure it for your environment, import some real data, install the system on the desks of your major functional departments, and then try to use it—*really* use it. This will not be an easy phase, and it will make demands on the participants. If this approach seems expensive, remember that nothing costs more than regret.

The I/S that you select should be easy to support, especially if yours is a small organization with limited resources. The tools used to develop the system should be standard and widely available. Selecting a system built with the vendor's proprietary tools will put your organization in the position of being dependent on your vendor alone for support, and this arrangement can make the system's future growth and enhancement difficult. Moreover, recruitment and training of staff will be much easier if your system's architecture is a common or popular one. If the vendor is your only source of contract support, then this is a good sign of a "closed" system architecture, and so the system should be avoided. A system developed with a common programming language known as Report Programming Generator (RPG) or with PowerBuilder (Powersoft's tool for access to databases) can be integrated with a wide variety of other systems and platforms, whereas a system developed with a custom-made computer-aided software engineering (CASE) tool or programming language cannot be easily integrated with other systems unless you have significant assistance from the vendor.

The system's database and its operating system should also have an "open" architecture. A system developed on any of the top databases (Oracle, Sybase, DB2, DB/400, Microsoft SQL Server) is much more likely to grow with your needs than is a system developed on a proprietary database that you've never heard of. The operating system that you select will also have a significant impact on your long-term costs. A system that runs on Unix or OS/400 may offer more flexibility but will also require more expensive hardware than a system running on NT.

Also consider the direction of the vendor's software company. The I/S that you buy has to grow with your organization, and it has to keep pace with changes in the technology sector. This is the only way to ensure that your organization will have access to the staff it will need for supporting the I/S and to people who can easily learn how to use it. For example, if a system is currently running on technology built in the 1980s, then its vendor may be unwilling to invest in and grow the software that will meet your future needs. A vendor who claims to be enhancing a system with new technology should be put on hold until the enhancement has actually been completed, lest your organization make an unwitting investment in "vaporware." For example, I/S vendors who are aligned with emerging trends should have developed browser technology by 2000. Much of a development officer's job is conducted out of the office, and access to the World Wide Web makes up-to-date information quickly available. Browser technology also significantly reduces the load that software puts on a personal computer (PC) and therefore may reduce the cost of the computer's support.

## Installing the Information System

The I/S installation process is rarely "over." For one thing, the needs of the development staff are constantly changing as the organization moves from one campaign to the next, and the installation process has to account for the ongoing enhancements that will be requested. For another, because the installation of a new system is a major distraction from building anything else, you should be aware that there is certain to be a backlog of priority projects waiting for your team after the I/S has been installed. Therefore, you should not imagine that you will be able to hire temporary staff just for the installation and then let them go. The keys to successful installation of the I/S are as follows (listed here in order of their importance):

### Leadership

From the most senior executive in development to the heads of each functional area, you must have solid leadership if the project is to be successful.

### Time

Your best friend is time—the time to do it right. Deadlines are important in maintaining a sense of urgency about the project, but unrealistic timelines will damage the project. It is better to say that the project will take three years and then finish it a year early than to say it will take one year and then finish it a year late. Do the math: in both instances, the project takes two years.

### Funding

Installing a new information system is expensive, no matter how good your staff is. The budget manager needs to be accountable at each stage of the project and must continue to demonstrate progress—real progress, not status reports and timelines. It is vital to know that you are getting the most for each dollar.

## Involvement

Nobody gets to sit on the sidelines and throw rocks at the project. For the capabilities of the I/S to be integrated with the processes in each functional area, the staff and managers of each area have to be involved. They should be involved in the definition of the processes, the data, and the interactions with other departments. This is the area where you are most likely to encounter resistance to change, but strong leadership and executive sponsorship can stifle it. Keep others involved, responsible, and accountable. Make it their project, too.

## Communicating and Managing Expectations

Constant, consistent, positive, honest communication has to be the rule. The installation of the I/S should not occur in the dark. Expectations need to be communicated clearly in the beginning. *Do not* let staff, employees, or executives believe that the system is going to be a panacea. *Do* tell them all the reasons why they should be excited, but also prepare them for the work associated with the changes they will encounter.

## Expertise of the Technical Team

Select an information system that your technical staff knows how to support. If that is impossible, then get your technical staff into training. Make sure that the "stars" on your staff know how to make the I/S work. Beware of simply hiring someone who has experience in the technical environment of the new I/S: doing that may get your system up and running faster, but it could hurt you in the long run because it takes time to learn and understand a development environment. Therefore, make sure that you recognize the value of the institutional knowledge in your existing staff. Contract with outside experts to coach, mentor, and guide you through the installation process, but do not hire contractors to install it for you. Contractors will not understand your environment, and, in the long run, turning installation over to contractors will not help your staff support the I/S. It is better to contract for education than to contract for labor. Bring in experts from other sites to check your project's quality and provide a reality check for your decisions. Your consulting support should ensure that you are asking the right questions, making the right decisions, and learning along the way.

## Pilot Testing

Nothing provides a better reality check than a good pilot test. Make it a real one. Be sure that there is ample time to conduct the test and evaluate the results before full installation of the I/S begins. Use real data, process parallel transactions, and then compare the results of these transactions. Most of all, build some reports that simulate your current ones.

## Education and Training

Invest time and money in training. If people lack skill and knowledge, they will either ignore the system or use it incorrectly. It is essential that key users as well as technical staff understand the functionality of the I/S. Conduct basic training courses after the system goes live, and conduct refresher training frequently and repeatedly until the users stop attending.

## Reports

No functionality is more important than the ability of the I/S to build and produce reports. The I/S should offer report capabilities to users at all levels of experience as well as to the system's programmers; any system that requires experienced programmers for the production of simple reports should send you running for the hills. As soon as the system goes live—not after—have several standard reports ready (for example, weekly giving activity, a month-by-month comparison of the current year to the previous year, donor profiles, completed pledges, campaign tracking, account balances). These reports will keep most users at bay while additional reports are being developed.

## Standards and Procedures

Nothing in a system is harder to fix than bad data. Therefore, standards and procedures must be defined before the system is installed because they are essential to converting and importing historical data, and they will be vital if your data-entry operations are decentralized.

## Coding Structure

The coding structure used throughout your I/S should be defined by people who understand both the business of the institution and its data. At this stage, it is also crucial to have someone on hand who is an expert in the particular I/S that has been installed. Therefore, the team defining the coding structure must include a representative from the vendor's company who knows the system inside and out—that is, who understands how information is processed on the screens and how data are processed by the programs. Failure to define the codes correctly may prevent entire modules of the system from functioning in response to your needs. This expert must also have experience using the system's software in an environment comparable to yours because the coding scheme used by a small institution may be significantly different from the scheme used by a large institution.

## Support of Core Processes

With every new decision, ask yourself, "Does this feature support a core process?" Many bells and whistles can be included in a development I/S system, and many among the sophisticated 20 percent of users believe they "gotta have it." The 20 percent will have a knack for quibbling and distracting the project from its purpose, and this is why strong, knowledgeable leadership is so important. An essential part of the leader's role is to ensure that the functions installed are those that support the institution's core processes. A new system also very often requires a fundamental change in mind-set, especially if you are making the change from an existing system: "We've always done it this way" could cripple your project. Your focus should always be the marriage of your functional needs with the capabilities of the system.

# Managing an I/S Group

Many factors—skillful leaders, executive support, ample funding, a talented technical staff—promote the successful management of an I/S group, but one factor stands out from the rest: the separation of day-to-day operational duties from project-related duties. In general, attempts to blend the staff responsible for day-to-day I/S support and the staff responsible for developing and upgrading I/S tools and services will prevent both functions from reaching their maximum potential (if they do not fail altogether). Operational duties include user support, service on the help desk, and report development and distribution. Project-related duties include software development, database development, systems integration, business process automation, and of course, the installation of a new I/S. To the extent possible, the operational staff, at least the help desk, should be physically separated from the other I/S staff. This area usually draws high traffic and open conversation and can be a major distraction to programmers.

The processing of ad hoc report requests and the production of reports should also be separated from the functions of the I/S programming and project staff. According to the kind of system you have, reports may be produced by support staff, programmers, or high-end users. Regardless of who produces the reports, however, the demands of report production are very different from I/S project-related demands and should be kept separate from them. User support is a chaotic environment, where the priorities and the focus change daily, and project-related staff will fail in this environment. They need a quiet area where focus, concentration, and teamwork are possible. Smaller organizations (those with fewer than twenty-five fundraising professionals) may be required to use programmers to produce ad hoc reports, but these organizations should still use dedicated programmers for this task, keeping it separate from the work of the project-related programmers.

## Setting Clear Priorities for the Information System

One of the key success factors in an efficient and effective I/S operation is the setting of clear priorities. These priorities must be set through a balance of the needs of the system's users and the needs of the infrastructure. The I/S staff is responsible for defining and clearly communicating the needs of the infrastructure; in order for the needs of users to be defined, however, organizational leaders must be involved. Organizational environments can be hotly political at times, and there is always a slate of high-priority projects under way. It should not be the responsibility of the I/S department to determine which projects will receive its attention; saying no is not a successful position to be in. Assigning an I/S director the job of saying no can quickly alienate the director and produce animosity between the departments that get top priority and those that do not. Cross-functional representation ensures that every priority is set with the best interests of the organization in mind and that all departments will understand why. Moreover, there are never enough I/S resources to implement every project, solve every emergency, or design every good idea introduced by users. Therefore, an empowered team of organizational leaders must be responsible for setting priorities.

The forum and process for establishing priorities can be very simple. It starts with a request form—a simple form that states the nature of the project, records who has requested it, says how it will benefit the organization, and provides a place where a programmer can make an assessment and estimate the time needed for the project. All requests should be logged in a database or spreadsheet so that a report of new requests can be produced. The team of organizational leaders should gather periodically to go over the new requests, review the status of current projects, and set priorities for the new requests.

This process has two clear benefits for both the I/S staff and the development staff. First, the programmers are given clear priorities: they know what to work on first and can complete projects in order. Second, this process ensures that limited programming resources are focused on the areas of most benefit to the organization as a whole. The needs of the infrastructure may or may not be discussed by way of this forum. These include upgrades to network and server equipment that will be transparent to the users. These needs must be factored into the discussion if a shared pool of staff is required for both project types and will have to be co-ordinated with upcoming projects, of course. But often the priorities for the infrastructure projects are defined or required by changes in the technology industry; solid leadership in the I/S function can ensure that the needs of the infrastructure are well orchestrated with other priorities.

## Updating and Maintaining Your Technical Environment

Updating and maintaining your technical environment is a strategic imperative of your development program. It costs less to maintain a position ahead of the advancement curve than it does to regain a position once it has been lost. As newer technologies have emerged and faster computers have been developed, the cost of maintaining a positive position in technology has actually been coming down. In the early 1990s, PCs had to be upgraded or replaced every three years in order to run current software. This meant that 30 percent of an organization's computers had to be replaced every year. In 1998, a PC with the best-valued processor and a fifteen-inch monitor cost between $2,000 and $2,500. A year later, a PC with twice the power and a seventeen-inch screen cost between $1,200 and $1,800. The newer PCs are able to last four to five years and even after five years will house enough power to satisfy low-end, occasional users. This means that now only 20 to 25 percent of your equipment needs to be upgraded every year. The price for very powerful PCs will continue to drop.

The updating and upgrading of your primary applications and your operating systems will need to be justified and handled with due diligence. Software vendors commonly try to force an organization to upgrade, but the value added to the system does not always justify the cost of the upgrade. Moreover, a software upgrade can accelerate the life cycle (that is, shorten the life) of your hardware. To protect your investment, control your staffing and support costs, and ensure that your priorities are focused on the projects that offer the most value to the organization, do not upgrade your software unless you have a real need to do so. Any plans for a software upgrade should justify the expense and guarantee that the upgrade will not make current hardware obsolete (this is not an issue, however, if your computer hardware has already outlived its usefulness).

Business managers should be involved in the planning process for a software upgrade, to ensure their understanding of the added functionality and the changes to their existing systems. Technical professionals should not be expected to make an upgrade decision alone. The key success factors for an upgrade are similar to those for selecting a new system. The involvement of everyone essential to making sure the decision that gets made is the right one for the organization.

The budget needed to maintain your technical environment needs to be in the baseline of your capital budget; it should not be an add-on. Technology is a strategic tool. Those who use it well will gain an advantage over those who do not. Effective use of technology provides the ability to reduce business costs, improve the efficiency of all processes, and increase fundraising. It is difficult to prove that adding technology increases success, but it is often very easy to spot cases in which poor technology or failed technology projects seriously hampered the success of a development program. Therefore, the baseline budget should include the funds required to maintain your position.

The budget for a new technology project should be independent of the operational budget. The funds for new technology should be justified and requested separately, on the basis of the value that the technology can add to the organization. The technology-related expenditures and returns should also be tracked separately so that the progress, success, or failure of the project can be monitored. This procedure ensures that the project's performance will not have an impact, positive or negative, on the operational budget (this precaution is most important, of course, when a new technology project runs over budget).

# Technologies That Serve Development

Some technologies serve development better than others. A few of these are emerging technologies; others are time-tested.

## Internet Technology

Information can be a strong asset for a development officer, if it is available when and where it is needed. The emergence of the Internet as an international communications pathway has opened the door for all institutions, large and small, to enhance their information sharing, both internally and with their peers. Most of the technologies relevant to the development function are now more useful because of the Internet. The truly helpful elements that all development organizations should consider—in addition, of course, to an in-office local-area network (LAN) and an information system—are access to the Internet (and to the World Wide Web), e-mail, laptop computers, remote access to databases, and palmtop devices. (If you do not have a LAN or an I/S, then you should not yet be looking at these other elements.)

Fortunately, most universities (and many other larger organizations) are wired, one way or another, for Internet access. Therefore, the first step is to get your office connected to your organization's Internet server via your LAN. Once that connection has been made, everything else is possible, and everyone in the development office will have access to a wide array of research services.

A staff constantly on the move, on the road, and in meetings can find e-mail extremely useful. It is an excellent tool for receiving and responding to messages. The disadvantage of e-mail, relative to the phone, is that you cannot have a real conversation; and, because a text message contains no audible emotional cues, messages can be misinterpreted. The advantage of e-mail over the phone is that you can read and respond at your own convenience (you are not interrupted), you do not have to take written messages, and you can easily keep a log of your correspondence. When I am asked which medium I would choose, the phone or e-mail, my answer is "I need both." An e-mail program usually also offers a suite of other tools (an officewide calendar, an officewide address book, a tool for contact management) that make life in the office easier.

If yours is a small development office, you can piggyback your e-mail on someone else's system (your organization's, for example). Supporting an e-mail system is expensive; do not install your own unless your office is large enough to afford the support staff, or unless you absolutely have no other choice. The advantage of using an organizationwide system is that you can share an address book and calendar with your colleagues and associates. If tying your e-mail to your organization's service is not an option, however, then often you can find an Internet service provider (ISP) in your area that provides e-mail service. One requirement for an e-mail system is that it be accessible via the Internet. Internet access to an e-mail account opens up a larger array of solutions for staff on the road.

## Portable Computing

Laptop computers have continued to drop in price while increasing in quality and power. Today, a full-powered laptop with a beautiful monitor costs the same as desktop computers did three years ago and provides five times the power. A laptop with a docking station (which allows it to be connected to your network), a full-size keyboard, and a full-size screen provides all the services of a desktop computer but offers the advantage of portability. After work, or as you head off on a trip, you can detach your laptop from your docking station and take it along. This means that you can take your tools and information—essentially, your whole office—with you.

A laptop becomes a mobile office once you have remote access to your servers and to the Internet. Remote access can be provided in three ways: through an organizational dial-up (another reason to connect your office with your organization's network), through an Internet service provider (the primary reason to ensure that your e-mail is accessible via the Internet), or through your own "modem pool" (a bank of dedicated phone lines for you to use in dialing in to the office). These options are listed in increasing order of cost. Supporting your own remote-access server (RAS) is much more expensive than piggybacking on your organization's.

The larger your organization, however, the easier it is to support your own RAS. Having your own RAS also provides you with dedicated lines and with the ability to connect a toll-free. A toll-free number can save your organization significant money in charges for calling over long distances while it simplifies the dial-in process for the staff.

Palmtop devices are providing increasing power and functionality in a small package. Many staff on the move prefer a palmtop to a laptop. A palmtop device will not serve as a fully mobile office, but it will provide many of the essentials (e-mail, an appointment calendar, a contact list, expense reporting, and other features helpful to the traveling development officer). The price of a palmtop is also one-tenth that of a laptop. For an office on a small budget, palmtops and a link to the Internet could provide a very cost-effective package of functionality.

Another helpful software product in the early stages of emergence is the system for geographical mapping and location finding. Such a system allows you to import a name and an address from your development database. It then plots the location of the address on an interactive map, showing you the how to drive to the location. The more advanced systems can work in your car and be integrated with a global positioning system (GPS) that actually tracks your current location and plots your position with respect to your destination.

## Automated Telemarketing

Automated telemarketing systems offer another kind of helpful technology. These systems come in all shapes and sizes, with prices ranging from $15,000 to more than $200,000. The cost depends on the system selected, the functionality it provides, and the size of your institution (that is, the number of callers). An automated telemarketing system, implemented correctly, can pay off handsomely. For example, Indiana University's installation of a telemarketing system (EIS's Centenium) cost nearly $400,000 for all the software, hardware, and installation services, but it paid for itself in one year through the increased donations and lower staff costs that it made possible. Complete installation took only twelve weeks: four to get the system live, and eight to get it fully integrated with the development system. Note that this telemarketing system took nearly one year to "select." Careful planning during the selection process made the short installation time possible.

An automated telemarketing system provides a wide range of functions. Those you require will depend on the current sophistication and philosophy of your calling program. Smaller systems offer convenient data-entry screens that allow you to load donors' data from your development I/S and update this information during a phone call. More advanced systems offer programming capabilities that enable you to "script" your calling programs and respond to the multitude of prospects' excuses. These advanced systems also suggest approaches to making calls, and they track the results of each call. An even more sophisticated system can be integrated with a phone system and will make calls by reading phone numbers from the donors' data. This feature, used correctly, can save enormous time by eliminating many of the no-answers, busy signals, answering machines, and wrong numbers, allowing your callers to spend the vast majority of their time talking to prospects instead of pushing buttons.

Like most technology projects, installation of an automated telemarketing system is a "process" project, not just a systems project. Its full benefits will be realized only if the telemarketing system is integrated with your development I/S at the front end, integrated with your development I/S at the back end, and able to provide its own statistical reports. These three features will ensure that minimal time is spent in supporting of the system and will save the majority of your time for using the system.

At the front end, the automated telemarketing system should accept data from your development I/S and allow you to pare it down and group it into calling programs. It should not only allow you to store data from your development I/S but should also allow the caller to update any and all data elements while the prospect is on the phone. At the back end, after the calling program is completed each night, pledges, gifts, and data should be uploaded back into your development I/S and posted with the daily gift batches. (Transactions received from the automated telemarketing system should be uniquely coded in the system, for later tracking purposes.) All updates to addresses, employment data, and other information should be reported to the records department for entry into the development I/S. (Whether entry of these data should be direct, automatically uploaded, or manual will depend on the quality of your calling staff, their understanding of data, and the priority of data in their jobs; not automatically uploading them will protect the integrity of the data and maintain high data standards.) Finally, after the total calling program is complete, the system should produce the pledge acknowledgments to be mailed to the donors, as well as all the statistical reports that will be needed in tracking the effectiveness of the program and each caller.

## Maintaining Data

Maintenance of the data in a development system can be a complex, time-consuming task. Many factors, among them those that follow, affect how complex this task will be:

- *The number of prospects and donors in the database.* Complexity increases as the number of records increases. A staff of two or three may be effective in maintaining a database of 25,000 constituents but cannot maintain a database of 250,000 with the same degree of efficiency. Likewise, a large organization may have 250,000 constituents but may not be able to afford to hire twenty people for its records department. Therefore, you must determine the priorities of your database, the technologies and techniques you plan to use, and the costs you are willing to incur in maintaining your data.

• *The number of gift and accounting transactions completed each year.* The more transactions you have in your system, and the more you add each year, the more efficient your data-maintenance processes need to be, especially if you have many years of historical data in your system. Maintaining accuracy in the files that contain the giving history, and in all the subtotal files, requires strict standards for your processes. The need for accuracy and for the ability to subdivide these data will increase as the number of transactions increases.

• *The number of fields important to the organization.* Maintaining only donors' home addresses makes for a simple data-maintenance process, no matter how many records you have. If your primary focus is on home mailings, then your staff can focus on strategies that enable this level of data maintenance. But if phone numbers and information about prospects' employment, activities, and affiliations are also required, then the complexity of the data-maintenance process increases. In sophisticated organizations—those with programs for annual giving, special giving, major gifts, planned and deferred giving, capital campaigns, donor relations, and prospect management—it is not uncommon to maintain more than a hundred data elements for each record.

• *Accuracy requirements.* Accuracy in constituents' records is often measured by addressability, and addressability is a moving target: more than 20 percent of your population may move in any given year. The costs and efficiency of your record maintenance will be closely tied to your need for accuracy. For example, although average addressability in the United States is around 80 percent (which means that 20 percent of the addresses in organizations' databases are not valid), one leading U.S. university's addressability exceeds 92 percent, a figure related to the strategic importance of valid addresses to that institution, given its large size and its decentralized structure. But that kind of accuracy comes at a price: $250,000 per year.

## Organizing the Records Department

There are many options for organizing your records department, and you should put your records staff in the department where they will receive the most support, regardless of that department's primary function. This may mean putting the records department in the research area, in the alumni association (if yours is an educational institution), in accounting, in another development office, or somewhere else. The essentially important thing is that they receive the tools, guidance, and direction they need and that they are not expected to carry out duties in addition to maintaining records (record maintenance is hard, tedious work, and if staff must choose among competing priorities, record maintenance will always be the first to go).

Several techniques and technologies can improve the process of maintaining records; what works at your organization may very well depend on a number of external factors. If you are in a large, complex environment, for example, you should take advantage of your large core of development officers in order to gather new data from a wide variety of sources (events, meetings, telemarketing, Web pages, and so on).

It is best not to decentralize data entry itself; centralized control of data-entry standards is very important for long-term integrity of the data. One key to ensuring its integrity is to have a single individual responsible and accountable for that task. This individual is in charge of all code definitions and oversees the data-entry process. It is vital that this individual understand the objectives of the organization and become an integral contributor to its business functions.

With strong and well-defined data standards, you can provide the ability for all users to contribute to the accuracy of information. If you do not already have this ability, consider adding a function to your system that allows every user to send updates to the records department directly through the system. Updates are made by the records department, but every user contributes to the update process. Decentralization of access to record maintenance is one of the key success factors in many large, complex organizations.

The future offers the use of e-mail and the World Wide Web as outstanding mechanisms for further decentralizing the collection of data from constituents. An organization-sponsored e-mail address gives your constituents an affinity mechanism and gives you a means of making contact with them electronically (thereby saving postage) throughout many career transitions. The Web also offers you the ability to post an on-line form that enables your constituents to update their own information as often as necessary. This electronic form should send the updated data to the records staff, who will then enter it in your system. A form like this one is easy to create and very cost-effective. Both of these services should be advertised on every publication and mailing that you send out.

Postage is an expensive part of record maintenance and development. Coordinating your mailing efforts can save expenses and increase your ability to update constituents' information. For example, if you are mailing a gift receipt to a donor, check to see if the phone number and employment data are complete. If not, then include a minisurvey form in the receipt envelope. In addition, pay for the returned postage on at least one major mailing a year. When you mail a receipt, solicitation, magazine, or invitation, make sure that you get the item returned with any address correction information from the U.S. Postal Service. If employment data and phone numbers are important to you, then send out a survey form for every address update you make. The logic here is "We noticed that your address changed—has anything else?"

Address information is available through several third-party sources that work with the U.S. Postal Service. Many universities use these services to update their addresses on a quarterly basis, more or less. This approach could save you money in data-entry personnel, but you will sacrifice some accuracy. Average accuracy at the Big Ten universities that use this approach is 80 to 85 percent, by comparison to more than 90 percent at some universities that do not use it (but some that do not use this approach also have much lower accuracy percentages). Cost versus accuracy is the decision that needs to be made here.

## The Technology Constant: Change

Commenting on trends affecting the future of capital campaigns in the first edition of this book in 1988, Kent Dove wrote: "Computers will be increasingly used to track prospects, build donor information, and process gifts. This is the unmistakable direction philanthropy is taking" (p. 162). How correct that statement was—but how limited its vision as we look back more than a decade later. Who could anticipate the technological explosion that was about to take place? Chapter Fifteen of this edition looks ahead to the next decade and beyond and predicts even greater and more rapid changes. It can truly be said that the only constant with technology is change—fast, evolutionary, even revolutionary change.

# CHAPTER THIRTEEN

# CREATING SUCCESSFUL PUBLICATIONS, PROMOTIONS, AND PUBLIC RELATIONS

Just how much value literature has to a campaign is hard to quantify. Publications and publicity alone do not raise money, but funds cannot be raised without them. It is interesting that they are especially helpful with those who are not institutional insiders; they also give confidence and provide support and security to volunteers and staff alike. Therefore, campaign literature must be planned in light of its specific purpose, and with the belief that it will be read and heeded.

## Types of Campaign Communications

The case statement and its derivatives are clearly the most important single pieces of campaign literature. Nevertheless, in addition to the case statement, the program brochure, and the question-and-answer folder, the campaign will also need several other written pieces:

- A pledge or contribution card or form
- A brochure on tax information and estate planning in making major gifts
- Instructions to workers
- A fact booklet on the institution
- An impact-of-institution brochure or a financial impact study
- A campaign or program newsletter

- Campaign reports
- Transcript materials (major gift presentations and foundation and corporate proposals)

For examples of such materials, see the following resources:

Resource D, "Sample Volunteer Kit"

Resource I, "Sample Monthly Financial Report"

Resource L, "Sample Communications Materials Checklist"

Resource M, "Sample Newsletters"

A brochure on tax information and estate planning and a companion piece on memorial or named gift opportunities are important pieces of campaign literature. Both are intended to raise sights and encourage larger gifts by pointing out tax advantages and offering an opportunity for personalizing gifts in a permanent and appealing way. These brochures will take a variety of forms, in keeping with the circumstances of an individual campaign. (See Resource D, "Sample Volunteer Kit.")

Another vital piece of campaign literature is an instruction booklet for workers. (See Resource D, "Sample Volunteer Kit.") Such a volunteer guide should provide a step-by-step program designed to educate volunteer solicitors and make them feel at ease. It should also describe the suggested procedure for cultivating prospects and securing major gifts. Some campaign directors also prepare information for volunteers that focuses on how to "close" the gift and that details the skills needed to close (opening, questioning, listening, presenting, overcoming objections, and asking for the gift; see Chapter Nine).

A fact sheet about the institution need not be elaborate. Nevertheless, it should be comprehensive and should provide a variety of important general information that will educate volunteers and provide answers to many of the routine questions that may be asked by prospects, especially by those who are not intimately familiar with the institution.

The campaign newsletter is another piece of literature that takes infinite shapes and forms. (See Resource M, "Sample Newsletters.") It is important that the campaign newsletter appear regularly. It should make liberal use of pictures of volunteers, donors, and others involved in the campaign and, within reason, should include the greatest possible number of people's names. The best campaign newsletter will also have a well-thought-out purpose. It serves not only to provide recognition and reward for volunteers and donors but also to set the tone for the campaign and to move the fundraising effort forward in an organized, efficient, effective manner.

Another important component of the campaign literature is pledge documentation. (See Resource K, "Sample Pledge Forms.") The first form of this documentation is the campaign pledge card. The typical pledge card provides a space for typing or printing the name and address of the prospect, a statement indicating that the donor's pledge is made "in consideration of the gifts of others and toward the campaign goal," a place to record the amount of the pledge, a statement of how it will be paid (if in some way other than cash), a statement of the payment period, and a description of the frequency with which payments are to be made including the starting date. It also includes a place for the donor's signature and a space for indicating both the amount paid, if any, at the time the pledge is made and the balance remaining. It is important that a statement appear on the face of the pledge card that contributions "are deductible for federal and state income tax purposes as provided by law." There should also be instructions on how to make checks payable.

Also to be included, usually on the back of the card, is a statement indicating whether the soliciting institution intends to treat the pledge as a legally binding obligation. (The majority of campaigns do not treat pledges as legal obligations.) There should be ample space for the donor to indicate a gift designation (if the gift is to be restricted) and any commemorative gift wording that the donor may wish to have used, as well as a place for other information. The pledge card should also include a place for the volunteer's name and the date of the solicitation.

In addition to the basic pledge card, most pledge instruments have two perforated, detachable pieces referred to as "ears." The first ear is used for a confidential statement indicating the gift rating of the prospect, to guide the solicitor in making the call. The information included here is highly confidential, and the volunteer should detach it before seeing the prospect; it should never be shown to a prospect. The other ear is a temporary acknowledgment form. If its use is required, this ear should be separated from the pledge card at the time the commitment is made. These forms usually include places for writing the name of the donor, the total amount of the gift, and the amount paid (if any) at the time of the pledge. There is also a place for the volunteer to sign and date the temporary acknowledgment. The temporary acknowledgment usually indicates that an official gift receipt will be mailed in the near future.

The second instrument used to record pledges is a letter of intent. A sample letter of intent is shown in Exhibit 13.1. The third form of pledge commitment is a letter written by the donor on personal or corporate stationery and giving the same information that would be recorded on a pledge card or included in a letter of intent.

## EXHIBIT 13.1. SAMPLE LETTER OF INTENT.

Date _____

Name, Chief Executive Officer
XYZ Institution
Everytown, NY 00000

Dear _____ :

   To assist (name of institution) in fulfilling its important responsibilities and in consideration of the gifts of others, I intend and expect to contribute the sum of $ _____ to (name of institution and title of campaign).
   My gift is:
   1. Designated for the following purpose(s):

   _____

or

   2. To be used at the discretion of the Board of Governors of (name of institution). I expect to make this gift over a period of _____ years, as follows:

   $_____ Herewith
   $_____ on or before _____ 19___
   $_____ on or before _____ 19___

or

   _____

   _____

   This statement of intention and expectation shall not constitute a legal obligation and shall not be legally binding in any way on me or my estate. While I consider that I have a moral obligation to make this gift, I reserve the right to adjust or to cancel it in the event of unforeseen circumstances.

Sincerely yours,

/s/ _____

The number, quantity, and costs of the publications needed to support a given campaign can and will vary; never skimp on quality, however. In addition to the various printed documents, appropriate audiovisual materials should routinely be prepared. These may include a synchronized sound/slide show, motion pictures, audiocassettes, videocassettes, flipcharts, graphs, posters, and building models.

It is also important to design the presentation of the case so that it is easy to interpret differently for various market segments. The same information about the organization may be viewed differently from the perspective of a corporate executive,

a wealthy philanthropist, a vendor, or a neighborhood group. In designing literature and institutional approaches to various constituencies, it is important to remain
flexible so that the approach can be specifically tailored to produce optimal results.
With the explosion of technology and the ever-widening possibilities for delivering
the message, all materials should be adaptable to distribution via the World Wide
Web and through telecommunications media and all the other emerging technologies, as well as through traditional, more conventional methods.

No function of the campaign literature and audiovisual material can be more
important than supporting and sustaining a mood of importance, relevance, and urgency and an atmosphere of optimism and institutional community. This function
becomes more and more important as campaign goals go higher and higher and as
schedules have to cover more and more time: as solicitation moves from the inside
out, from one group of potential givers to another, and as the few traveling teams of
official advocates go from group to group—and, in wide-area campaigns, from city to
city—the risk of having the campaign die on the vine becomes real indeed.

The key to avoiding this problem is for the campaign chair, the chief executive officer, and others to keep delivering the message of the campaign, actively
and continuously engaging in the case-stating process and never letting up until
the job is done. They should never make speeches or write reports without referring to the unfinished task, doing so with all the gravity due its importance and
with the confidence of certain and complete success.

What they and the campaign publications say, and keep saying, is important
in itself; almost equally important is that everything and everyone say it again and
again and carry the same message, even if it is stated with different emphases for
different constituencies. Continuity is the business of all institutional communications, whether they are disseminated via magazines, newsletters, or Web sites.
Indeed, this is the principal business of campaign bulletins or newsletters, which
nevertheless sometimes make the mistake of dealing almost solely with progressive statistics. These bulletins deserve careful planning so that every issue deliber-
ately plays up the attainment of higher standards, the involvement of respected
people, praise from outside the institution, significant growth in the campaign,
quotations worthy of repetition, and every good thing to be thought of that can
make for confidence.

## Preparing Campaign Publications

If an institution does not have a top-quality publications department, it should seriously consider hiring outside help to produce its campaign publications, especially the major ones. If outside help is used, do not relinquish control over the

finished product. Monitor progress, and require periodic checks with the campaign leaders. Do not scrimp on campaign publications. Prestige pieces are a necessity, and they will pay for themselves. In creating the communications package for a campaign, review the proposed strategy, audience message, and goal for each piece. If necessary, restate the message as it should appear in each communication, remembering that different communications are written to address and to reach different audiences.

Always develop logic to support the request or message in each communication. Analyze what the audience has indicated it would like to hear; make sure to use the feedback process to secure important information. Write, dictate, or design the first draft of a communication, and then edit to eliminate triteness, fuzziness, and pet phrasing. Then test the communication with a segment of its target audience, and listen for a response. It may be necessary to revise this communication after audience feedback and review.

A word about style is also in order here: the principles of clear, concise, idiomatic writing that apply to other nonfiction can be the guide for brochures as well. Campaign literature too often contains a good deal of specialized language—professional jargon that is familiar to educators, medical staff, or seminary scholars but a deep mystery to almost everyone else. Try to avoid it. Keep in mind that most donors, and all major ones, will be laypeople who respond best to plain language, short sentences, and familiar usage. One rule of good writing that particularly applies to fundraising brochures is to avoid generalities and look for specifics. Every institution has its own history, achievements, and vital statistics. Know them, and include them in the writing.

David W. Barton Jr., former president of Barton Gillet, is fond of reminding people that the characters in Mark Twain's *Huckleberry Finn* speak in five distinct dialects. He specifically mentions that Twain pointed to this phenomenon in the book's introduction because he had taken pains to get the dialects right: the characters speak authentically, and Twain wanted the reader to appreciate what he had accomplished; what he wrote is a masterpiece because he respected his characters enough to get their language right. In the same way, every institution speaks in a different voice, with a different tone and a different stylistic emphasis. If an institution can capture its own flavor and essence in its campaign literature, its constituents will respond to it. The difference between the right word and the nearly right word is the difference between lightning and a lightning bug; in the same way, the right word and the right image aimed at the right person at the right time and in the right way can produce lightning.

The institution must also be concerned about the layout and design of its publications and on-line presentations. Graphics should be done by a professional designer, but it is the writer's responsibility to gather the necessary material and guide the designer on tone and style. It is helpful to give the designer a few samples of the institution's recent literature as a guide to its taste (unless the pieces are particularly poor and the institution wants to start over). Try to give the designer more illustration material than can actually be used so that he or she will have a range of choice. Avoid extremes, being neither too conservative nor too modern; the institution wants to raise money, not win graphics or arts awards. Clean, readable, attractive campaign communications are the goal.

Photographs, because of their immediacy, are generally favored over artwork. They should be informal, candid, and unposed. Use pictures that add warmth to the story and bring the institution to the donors. In today's publications, larger pictures are generally favored over smaller ones, and an uncluttered look is preferred to a cluttered look. Institutions occasionally have orderly, up-to-date picture files and can simply provide a selection for the designer. If that is not the case, hire a professional photographer to take a fresh set of pictures for the campaign.

Architectural drawings are essential when an objective of the campaign is a new building. Nobody would contract for a building without some idea of what it would look like, and the same applies to those who put up the funds. Further, an attractive rendering dramatizes the building, and floor plans help to explain the named and memorial gift opportunities. Sometimes there is a problem getting renderings for the brochure because of delays in making decisions about the components. The architects thoroughly understand this problem and are usually willing to cooperate. Blueprints are not essential. Most people cannot "read" them anyway, and so they tend to confuse rather than clarify.

In preparing information for campaign workers, package the materials conveniently and compactly. Summarize key information, and do not overload volunteers with unnecessary facts. Provide sample questions and answers as well as simple charts and graphs to aid them in their understanding and acceptance of the campaign.

## Developing a Realistic Plan for Marketing and Public Relations

Effective campaign communications are not enough; for a campaign to succeed, a comprehensive plan is also required for public relations and marketing. The objective of any public relations plan in support of a capital campaign should be to increase awareness, understanding, and appreciation on the part of targeted audiences in selected geographical areas, with the aim of motivating support for the campaign. Target audiences will vary according to the size and kind of institution conducting the campaign. In a capital campaign, with respect to these targeted audiences, the ultimate public relations challenge for an institution seeking to maintain and enhance its reputation is to bring sharp focus to those of its past achievements that have contributed to its current high stature, its current achievements in its area of interest, and its future hopes and aspirations.

Donors at all levels and from all sources are more inclined to contribute to institutions that can make this part of their case. Effective public relations programs produce a climate for fundraising but should not be expected to attract gifts or volunteers directly. As is true in every other phase of the capital campaign, it is paramount that those involved with developing and implementing a public relations plan learn the organization and its cause very well.

Once the institution has done its homework—defined its mission and priorities—and once a fundraising strategy has been established, it becomes a task of the public relations program to identify the audiences to be informed and cultivated, state the campaign's message (understanding what response is being sought from each target audience), and identify potential methods for communicating this message to the selected audiences. Among the instruments available for communicating the message are personal visits; open houses; speeches; slide presentations; letters (personal letters or mass mailings); brochures; leaflets; graphs, charts, and other visual displays; special press conferences to announce significant gifts; films; radio and television public service announcements or purchased time; groundbreaking or dedication events; regional campaign announcement events (in wide-area campaigns); news and feature stories in newspapers or magazines; newsletter, magazine, or newspaper advertisements; and creative use of technology.

It is not enough simply to block out the period of time when the capital campaign will be conducted and say that during this time the institution is going to have a good public relations program. Good public relations should precede the fundraising activity, accompany it, and go on after the active fundraising period has passed—and good public relations should exist inside the institution as well as outside.

## Naming the Campaign

Whatever the campaign is called, its name should have dramatic impact and meaning for the institution as well as its constituents. Symbols, logos, titles, themes, and other identifiable marks should be developed for and used throughout the campaign. In this area, a communications advisory committee can often be extremely helpful (Perkins, 1985).

After the campaign has been thoroughly planned—and a significant portion (30 to 50 percent) of the campaign goal should have been achieved before the formal announcement—it should be formally announced through a major media event, such as a formal dinner, a major press conference, or both. (See Resource J, "Sample Public Announcement Event Invitation and Program.") The media should be used to keep the campaign's progress before the public. In addition to cultivating newspaper and broadcast media coverage, the institution should use its publications to provide continuing publicity for the campaign. Printed materials (such as the chief executive officer's report) and other, external magazines, bulletins, and announcements for athletic events should all be used to keep the campaign before the institution's publics. When the campaign has been completed, a victory dinner should be held, and a final report should be issued to everyone who was involved in the campaign.

It is important that community leaders be involved in making decisions about the public relations program. To this end, according to Perkins (1985), a communications advisory committee should be established. This committee is of great importance in any well-planned and professionally administered campaign. Committee members should be experts—public relations executives, marketing experts, media professionals, Webmasters, and senior members of advertising firms. This group should review and recommend program materials, media coverage, and special events. Not only can the members of this committee give professional advice, they can also offer active assistance in working with the media. They can publicize the institution's efforts in areas where it is not known, accompany representatives of the institution on visits to media outlets and representatives, and make phone calls to say that a story or an idea for one is on the way.

In establishing such a committee, the institution should select members for specific purposes—for areas to be reached, or for the kinds of stories that the institution is apt to produce more abundantly. Bring these committee members to the institution, if at all possible, to orient them to the institution as it is now, not as it was when they last visited. Be professional, and do not ask members of the committee to help sell what is not legitimate news. Keep the committee informed about successes, and give credit to those who helped. Make sure that committee members know they are appreciated—send letters from the chief executive officer welcoming them to the committee and, at the end of the first year, thanking them for their time and effort and noting their successes. Give them recognition for their efforts in institutional publications, and invite them to institutional events.

The basic steps, generally stated, in a public relations program for a capital campaign are as follows:

1. To gain support for the campaign from all the organization's constituencies, beginning with members of the institutional family (and making sure to keep all constituencies adequately informed about the campaign's progress)

2. To secure broad agreement on the plan from all the major parties involved in the campaign
3. To work closely with all elements of the development or advancement structure within the organization, to secure their support and cooperation.

If all the advancement efforts are not already combined, it is highly recommended that the organization seriously consider combining them (at least temporarily) in preparation for a capital campaign. If combining these efforts is impossible, at least a pledge of complete cooperation in working toward the campaign goal should be secured from all the members of the institutional advancement program. There should be enough incentive to overcome any future territorial conflicts about who is going to call the shots.

Public relations in a capital campaign cannot operate in a vacuum. The person responsible for the campaign's public relations must be considered an important and integral part of the campaign team. The campaign's public relations director should attend all meetings and special events connected with the campaign—especially meetings held at the highest levels. The public relations director should be allocated time, as appropriate, to discuss the campaign's public relations plans and to report on progress. This person must be thoroughly familiar with the master fundraising plan and should know when, where, and how funds are to be raised. It is also important for him or her to know what strata of the population are expected to make contributions, in order for him or her to determine what those people read, watch, and listen to and to develop strategies for reaching them effectively.

Above all, every public relations effort connected with a capital campaign must be planned and carried out with the dignity and sophistication that the institution merits. A campaign's public relations effort, well done, will pay dividends far into the future.

# CHAPTER FOURTEEN

# CONCLUDING THE CAMPAIGN AND BUILDING ON THE MOMENTUM

Perhaps the greatest enemy in a capital campaign is volunteers' procrastination. Maintaining volunteers' effort can be frustrating, especially during the campaign's "dog days"—that period after the public announcement, when the initial excitement and enthusiasm of the campaign have long since passed, the arduous, detailed work of concluding the campaign is at hand, and everything seems to have come to a halt. Procedures for maintaining momentum should be planned well in advance. The following suggestions from Picton (1982) should prove helpful:

• Use the campaign organizational structure. Require all chairs to keep in touch with the volunteer leaders [in] their part of the organization, and [those leaders to keep] in touch with their workers, by visit or by phone on a regular basis. Push for the successful completion of each prospective gift. Each chair, co-chair, and worker is responsible for regularly reviewing the assignments of each volunteer under them. Caution: do not push volunteers for gifts per se. Keep volunteers aware that the suggested level of giving or rating of each prospect [must] be asked for and received if the campaign is to be successful.

• Try to keep everyone aware of deadlines—whether it is a regular, scheduled report meeting or the final report meeting, push constantly so that each person will complete assignments on schedule. Most people need deadlines. Arrange to have each worker called and reminded of report meetings a day or so in advance and ask if they will have a report. If not, when?

- Particular attention should be given to uncompleted assignments which are of significant importance to the campaign's success . . . the top 10 to 20 percent of the prospects expected to give the majority of the campaign objective. Although it is rare when all major gift assignments are completed by the deadline, every effort should be extended to push for this conclusion. Major gifts sometimes take a long time to gel. However, careful, thoughtful follow-up is essential. [No matter how often they are reminded of] the importance of the top few prospects to the success of the campaign, staff and volunteers are still inclined to spend an undue amount of time and effort on the smaller donors. Do not neglect them, but concentrate efforts where the returns can be greatest. [Remember Seymour's theory of thirds; see Chapter Six.]

- A major gifts committee composed of the chief executive officer, chief development officer, campaign chair, and selected key volunteers already committed should be included as a part of the campaign cabinet to concentrate on these key problems and other major obstacles which will arise. Having a troubleshooting committee should make it easier to enlist the campaign chair, since that individual can accept the position knowing there will be someone to turn to, if necessary. And this committee is a good vehicle to have available when attempting to enlist a powerful individual who may not want or be able to accept major campaign responsibilities.

- Regular reports indicating the status of the program will, of course, be given at report meetings. Be certain the official report is mailed to all volunteers immediately as a follow-up. Showing comparative results by division or teams can be a helpful tool to help overcome procrastination. Keep deadlines before volunteers. Most people work better when under pressure. Also send reports to major donors and prospects. It keeps them attuned to the campaign. And remember that many a major donor has increased an original gift, so continued cultivation of donors as well as prospects is essential during the campaign.

- If media attend key report meetings it will be helpful, especially if there is something eventful to report. If the media will not come, see that a report is filed with them. Widespread word of success adds momentum. Any announcement of a significant gift for a special purpose, like a portion of a building, or for some other major objective should be carefully planned so that it is featured properly.

Even the best leaders and volunteers, those well trained and committed to the cause, will sometimes find fundraising challenging and difficult. It is the job of the staff to help everyone fight through these periods, to maintain momentum, to encourage and lift those who are flagging, and to express the right mixture of confidence and enthusiasm, tempered by sober reality, to carry the campaign through to victory.

## Victory on Schedule

Picton (1982) shares the following thoughts on celebrating a victory. Ideally, success on schedule will be the campaign's good fortune, and it is important to plan the victory celebration carefully in the event that this good fortune does come about. Continue to feature the campaign's leaders. All the credit and limelight should be theirs, not the staff's. Be certain that each person who has had a major campaign responsibility or who did an outstanding job is appropriately recognized. Encourage the attendance of major donors who really made success possible. Be certain that all volunteers are invited and recognized, too. The celebration should be a well-organized, happy occasion.

Recognize those major donors who will agree to be recognized. How they are recognized depends on the institution and on the individual donor. Being recognized from the dais is enough for some; others like certificates, plaques, or some other imaginative, tangible symbol of their generosity. The institution may want to honor some donors at other, smaller occasions—private affairs. A campaign also provides chances to give recognition while the campaign is in progress. This kind of recognition may mean naming a facility after a donor, placing plaques and offering citations, presenting distinguished service awards (or, in the case of a college or a university, awarding honorary degrees), and electing advisory groups or governing boards. Each situation should be examined separately. But, by all means, do give recognition, no matter how you choose to do so. Maintain friendly contact with donors, and use direct mail, the telephone, and face-to-face opportunities to report on what their gifts have accomplished. Doing so reinforces donors' appreciation and gives the institution an opportunity to keep donors aware of continuing needs. Additional gifts are often a by-product of the pleasure derived from being recognized and receiving information.

It is equally important to honor campaign workers. In all campaign announcements, reports, and news releases, praise the volunteers for their efforts, and invite them to special events along with donors and prospects. Maintain contact with and seek advice from important workers as well as from major donors.

Prepare media handouts concerning what the capital campaign gifts have accomplished and will accomplish, and recap the highlights of the campaign. Once again, feature leaders and major donors if they will permit you to do so. If media representatives attend the victory event, a larger audience will be informed of the campaign's triumph, and that will help develop public relations for the institution. Whatever the celebration program, it should be carried out in a thorough but light and entertaining way, leaving everyone feeling good about what has been accomplished. Go first class! Everyone wants to be recognized for accomplishments, and everyone wants to be on a winning team. When these factors are recognized in plans for the victory celebration, volunteers will be more likely to say yes when the organization asks for their assistance in future fundraising activities, whether these efforts are campaigns for annual support, capital campaigns, or other specific kinds of programs.

Donors should not be forgotten after the victory is celebrated. They should be invited to special occasions at the institution—lectures, research symposia, special luncheons or dinners, plays or musical productions, gallery openings; whatever brings them on site is sound cultivation. If a capital campaign was conducted for a specific construction or renovation project, be certain to invite all donors to the dedication or opening. If a donor gives a scholarship, it is nice to have the donor meet the student recipient. This is just common sense, but sometimes institutions get so involved in daily activities that they overlook these possibilities for continued cultivation.

If you ask volunteers to do something today, do not forget them tomorrow. Workers and donors have the right to expect to be remembered forever for what they have done. Responsibility for remembering them belongs to the public relations and development departments. All past good deeds should be regarded as promises for the future. The best way to remember your people is to give them further opportunities to serve the institution. Never write anyone off as a future prospect—at least not until the day the will is probated.

# Final Reports

At the conclusion of the campaign, two types of final report should be prepared. The first is an internal report (see Resource O, "Sample Final Report"); the second is a public document (see Resource P, "Sample Post-Campaign Assessment").

## Internal Report

The internal report should include a cover letter from the campaign director to the general chair of the campaign (with a copy to the chair of the board) summarizing the major accomplishments achieved by the campaign and the problems that were encountered. This report should also include any recommendations or suggestions that the campaign director would like to make. It should provide a plan for stewardship, describing activities that can be developed both to recognize donors and keep them informed about the benefits being derived from their contributions. It may also include other suggestions designed to prepare the institution for a more fruitful long-range development program. The report should contain a list of prospects who have not yet committed themselves to the campaign, a brief plan for approaching those prospects who can still be seen and solicited, and a report on the volunteers, indicating the assignments they have taken, the assignments they have completed, and the assignments that have yet to be completed. It should also include a suggested collections procedure for any outstanding pledges to the campaign, along with a cash-flow projection, indicating the amount already received and income projections for each of the following years during which pledge payments are scheduled. It may also provide a list of the named and memorial gift pledges that were recorded during the campaign.

Another part of this report should be a statistical review of the campaign, listing the campaign goal, the total subscribed by particular donor groups (corporations, foundations, individuals), the total number of donors, the total cash received to date, and the number of volunteers involved with the project. In larger and more complex campaigns, there may also be an analysis of the prospects by campaign division. The report should also contain an expense summary, showing expense accounts, budget allocations, and expenditures made against budget allocations.

One of the most important parts of the internal final report is a scrapbook that will serve as a visual record of campaign activity. It should be organized chronologically and should show how the campaign and all its aspects were built. Early in the preparation for the campaign, the institution should prepare a file folder so that materials can be automatically collected in the scrapbook file as they are generated. The responsibility for preparing the scrapbook is usually assigned to a member of the office staff. It is important to understand that this scrapbook should be compiled as the campaign goes along; the materials should not be reconstructed and assembled at the end of the campaign.

## Public Document

The second kind of final report is circulated widely to donors, workers, key constituents, and, according to the circumstances, prospective donors and workers as well. If this type of report is used, it can be designed as part of the transition from the current campaign to the continuous development effort. This report, which can take infinite shapes and formats, should include a listing of all donors unless the campaign has been comprehensive, with all annual gifts also counted in the campaign goal. In this case, the organization may opt to list only donors of a certain amount—say, $1,000 or more. It is equally important to consider segregating listings of donors, especially if the campaign has encompassed several separate objectives under a total goal, and to provide recognition according to the size of the donation: obviously, more attention will be given to donors of $100,000 than to donors of $1,000. Give recognition to key volunteers and workers as well as to donors. A campaign cannot succeed without both groups. The report should also provide an adequate amount of financial detail—amounts pledged, amounts collected to date, and plans for expenditures—to satisfy donors and volunteers alike that their efforts are indeed providing the benefits that the campaign aimed to provide.

There is sometimes a temptation to eliminate this report, with the rationale that the campaign is already over and that the report represents an additional expense that can be avoided. Do not be rationalized out of preparing this report! Whatever the institutional investment required, it assuredly will be returned in full and plentiful measure in the future.

## Post-Campaign Assessment

At the end of the campaign, the institution should analyze its effort. According to John Grenzebach & Associates, Inc. (1986), this analysis should be geared to answer the following questions:

- Was the campaign on the whole well received?
- [Which expenditures] proved the most beneficial and [which] the least effective?
- What promotional materials and events were the most effective?
- What was the best method of solicitation?
- What procedures should be repeated, and [which] ones should be abandoned?
- What key leadership developed during the campaign?
- What key prospects appeared?
- Has the institution recorded all the data that turned up during the solicitations?
- Should it publish a final report on the effort?
- How well did the campaign, volunteers, staff, and consultants, if used, perform?
- Did any individuals identify themselves as prospective board members during the campaign?
- Did others who might serve on important institutional committees surface?
- Was the goal met, but did some of the objectives of the campaign fail to be fully funded?
- Did the efforts of the campaign bring about a need for increased staff and greater budget to undergird the development effort in the future?

The institution may think that the conclusion of its campaign marks the conclusion of its intensive work. Actually, its work should just be beginning. The end of a campaign is the time for the institution to capitalize on its success and move its development efforts to a new and higher level for the future. It is the time to establish and begin to sustain an ongoing major gifts program. Conducting an audit to find answers to the important questions just listed is a vital step in this process. Even more vital is taking action once the answers have been obtained.

# Only the Beginning

In almost every campaign in which more than one objective has been included in the overall fundraising goal, not every objective is fully funded during the campaign. This shortfall provides an opportunity, at the end of the announced campaign period, to carry over the funding of an important facility or other unmet needs into an ongoing development program or to develop a short-term campaign separate from the original one. It also presents an excellent opportunity to reconstitute a new, smaller working group of volunteers specifically dedicated to completing the task at hand. In this way, the institution has an opportunity to begin integrating into the working group of key volunteers those people who emerged during the campaign as major donors or able workers. This transition period is the time to clean up old business and establish the basis for new, future relationships.

Even as an institution concludes its current campaign, it is planning the next. The ongoing program for major gifts development never truly ends. The methods and contacts developed must sustain the institution and prepare it for its next campaign or special effort. Workers who develop in one campaign are the leaders of the next. They need to be continually developed through active, meaningful, appropriate, increasingly responsible involvement from the time one effort ends until the next one begins. Ask volunteers to continue serving by becoming involved in the ongoing program for annual giving. Many will now be ready and able to solicit top gifts, either on a face-to-face basis or through telephone solicitation programs during the annual campaign. Ask them to continue working as volunteers in single-purpose capital campaigns that may be undertaken after the comprehensive or historical effort is completed. And ask them to continue working in the program for planned and deferred gifts. Find a niche for each and every one, and use them—or risk losing them, possibly to the organization down the street! The cultivation of prospects needs to continue, and weaknesses in the campaign need to be identified and corrected as part of the continuing development effort. It is also important to maintain the abilities of the staff beyond the current campaign period as the institution looks to the future.

In most cases, as we have seen, 90 percent of the dollar objective will come from 10 percent of the constituency. This fact makes it vitally important that the institution treat its potential and actual major donors with extreme care. When a campaign has been successful and celebration is at hand, it is time to begin a new period of cultivating current donors and to continue cultivating the prospective major donors to future campaigns. Chances are that the institution will have found new top prospects for continued support because of their gifts to the campaign. A number of major donors may also have disappointed the institution and will need special attention. What will emerge, however, is a new listing of the top 10 to 20 percent of the institution's constituency, and those prospects are the key to future fundraising success, as well as a major source of future institutional leadership.

How this new list is treated is important. First, it must be acted on, not just drawn up. Second, room must be made in the organization to accommodate these people. It is often hard to effect the succession of leaders or make room for new faces, but it is important that this be done, and that it be done in creative, enthusiastic, energetic ways so as to let everyone, old and new, feel wanted and welcome.

The key is involvement; that begets investment. The secret to involving volunteers and donors, old and new alike, is simple, well known, and timeless: give them something meaningful to do; earnestly seek their counsel, advice, and support. What is most important is that the institution proactively and systematically go about involving its key donors and volunteers. *Do not leave involvement to chance.* There should always be a place in the organization for someone who is willing to work and who agrees to give. Further, outstanding volunteers will have come to light during the campaign because of their excellent performance. Do not overlook or forget them. Be certain they are brought into the institution's planning and that they have a voice in its future activities, and make this a certainty as soon as possible. Name them to committees; nominate them for positions on the board. By tying up all the loose ends, by following through, the institution will have prepared a neat package for its future activities.

# CHAPTER FIFTEEN

# TRENDS AFFECTING THE FUTURE OF FUNDRAISING AND CAPITAL CAMPAIGNS

According to the American Association of Fund-Raising Counsel Trust for Philanthropy (1997), in 1995 there were 626,226 organizations registered with the Internal Revenue Service as charities, up from 422,103 in 1987. One year later, the same organization reported that by 1996 the number had risen to 654,186—up 4.5 percent in one year, and a 55 percent increase since 1987 (American Association of Fund-Raising Counsel Trust for Philanthropy, 1998).

## Implications of Growth in the Nonprofit Sector

These impressive numbers are just the tip of the iceberg in measuring the size of the nonprofit sector in the United States. For example, these totals do not include many religious congregations—religious congregations are not required to register, although some do—nor do the local affiliates of such national organizations as Boys and Girls Clubs or the American Cancer Society register separately.

Even if religious congregations and local affiliates were counted, however, the picture of voluntary associations in the United States would still be incomplete. Entities with gross revenues of less than $25,000 do not have to register, and there are more of them than one might imagine. Smith (1997) estimates that there are between thirty and one hundred organizations for every one thousand citizens. This estimate implies that at least 90 percent of the voluntary associations in the

United States are not counted in IRS registration data, nor is giving to most of these organizations included in national statistics.

As the number of nonprofits grow, so do the number of organizations conducting capital campaigns. In August 1998, the Indiana University Center on Philanthropy (1998) released a new biannual report, *The Philanthropy Giving Index (PGI)*, which says that some 33 percent of three hundred fundraising executives who were polled indicated that their organizations were engaged in capital campaigns, and that another 21 percent indicated plans to begin capital campaigns within the next six months. Put all of this together and you get the picture of a sector that has grown at the rate of nearly 50 percent over the past decade, with the real possibility that more than 50 percent of organizations in the third sector are conducting or planning capital campaigns. In this very large, rapidly growing field, the number of campaigns will continue to increase and goals will go higher, even though they may level off for a period if present-value reporting methods are fully adopted (see Chapter Seven). This growth points emphatically to the need for strategic institutional planning, for solidly drawn, carefully documented cases for support, and for volunteer campaign leaders of the first caliber.

## Women's Expanding Role

The role that women play in all phases of philanthropy will also continue to grow. Women have long controlled the majority of wealth; they outlive men, on the average. Only in the past twenty-five years, however, have they emerged in large numbers as an active, independent force in philanthropy. Today's nonprofit boards are heavily populated, in some situations dominated, by women. Corporate boardrooms are seeing more and more women, too. Women in growing numbers are rising to the topmost rungs of the corporate ladder, and they are populating the executive and staff ranks of nonprofit organizations and development programs as well.

Women, too, are now giving big. For example, Miller and Nayyar (1998) report on a recent Princeton University study (Capek, 1997) showing that the number of women whose net worth exceeds $600,000 increased 28 percent between 1992 and 1995 and on research by INDEPENDENT SECTOR (1996) showing that average charitable contributions by women increased 26 percent between 1993 and 1995.

According to an interview in *Counsel*, the Marts & Lundy newsletter, with Gwinn Scott ("Exploring Women and Philanthropy," 1998), for more than a century women philanthropists have been bringing dramatic change about in America, whether they were creating colleges, as Sophia Smith did in 1871 with a gift of $393,000, or working to save the planet, as Harriet Bullitt and Patsy Bullitt Collins did when they announced in 1994 that they would give most of their $375 million fortune to fund environmental causes. In fact, women respond to a wide variety of needs and give to all kinds of institutions and organizations, and yet only recently have they begun to realize their full potential as philanthropists—and only recently have many nonprofits taken action to identify and cultivate women as key sources of financial support. Scott finds that women tend to prefer outright gifts over multiyear commitments, are driven more by causes than by competition between and among themselves, base their choices on where they can have the most impact, are moved to respond to cases that stir their hearts and evoke passion, are more likely to give anonymously or to name things for others, and give most readily to organizations that include them and target programs toward them.

# The Importance of Volunteers

Chapter Four of this volume focuses on volunteers, and some may question the need to place such importance on this topic; the trend, they will suggest, is away from using volunteers and toward having staff-driven campaigns. They will say that volunteers today ask too many questions, express too many opinions, and sometimes forget their place. There is also an obvious and growing problem of supply and demand: good volunteers are in short supply and in great demand. But do not be seduced by the short term simplicity of believing, or especially of trying to convince others in your organization, that identifying, training, and staffing volunteers is more trouble than it is worth. Over time, nothing could be further from the truth. Research on this point stretches over time and is abundant, and the results are abundantly clear. Included among the most recent research in this area is the data collected by the Gallup Organization, which can be found in INDEPENDENT SECTOR (1996) as well as in American Association of Fund-Raising Counsel Trust for Philanthropy (1997). The latter source, that organization's fifth biennial household survey of giving and volunteering, highlights these findings:

• Among individuals who volunteer for nonprofit organizations, 90 percent also make financial contributions to charities; among those who do not volunteer, 59 percent contribute. These percentages have been relatively stable over time. These results indicate that nonprofits able to increase volunteers' participation can boost giving levels—moderately during recessions, and measurably when the economy improves.

• In 1993, the average gift among households with volunteers was 55 percent higher than among households with no volunteers. Among volunteers, the average contribution represented 2.6 percent of household income, whereas in households without volunteers the average was 1.1 percent of income.

Volunteers are at least as valuable as major gift prospects. Good ones are fewer in number and will have multiple impacts that go beyond making gifts. Organizations that incorporate volunteers meaningfully into the campaign structure will make the giving environment immeasurably more conducive to the acquisition of lead gifts. Genuine involvement of volunteers includes their proper orientation, personalized professional staffing, shared planning and decision making, and allowance for honest differences of opinion. It means making a conscious decision about the selection of each volunteer for every role that the institution envisions. It requires the same thoughtful commitment to peer-to-peer personal recruitment as used in solicitation of major donors, and it takes account of the fact that volunteers' time is often more valuable to them than money. Volunteers' active participation in guiding the development of the case statement, creating strategies for others' involvement, and providing peer influence and leverage on solicitation calls all lead effectively to the attainment of large gifts. Use your volunteers or risk losing them—and if they go, realize that your donors, who are also volunteers, are also being lost.

## The Impact of Regulation

The third sector is increasingly coming under scrutiny. This trend began to develop a decade ago. Unfortunately, it will continue unless nonprofits step in and do a better job of regulating themselves. Pat Lewis, past president and chief executive officer of the National Society of Fund-Raising Executives, comments as follows:

> The nonprofit sector must continue to be proactive regarding the federal and state governments' heightened interests in the activities of charitable organizations. Charges of misuse of funds at several highly visible organizations, and the search for new sources of revenue[,] have led regulators to look critically at charitable tax exemptions and activities.
>
> Some states are examining cause-related marketing and questioning both the corporate expense claim and the tax exemption. They are exploring whether corporate contributions and sponsorships are unrelated business income and therefore, subject to taxes ["Pat Lewis on Fund Raising in the 1990s," 1994, pp. 8–9].

Hartsook has this to say on the subject:

> Government oversight, which currently has emerged with regard to telemarketing sales, will be enforced prominently with regard to philanthropic

solicitations—especially solicitations relating to high-cost telephone solicitations made by fringe philanthropic groups. Unfortunately, telemarketing for nonprofit organizations has received a bad name because of fringe philanthropic organizations that solicit and collect large sums of money—while dedicating most of those funds to the costs of fund raising and salaries.

State regulators are responding to calls from the public, which is expressing concern about charities. Registration requirements for fund raisers and consultants, which sometimes require large bonds, are being enacted. Questions about charitable annuities and charitable life insurance gifts are being raised [Hartsook, 1997, p. 48].

At the end of the 1990s, the situation has come to this: only three states—Idaho, Montana, and Wyoming—have no laws regulating nonprofits. The American Association of Fund-Raising Counsel Trust for Philanthropy ("Annual Survey of State Laws," 1998, pp. 1–7) lists the following seven general categories of regulation (the number of states where such regulation exists is shown in parentheses):

1. Registration or licensing requirements for charitable organizations (40)
2. Reporting dates and requirements for charitable organizations (41)
3. State acceptance of uniform registration form (18)
4. Solicitation disclosure requirements for charitable organizations (17)
5. Requirement for organizations using paid solicitors to note additional disclosure requirements if paid solicitors are used (28)
6. Requirement for organizations using fundraising counsel to note registration/licensing/bonding requirements for counsel (28)
7. Need for organizations using paid solicitors to note that the state imposes additional requirements for solicitors (42)

Funds spent on legal services and on administration to satisfy the growing number of rules and regulations cannot be used to fulfill the primary missions of third-sector organizations. The creation of and adherence to acceptable standards and practices should be determined by the nonprofits themselves. It should remain the vigilant business of the American Association of Fund-Raising Counsel, the National Society of Fund Raising Executives, the Council for Advancement and Support of Education, the Association for Healthcare Philanthropy, and other such bodies to impose self-discipline in this field, lest legislators and the general public impose their views on the third sector to an even greater extent.

# New Roles for Technology

Information services and products constitute the world's largest and fastest-growing economic sector. Computers, computer systems, networks, and digital information increasingly dominate every facet of our lives. This growing dependence on digital information and information technologies is dramatically altering fundraising and will continue to do so. Warwick has the following comments on this development:

> It's impossible to foretell the shape or direction of the future—especially where technology is concerned. But this much I'll predict: the direct response fundraising systems we'll depend on twenty years from now will share the following six characteristics.

> 1. INDIVIDUALIZED. Our appeals will be "individualized." By and large, we won't be dealing with donor file "segments" anymore but with individuals—responding to their unique, personal interests and capabilities. We'll know a lot more about our donors, because we'll ask them for more information through frequent surveys and questionnaires and because our information management systems will be capable of storing much more data than most charities now find practical to retain.
> 2. MULTI-SENSORY. Our appeals will be "multi-sensory," using forms of what today are called "multimedia" technologies. We won't be limited to paper, or to voice communications, or to pre-recorded sounds or video images. A single fundraising appeal might consist of sights, sounds and data, and be delivered, separately or simultaneously, through several communications channels: a wallscreen, perhaps, with full-motion sound and video, or a pocket communicator bearing a simplified, two-dimensional version, or a hardcopy printout a little like what today we call a "fax." Donors will choose which method they prefer, and open it up when and where they wish—suiting the mood or constraints of the moment, or following long-established preferences for one form or another.
> 3. INFORMATION-RICH. Twenty years from now, our appeals will be "information-rich." On-line databases and super-high-speed data transmission will permit us to make veritable mountains of information available to every prospect or donor—and the demands of competition will force us to do so. Meanwhile, flexible database management software will permit every prospect and every donor to select precisely those bits of information they want—and not one word or one image more.

4. REAL-TIME. Within two decades, "real-time" transactions will be common in direct response fundraising. "Real-time" is computer jargon for "right now." For example, by authorizing a gift in the course of an on-line videoconference with her favorite charity, a donor may instantaneously transmit funds from her bank account to the charity—before the conference is even over. The response curves we measure today in weeks and months may be viewed in terms of hours or even minutes twenty years from now.

5. INTERACTIVE. Fundraising thirty years from today will be highly "interactive." Donors will actively participate, not just in selecting the amount and the format of the information they receive, but [in] the role they'll play in the life and work of the charities they support. Today's dedicated donor "hotlines" will become multimedia gateways that offer donors a multitude of new options: to participate in the latter-day equivalent of focus group research, for example, or to share their specialized expertise with program staff, or to integrate what they're learning from us into ongoing educational programs. Both two-way and small-group communications will be an integral part of the process—freeing fundraisers from the constraints of time and geography, and permitting us to develop rich and rewarding relationships with donors we may never actually meet.

6. COMMUNAL. The nonprofits that flourish in the fast-moving environment of the twenty-first century will be those that provide their supporters with the experience of community. Today's fast-multiplying computer networks, bulletin board systems, local access cable TV, video teleconferencing and E-mail facilities foreshadow the integrated technologies of the twenty-first century. Within twenty years, charities will be able to engage thousands of their donors in a profoundly personal and meaningful way—simultaneously, and over great physical distances. Meanwhile, as individuals, many donors will find the nearly instantaneous, broadband communications of the New Age will permit them to turn a shared commitment to a charity's work into personal relationships with many of their fellow donors. Just as users of today's converging technologies are forming "virtual communities," often spanning continents and oceans, donors by the thousands may eventually be able to join with a charity's other constituents—staff, board, clients, alumni—in shared access to the daily experience of the charity's work. How? Through a latter-day equivalent to "personals" ads in the newsletters or public forums on the Network of the future. That experience and the personal relationships that result may enrich daily life in the twenty-first century for tens of millions of people [Warwick, 1994, pp. 39–41].

# The Capital Campaign: Pros and Cons

In 1980, a thought-provoking seminar for senior development professionals included a discussion of the capital campaign. The presenter, Joel P. Smith, left those he was addressing with two questions: Is a capital campaign the right way to do fundraising? If not, how will fundraising get done?

In the essay that grew out of the ideas presented there, Smith (1981) developed the point that capital campaigns entail pros and cons. For twenty-five years, it has been an almost unchallenged axiom of fundraising that capital campaigns are a good idea. They are the centerpiece of fundraising programs in most institutions, and many institutions judge the success of fundraising programs by the magnitude and frequency of the campaigns they conduct. There is quite a persuasive case to be made for capital campaigns. Nevertheless, there is also room for more skeptical observations.

## Pros

Capital campaigns provide valuable discipline in terms of planning, setting schedules, establishing goals, and providing an opportunity to manage by objectives—a rare opportunity in fundraising. Campaigns also inspire donors to make larger commitments than they otherwise would—commitments, to be sure, that may be spread over a considerable time but that are nevertheless larger than in the ordinary course of events.

A campaign produces results with long-term effects; the institution's ability to enjoy these results is not limited to the campaign period itself. Because standards have been raised during the campaign effort, it is reasonable to expect a higher level of giving afterward than was the case beforehand.

A campaign also provides valuable, intensive experience for the development staff. Because there is so much going on, and at such a level of intensity, there is an opportunity for dramatic professional growth that otherwise would not occur. There is so much to do that the staff, one way or another, learns how to do it and get it done, emerging as a group of more experienced professionals. Moreover, campaigns provide not just discipline but also esprit de corps. They create a climate in which team members come together emotionally to accomplish some mutual objective. And, because fundraising is a human, emotional activity, that spirit is a very valuable component in getting the job done.

These arguments amount to a really quite persuasive case. Therefore, it is not at all surprising that so many institutions have accepted these arguments and gone forward with campaigns. Indeed, some have gone forward with several campaigns within the last few decades. Nevertheless, there are some other, seldom aired, considerations.

## Cons

When it comes down to the day of decision, a great many institutions are forced to conclude, reluctantly, that they simply do not have staff members with the requisite competence and experience to conduct a successful campaign. As a result, they turn to consultants or to short-term contract employees to conduct their campaigns. This is not to denigrate consultants or contract professionals—there are many honorable, able people who help numerous institutions in those roles—but turning to temporary help does have serious drawbacks. For one thing, the consultants and contract professionals will leave after the campaign. Therefore, the opportunity for professional growth, which is one of the most forceful arguments in favor of the campaign, is forfeited to some degree. Instead of building a professional staff that will be in place to conduct a refined fundraising program when the campaign is over, the institution has set up a situation in which some of the key players will leave, taking with them valuable knowledge and experience, no matter how conscientious they are about recording their knowledge in the institutional files. Furthermore, no matter how sophisticated consultants and contract professionals are, they may not be able to represent the institution with the same understanding, conviction, and depth of experience and local knowledge that the institution's professional staff can. And if there is a sine qua non of being a first-rate fundraiser, it is to have conviction and understanding about the place that is being represented.

Campaigns, almost by definition, place terrific emphasis on current results. The point of a campaign is to force as many gifts as possible over a prescribed period in order to achieve a goal that is often a terrific stretch. Really sophisticated fundraising is patient, and campaigns do not permit patience. Campaign deadlines, although they provide discipline, sometimes also cause impatience. The emphasis on getting gifts now in order to reach the goal may cause an institution to accept, for example, a $50,000 gift when a larger gift would have been available had the institution been more patient. There is a definite risk of haste and waste in campaigns.

It is difficult during a campaign to maintain the appropriate focus on an institutional agenda because there is so much attention directed to the bottom line, as well as such enthusiasm, eagerness, and determination to make the number on the bottom as large as it can be. But what is more important than amount is utility—not just bringing gifts to the institution, but bringing in gifts that underwrite the institution's most important purposes. It is ironic that institutions lose this focus during campaigns, because campaigns are almost always preceded by months of discussion and planning about what it is important to raise money for. But the product of such discussion often is a comprehensive wish list rather than a rigorous evaluation of whether it is more important to have gifts for improving facilities or for expanding services. Assuming that the institution cannot have both, how is it to make the choice? Campaigns rarely force this kind of trade-off thinking; instead, they encourage the optimistic attitude that the longer the laundry list of desirable objectives, the more probable it is that the institution will achieve the vast dollar amount representing the total objective.

Campaigns make fundraising episodic. The institution pulls out the throttle and really goes for it for two, three, or four years, and then there comes a respite in which it falls back, gives the volunteers and others some time off, and then regroups to think about another campaign. Most refined fundraising programs are not episodic, however. They are patient and sustained, they look to the long term, and they resist the temptation to be proud of their immediate accomplishments.

Then there is the matter of taking time off when a campaign is over. The conventional wisdom is that campaigns are so intensive and call for such effort, not only from the institutional team but also from volunteers, that everybody needs a rest. Furthermore, the argument runs, if the institution is successful in a really ambitious campaign, it will have picked all the pears there are on that particular tree and is going to have to take some time off to let new pears grow.

This is a really dangerous fallacy. It assumes that the body of prospects with whom the institution works is finite, that there is a certain number of interested people, loyal to the institution, from whom it is reasonable to expect gifts, and that the institution will go to them during the campaign and get an answer, yea or nay, so that when the campaign ends it is important to take time off, renew and regroup, and give these loyal supporters a rest.

But that is not what happens during a campaign. What happens is that a significant portion of the prospects give the institution an ambiguous answer. When the institution concludes its campaign and takes time off, it forfeits the opportunity to follow through with those people. Moreover, a campaign that covers three years lasts a long time, and the body of prospects is not some fixed constellation of individuals that remains static over that time. It changes by 20, 30, or 40 percent during the campaign. During that period, alliances emerge with people who become interested in and enthusiastic about the institution for the first time. To let down immediately after a campaign is to forfeit the opportunity to nurture alliances with these people, who have the potential to become important prospects over the next several years.

Campaign goals are also getting terribly large. The needs listed in a capital campaign today add up to a number likely to startle most people who care about the institution. For those who are understanding and who are really close to the institution, an explanation of those needs will be received sympathetically. But with many, many people, the institution has the burden of making a case that is awfully difficult to make convincingly. How much credibility can there be in the claim that an unusually large goal is a realistic reflection of what an institution needs—that the institution has done the kind of soul-searching that warrants the assertion that these really are worthy objectives crucial to the quality of the institution? Is the institution coming across as grasping, as reaching for some dramatically large amount, hoping that somehow it might get it but willing to settle for less?

Clearly, whether to have a capital campaign is not the only issue. There is another very significant question: If a capital campaign will not be conducted, what are the alternatives? Surely no one can be satisfied with less than the most ambitious fundraising program appropriate to the institution's situation. The quality of all institutions is in jeopardy, and most have reached the point where their health can no longer be improved by the reduction of expenditures. The road to survival is not to sacrifice the quality of the organizations that constitute the third sector through radical cost cutting. The road to survival—for some, literal survival; for most, survival with a respectable level of quality—is somehow to bring in enough funds to underwrite the critically important objectives, the objectives that define quality for each institution and its mission.

## A Proposed Solution

The best answer to Smith's question, and one that addresses many of his concerns, is the development program based on continuous lifetime giving. This approach requires many of the essential components of any successful campaign to be incorporated into the everyday life of the organization. The result of this approach is shown in Table 15.1. It presupposes that an organization's administrative leaders have done careful, thoughtful analysis and planning and that the resulting objectives, in terms of both operations and capital, fit into the overall long-range strategic plan. It mandates that the board approve plans and, through the approval process, accept leadership responsibility. It requires that needs be real and compelling, and the case for them be articulate and stimulating. It directs that the case and the goal be tested and validated in the market before the campaign (annual or capital), insists that proper internal preparation take place, and, finally, appreciates that there must be a prospect pool able and willing to meet the fundraising goals that have been established.

## TABLE 15.1. CONTINUOUS LIFETIME GIVING PROGRAM—BROAD OUTLINE.

| Type of Giving | Age of Prospects | | | | | | | | | | |
|---|---|---|---|---|---|---|---|---|---|---|---|
| | 20–25 | 25–30 | 30–35 | 35–40 | 40–45 | 45–50 | 50–55 | 55–60 | 60–65 | 65–70 | 70+ |
| **Annual gifts** | | | | | | | | | | | |
| less than $1,000 | X | X | X | X | X | X | X | X | X | X | X |
| $1,000–4,999 | | | X | X | X | X | X | X | X | X | X |
| $5,000–24,999 | | | | | X | X | X | X | X | X | X |
| $25,000+ | | | | | | | X | X | X | X | X |
| **Special gifts** | | | | | | | | | | | |
| Programs, events (e.g., reunions) | | | X | | X | | | X | | X | |
| Major and planned gifts | | | | | | X | X | X | X | X | X |
| Wills and bequests | | | | | | | | X | X | X | X |
| Capital gifts | | | | | | | X | X | X | X | X |

## The A. T. Kearney Study

A. T. Kearney, based in Chicago and in operation since 1926, is one of the premier management consulting firms in the United States. In 1997, the firm performed a pro bono analysis of the giving trends, marketing practices, and strategic direction of the Indiana University Foundation (IUF). (The analysis was done under the direction of Fred G. Steingraber, chief executive officer at A. T. Kearney and a member of the IUF board of directors; for more information about the firm, go to http://www.atkearney.com.)

The study was the first of its kind for Kearney. Although Kearney typically consults more with major corporations, commercial and service industry clients than with institutions of higher education, which market "intangibles" in their giving programs, the firm's expertise in analyzing data and data trends was readily applied to over 200,000 donor records provided by the IUF. In addition to analyzing these data, Kearney gained insight into the institution and its sector by interviewing Indiana University (IU) and IUF administrators, officers, and deans, as well as the presidents of five peer universities' fundraising foundations. Kearney gave IUF a rare opportunity to see how taking a for-profit approach to fundraising can bring it closer to achieving its objectives without compromising its nonprofit identity and integrity.

Overall, Kearney concluded, IUF does an excellent job of securing large gifts from top donors, but it does not spend adequate time and resources on younger, less mature donors, who represent a sizable source of untapped funding. Kearney recommended that IUF work toward developing a "lifetime giving" program—one that begins simply with participation when a student graduates from IU but evolves into a major and/or planned gifts effort over the life of the donor. Young donor acquisition and retention, coupled with continuous contact and cultivation, are essential phases in moving donors along in this giving cycle. It is recognized that each of IU's many schools and campuses is at its own level of fundraising sophistication. To maximize giving to each school, IUF needs to implement a more strategic, tailored, targeted marketing effort than it currently has in place. In summary, developing a lifetime giving program requires IUF to change the way it thinks about marketing to its various donor segments.

This approach will be required if our organizations are to move to the next level of support. It is true that giving in the United States goes up nearly every year; and, over the past fifty years, giving as measured by three-year rolling averages has always gone up. It is also true that, over more than a quarter-century, the percentage of gross domestic product and the percentage of household income given to nonprofits have remained fairly constant. Between 1966 and 1996, according to the American Association of Fund-Raising Counsel Trust for Philanthropy (1997), giving as a percentage of gross domestic product varied between 1.8 percent and 2.1 percent, and it was 2.0 percent in 1966 but only 1.9 percent in 1996. It fell to 1.8 percent in 1997, and giving by individuals as a percentage of personal income ranged from 1.8 percent to 2.1 percent over the same period (American Association of Fund-Raising Counsel Trust for Philanthropy, 1998). According to the latter report, giving by individuals as a percentage of personal income was 2.1 percent in 1966 and 1.9 percent in 1996, and a further drop is reported for 1997—down to 1.6 percent, the lowest point in the past thirty years. Giving is going up as the economy grows; measured against these significant baselines, however, it is not growing.

Kearney opened IUF's eyes. IUF's development staff members, like those at most other institutions, were hired for their people skills and their fundraising expertise, not for their analytical and marketing skills. *Marketing* is a term that is broadly defined. To some it means sales or advertising; to others it means public relations or communications. IUF does have people with all these skills. What is needed are analytically skilled people—marketers, statisticians, mathematicians, programmers—who can combine the expertise of their disciplines with the experience of the fundraisers to produce a new, more strategic, more focused, more productive, more cost-effective way of raising money.

Like most of our organizations, IU, in looking for the next major donor prospects, is combing through a haystack and looking for needles. A better way is to do the looking with a magnet, a highly powerful one. The combination of technology and analytical marketing skills will create that magnet in the future.

But does this mean that we have to give up the old prospects for the new ones, or the new for the old? We will not have to give up either group if we can incorporate a sophisticated marketing department into our organizational structure. By identifying the most promising prospects, old and new alike, a marketing department will increase the efficiency and success of the development team: instead of having to find the prospects, fundraisers will be able to devote maximum time and resources to developing and cultivating the relationships that are most likely to result in private support.

The mission of the marketing department is to facilitate and support IUF's development division in its ongoing effort to maximize private support for IU through the systematic, intentional implementation of a lifetime giving program. This program will identify the varied financial resources and personal goals of IU's alumni and friends and will then match them with corresponding priorities of the university.

The uniqueness of the IUF "customer" is significant, according to a report (Thiede, 1998) that deals with the need to establish a marketing department at

IUF. For IUF to be successful, it must convince its constituents to *give away* their resources, not for the sake of a tangible product that could benefit them directly, but rather for the satisfaction of knowing that their gifts have enhanced the lives of others. This approach makes fundraising a very emotional business—and different people are emotional about different things. IU alumni and friends may be emotional about a particular campus, athletics, faculty research, music, or financial aid for students. The marketing department's job will be to identify who is emotional about what, and then to match appropriate prospects with the needs of the university.

The overall objective of the marketing department, then, will be to help development professionals throughout the IU system secure private gifts for the university. Within this framework, the specific objectives and responsibilities of the marketing department are defined by the five-part GIFTS program, as outlined by Thiede (1998):

1. *Gathering* information on current and prospective donors
   - Keeping the database updated with pertinent demographic data
   - Systematically recording all pre- and postgraduate affiliations and activities
   - Writing, conducting, and analyzing survey projects for all IUF departments, IU campuses, schools, colleges, departments, and units
2. *Identifying* donor segments for various giving programs
   - Obtaining demographic information (age, income, property, names and number of children, and so forth)
   - Establishing levels of loyalty (gift amounts and gift frequency)
   - Making connections with donors (matching institutional needs with donors' affiliations, activities, and interests)
3. *Fostering* lifelong IU-donor relationships through consistent, targeted communication
   - Increasing emphasis on targeted direct-mail marketing programs
   - Developing IU "brand loyalty" by increasing the quality and frequency of communications from IU
   - Developing donor- and/or project-specific marketing materials
   - Personalizing communication materials whenever possible
   - Using the IU and IUF Web site to maximize constituents' exposure to IU
4. *Tracking* performance through systematic statistical analysis
   - Noting response rates to direct mail, customized correspondence, and personal solicitations
   - Calculating median gift amounts
   - Noting participation levels
   - Noting trends in giving (increases, decreases, or stagnation)

5. *Sharing* results and information
   - Disseminating "best practices" information throughout the organization, to help development professionals and programs achieve their own objectives

The Kearney report found that the groupings used to segment age (under 45, 45–65, and over 65) and income (under $75,000 and over $75,000) gave a good general illustration of how a donor's life stage and income level can influence their level of support. (See Table 15.2.) Nevertheless, there are segments within these segments, and each segment represents an opportunity to develop a more targeted and more effective marketing strategy. For instance, consider, on the one hand, a recent college graduate starting a first job, and, on the other, a forty-year-old who has a successful business. Both donors might fall into the "under 45, single, under $75,000" segment, but their circumstances are obviously different, and each should be approached differently. This example shows the need for IUF to divide its donors into smaller segments that keep relationships between age and lifestyle in mind (Thiede, 1998).

The Kearney report also recommends that donors' loyalty be examined to identify trends in giving (upward, downward, or constant) for IUF's use in developing targeted marketing strategies for specific donor segments. In analyzing donors' loyalty, it is important to remember, once again, that fundraising is different from selling products like soap, bread, gasoline, or milk, which consumers generally are obliged to buy. IUF "consumers" are people who give their money away, and so they are a unique kind of customer. The Kearney report defined three levels of loyalty:

1. Loyal (donor has given to IUF four to five times in the past five years)
2. Supportive (donor has given to IUF two to three times in the past five years)
3. Erratic (donor has given to IUF one time or not at all in the past five years)

### TABLE 15.2. SEGMENTING DONORS INTO NINE DEMOGRAPHIC GROUPS.

| Group | Age | Income Level | Marital Status |
|-------|-----|--------------|----------------|
| 1 | under 45 | under $75,000 | N.A. |
| 2 | under 45 | over $75,000 | N.A. |
| 3 | 45–65 | under $75,000 | single |
| 4 | 45–65 | under $75,000 | married |
| 5 | 45–65 | over $75,000 | single |
| 6 | 45–65 | over $75,000 | married |
| 7 | over 65 | under $75,000 | single |
| 8 | over 65 | under $75,000 | married |
| 9 | over 65 | over $75,000 | N.A. |

N.A., not applicable.

Basing loyalty analysis on the consistency and frequency of gifts given over a period of time is likely to paint an incomplete picture of loyalty, however (Thiede, 1998). To illustrate, Table 15.3 shows the gifts of two different donors over the same five-year period. Both donors have given five gifts over five years, and each donor has given a total of $750. If they were evaluated by the number of gifts alone, both donors would be deemed loyal, and IUF would spend equivalent time and resources to retain their gifts. But the trends in their gift amounts reveal very different levels of loyalty, and these should be factored into the marketing strategy for each donor:

- Donor 1 has steadily increased his gift amount. Therefore, he should be thanked for consistent giving and asked either to maintain or slightly increase his gift.
- Donor 2 seems to have lost interest in IU after year 2. Therefore, he requires cultivation to return him to his previous level of giving.

Determining a donor's loyalty requires a more comprehensive look at the donor's giving history than can be gleaned from a single factor. Additional questions to be asked in determining a donor's loyalty include but are not limited to the following:

- Has the donor's gift amount decreased, increased, or remained constant over the years?
- Has the donor been solicited every year?
- How was the donor solicited? By direct mail? Telefund? A personal visit? Some combination?
- Has the donor given in each year, or did the donor make multiple gifts in one year?

### TABLE 15.3. COMPARISON OF TWO DONORS' GIFTS OVER FIVE YEARS.

|         | Year 1 | Year 2 | Year 3 | Year 4 | Year 5 | Total |
|---------|--------|--------|--------|--------|--------|-------|
| Donor 1 | $50    | $100   | $150   | $200   | $250   | $750  |
| Donor 2 | $350   | $250   | $50    | $50    | $50    | $750  |

Simultaneous evaluation of these kinds of questions will help IUF develop more effective marketing strategies for different donor segments (Thiede, 1998).

When A. T. Kearney and IUF decided to conduct this study, each party understood that the other had a steep learning curve ahead: IUF was no more expert in marketing than Kearney was in fundraising. The techniques used in Kearney's analysis were a far more sophisticated approach to marketing than any IUF had ever taken. IUF staff members were quick to admit that a great portion of Kearney's statistical analysis was over their heads. This gap in understanding can be likened to the gap in understanding between a professor and a student. In this case, A. T. Kearney held a D.B.A. in marketing, and IU was a freshman with limited experience; Kearney had volumes to teach, but there was only so much IUF could absorb at once. But IUF will continue studying and learning how to apply and implement these new marketing techniques. IUF, because it wants to gain the maximum benefits from the Kearney study, is committed to bringing together a team of people who understand marketing, statistical analysis, and development and having them do "Kearney-type" analysis on a regular basis. Their end product will be a truly powerful fundraising tool that the IUF staff can easily access, interpret, and apply—a model that other thoughtful nonprofits will be able to study and adapt to their own individual situations.

## A Final Thought

In the past, too many organizations have succumbed to the temptation to proceed with campaigns even though the signals warned against this course. In the future, more discipline needs to be exercised by boards and institutional managers. Facts, not whims, must set an institution's fundraising course, whether the campaign is conducted in Vancouver, British Columbia; Peru, Indiana; or New York City. It is true whether the goal is $250,000, $50 million, or $250 million. It is true for colleges and universities, for hospitals, for social, community, and health and welfare organizations, and for churches and synagogues.

But, no matter how much technology and marketing influence our lives and change our worlds, one thing is not going to change. Fundraising will continue to be of, by, about, and for people. Welcome to the new millennium.

# PART TWO

# THE CAPITAL CAMPAIGN RESOURCE GUIDE

## RESOURCES FOR PREPARING FOR THE CAMPAIGN

## RESOURCES FOR IMPLEMENTING THE CAMPAIGN

## RESOURCES FOR MOVING FORWARD

## SAMPLE STRATEGIC PLAN

<u>Confidential</u>

# STRATEGIC PLAN

◆

## INDIANA UNIVERSITY FOUNDATION

BUILDING SUSTAINED GROWTH
IN PRIVATE FUNDING
FOR THE YEAR 2000 AND BEYOND

_____

## June 12, 1998

# Table Of Contents

◆

## I. Situation Analysis: The Need for Sustained Growth in Private Funding

The Indiana University Foundation has maintained a position of strength over many years, with particular success during recent years in the areas of major gifts, consolidation of the annual giving program, investments, administrative processes, and technology. Going forward, the number of private funding opportunities appears significant with alumni, friends, corporations, and foundations.

### Current Situation and Challenges

- The Indiana University Foundation (IUF) continues to build from a position of strength. In partnership with the campuses and schools, it has achieved significant growth in private support for IU and is a leader among university and college foundations. Achievements include:
- A consistent ranking in the top 3 percent among all universities and colleges in the U.S. in total voluntary support.
- A consistent top 10 ranking among public universities in market value of endowment.
- The Endowment Campaign for IU Bloomington has doubled giving to that campus. In the eighteen months between July 1, 1994 and December 31, 1995, $53.4 million was committed in gifts, pledges, and expectancies; in calendar 1996, nearly $89 million; and in calendar 1997, more than $105 million.
- Consistent growth in giving for IU, from $40.4 million 1989–90 to more than $70 million in 1997–98, an increase of approximately 73 percent.
- Consistent growth in number of donors to the University, from 62,400 in 1989–90 to 92,000 in 1997–98, an increase of 47 percent.

However, continued growth in private sector funding through the Foundation is essential. Competition for limited funds from the private sector has intensified, with a general decline in corporate and governmental support. Moreover, public funding of the University from the State is under pressure, and the University must look for increased private funding. Therefore, the Foundation must continue to build on its current strengths to achieve considerable growth in private sector support for IU, in order to help enable IU to realize its overall mission and each campus to realize its strategic initiatives. Fortunately, the Foundation's ability to meet the challenge of increased private funding is made easier by our strengths, including:

- Development efforts that have built a superior major gifts and campaign capability and integrated the annual fund;
- Administrative initiatives and policy changes that have resulted in state-of-the-art information databases, compliance with donor intent, and overall efficiencies and work flow improvements;
- An investment program that has generated attractive returns within reasonable risk parameters, helping to stabilize our financial resources;
- An experienced and expert staff dedicated toward achieving even better performance in the future.

## II. Our Strategic Vision: Why We Exist

To be a catalyst for maximizing private sector for Indiana University so that IU can contribute to the betterment of individuals and of the human condition.

### Our Strategic Purpose: What We Do

Our strategic purpose is, therefore, to develop and implement an institution-wide strategy for maximizing private-sector support of Indiana University.

### Our Mission: How We Do It

Designated by the Trustees of Indiana University as the sole fund-raising entity for the University and directed by its priorities:

The Indiana University Foundation seeks to maximize the University's private-sector resources by:

- Developing comprehensive strategies and programs for building lifetime donor relationships;
- Preserving the purchasing power of gifts and providing a major source of consistent, ongoing support to the University;
- Administering these resources for the benefit of the University, in a way that inspires continuing trust and commitment from donors and enhances our partnership with IU.

### Institutional Values

The Indiana University Foundation endorses a set of institutional values that govern our conduct and our relationship with donors and with IU.

*We will always represent the priorities of the University to the donors.* Indiana University rightly sets its own academic and program agenda and, in light of the feasibility of raising private-sector funds for various projects at each of the campuses, presents its fundraising requests to the Board of Directors of the Foundation for review. It is the Foundation's responsibility to present these priorities fully and fairly to donors, with an awareness of and respect for donors' interests, abilities, and welfare.

*We ensure compliance with donor intent.* We listen to, represent, and recommit ourselves to donors across all segments. This focus on donor stewardship drives all of our development, investment and administrative activities. We will continually seek to reach out to donors, communicate their needs, concerns, and desires, and translate them into effective development, service, and investment programs. In this process, we will celebrate the diversity of donors and treat each donor as an individual, not simply as source of funds.

*We respect the privacy of donors.* We value the consistent collection and capture of information regarding donors and their relationships with the University and with each campus, and develop and adhere to ethical guidelines regarding the kind of information collected and its use. To serve donors cost effectively, we need to gather information regarding giving patterns and aspects of their University relationships. In the process of using this information, we always respect a donor's request for control, security, and privacy. Ultimate approval for the use of information rests with donors.

*We continue to enhance our partnership with the University.* To maximize private resources and to extend the best practices across the University, we must continue to build an integrated planning process with campuses, schools, and departments. Although we will initiate the process and develop recommendations proactively, we recognize that the Foundation's goals can be met only through the spirit of active listening and participation in planning and execution of programs and events. Therefore, the Foundation is simultaneously a leader and a partner in this process.

## Organizational Values

These beliefs shape the essential character of the Foundation, creating our unique organizational culture and becoming the criteria for shaping policy, making decisions, and for directing our day-to-day behaviors and attitudes.

*All our interactions are based on mutual respect and a recognition of the value of each individual.* Within the Foundation and in interactions and communications with our Foundation colleagues, our partners at IU on all the campuses, donors, and all others, we are appreciative of each person's contributions and achievements, eager to work with others to accomplish goals and solve problems, open in expressing and hearing differences of opinion, and committed to making our best effort once a course of action has been chosen. We reach out to our colleagues, partners, and friends, delighting in their successes and encouraging them in times of difficulty.

*We accept our individual accountabilities and acknowledge our responsibilities to organizational success.* Growth and the increasing complexity of our business require greater specialization and expertise. Individually, we must specialize. Collectively, we must work in teams to meet our goals. By means of effective program and functional teams and of training, we gather the collective expertise needed for success in execution. As much as collaboration, success requires individual accountability within these teams.

*We commit to achieving individual and organizational potential.* Without staff commitment and a sense of ownership, we cannot build donor commitment and loyalty or offer our best service to the University and to each campus. Without commitment to professional growth and service to the Foundation, we cannot find better ways to achieve our goals. We therefore strive to create an environment that strengthens individuals, relationships, and the organization, and that promotes effectiveness and efficiency. We aim high, realizing that courage and perseverance will be needed to realize our aspirations.

*We believe in integrity and ethical behavior.* We are committed to the consistent expression of the core values of the Foundation and manifest those values daily. Whether complying with regulations or navigating a difficult and complex ethical dilemma, we remain steadfast in adhering to our core values and encourage others in their efforts to do so, even at the risk of the displeasure of others.

## Our Responsibilities

The Foundation has responsibilities to a wide range of individuals and constituencies—to Indiana University and its leadership, faculty, staff, development officers, and students on all campuses; to donors and prospects; to our Board of Directors and other volunteers; and to our own staff.

The Foundation's responsibilities to these constituencies have a number of common threads. We must communicate the importance of private funding to the success of Indiana University; maximize private resources for IU, providing increased gift income and maintaining the purchasing power of gifts; respect the interests, privacy, and individuality of donors; represent the University's interests and priorities; provide for the financial stability of the Foundation without unduly calling on University resources; adhere to the highest standards of service; and meet or exceed the obligations and expectations of a not-for-profit corporation partnering with a great public university.

*To Indiana University:* We must increase private resources by means of a comprehensive development program based on continuing lifetime relationships, with donors; plan and coordinate an institution-wide strategy for building private support; be guided by the academic mission of the University, as articulated to us by University administration; be sensitive to the needs and concerns of the faculty, staff, and students; represent accurately the University's interests and priorities to donors, prospects, and others; advise the University on the feasibility of proposed projects; manage assets, making every effort to maximize return on gifts; administer funds efficiently and with excellent service; and educate IU staff about our programs, policies, and strategies.

*To donors and prospects (alumni, individuals, corporations, foundations, and other organizations):* We must communicate to donors and prospects the importance of private resources, fundraising priorities, and avenues for giving; elicit their interests and their perceptions of the University and relay these comments to the appropriate person or group; preserve donors' and prospects' confidentiality by collecting and distributing only appropriate information; in cooperation with the University, have administrative controls in place to ensure that donors' gifts are directed by the Foundation and by the University to the purposes specified; ensure a reasonable return on donors' contributions; report regularly and fully to donors about the use and status of their gifts; and encourage their continuing involvement in the life of the University.

*To our Board of Directors:* We must keep the Board informed regarding the operation and management of the Foundation; seek its guidance; follow its policies; and reconcile requests from the University with those policies. We continue to encourage the representative mix of members that has provided the Board with a diversity of perspectives and experiences to draw upon.

*To our other volunteers:* We must inform and educate them about the University and its fundraising priorities; train them as needed; provide logistical support, feedback, and reports on results; recognize volunteers' contributions of time and talents on behalf of the University in an appropriate manner; and make them aware of opportunities for continuing involvement.

*To the Foundation staff:* We must treat each other fairly and with respect; train and educate; set realistic and appropriate performance expectations with reasonable regard to each individual's personal situation; match talents with tasks to be done and adjust the match if necessary in light of the Foundation's expectations and the person's potential; provide recognition of achievements; communicate openly and freely with one another; and provide a working environment that promotes work-related growth and development and that fosters employee health and well-being.

# III. Goals and Priorities: Fiscal Years 1998 through 2002

## Goal 1: Fundraising

*Maximize private sector support for Indiana University, guided by the priorities of Indiana University and complying with donor intent.*

### 1.1 Total Gift Income

From the base year, 1995–96, increase the three-year moving average of gift income 50 percent by 2002.

### 1.2 Major Donors

Increase the number of major donors to 300 in FY 1998, 325 in FY 1999, and 350 in FY 2000.

### 1.3 Planned Giving

Complete 25 planned giving instruments per year, per planned giving officer, for a total of 150 gifts in 1997–98, 175 gifts in 1998–99, and 200 gifts in 1999–2000. Also, realize 120 bequests in 1997–98, 130 in 1998–99, and 140 in 1999–2000, for the total University development effort.

### 1.4 Annual Giving

Increase the three-year moving average of all annual gifts via best practices by 2,800 donors in 1998, 2,950 in 1999, and 3,100 in 2000, a 5 percent increase each year.

### 1.5 Alumni Giving

**1.5.1 Loyalty Migration:** Increase the five-year moving average of loyal alumni by 8.8 percent in 1999 and 8.2 percent in 2000. (Loyal alumni are defined as those who gave in either four or five of the last five years.)

**1.5.2 Retention** of alumni through continuous lifetime giving: Retain 65 percent of alumni who give in each of the next three years, generating $3.5 million 1998, $3.8 million in 1999 and $4.0 million in 2000.

### 1.6 Corporations and Foundations

Realize funding of 40 percent of proposals submitted.

### 1.7 IU Faculty

Continue to work with IU faculty in appropriate ways, respecting the academic culture and its sensitivities to the proper handling of the development process so as to instill confidence in the IUF and to maximize private support from the faculty in support of IU.

### 1.8  IU Students

Challenge each professor and dean at every school and program to increase participation in specific events.

### 1.9  Friends

From the base year 1995–96, in which contributions from friends totaled $18.9 million, increase the three-year moving average of friends' donations by $2.0 million in 1998, $2.5 million in 1999 and $3.0 million in 2000.

**1.9.1**  Develop targeted programs aimed at specific friend segments, both to acquire new donors and cultivate ongoing relationships with the University.

### 1.10  Best Practices Partnership

Capture and institutionalize best practices that can be used broadly with all campus and degree programs.

**1.10.1**  Implement the Comprehensive Integrated Development Program (CIDP) begun in 1996.

### 1.11  Volunteers

Work with the campuses and schools to engage 900 more individuals who are actively involved in fundraising on their behalf. Further educate, engage in service, and staff a volunteer support group for the Foundation of 100 individuals actively involved in fundraising, and maintain this level of volunteerism going forward.

### 1.12  Contact Management

Develop appropriate and effective contacts to maintain a continuous lifetime giving program.

## Goal 2: Investment Management

*Preserve and enhance the real purchasing power of contributions, and provide the University with a stable and growing source of income.*

**2.1**  Achieve, within acceptable risk levels, an average total return that meets or exceeds the sums of the Foundation's spending (distribution) rate, plus the inflation rate, plus the investment management and related fees over a long period of time.

## Goal 3: Financial Stability

*Develop operating fund resources sufficient to achieve the goals and objectives of the strategic plan; minimize the vagaries of changing conditions by identifying multiple, stable sources of income; provide an acceptable return on investment in fundraising; provide funding for future expenditures for technology, campaigns, facilities and related infrastructure, and other contingencies; and build trust and strengthen relationships with constituents by developing a funding structure that is fair and is perceived as fair, and that is consistent with good business practices.*

## Goal 4: Service and Compliance

*Offer exemplary service to our constituents while complying with all regulatory and other external requirements.*

**4.1**   Comply with or exceed mutually agreed upon expectations and requirements of outside agencies and of our constituents; Indiana University and its administrators, faculty, students, and staff; donors and prospects; our Board of Directors; other volunteers; and Foundation staff.

**4.1.1**   In coordination with IU, establish procedures to obtain documentation of compliance with donor intent for all transfers to IU.

**4.2**   Adhere to professional standards, monitor compliance with federal and other regulations, perform all business operations in a timely and accurate manner.

## Goal 5: Efficient and Effective Management of Resources

*Create and enhance internal programs and processes to add value to the Foundation's services and operations, increase efficiency and effectiveness, and further the mission and goals of the Foundation.*

**5.1**   **Technology**

The Foundation must provide superior technology services that support the achievement of the missions of the organization. New technology will be cost justified and proven. Information will be timely, accurate, easy to use, and easy to support. Services will be outsourced as appropriate.

**5.1.1**   Score the database annually with proven variables that can be leveraged to build targeted marketing programs.

**5.1.2**   Provide tools and training that enable quick and accurate analysis for prospective programs.

**5.1.3**  Continue to eliminate redundant systems and streamline processing throughout the Foundation and University.

## 5.2 Facilities

The Foundation will provide professional and functional work facilities that will support the staff in achieving the Foundation's goals. Buildings and grounds will be maintained in ways that support professionalism, quality, and security.

**5.2.1**  For both Bloomington and Indianapolis, renovate, expand, and/or build new facilities with adequate space to accommodate the Foundation's needs for the next 20 years.

**5.2.2**  Establish regular maintenance programs for buildings, grounds, and equipment.

**5.2.3**  Ensure correct ergonomics for all offices and workstations.

**5.2.4**  Develop a Facilities disaster plan.

**5.2.5**  Reorganize maintenance staff to prove more flexibility, cost efficiency, and security.

**5.2.6**  Implement a new purchasing and inventory policy.

**5.2.7**  Research and implement bar coding on outgoing mail where cost effective.

**5.2.8**  Fully implement records retention schedule.

## 5.3 Work Flow

The Foundation will periodically assess key processes to ensure that they meet all standards yet flow as efficiently as possible and accommodate current needs.

**5.3.1**  Conduct a review of all key processes and develop a timeline to evaluate and make appropriate adjustments to every key process over the next three years.

**5.3.2**  Implement a system-wide Acknowledgment/Receipt Process, which receipts/acknowledges gifts within 72 hours of deposit. Consider sending an annual contribution statement to donors.

**5.3.3**  Complete review of Gift Agreement or Account Agreement for 3,200 accounts.

**5.3.4**  Issue annual statement to donors for all endowment accounts on a timely basis, including a report from the unit on how the funds benefited IU, by fall 1998.

**5.3.5**  Automate gift processing for certain units at IU. Improve efficiency and accuracy of data-entry procedures.

**5.3.6**  Add capability of filing prospect tracking and contact reports electronically.

**5.3.7**  Continuously upgrade and refine systems available to users on Benefactor and Affinity.

## Goal 6: Organizational Development

*Continually evaluate the organization's environment and capabilities to assure its ability to meet its strategic goals and objectives. Align individual and organizational capabilities with the strategic mission and direction.*

**6.1**  Employment practices: Assess, diagnose, and develop practices that attract and retain superior employees.

**6.2**  Learning: Provide appropriate programs/systems for new and existing employees that focus on business and organizational knowledge, interpersonal proficiency, and the ability to analyze and solve problems.

**6.3**  Develop an organizational environment which will attract, develop, and retain managers and development professionals whose vision and values are aligned with the organization.

**6.4**  Communication: Assure that employees have continuous access to accurate and up-to-date information on matters related to their Foundation employment.

## Goal 7: Excellence

*Be recognized at the local, regional, and national levels for excellence and as a leader among peer organizations. Create strategic alliances to improve our ability to achieve our mission and goals.*

**7.1**  Rank in the top 3 percent of universities and colleges nationwide in total voluntary support.

**7.2**  Rank among the top 10 public universities in market value of endowment.

**7.3**  Plan professional volunteer service and other commitments in accordance with our information needs and plans for achieving our goals.

**7.4**  Benchmark against outstanding organizations in the public and private sector.

**7.5**  Create communications and activities that facilitate the achievement and recognition of the Foundation's goals and objectives.

In the appendices section of a strategic plan, you would elaborate on some but not all of the goals. Below is an example of more in-depth information provided for two of the goals in this plan.

## IV. Appendices

Appendices of the Foundation's strategic plan amplify discussions of the plan's goals and objectives. The number of each item in the Appendix corresponds to its objective number in the plan. Not every objective is discussed in the appendices.

## Objective 3: Financial Stability

- The Foundation's resources are all directed to maximizing private support for IU and providing the highest level of service to our constituents. These goals determine our requirements for resources, including expert staff, adequate facilities, and state-of-the-art technology.
- Guidelines and assumptions:

  Assets under management will grow to $1.1 billion by the end of our five-year planning period.

  The fee on the Long Term Pooled Fund is 1.32 percent as of July 1, 1997.

  The Development Services Fee from the University is not expected to grow by more than 2.5 percent per year.

  The Foundation will develop efficient key processes that will allow the organization to reduce expenditures in certain areas or accommodate 10 percent growth while maintaining growth in expenditures at the rate of inflation, which is assumed to be 4 percent over the planning period.

  Contributions will grow by 50 percent in five years.

  Effectiveness should be measured as a relationship between resources expended and returns achieved. Compare our effectiveness to both education-related and non-education-related institutions.

## Objective 6: Human Resources

Human Resources has a responsibility to assure value-added services to IUF's customers and employees utilizing fiscal common-sense. HR practices are to be incorporated into business strategy.

The employee dimension is defined in terms of employee attitude and organizational processes that affect employee attitudes (leadership, teamwork, communication, empowerment, shared values, treating with dignity).

### 6.1    Employment Practices

1. Assess, diagnose, and develop practices that attract and retain superior employees.

   - Analyze effectiveness of current search techniques by comparing recent hires and the search methods used to find the candidate.

   - Investigate alternative search approaches that have the potential for increasing the quality of the candidate pool and the diversity of that pool.

   - Work with hiring managers to design interview strategies that effectively identify candidates that can accomplish the strategic goals of the organization and work effectively in the IUF culture.

- Work with IUF managers to assist them with their future staffing needs in order to project and plan staffing costs and strategies.
- Review the total compensation program. Determine which components of the program are most important to our employees. Utilizing the employee benefit committee, identify key improvements to the program. Promote the total compensation program among employees as a retention tool.

2. Assure that job descriptions are clearly written and accurately summarize the duties and responsibilities of the job and are properly aligned with business strategy.
   - Increase flexibility and usage efficiency of the job descriptions by combining jobs wherever practical.

### 6.2  Learning

Provide appropriate program/systems for new and existing employees that focus on business and organizational knowledge, interpersonal proficiency, and the ability to analyze and solve problems.

- Continue the supervisor training programs with a more pronounced focus on the strategic plan and management's role in the success of the plan.
- Provide individual coaching and guidance to managers as needed. This practice must be a priority of the HR Director to maintain consistency with IUF HR practices.
- Devise ways for managers to share ideas and problems in a nonthreatening environment and learn from each other.
- Continue to facilitate meetings with secretaries and other employee groups that assist them with job enhancement strategies, problem-solving, and conflict resolution.
- Develop a skills/knowledge inventory of our employee base. Knowing which individuals possess the talent to work on specific problems can help minimize the need to hire outside talent.

### 6.3  Organizational Environment

1. Develop an organizational environment which will attract, develop, and retain managers and development professionals whose vision and values are aligned with the organization.
   - Identify key performers and hard to fill positions.
   - Design strategies for individuals and positions identified above that increase retention potential and the potential for filling key positions when needed.

- Design a succession plan that incorporates key performers into a long-range strategy of planning for replacement of key management positions and targeted projects (A/FIS in particular must be prepared with the correct talent for rapidly changing technical needs).

- Develop a horizontal progression plan for job rotation and transfer that assures the continuous development of technical and managerial skills for key employees.

- Maintain an interest inventory of our employee base to identify the projects they would like to work on and the skills they would like to develop.

2. Assist managers with the development of learning strategies for their employees that helps increase knowledge sharing and the application of that knowledge.

3. Assure that managers identify their key positions and then identify and develop the individuals targeted to fill those positions should they become vacant.

4. Investigate ways to enhance our reward systems to assure employees feel recognized for their efforts and years of dedication to IUF.

- Improve the service award program

- Continually look for ways to enhance the EOM program

- Investigate ways to recognize and reward community volunteer efforts

- Increase usage of the employee relations committee to identify efforts that the employees feel would be meaningful ways to recognize employee efforts

## 6.4 Communication

Assure that employees have continuous access to accurate and up-to-date information related to issues related to their IUF employment.

## SAMPLE STRATEGIC PLAN PROGRESS REPORT

# STRATEGIC PLAN: PROGRESS TOWARD GOALS AND OBJECTIVES IN FISCAL 1998–99

## INDIANA UNIVERSITY FOUNDATION
as of October 6, 1998

◆

*Action plans developed by the staff of the Indiana University Foundation in support of the goals and objectives established through the strategic planning process and approved by the Foundation's Board of Directors on June 12, 1998*

## GOAL 1: FUNDRAISING.

| Goal | Obj. | Dept. or Program | Staff | Action Plans | Time Frame | Budget | Progress/Evaluation |
|---|---|---|---|---|---|---|---|
| 1 | 1 | Maximize private sector support for Indiana University, guided by the priorities of IU and complying with donor intent. Total gift income: From the base year, 1995–96, increase the three-year moving average of gift income by 50 percent by 2002. | | | | | |
| 1 | 1 | President | Simic | Work with a select group of major gift donors and prospective donors | 7/1/98–6/30/99 | | 1996–97 116,422,088 1997–98 139,210,524 19.57 percent increase in 1st year |
| 1 | 1 | VP Development | Dove | Increase private support 50 percent over five-year period | 7/1/97–6/30/02 | | |
| 1 | 1 | Endowment Campaign | Dove | Complete campaign successfully by 6/30/00 | 6/30/00 | | $297,041,791 toward $350,000,000 goal (84.9 percent) as of 8/98 (69.4 percent of the timeline.) |
| 1 | 1 | VP Development | Hardwick | Campaign for IUPUI campus | | | |
| 1 | 1 | Special Gifts & Annual Giving Programs | Madvig | 1. Bring together staff to form new office of Special Gifts & Annual Giving Programs | 7/1/98 | $0.00 | Complete |
| | | | | 2. Provide staff opportunities to brainstorm and implement new initiatives that will encourage continuous lifetime giving, and form the nucleus necessary to identify and cultivate the next generation of major gift prospects | 12/31/98 | $0.00 | Ongoing |
| | | | | 3. Provide support and advice to each program within the department, ensuring present and future success | 7/1/98 | $0.00 | Ongoing |
| 1 | 1 | Well House Society | Muehling, Bomba | 1. Market New Under 40 level. | 7/1/98 | $5,000.00 | Complete |

| | | | | | | | |
|---|---|---|---|---|---|---|---|
| 1 | 1 | Well House Society | Muehling, St. John | 1. Concentrate additional energies on integrating support for the arts and academics into the Well House Society. | 9/1/98 | $3,000.00 | Ongoing |
| 1 | 1 | Class Campaigns Program | Stuckey, Ellis | 1. Use Fiscal Year '98 successes as challenge/benchmark for upcoming classes. | 6/30/99 | $0.00 | Ongoing |
| 1 | 1 | Parent/Student Programs | Madvig, Rogers, Ingersoll | 1. Raise funds for Armstrong Stadium renovation and Armstrong Student Foundation Endowment in Bill Armstrong's memory. | 12/31/98 | $5,000.00 | Ongoing |
| 1 | 1 | Regional Campus Services | Lindauer | Increase regional campus development officers' knowledge of and use of IUF resources (i.e., the Major and Planned Giving Office, the Department of Research, the Corporate and Foundation Relations Office, the Prospect Management Program, etc.) | 6/30/99 | $0.00 | Ongoing |
| 1 | 1 | Regional Campus Services | Dove | Conduct campaign for Danielson Center in New Castle for IU-East | 6/1/98–12/31/98 | $0.00 | Goal Met |
| 1 | 1 | Regional Campus Services | Dove | Conduct market survey for IU-Southeast | 11/1/98–3/31/99 | $0.00 | |
| 1 | 1 | Student Foundation | Rogers | Identify plan for renovation of the Armstrong Stadium<br>1. Work with proper university officials to identify all needs<br>2. Develop time schedule to meet 50th running celebration | 6/30/99 | | |

# GOAL 1: FUNDRAISING, Cont'd.

| Goal | Obj. | Dept. or Program | Staff | Action Plans | Time Frame | Budget | Progress/Evaluation |
|------|------|------------------|-------|--------------|------------|--------|---------------------|
| 1 | 2 | Major donors: Increase the number of major donors to 300 in FY 1998, 325 in 1999, and 350 in FY 2000. | | | | | |
| 1 | 2 | Student Foundation | Rogers | Develop strategy for the Armstrong Endowment<br>1. Identify key members for steering committee<br>2. Identify major donors for plan<br>3. Develop plan for participation of past steering committees<br>4. Develop plan for participation of past riders<br>5. Work with athletics for proper recognition of soccer program | Spring 1999 | | |
| 1 | 2 | Dev. Services | <br><br><br><br><br>Wilson, K.<br>Wilson, K.<br><br><br>Wilson, K. | Establish and formalize policies and procedures for regular reporting to donors of endowed funds account balances, use of funds, identity of recipients, and other such information as may be requested by Development Services and donors.<br>1. Develop a donor statement acceptable to Sr. Management<br>2. Create cover letter for statements<br>3. Create proposal for Sr. Management; e.g., how many will be mailed, what will the package look like, what units do not want to mail, etc. | <br><br><br><br><br>12/98<br>2/99<br><br><br>6/99 | | <br><br><br><br><br>in process<br>not yet started<br><br><br>not yet started |
| 1 | 2 | Dev. Services | Wilson, K. | Actively encourage and assist in identification and carrying out of stewardship activities within units, with particular emphasis on donors of endowed scholarships, lectureships, professorships and chairs. Follow-up interviews. | 6/2000 | | in review process |

| | | | | | | |
|---|---|---|---|---|---|---|
| 1 | 2 | Dev. Services | | Identify ways to promote stewardship messages to large numbers of donors to augment those of the IUF Annual Report and individual unit reports to donors | | |
| | | | Wilson, K. | 1. Identify possibilities | 12/98 | |
| | | | Wilson, K. | 2. Document, test and implement plan(s) in consultation with others | 12/2000 | |
| 1 | 2 | Dev. Services | | Establish and implement policies and procedures for a "moves management" program working closely with milestones committee | | |
| | | | Wilson, K. | 1. Determine PMP "Moves Mgmt" needs based on current goal(s) of milestones cmte. | 2/99 | in process |
| | | | Wilson, K. | 2. Document desired enhancements of current PMP reports to meet policy and provide to programmers. | 3/99 | in process |
| | | | Wilson, K. | 3. Test reports with key development officers. | | |
| | | | Wilson, K. | 4. Roll out policies, procedures, implementation plan to Sr. Mgmt then to development officers. | 6/99 | not yet started |
| | | | Wilson, K. | | 9/99 | not yet started |
| 1 | 2 | IUPUI Campaign | IUPUI Campaign | 1. Prepare for the market survey for the comprehensive campaign for IUPUI.<br>• Work with the schools/units to develop priorities and goals into case statements to be tested in the Grenzebach Glier market survey and follow-up interviews.<br>• Work with the schools/units to develop the prospect list for the market survey.<br>• Work with IUPUI administration to develop a concise campaign prospectus which defines campus projects, states campus priorities, and summarizes the themes of the school/unit case statements. | 6/98–9/98 | $671,143 |

## GOAL 1: FUNDRAISING, Cont'd.

| Goal | Obj. | Dept. or Program | Staff | Action Plans | Time Frame | Budget | Progress/Evaluation |
|---|---|---|---|---|---|---|---|
| 1 | 2 | IUPUI Campaign | IUPUI Campaign | 2. Work with Grenzebach Glier as they conduct the market survey for the comprehensive campaign for IUPUI.<br>• Prepare and send letters to all prospects introducing the market survey and requesting the interview.<br>• Schedule appointments with interview prospects for Grenzebach Glier.<br>• Prepare and send follow-up letters and gifts to all interviewees.<br>• Provide other assistance, as appropriate. | 10/98–1/99 | | |
| | | | | 3. Review report from Grenzebach Glier market survey and facilitate dissemination of the findings to the campus. | 1/99 | | |
| | | | | 4. Conduct follow-up interviews to supplement the Grenzebach Glier market survey and to provide additional, more detailed market information to the schools/units. | 2/99–4/99 | | |
| 1 | 2 | IUPUI Campaign | Sloan, McGuffey Hardwick | 1. Develop a formal campaign plan.<br>2. Working with campus administration, campus development staff, and IUF staff, initiate the silent phase of the IUPUI comprehensive campaign. | 2/99–3/99<br>3/99 | | |
| | | | | 3. Develop campaign theme/logo.<br>4. Begin development of campaign marketing materials. | 2/99<br>3/99 | | |
| 1 | 2 | School of Law, Indianapolis | Jones | 1. Work with the School of Law on the completion of their capital campaign. | Ongoing | | |
| 1 | 2 | Herron School of Art | Cornacchione | 1. Work with the Herron School of Art on the silent phase of their capital campaign. | Ongoing | | |

| | | | | | Date | Status |
|---|---|---|---|---|---|---|
| 1 | 3 | | Planned Giving: Complete 25 planned giving instruments per year, per planned gift officer, for a total of 175 gifts in 1998–99, and 200 in 1999–2000. Also, realize 130 bequests in 1998–99, and 140 in 1999–2000, for the total University development effort. | | | |
| 1 | 3 | Dev. Services | Establish and formalize policies and procedures for regular reporting to donors of endowed funds account balances, use of funds, identity of recipients, and other such information as may be requested by Development Services and donors. | | | |
| | | | 1. Develop a donor statement acceptable to Sr. Management | Wilson, K. | 12/98 | in process |
| | | | 2. Create cover letter for statements | Wilson, K. | 2/99 | not yet started |
| | | | 3. Create proposal for Sr. Management, e.g., how many will be mailed, what will the package look like, what units do not want to mail, etc. | Wilson, K. | 6/99 | not yet started |
| 1 | 3 | Dev. Services | Actively encourage and assist in identification and carrying out of stewardship activities within units, with particular emphasis on donors of endowed scholarships, lectureships, professorships and chairs. | Wilson, K. | 6/2000 | in review process |
| 1 | 3 | Dev. Services | Identify ways to promote stewardship messages to large numbers of donors to augment those of the IUF Annual Report and individual unit reports to donors. | | | |
| | | | 1. Identify possibilities | Wilson, K. | 12/98 | in process |
| | | | 2. Document, test and implement plan(s) in consultation with others | Wilson, K. | 12/2000 | not yet started |
| 1 | 3 | Major Gifts | Develop a strategic plan for major gifts. | Spears | 4/30/99 | |

## GOAL 1: FUNDRAISING, Cont'd.

| Goal | Obj. | Dept. or Program | Staff | Action Plans | Time Frame | Budget | Progress/Evaluation |
|------|------|------------------|-------|--------------|------------|--------|---------------------|
| 1 | 3 | Planned Gifts | Spears | Identify new and solicit existing planned giving prospects. | | | |
| | | | | 1. Provide ongoing assistance to development staff with individual planned giving prospects. | Ongoing | | |
| | | | | 2. Identify and meet with existing donors to show them new planned giving calculations and solicit additional gifts. | 12/31/98 | | |
| | | | | 3. Begin annual effort to upgrade selected bequest donors by cultivating them for a life-income gift. | 12/31/98 | | |
| | | | | 4. In cooperation with Class Campaigns, approach appropriate members of classes celebrating their reunions to identify prospects for planned gifts. | 6/30/99 | | |
| | | | | 5. In cooperation with prospect research, identify a minimum of 200 new planned giving prospects each year. | Ongoing | | |
| 1 | 3 | Planned Gifts | Spears | Establish a strong marketing effort to promote Planned Giving. | | | |
| | | | | 1. Draft planned giving advertisements and articles for existing development newsletters, publications and alumni magazines. | 12/31/98 | | |
| | | | | 2. Develop a marketing brochure which includes testimonials from current planned giving donors. | 4/30/99 | | |
| | | | | 3. Develop our own planned giving newsletter which will be sent at least three times a year to a targeted group of prospects and donors. | 12/31/98 | | |
| | | | | 4. Revise "Guide to Giving" and "Gifts of Retirement Plan" brochures for general use. | 6/30/99 | | |

5. Mailings

a. Segment the database to identify a targeted population of donors who have made annual gifts of $100 or more for three consecutive years to receive planned giving mailings. — 12/31/98

b. Segment the database to send our planned giving newsletter to prospects and donors age 65 and above. — 6/30/99

c. Begin an annual mailing to select donors or prospects age 75 or older to provide information on charitable gift annuities. — 4/30/99

d. Begin an annual mailing targeted to donors 45–60 years old for a deferred gift annuity. — 4/30/99

e. Identify all donors who have cumulatively given $5,000 or more to the Foundation to receive planned giving information. — 4/30/99

f. At year-end send a letter soliciting stock gifts from existing donors who have made a gift of stock in the past five years or have cumulative gifts of at least $2,000. — 12/31/98

6. Events

a. Annually, host seminars for IU faculty. Focus will be on pre-retirement planning, retirement planning, and financial planning, to inform the faculty and motivate those who are capable of making a planned gift. — 2/28/99

b. In conjunction with our out-of-town Board meeting, conduct a seminar on planned giving opportunities for prospects, donors, friends, and alums living in that area. — 03/31/99

c. Host annual Arbutus Society recognition event. — 06/30/99

## GOAL 1: FUNDRAISING, Cont'd.

| Goal | Obj. | Dept. or Program | Staff | Action Plans | Time Frame | Budget | Progress/Evaluation |
|------|------|------------------|-------|--------------|------------|--------|---------------------|
| 1 | 3 | Planned Gifts | Spears | Raise the visibility of the Planned Giving Program internally and externally. | | | |
| | | | | 1. For internal constituents. | | | |
| | | | | a. Educate development officers about trends in planned giving so that they are comfortable in presenting planned giving options to donors and prospects. | Ongoing | | |
| | | | | b. Educate and train researchers, tele-fund callers, annual fund staff, and Class Campaigns staff to identify planned giving prospects. | 6/30/99 | | |
| | | | | c. Assign Planned Giving Services staff members to serve as the liaison to specific units. | 6/30/99 | | |
| | | | | d. Develop planned giving strategies for each academic unit and regional campus. | 12/31/98 | | |
| | | | | 2. For external constituents. | | | |
| | | | | a. Continue mailings of newsletter to representatives of the banking, fi-nancial, and legal communities. In-stitute personal follow-up with those who request additional information from response cards. | 12/31/98 | | |
| | | | | b. Create professional advisory com-mittees in Bloomington, Indianapo-lis, and each regional campus to assist in marketing planned gifts. | 6/30/99 | | |
| | | | | c. Create professional advisory com-mittees in those areas with large concentrations of IU alumni, includ-ing Chicago, Florida, and the East and West Coasts. | 12/31/99 | | |

| | | Program | Strategy/Action | Date | Amount | Status |
|---|---|---|---|---|---|---|
| | | | 3. Conduct an Annual Charitable Gift Planning, Estate Planning, and Financial Planning Seminar for donors and prospects. | 4/30/99 | | |
| | | | 4. Conduct Annual Continuing Education Seminars focusing on charitable giving for professionals. One held in Indianapolis and one held in Bloomington. | 4/30/99 | | |
| | | | 5. Host two receptions per year for outside professionals to educate them about the organization and foster social interaction. | 12/31/98 | | |
| 1 | 4 | Annual Giving: Increase the three-year moving average of all annual gifts via best practices by 2,950 donors in 1999 and 3,100 in 2000, a 5 percent increase each year. | | | | |
| 1 | 4 | Parents Fund Program | Rogers, Ingersoll | | | |
| | | | 1. Change Solicitation Cycle to Fall. | 8/1/98 | $0.00 | Complete |
| | | | 2. Work with IU to find alternate ways to get parent phone numbers. | 6/30/99 | $0.00 | Ongoing |
| 1 | 4 | Special Gifts & Annual Giving Programs, Annual Giving: Telefund | Madvig, Lindauer | | | |
| | | | 1. Enter affiliation/activity codes for all IU graduates of 180 and after. Use Statistician's input to assist in determining additional target pools. | 12/31/98 | $5,000.00 | Project is 60 percent complete as of 9/30/98. |
| | | | 2. Test three target pools: Residence Hall Association, Singing Hoosiers and IU Student Foundation Steering Committee. | 6/30/99 | $0.00 | Calling to these segments will commence in the Spring of '99. |
| | | | 3. Plan and implement quarterly phone look-ups. | 9/1/98 | $28,000.00 | Complete |
| 1 | 4 | Special Gifts & Annual Giving Programs, Annual Giving: Direct Mail | Madvig, Higgins | | | |
| | | | 1. Segment currently planned mailings additionally. | 8/1/98 | $0.00 | Complete |
| | | | 2. Use Kearney Report and Statistician to target new donor acquisition pools. | 6/30/99 | $0.00 | Ongoing |

## GOAL 1: FUNDRAISING, Cont'd.

| Goal | Obj. | Dept. or Program | Staff | Action Plans | Time Frame | Budget | Progress/Evaluation |
|------|------|------------------|-------|--------------|-----------|--------|---------------------|
| 1 | 4 | Regional Campus Services | Lindauer | Integrate regional campuses into the centralized annual giving program, leaving development officers free to focus on major gifts and other activities. | 3/31/99 | $0.00 | Ongoing |
| 1 | 4 | Annual Giving-IUPUI | Bosch | Develop and implement a Direct Mail program with the schools of the IUPUI campus. | 6/31/99 | $11,000 | |
| 1 | 4 | Annual Giving-IUPUI | Bosch | Chancellor's Circle: Hold three cultivation events for this major donor's group and increase membership from 43 to 65 | 6/31/99 | | |
| 1 | 4 | Annual Giving-IUPUI | Bosch | Campus Campaign: Duplicate procedures from the 1998 campaign while enhancing promotion techniques. Increase dollar return by 10 percent over 1998 and number of donors by 5 percent. | 1/99–5/99 | $2,148 | |

## GOAL 2: INVESTMENT MANAGEMENT.

| Goal | Obj. | Dept. or Program | Staff | Action Plans | Time Frame | Budget | Progress/Evaluation |
|------|------|------------------|-------|--------------|------------|--------|---------------------|
| 2 | | | | Preserve and enhance the real purchasing power of contributions, and provide the University with a stable and growing source of income. | | | |
| 2 | 1 | | | Achieve, within acceptable risk levels, an average total return that meets or exceeds the sum of the Foundation's spending (distribution) rate, plus the investment management and related fees over a long period of time. | | | |
| 2 | 1 | Investments | Koon | Review alternative investment classes for possible inclusion in the endowment portfolio | 6/30/99 | | |
| 2 | 1 | Investments | Stratten | | 6/30/99 | | |
| 2 | 1 | Real Estate | Koon Stratten | Review and recommend necessary changes to streamline and increase returns in the management of daily cash balances | 12/31/98 | | |
| | | | Koon | Complete process to replace Director of Real Estate | | | |

## GOAL 3: FINANCIAL STABILITY.

| Goal | Obj. | Dept. or Program | Staff | Action Plans | Time Frame | Budget | Progress/Evaluation |
|---|---|---|---|---|---|---|---|
| 3 | | President | Simic | Ensure the long-term financial stability of the Foundation, including an operating endowment | | | |
| 3 | | FINANCE | Claflin | 1. Continue benchmarking with Big Ten/Big Twelve/PacTen Universities to develop best practices. | Ongoing | | Meet regularly with peer group (University Financial Officers [UFO]). |
| | | | | 2. Work with CASE to develop set of three standard surveys. | 1999 | | UFO group will develop surveys on a one year test basis. IUF's share of cost will be approximately $500—paid to CASE. |
| | | | | 3. Continue working with FASB and GASB to develop reporting guidelines that favorably and fairly present Foundation's financial position. | 1999 and ongoing | | Have been in close contact with FASB representative who is drafting regulation. |
| 3 | | FINANCE | Claflin/Kerstiens | 4. Develop 5 year budget models that provide for contingency plans should revenue sources fall short of projections. | 1999 | | |
| 3 | | FINANCE | Kerstiens | 1. Work with IDFA and Bond Counsel to issue second series of tax exempt bonds for the construction of an IUPUI facility. | 2000 | | |

## SAMPLE MARKET SURVEY MATERIALS
## (FACE-TO-FACE AND DIRECT MAIL)

**INDIANA UNIVERSITY BLOOMINGTON**
**ENDOWMENT CAMPAIGN**

# FACE-TO-FACE
# MARKET SURVEY QUESTIONNAIRE

Before we address the questions in this survey, what association, if any, have you had with Indiana University Bloomington?

Over what period of time?

Has your association been satisfactory (pleasing)?

Who is your closest contact at Indiana University Bloomington?

When do you have occasion to see this person?

When did you last have a conversation with him or her?

1. When you think about the future of Indiana University Bloomington, how interested and concerned are you about its welfare?

   ( ) Very interested

   ( ) Somewhat interested

   ( ) A little interested

   ( ) Not at all interested

2. Compared to others you know who are associated with Indiana University Bloomington, how knowledgeable do you think you are about the University as a whole?

   ( ) Much more knowledgeable

   ( ) Somewhat more knowledgeable

   ( ) About as knowledgeable as most people I know

   ( ) Somewhat less knowledgeable

   ( ) Much less knowledgeable

3a. Regardless of how much or how little you actually know about Indiana University Bloomington, please give me your impression of each of the following.

| | Excellent | Good | Fair | Poor | No Impression |
|---|---|---|---|---|---|
| A. The quality of IUB's faculty | | | | | |
| B. The overall academic quality of IUB | | | | | |
| C. The performance of the current president | | | | | |
| D. The general quality of IUB's administrators | | | | | |
| E. The quality of IUB's fundraising program | | | | | |
| F. How does IUB rank with other universities in the Midwest? | | | | | |
| G. How does IUB rank with other universities in the United States? | | | | | |

3b. What area(s) stand out among its greatest strengths?

3c. What area(s) need improvement?

4. I would like to suggest some different ideas others have expressed. For each one, please indicate how much you agree or disagree.

|  | Agree Strongly | Agree Somewhat | Disagree Somewhat | Disagree Strongly |
|---|---|---|---|---|
| A. Unless IUB receives endowment funds, it will not be possible to maintain its standard of excellence |  |  |  |  |
| B. Private funding is critical to meeting IUB's endowment goals |  |  |  |  |
| C. Above all else, IUB's excellence depends upon the quality of its faculty |  |  |  |  |
| D. It's up to the State of Indiana to provide most of the funding for building improvements at IUB |  |  |  |  |
| E. Matching funds are important in encouraging private support |  |  |  |  |
| F. Today, even private universities are very dependent upon government funding |  |  |  |  |

5.  The University has set forth seven major areas of proposed improvements. Please tell me how important you consider each of the following proposed campaign projects at Indiana University Bloomington.

| | Essential | Important but not Essential | Somewhat Important | Not Important |
|---|---|---|---|---|
| Faculty Support | | | | |
| Student Support | | | | |
| Library | | | | |
| Technology | | | | |
| Special Programs | | | | |
| Executive Education Center | | | | |
| Discretionary Funds | | | | |

6.  Now, please indicate which you think deserves top priority, second priority, and third priority in the allocation of funds.

| |
|---|
| Faculty Support |
| Student Support |
| Library |
| Technology |
| Special Programs |
| Executive Education Center |
| Discrete Funds |

1. _____

2. _____

3. _____

7.  Are there any other campus needs and goals (not included in question 5) that you consider important?

( ) Yes    ( ) No

If yes, what?  _____

_____

_____

8a.  In order to accomplish the goal outlined, private funds totaling approximately $224 million will be needed over the next three to five years. Please refer to the Table of Gifts which allows the number and size of gifts that are needed to meet these goals.

**TABLE OF GIFTS NEEDED TO RAISE $224 MILLION.**

| Size of Gift | Number Needed | Total |
|---|---|---|
| $25,000,000 | 1 | $25,000,000 |
| $15,000,000 | 1 | $15,000,000 |
| $10,000,000 | 3 | $30,000,000 |
| $5,000,000 | 7 | $35,000,000 |
| $2,500,000 | 10 | $25,000,000 |
| $1,000,000 | 25 | $25,000,000 |
| $500,000 | 50 | $25,000,000 |
| $100,000 | 100 | $10,000,000 |
| $50,000 | 250 | $12,500,000 |
| Under $50,000,000 | Many | $9,250,000 |

8b.  Do you consider this configuration of gifts to be feasible?

( ) Yes (Skip to 9a)     ( ) No (Skip to 8c)     ( ) Don't know (Skip to 9a)

8c.  What is the *main* reason you feel that way? (Please check only one)

1. _____ Because the dollar amount of the top gift levels is too high.

2. _____ Because the dollar amount of most of the gift levels is too high.

3. _____ Because the number of gifts required at the top gift levels is too high.

4. _____ Because the number of gifts required at each level is too high.

5. _____ Some other reason (Please explain): _____

_____

_____

_____

_____

8d. If no, then what dollar goal would you consider to be realistic?


9a. Do you think there are any reasons why Indiana University Bloomington *should not* undertake a major capital fundraising campaign at this time?

( ) Yes  ( ) No


9b. Please tell me the reason:


10. Are there other major fundraising campaigns that are currently vying for your support? If yes, what are they?

( ) Yes  ( ) No

( )  A fundraising campaign for another college or university

(If so, which one(s)?) _____

_____

_____

( )  A fundraising campaign for a medical center or hospital

(If so, which one(s)?) _____

_____

_____

( )  A campaign for an arts organization (If so, which one(s)?)

_____

_____

_____

( )  Some other type of campaign? Please describe:_____

_____

_____

_____

11. People have many different reasons for wanting to work for or make a significant financial contribution to a capital campaign. Which of the reasons listed below would provide the *strongest motivation(s)* for you personally to participate in such a campaign for Indiana University Bloomington?

    (   )    Loyalty to Indiana University Bloomington

    (   )    Well-documented needs and rationale

    (   )    Recognition for myself or another person I wish to honor

    (   )    Being part of a prestigious leadership group

    (   )    Being able to make an anonymous gift

    (   )    Having input in the setting of goals

    (   )    Having a major responsibility in the campaign

    (   )    Having a limited responsibility in the campaign

    (   )    Indiana University Bloomington's reputation as an educational institution

    (   )    Income tax considerations

    (   )    Some other reason, please describe: '

    (   )    I probably would not be motivated to participate in a campaign for Indiana University Bloomington.

12. Were Indiana University Bloomington to launch a campaign, who would make a good volunteer chair for this effort? _____

_____

13. If asked, would you personally consider taking a leadership position in the campaign?

    (   ) Yes    (   ) No

14. Have you ever participated in any way in a major capital fundraising campaign for a non-profit organization?

    (   ) Yes    (   ) No

15. Do you know any individuals or organizations who you believe might be willing to make a contribution of $50,000 or more?

( ) Yes ( ) No

NAME                                    NAME

_____        _____

_____        _____

_____        _____

16a. While I am not here to present a solicitation proposal today, some sense of our own participation in this project is important to our study. If properly approached, would you personally consider making a significant contribution to Indiana University Bloomington?

( ) Yes (Ask 16b)        ( ) No        ( ) Don't know

16b. If you would, could you tell me where on the gift range chart you might fall?

17. Do you personally have ties to any corporations or foundations that might be willing to support a campaign for Indiana University Bloomington?

( ) Yes ( ) No (Please skip to question 18)

Corporation/Foundation          My relation to it is:

_____        _____

_____        _____

_____        _____

18. Do you have any specific suggestions to offer regarding any aspect of Indiana University Bloomington that we have not already discussed which you feel would assist us in preparing our report for IUB?

# DIRECT MAIL SURVEY #1
## Letter

INDIANA UNIVERSITY

March 10, 1995

THE PRESIDENT'S
OFFICE

Dear Friend:

You are among a select group of leading alumni and friends who are being asked to give your candid opinion, on a confidential basis, about our plans for achieving Indiana University-Bloomington's goals over the next five years.

All of the goals outlined in the enclosed brochure are aimed at ensuring IUB's strength in many diverse disciplines—the strengths that make the Bloomington campus such a tremendous resource to the state, the nation, and the world.

In order to ensure our ability to meet the needs of our constituents, we need to enhance our permanent, stable base of support—*the endowment*. Increased endowment in the areas of faculty support and student aid, for both graduates and undergraduates, is required in addition to endowment support for our libraries. Support for special programs, technology enhancement, the Art Museum, and the creation of an Executive Education Center is also being considered.

Estimates of the funds required to achieve these objectives are included; together they total approximately $224 million, an amount that must be raised entirely from private sources. We are preparing to undertake an ambitious capital campaign to reinforce IU-Bloomington's traditions of excellence and service to society.

I would appreciate it if you took the time to answer the questions in the enclosed booklet regarding Indiana University-Bloomington. The information you provide will be helpful to me as a means of measuring potential participation in a campaign for the Bloomington campus.

Part One of the survey, to be returned to the IUB Survey Research Center, is designed to elicit your opinions about the campus, its needs and its priorities. Please return Part One to the Survey Research Center in the prepaid envelope that accompanies it. The Survey Research Center will tabulate the data and prepare statistical summaries only. Their procedures ensure absolute anonymity, so that no one will ever know who said what on Part One.

Part Two is a brief supplement to the survey. Any information you can provide will be helpful to me and my campaign planning counsel as a means of measuring potential participation in a campaign for Indiana University-Bloomington. A separate prepaid envelope, addressed to me, is included for Part Two of the survey. Please be assured that we will hold any information you provide in Part Two in the strictest confidence.

Bryan Hall 200
Bloomington, Indiana
47405–1201

(812) 855–4613
Fax (812) 855–9586

I am very grateful for your interest and help.

Sincerely yours,

Myles Brand
President

Preliminary Case Statement

# THE FACES OF INDIANA UNIVERSITY: AN ENDOWMENT CAMPAIGN FOR THE BLOOMINGTON CAMPUS

## INDIANA UNIVERSITY, BLOOMINGTON
### January 1995

# Introduction

In his book, *Being Lucky,* Herman B Wells wrote:

*"A university can be distinguished only as its faculty is distinguished. . . ."*

Dr. Wells' vision contains a great truth: *It is the people of Indiana University that create this distinguished institution, whether they are first-rate faculty, bright graduate students, or sought-after undergraduates.* Indiana University has been such an institution for a very long time.

Indiana has always done more with less. It is quite remarkable—given limited funding—to see what Indiana University has achieved. For example, in recent years the *Gourman Report* (an objective, comprehensive rating of American universities) ranked 26 departments of the College of Arts and Sciences in the top 20 nationally. The School of Music has been ranked number one consistently in four independent surveys over a 20-year period, and *Business Week* places the School of Business seventh in the country. One of the ten best university art museums in the U.S. is right here, as is the thirteenth best university research library in all of the U.S. and Canada. The Schools of Journalism; Education; Library and Information Science; Public and Environmental Affairs; Law; Optometry; and Health, Physical Education and Recreation—all have programs that are among the best in the country in their respective disciplines. Their quality, and what they can do for their students, is increasingly threatened as resources become more scarce.

Indeed, while some surveys place IU in favorable company, others do not. The latest reports also show that faculty salaries, graduate student stipends, and student/faculty ratios at IU have all drifted to the bottom of the Big Ten. Dr. Wells also stated:

*". . . So keen is the competition everywhere for outstanding faculty that they are difficult to secure, even for institutions with adequate resources; but for institutions such as ours, with limited revenues, the problem is unusually acute."*

The same is true for outstanding graduate students and undergraduates. In this competition with some of the best universities in the nation, we are losing as often as we are winning.

The State of Indiana has been generous within its means. In the 1950s it provided IU Bloomington with more than 50 percent of its total budget. Today, *only 26 percent* comes from the state. This change reflects the growing pressure our legislators and state leaders are under to meet other state needs in health care, social services, the schools, and the criminal justice system.

*IU is no longer a state-supported university. Now, at best, it is a state-assisted university.* It is clear: as we look to the future, we cannot build our strategy for shaping an even greater Indiana University by relying primarily on state support.

Indiana University must supplement fluctuating and uncertain funding with a steadier source of income. As Dr. Wells observed,

*"Peaks of excellence are provided typically by private money."*

The program that now bears his name stands out as an example of how *private endowments* can affect the academic quality of the University. The Wells Scholars Program, created and endowed through a successful fundraising campaign, brings 20 of the nation's best and brightest undergraduates each year to the Bloomington campus. These students have turned down full scholarships to universities such as Harvard, Yale, and Michigan. The high caliber of these young scholars, and the other talented students they attract, has had a positive influence on the entire student body.

*Endowments are among the best assets a university can use to build and maintain long-term quality. Endowments mean money invested for future growth, with only a portion of the return being used today. Investment returns that exceed the amount needed for distribution are reinvested to add to the growth of the fund. Endowments therefore provide stable, dependable sources of financial support, protected from the uncertainties of state funding, the economy, tuition, or other factors.* Endowment funds give the University the ability to retain and recruit great professors; to provide competitive stipends for the next generation of teacher/scholars—graduate students; to attract more undergraduates like the Wells Scholars; and to build strong library collections and furnish modern technology for these talented people to use.

By building Indiana University's endowment now, we seek to strengthen our ability to serve future generations of Hoosiers, as well as people across the country and around the world. IU's traditions, its history, its core values, all lead us to embrace and renew the University's strong commitment to the ideals of a *public* university: one that daily touches all our lives and helps all members of our community reach their potential.

*To realize fully all these possibilities, we seek your financial assistance. We propose to embark upon a $224 million endowment campaign—a campaign that is about people and the tools they need to succeed.* What follows are brief descriptions of the priority areas where funding is critical to the future well-being of our University.

## Faculty Support

Faculty are the heart of any great university. As teachers and mentors, in classrooms and through one-on-one projects, they guide students through the best that has been thought, said, written, and discovered. As scholars and artists, they help assure that knowledge and ideas live, grow, adapt.

State funds, which help pay faculty salaries and benefits, constitute a diminishing share of IU's support. To compensate, we turn to fundraising—and endowments.

Chairs and professorships are among the most important resources any university can have in assembling and maintaining a distinguished faculty. Such positions provide honor and recognition for the faculty members who hold them, of course. But they provide something more important: stable, dependable sources of income for special teaching and research materials, library acquisitions, salary supplements, and travel assistance, protected from the vicissitudes of state funding, the economy, fee income, or other factors. They are an insurance policy for our excellence.

Indiana University is lagging far behind its peers in establishing these valuable assets. IU has 19 faculty endowments with market values of $1 million or more. Among Big Ten schools alone, Michigan has nearly 100 such endowments; Minnesota has 223.

In appointing faculty to endowed positions, we seek to retain and recruit scholars, scientists, and artists who help set the standards in their disciplines. And we expect each to set another standard: distinction in research, distinction in teaching, and commitment to the University community.

*Goal: $84 million*

# Graduate Student Support

As a top public university in a higher education system that is the envy of the world, IU provides an incomparable range of resources to the state and country. This success is directly tied to our graduate programs (IU has more than any other institution in the state), and particularly to the interactions between students and faculty. Graduate students are the life force of academia and innovations for the future. They come here to assist faculty in research and teaching, bringing new and creative ideas. They help open doors of learning to thousands of undergraduate students; they participate in the discovery and dissemination of new knowledge.

Unfortunately for us, the competition for new graduate students, especially at the PhD level, is intense. Our stipends for fellowships, and teaching and research assistantships, just are not adequate to meet basic living expenses. The most promising graduate students will go to the universities that can offer them sufficient compensation to allow them to devote themselves entirely to study, research, and teaching. We cannot allow Indiana University to fall behind in its ability to attract the best and brightest graduate students, and thereby jeopardize our over-all strengths. The links are clear: outstanding faculty attract outstanding graduate students; both participate in the education of undergraduates.

*Goal: $29.5 million*

# Undergraduate Student Support

As the costs of higher education rise, more and more good students are forced to delay or abandon their degree goals, or take on very heavy debts. Over the past decade, as state funds have diminished, tuition increases have taken their place. At the same time, federal assistance for undergraduates has dramatically declined. Students increasingly must borrow to pay the costs of their schooling. Within the last six years, the loan portion of the typical student aid package has jumped from 49 percent to 70 percent. If these trends continue, we risk pricing students out of the education they deserve. When only prosperous families can afford higher education, we will have helped to create a permanent underclass that cannot add value to the economy of the future.

Endowed funds can provide scholarships to help undergraduates stay on a more productive track. These funds will be used especially for students who work part-time to finance their educations. Keeping these students enrolled at IU and making progress toward their degrees is important to the future of Indiana. The large majority of undergraduates, especially those already working, remain to pur-sue their careers in the states where they earn their degrees. Endowments can help IU students make better academic and career progress and help prevent a "brain drain" of the best young minds.

*Goal: $22.3 million*

# Libraries

When your purpose is acquiring, transmitting, and preserving knowledge, you can only be as good as your information source: your libraries. The success of our teach-ing, research, and service programs depends on outstanding library collections, high quality information services, and talented personnel. In a world exploding with information, the Libraries enrich learning and scholarship by bringing faculty and students in touch with the resources they need to answer questions, to solve problems. These capabilities are shared by thousands of individuals and businesses across Indiana and the nation, for whom the Libraries serve as a vital resource.

As one of the top teaching and research collections in the world, the Bloomington Libraries are recognized for distinguished holdings in many fields, innovative services, important participation in national cooperative programs, leadership in the use of technology, and valuable contributions to professional research. But this excellence is challenged by the escalating cost and diversity of information; the need to invest in new technology; the demand for librarians and staff with a wide variety of subject, language, and computer skills; and a requirement for modern facilities.

Endowments for the collections will enable the expanded purchase and preservation of books, journals, and the rich electronic resources so central to the work of students and faculty. Endowments for specialized librarian positions will make the Libraries more competitive in the recruitment and retention of experienced professionals and provide the resources to enhance their work. And support for technology equipment and electronic services will enhance dramatically the ability of our students and faculty to take advantage of extraordinary information opportunities.

*Goal: $8.5 million*

## Special Programs and General Endowments

Each school and department has unique needs that do not fit under a simple heading of faculty endowments, scholarships, or technology needs. Many schools have responded to their faculty or students by creating programs that meet a special need. For example, a program in the College of Arts and Sciences is attempting to prepare its students for the workplace by offering classes taught jointly by liberal arts and School of Business faculty.

Or the School of Education, which has created programs to foster new thinking in teacher education. Or the School of Health, Physical Education and Recreation, which is investigating new measures and improvement of human performance. Or the School of Library & Information Science, which hopes to build an observational laboratory to study how people interact with new technology. This is the type of creative programming that has marked Indiana University as a great university in the past. Endowments will ensure it continues.

*Goal: $25.65 million*

## Technology

Two things are certain about IU and technology. First, needs will increase as the role of technology increases and diversifies throughout society. Second, opportunities for students, faculty, and the public will also expand. Communication networks will bring enormous amounts of information to the student's or the professor's fingertips while carrying IU's vast resources to the public.

We must prepare our students for a world increasingly dominated by sophisticated information technologies. Information-seeking and information-management skills must become integral parts of our students' educations. Further, to maintain our prominence in teaching and research, the University must provide access to global networks that will enhance students' and faculty's learning.

For example, in the School of Journalism, students no longer can rely on a sharp pencil and a clean notebook. New communication equipment has reshaped the journalism major. Technology also has reshaped the future of the business student, for whom international communication may be a way of life. Interactive TV and distance learning equipment will be necessary to prepare these students, but it will not come cheaply—nor will the vital scientific equipment needed by students in the College of Arts and Sciences to perform relevant research.

But perhaps nowhere do we become more aware of technology's effect on academia than in the University library system. Electronically connecting IU students and faculty to the vast network of international databases is an exciting vision. And the IU Library System also serves all of the citizens of Indiana, and indeed the nation.

Efforts to create a technology environment are expensive. An interactive university requires major investments for classrooms, learning centers, and libraries.

*Goal: $26.5 million*

## IU Art Museum

Among the best university art museums in the country, this facility brings important international exhibitions, publications, and treasures of the global art community to the people of Indiana. A successful endowment campaign will help keep this jewel in the University's crown polished by supporting new acquisitions, conserving current holdings, planning educational programs, and mounting exhibits.

The excellence of the Museum staff, the quality and depth of the collections, and the leadership roles the staff have taken within the larger Museum community all attest to the Museum's level of excellence.

One of our faculty members recently wrote to the chair of the Museum's advisory board expressing sadness that we live in a time where so many people focus on the differences among human beings. He wrote that the Museum's collection "bears witness to the common desires that all people in all times have had to touch the eternal, to seek the beautiful, and to express their experience of this mystery we call life." This endowment would help us meet those aspirations, those desires.

*Goal: $10.8 million*

## Executive Education Center

As the IU School of Business extends its mission to include life-long partnership with business, it must dedicate more resources to serving the needs of practicing professionals. The Executive Education program was created to meet this need. Upper management professionals from national and international business come to the IU Bloomington campus 38 weeks a year. They participate in stimulating programs designed to refresh their educational background, learn how to work in teams, resolve conflict, increase productivity, discuss international business, and many other topics.

As the program has grown, so have housing, space, and technology needs. Currently, meeting and hotel space are relegated to wherever space allows in Bloomington or Indianapolis. Often, only outdated equipment is available in these hotel meeting rooms. To meet the growing demands of the program, the School proposes to renovate an existing building on the Bloomington campus. The new Executive Education Center would have 50 hotel rooms, office space for the staff, adequate meeting rooms, and state-of-the-art audio-visual equipment.

*Goal: $10 million*

## Chancellor's Initiatives

Organizations require discretionary funds to pursue new opportunities. Flexible resources free leaders to expand organizational reach or fund special one-time projects. IU faces these very demands. Circumstances arise after budgets are set. Urgent needs and great opportunities require immediate action.

As a public institution, IU operates with a fixed, two-year budget. Yet the campus chancellor must be able to move quickly and decisively when there is an opportunity to provide seed money for a promising program, to develop the interdisciplinary work which opens new fields of learning, to assist a new faculty member at the start of her career, to help a student through an emergency. The chancellor's fund will provide this vital flexibility.

*Goal: $7.5 million*

As the campaign proceeds, the University may discover other targets of opportunity as well. When possible, gifts will also be sought where specific donor interests coincide with special campus programs, such as the Indiana University Press and WFIU public radio.

## SUMMARY OF PRELIMINARY OBJECTIVES FOR A BLOOMINGTON CAMPUS CAMPAIGN BY UNIT AND PURPOSE (IN MILLIONS OF DOLLARS).

| | Faculty Support | Student Support | Library | Special Programs | Tech | Art Museum | Facilities | Unrestricted Funds | Total by Unit |
|---|---|---|---|---|---|---|---|---|---|
| Art Museum | | | | | | 10.8 | | | 10.8 |
| Business | 24.3 | 6.0 | | 4.0 | 7.0 | | 10.0 | | 51.3 |
| Chanc.'s Fund | | | | | | | | 7.5 | 7.5 |
| College of Arts & Sciences | 25.0 | 11.0 | | 12.0 | 7.5 | | | | 55.5 |
| Cont. Studies | | 0.3 | | 0.1 | | | | | 0.4 |
| Education | 3.0 | 3.0 | | 6.0 | | | | | 12.0 |
| Health, P.E. & Recreat. | 1.2 | | | 1.3 | | | | | 2.5 |
| Journal. | 1.0 | 1.5 | | | 1.0 | | | | 3.5 |
| Law School | 5.0 | 8.0 | 2.0 | | | | | | 15.0 |
| Library | 6.0 | | 6.0 | 2.0 | 11.0 | | | | 25.0 |
| Music | 10.0 | 20.0 | | | | | | | 30.0 |
| Library & Inform. Science | 1.0 | | | .25 | | | | | 1.25 |
| Public Environ. Affairs | 7.5 | 2.0 | 0.5 | | | | | | 10.0 |
| Total by Purpose | 84.0 | 51.8 | 8.5 | 25.65 | 26.5 | 10.8 | 10.0 | 7.5 | 224.75 |

## TABLE OF GIFTS NEEDED TO RAISE $224 MILLION.

| Size of Gift | Number Needed | Total |
|---|:---:|---|
| $25,000,000 | 1 | $25,000,000 |
| $15,000,000 | 1 | $15,000,000 |
| $10,000,000 | 3 | $30,000,000 |
| $5,000,000 | 7 | $35,000,000 |
| $2,500,000 | 10 | $25,000,000 |
| $1,000,000 | 25 | $25,000,000 |
| $500,000 | 50 | $25,000,000 |
| $100,000 | 100 | $10,000,000 |
| $50,000 | 250 | $12,500,000 |
| Under $50,000,000 | Many | $21,500,000 |

# QUESTIONNAIRE, Part 1

## SURVEY OF LEADING ALUMNI AND FRIENDS

## INDIANA UNIVERSITY–BLOOMINGTON

Center for Survey Research
1022 East Third Street
Indiana University
Bloomington, IN 47405

Before you complete this questionnaire, please read the packet titled
*"The Faces of Indiana University: An Endowment Campaign for the Bloomington Campus."* Some of the questions in this survey will refer to information in the packet.

Feel free to add notes if you think an answer might be unclear or require more explanation.

As soon as you finish filling out the questionnaire, please mail it back to the Center for Survey Research in the enclosed prepaid envelope.

1.   When you think about the future of Indiana University–Bloomington, how concerned are you about its welfare? (Please circle one number.)

   1  Very concerned

   2  Somewhat concerned

   3  A little concerned

   4  Not at all concerned

2.   Compared to other people you know who are associated with Indiana University–Bloomington, how knowledgeable do you think you are about the campus as a whole? (Please circle one number.)

   1  Much more knowledgeable

   2  Somewhat more knowledgeable

   3  About as knowledgeable

   4  Somewhat less knowledgeable

   5  Much less knowledgeable

3a.  Regardless of how much or how little you actually know about Indiana University–Bloomington, please give your impression of each of the following. (Please circle one number for each item.)

|  | Excellent | Good | Fair | Poor | No Impression |
|---|---|---|---|---|---|
| The quality of IU-B's faculty | 1 | 2 | 3 | 4 | 5 |
| The overall academic quality of IU-B | 1 | 2 | 3 | 4 | 5 |
| The performance of the current President | 1 | 2 | 3 | 4 | 5 |
| The performance of the current Chancellor | 1 | 2 | 3 | 4 | 5 |
| The general quality of IU-B's administrators | 1 | 2 | 3 | 4 | 5 |
| The quality of IU-B's fundraising program | 1 | 2 | 3 | 4 | 5 |
| How IU-B ranks with other universities in the Midwest | 1 | 2 | 3 | 4 | 5 |
| How IU-B ranks with other universities in the United States | 1 | 2 | 3 | 4 | 5 |

3b.  In your opinion, what areas stand out among Indiana University–Bloomington's greatest strengths?

_____

_____

_____

3c.  In your opinion, what areas need improvement?

_____

_____

_____

> The next set of questions refers to information in the packet "*The Faces of Indiana University: An Endowment Campaign for the Bloomington Campus.*" If you have not already done so, please read the packet <u>before</u> answering the next few questions.

4. Below is a list of ideas others have expressed. For each one, please indicate how much you agree or disagree. (Please circle one number for each item.)

|  | Strongly Agree | Somewhat Agree | Somewhat Disagree | Strongly Disagree |
|---|---|---|---|---|
| Unless IU-B receives endowment funds, it will not be possible to maintain its standards of excellence | 1 | 2 | 3 | 4 |
| Private funding is critical to meeting IU-B's endowment goals | 1 | 2 | 3 | 4 |
| Above all else, IU-B's excellence depends upon the quality of the faculty | 1 | 2 | 3 | 4 |
| Today, even private universities are very dependent on government funding | 1 | 2 | 3 | 4 |
| It's up to the State of Indiana to provide most of the funding for building improvements at IU-B | 1 | 2 | 3 | 4 |
| It's up to the State of Indiana to provide most of the funding for technology improvements at IU-B | 1 | 2 | 3 | 4 |
| Matching funds are important in encouraging private support | 1 | 2 | 3 | 4 |

5a. The University has set forth several major areas of proposed improvements in the packet materials. Please indicate how important you consider each of the following proposed campaign projects at Indiana University–Bloomington. (Please circle one number for each item.)

| | Essential | Important but not Essential | Somewhat Important | Not Important |
|---|---|---|---|---|
| Art Museum | 1 | 2 | 3 | 4 |
| Executive Education Center | 1 | 2 | 3 | 4 |
| Faculty support | 1 | 2 | 3 | 4 |
| Graduate student support | 1 | 2 | 3 | 4 |
| Library | 1 | 2 | 3 | 4 |
| Technology | 1 | 2 | 3 | 4 |
| Special programs | 1 | 2 | 3 | 4 |
| Undergraduate student support | 1 | 2 | 3 | 4 |
| Unrestricted funds | 1 | 2 | 3 | 4 |

5b. Please indicate which area from question 5a you think deserves top priority, second priority, and third priority in the allocation of private gift funds.

1 _____

2 _____

3 _____

6. Are there any other campus needs and goals (not included in question 5a) that you consider important?

1 Yes → If yes, what are they? _____

_____

_____

2 No

In order to accomplish the goals outlined in the enclosed preliminary case statement, private gift funds totaling approximately $224 million will be needed over the next three to five years. Please refer to the Table of Gifts below which suggests the number and size of gifts that are needed to meet these goals.

## TABLE OF GIFTS NEEDED TO RAISE $224 MILLION.

| Size of Gift | Number Needed | Total |
|---|---|---|
| $25,000,000 | 1 | $25,000,000 |
| $15,000,000 | 1 | $15,000,000 |
| $10,000,000 | 3 | $30,000,000 |
| $5,000,000 | 7 | $35,000,000 |
| $2,500,000 | 10 | $25,000,000 |
| $1,000,000 | 25 | $25,000,000 |
| $500,000 | 50 | $25,000,000 |
| $100,000 | 100 | $10,000,000 |
| $50,000 | 250 | $12,500,000 |
| Under $50,000,000 | Many | $21,500,000 |
|  | Total | $224,000,000 |

7a.  Do you consider this configuration of gifts to be realistic? (Please circle one number.)

1  Yes → *Please go to question 8*

2  No → *Please go to question 7b*

3  Don't know → *Please go to question 8*

7b.  What is the *main* reason you feel this way? (Please circle one number.)

1  Because the dollar amount of the *top* gift levels is too high

2  Because the dollar amount of *most* of the gift levels is too high

3  Because the number of gifts required at the *top* levels is too high

4  Because the number of gifts required at *each* level is too high

5  Some other reason (Please describe): _____

_____

_____

7c.  What dollar goal would you consider to be realistic?

8.   Do you think there are any reasons why Indiana University–Bloomington *should not* undertake a major capital fundraising campaign at this time?

    1  Yes → If yes, please describe: _____

    _____

    _____

    2  No

9a.  Are there other major fundraising campaigns that are currently vying for your support?

    1  Yes

    2  No → *Please go to the instructions in Box 1*

9b.  If yes, what are they? (Please check all that apply.)

    ___  1  A fundraising campaign for another college or university.

         If so, which one(s): _____

         _____

         _____

    ___  2  A fundraising campaign for a medical center or hospital.

         If so, which one(s): _____

         _____

         _____

    ___  3  A campaign for an arts organization. If so, which one(s):

         _____

         _____

         _____

    ___  4  Some other type of campaign. (Please describe.)

         _____

         _____

         _____

*Box 1*
*In order to compare the opinions of different groups of people, we would like some information about you. Please answer as many of the following questions as you can, knowing that all the data you provide will be treated in strict confidence.*

10a. Did you ever attend Indiana University–Bloomington?

1  Yes

2  No → *Please go to question 11a*

10b. How long were you enrolled at Indiana University–Bloomington? (Please circle one number.)

1  Less than one year

2  At least one year, but less than two

3  At least two years, but less than three

4  At least three years, but less than four

5  At least four years, but less than five

6  At least five years, but less than six

7  Six years or more

11a. Did you ever attend any *other* college or university?

1  Yes

2  No → *Please go to the instructions in Box 2*

11b. Which other colleges or universities did you attend?

_____

_____

_____

*Box 2*
*If you* never *attended a college or university, please go to question 15.*
*If you* have *attended a college or university, continue with question 12.*

12. When you were in college, at Indiana University–Bloomington or elsewhere, in which school or college did you complete the *majority* of your degree work? (Please circle one number.)

    1  I did not have a major

    2  Allied Health

    3  Business

    4  College of Arts & Sciences

    5  Continuing Studies

    6  Education

    7  Health, Physical Education & Recreation

    8  Journalism

    9  Law

    10  Library & Information Sciences

    11  Music

    12  Nursing

    13  Optometry

    14  Public & Environmental Affairs

    15  Social Work

    16  Other (Please describe): _____

13a. Did you pursue graduate studies either at Indiana University–Bloomington or elsewhere? (Please circle one number.)

    1  Yes, at Indiana University

    2  Yes, at another college or university

    3  No → *Please go to question 14a*

13b. What was your field of specialization? (Please circle *all* numbers that apply.)

| | |
|---|---|
| 1  Biology | 14  Languages |
| 2  Business | 15  Law |
| 3  Chemistry | 16  Mathematics |
| 4  Communications | 17  Medicine |
| 5  Computer Science | 18  Music |
| 6  Dentistry | 19  Optometry |
| 7  Education | 20  Political Science |
| 8  English | 21  Psychology |
| 9  Environmental Programs | 22  Public Affairs |
| 10  Health, Physical Education & Recreation | 23  Religious Studies |
| | 24  Sociology |
| 11  History | 25  Theater & Drama |
| 12  Jewish Studies | 26  Other (Please describe): |
| 13  Journalism | _____ |

14a. Have any members of your family, other than yourself, ever attended
Indiana University–Bloomington?

1  Yes

2  No → *Please go to question 15*

14b. What members of your family? (Please circle one number for each item.)

| | Yes | No |
|---|---|---|
| 1  Parent | 1 | 2 |
| 2  Child | 1 | 2 |
| 3  Spouse | 1 | 2 |
| 4  Brother or sister | 1 | 2 |
| 5  Grandchild | 1 | 2 |
| 6  Some other relative | 1 | 2 |

15. Where is your principal place of residence? (Please circle one number.)

    1 Northern Indiana          7 Southwest U.S.

    2 Southern Indiana          8 Great Plains

    3 Indianapolis area         9 Midwest

    4 East Coast                10 Southeast U.S.

    5 West Coast                11 Northeast U.S.

    6 Northwest U.S.            12 Other (Please describe):

    _____

16. How old were you on your last birthday? (Please circle one number.)

    1 Under 35

    2 35– 44

    3 45– 54

    4 55– 64

    5 65– 74

    6 75 or older

17. What is your gender?

    1 Male

    2 Female

18. What was your approximate household income (before taxes) in 1994? Please include income from all sources. (Please circle one number.)

    1 Under $30,000

    2 $30,000–$49,999

    3 $50,000–$99,999

    4 $100,000–$199,999

    5 $200,000–$499,999

    6 $500,000 or higher

19. Have you ever participated in any way in a major capital fundraising campaign for any college, university or other organization?

    1 Yes

    2 No

20. Would you consider participating in a future fundraising campaign (by working in the campaign and/or making a gift) for Indiana University–Bloomington?

    1 Yes

    2 No

21. Please use the space below to tell us anything else you think we should know about your feelings regarding the proposed campaign.

    _____

    _____

    _____

    _____

    _____

    _____

    _____

    _____

    _____

    _____

    _____

---

*Thank you for your help. Please return this questionnaire to The Center for Survey Research in the prepaid envelope provided.*

*We would appreciate it if you would take a few minutes to complete Part Two of this survey. The information you can provide will be very helpful.*

# QUESTIONNAIRE, Part 2

## SURVEY OF LEADING ALUMNI AND FRIENDS

## INDIANA UNIVERSITY–BLOOMINGTON

President Myles Brand
Indiana University
P.O. Box 500
Bloomington, IN 47402

Volunteer leadership and private gift support are essential to the success of a campaign to meet Indiana University–Bloomington's needs. In order to give us a *preliminary indication* of the level of interest in supporting a campaign, please take a few minutes to complete this survey.

Most of these questions ask about personal interest in providing leadership or financial support to a fundraising effort. In addition, if you know other individuals, foundations or corporations that you believe might consider participating in a campaign, we would appreciate knowing about them as well. Any information you give us will be extremely helpful.

PLEASE return this form in the enclosed prepaid envelope addressed to President Myles Brand. DO NOT return it to the Center for Survey Research with your larger questionnaire.

You need not put your name on this form, but you are welcome to do so. The information you provide here will be held in strictest confidence by the President and his development counsel. It cannot be linked to the information you provided in Part One.

Again, thank you very much for your help.

1.  People have many different reasons for wanting to work for or make a significant financial contribution to a capital campaign. Which of the reasons listed below would provide the *strongest motivation(s)* for you personally to participate in such a campaign for Indiana University–Bloomington? (Please circle one number for each item.)

| | Yes | No |
|---|---|---|
| Loyalty to Indiana University–Bloomington | 1 | 2 |
| Well-documented needs and rationale | 1 | 2 |
| Recognition for myself or another person I wish to honor | 1 | 2 |
| Being part of a prestigious leadership group | 1 | 2 |
| Being able to make an anonymous gift | 1 | 2 |
| Having input in goal setting | 1 | 2 |
| Having a responsibility in the campaign | 1 | 2 |
| Indiana University–Bloomington's reputation as an educational institution | 1 | 2 |

|                                                                                          | Yes | No |
|------------------------------------------------------------------------------------------|-----|-----|
| Income tax considerations                                                                | 1   | 2   |
| Believe it is important to emphasize the tradition of giving within the community        | 1   | 2   |
| Believe non-profit organizations are the most efficient way to solve society's problems  | 1   | 2   |
| Enjoy giving to organizations that are supported by my social network                    | 1   | 2   |
| Give out of a sense of obligation and gratitude                                          | 1   | 2   |
| Believe it is my moral obligation to give back to non-profit organizations               | 1   | 2   |
| Enjoy giving as a way to achieve personal development and self-fulfillment               | 1   | 2   |
| Feel it is important to emphasize the tradition of giving within my family unit          | 1   | 2   |

Some other reason (Please describe): _____

_____

| | Yes | No |
|---|---|---|
| I probably would not be motivated to participate in a campaign for Indiana University–Bloomington. | 1 | 2 |

Sometimes Indiana University–Bloomington alumni and others who support the University have helped us by providing names of corporations, foundations or individuals who might be interested in participating in a fundraising campaign.

2a.  Do you personally have ties to any corporations or foundations that might be willing to support a campaign for Indiana University–Bloomington?

1  Yes

2  No → *Please go to question 2b*

Please give us the name(s) and address(es) in the space below.

| Corporation/Foundation | Your Relationship or Connection |
|------------------------|----------------------------------|
| _____  | _____  |
| _____  | _____  |
| _____  | _____  |

2b. Do you know any individual who might consider taking a volunteer *leadership position* in a capital campaign for Indiana University–Bloomington?

1  Yes

2  No → *Please go to question 2c*

Please give us the name(s) and address(es) in the space below.

| | |
|---|---|
| _____ *Name* | _____ *Name* |
| _____ *Street* | _____ *Street* |
| _____ *City* _____ *State* ___ *Zip* | _____ *City* _____ *State* ___ *Zip* |
| _____ *Name* | _____ *Name* |
| _____ *Street* | _____ *Street* |
| _____ *City* _____ *State* ___ *Zip* | _____ *City* _____ *State* ___ *Zip* |

2c. Do you know any individuals or organizations who you believe might be willing to make a contribution of $50,000 or more?

1  Yes

2  No → *Please go to question 3*

Please give us the name(s) and address(es) in the space below.

| | |
|---|---|
| _____ *Name* | _____ *Name* |
| _____ *Street* | _____ *Street* |
| _____ *City* _____ *State* ___ *Zip* | _____ *City* _____ *State* ___ *Zip* |

3. If properly approached, would you personally consider making a contribution or pledging $50,000 or more to Indiana University–Bloomington? The contribution or pledge could be paid outright over the next three to five years or through a planned gift (e.g., trust, bequest). (Please circle one number.)

1  Yes

2  No

3  I cannot make a commitment at this time

4a. If asked, would you personally consider taking a volunteer leadership position in the campaign?

   1 Yes

   2 No → *Please go to question 5*

4b. On which of the following committees would you most like to work in a leadership capacity? (Please circle one number.)

   1 National committee

   2 State committee

   3 Local committee

   4 Other (Please describe): _____

5. Please use the space below to give us any comments about the proposed campaign or any other aspects of this effort.

   _____

   _____

   _____

   _____

   You need not put your name on this form, but you are welcome to do so. The information you provide here will be held in strictest confidence by the President and his development counsel. It cannot be linked to the information you provided in Part One.

   _____
   *Your Name*

   _____
   *Street*

   _____
   *City*          *State*     *Zip*

   _____
   *Telephone (Please include area code)*

   ---

   *Thank you again for your help. Please return this part of the survey to President Brand in the prepaid envelope provided.*

# DIRECT MAIL SURVEY #2
## Letter

UNIVERSITY OF CALIFORNIA, BERKELEY

BERKELEY • DAVIS • IRVINE • LOS ANGELES • RIVERSIDE • SAN DIEGO • SAN FRANCISCO          SANTA BARBARA • SANTA CRUZ

OFFICE OF THE CHANCELLOR                                   BERKELEY, CALIFORNIA  94720

July 1985

Dear Friend of UC Berkeley:

You are among a select group of leading alumni and friends who are being asked to give your candid opinions, on a confidential basis, about our plans for achieving Cal's goals over the next five years.

A two-part questionnaire is enclosed, along with a booklet that describes what I consider to be Cal's most critical needs in the areas of new construction, renovation and endowment. All of the goals addressed in the enclosure are aimed at ensuring Cal's strength in many diverse disciplines—the strengths that make Cal such a tremendous resource to the state, the nation and the world.

Fourteen projects are outlined. Five are new buildings, three are renovation projects, six are endowments for faculty and research support. Estimates of the funds required to achieve each objective are included; together they total approximately $270 million, an amount that would have to be raised almost entirely from private sources.

Therefore, we are preparing to undertake an ambitious capital campaign to reinforce Cal's traditions of excellence and service to society. Your participation in this survey will help me to evaluate how realistic and germane our aspirations are.

Part One of the survey, to be returned to the UC Berkeley Survey Research Center, is designed to elicit your opinions about the campus, its needs and its priorities. Please return Part One to the Survey Research Center in the prepaid envelope that accompanies it. The Survey Research Center will tabulate the data and prepare statistical summaries only. Their procedures ensure absolute anonymity, so that no one will ever know who said what on Part One.

Part Two is a very short optional supplement to the survey. Any information you can provide will be helpful to me and my campaign planning counsel as a means of measuring potential participation in a campaign for UC Berkeley. A separate prepaid envelope, addressed to me, is included for Part Two of the survey. Please be assured that we will hold any information you provide in Part Two in the strictest confidence.

I am very grateful for your interest and help.

Sincerely,

Ira Michael Heyman
Chancellor

# QUESTIONNAIRE, Part 1

## SURVEY OF LEADING ALUMNI AND FRIENDS

## UNIVERSITY OF CALIFORNIA, BERKELEY

Survey Research Center
University of California
Berkeley, CA 94720
I.D. #

CONFIDENTIAL            CONFIDENTIAL

---

- Before you complete this questionnaire, please read the booklet titled "Preliminary Statement of Goals for a Proposed Capital Campaign." Some of the questions in this questionnaire refer to information contained in the booklet.
- Please *do not* write your name anywhere on this questionnaire. The number will help tell the Survey Research Center who has returned their questionnaire and who needs reminder letters. But no one will ever know who said what.
- Feel free to add notes if you feel an answer might be misleading or require more explanation.
- As soon as you finish filling out the questionnaire, please mail it back to the Survey Research Center in the enclosed prepaid envelope.

---

1.  When you think about the future of the University of California, Berkeley, as a whole, how interested and concerned are you about its welfare?

    1  ☐  Very interested

    2  ☐  Somewhat interested

    3  ☐  A little interested

    4  ☐  Not at all interested

2.  Compared to most people you know, how knowledgeable do you think you are about UC Berkeley as a whole?

    1  ☐  Much more knowledgeable

    2  ☐  Somewhat more knowledgeable

    3  ☐  Somewhat less knowledgeable

    4  ☐  Much less knowledgeable

    5  ☐  About as knowledgeable as most people I know

3.  Regardless of how much or how little you actually know about UC Berkeley, please give us your impression of each of the following. *(PLEASE CHECK ONE BOX FOR EACH.)*

| | Excellent | Good | Fair | Poor | No Impression |
|---|---|---|---|---|---|
| | 1 | 2 | 3 | 4 | 5 |
| A. The quality of UC Berkeley's faculty | ☐ | ☐ | ☐ | ☐ | ☐ |
| B. The overall academic quality of UC Berkeley | ☐ | ☐ | ☐ | ☐ | ☐ |

C. The performance
   of the current
   Chancellor                 ☐      ☐      ☐      ☐      ☐

D. The general quality
   of UC Berkeley's
   administrators             ☐      ☐      ☐      ☐      ☐

E. The quality of UC
   Berkeley's fundraising
   program                    ☐      ☐      ☐      ☐      ☐

> *THE NEXT QUESTIONS REFER TO INFORMATION IN THE BOOKLET "PRELIMINARY STATE-MENT OF GOALS FOR A PROPOSED CAPITAL CAMPAIGN." IF YOU HAVE NOT ALREADY DONE SO, PLEASE READ THE BOOKLET BEFORE YOU ANSWER THE NEXT QUESTIONS.*

4.   Below is a list of different ideas some people have expressed. For each one, please indicate how much you agree or disagree.

| | Agree Strongly 1 | Agree Somewhat 2 | Disagree Somewhat 3 | Disagree Strong 4 |
|---|---|---|---|---|
| A. Unless UC Berkeley receives capital improvement and endowment funds, it will not be possible to maintain its standards of excellence | ☐ | ☐ | ☐ | ☐ |
| B. *Private* funding is critical to meeting UC Berkeley's building and endowment goals | ☐ | ☐ | ☐ | ☐ |
| C. Above all else, UC Berkeley's excellence depends upon the quality of its faculty | ☐ | ☐ | ☐ | ☐ |
| D. Today, even private universities are very dependent on government funding | ☐ | ☐ | ☐ | ☐ |
| E. It's up to the State of California to provide most of the funding for building improvements at the University of California's various campuses | ☐ | ☐ | ☐ | ☐ |

5.  Below is a list of the three major areas of proposed improvements at UC Berkeley. In each column, please check *one and only one* box, indicating which of these areas you think deserves top priority, second priority, or lowest priority in the allocation of funds. Please do not check two in the same column, even if you think two areas are almost equally important.

| | Top Priority | Second Priority | Lowest Priority |
|---|:---:|:---:|:---:|
| | 1 | 2 | 3 |
| A. New buildings and facilities | ☐ | ☐ | ☐ |
| B. Renovation of existing buildings and facilities | ☐ | ☐ | ☐ |
| C. Academic enrichment | ☐ | ☐ | ☐ |

6.  Now please tell us how important you consider each of the following proposed campaign projects at UC Berkeley. (These projects are briefly described in the companion booklet.)

| | Essential | Important but not essential | Somewhat important | Not important |
|---|:---:|:---:|:---:|:---:|
| | 1 | 2 | 3 | 4 |
| **BUILDINGS** | | | | |
| A. Biological Sciences Complex | ☐ | ☐ | ☐ | ☐ |
| B. Business School | ☐ | ☐ | ☐ | ☐ |
| C. Chemistry Building | ☐ | ☐ | ☐ | ☐ |
| D. Computer Science Building | ☐ | ☐ | ☐ | ☐ |
| E. Faculty Housing | ☐ | ☐ | ☐ | ☐ |
| F. Law School Renovation | ☐ | ☐ | ☐ | ☐ |
| G. Music Additions | ☐ | ☐ | ☐ | ☐ |
| H. Student Services Building | ☐ | ☐ | ☐ | ☐ |
| I. Other (*PLEASE DESCRIBE:* _____ _____ _____ ) | ☐ | ☐ | ☐ | ☐ |

ENDOWMENTS

| | | | | |
|---|---|---|---|---|
| J.  Faculty Chairs | ☐ | ☐ | ☐ | ☐ |
| K. Humanities Institute | ☐ | ☐ | ☐ | ☐ |
| L.  Latin American Studies | ☐ | ☐ | ☐ | ☐ |
| M. Moorea Biological Station | ☐ | ☐ | ☐ | ☐ |
| N. Soviet Studies | ☐ | ☐ | ☐ | ☐ |
| O. Cal Futures Fund | ☐ | ☐ | ☐ | ☐ |
| P.  Other (*PLEASE DESCRIBE:* _____ _____ _____ ) | ☐ | ☐ | ☐ | ☐ |

In order to accomplish the goals outlined in Question 6, private funds totalling approximately $270 million will be needed over the next three to five years. Please refer to the Table of Gifts below which shows the number and size of gifts that are needed to meet these goals.

### TABLE OF GIFTS NEEDED TO RAISE $270,000,000.

| Gift Amount | Number of Gifts Needed | Total |
|---|---|---|
| $20,000,000 | 2 | $40,000,000 |
| 15,000,000 | 2 | 30,000,000 |
| 10,000,000 | 3 | 30,000,000 |
| 5,000,000 | 6 | 30,000,000 |
| 2,500,000 | 10 | 25,000,000 |
| 1,000,000 | 20 | 20,000,000 |
| 750,000 | 30 | 22,500,000 |
| 500,000 | 40 | 20,000,000 |
| 250,000 | 75 | 18,750,000 |
| 100,000 | 100 | 10,000,000 |
| Under 100,000 | Many | 23,750,000 |
| | Total | $270,000,000 |

## SAMPLE VOLUNTEER KIT

INDIANA UNIVERSITY FOUNDATION

# ENDOWING THE

# FUTURE

Indiana University Faculty Endowment Income Matching Program

## ONE OUTSTANDING TEACHER CAN ENRICH THE LIVES OF THOUSANDS OF STUDENTS.

*PERHAPS YOU WERE FORTUNATE ENOUGH TO HAVE ONE OF THESE PROFESSORS WHILE YOU WERE IN COLLEGE.*

The kind of teacher who challenged you to set your sights higher, who settled for nothing but your best effort, who helped you to see things in a new light. These educators have always been hard to find, and harder to keep. Today, it's even more difficult.

Consider the following:

*Big Ten Public Universities*

*Number of Endowed Faculty Positions (reported by main campuses in 1995)*

| | | |
|---|---|---|
| 1. | Minnesota | 239 |
| 2. | Wisconsin | 226 |
| 3. | Michigan | 186 |
| 4. | Penn State | 118 |
| 5. | Iowa | 115 |
| 6. | Ohio State | 67 |
| 7. | Illinois | 62 |
| **8.** | **Indiana** | **31** |
| 9. | Michigan State | 27 |
| 10. | Purdue | 14 |

*AS YOU KNOW, WELL-DESIGNED FACULTY ENDOWMENTS DO MUCH MORE THAN FUND SALARIES.*

They strengthen libraries, laboratories, and computing resources; they attract talented undergraduate and graduate students. We're seeking faculty endowments that will help us address all of these needs and more.

The entire Indiana University family is grateful for the loyalty and generosity of so many donors. And now we can show our appreciation in a different way as we prepare for the future: by matching the income your new endowment generates.

We invite you to establish a legacy at IU by becoming a member of this select group of supporters. And we pledge our commitment to you by matching your gift's income. By helping IU attract and keep more distinguished faculty members, you provide more of today's and tomorrow's students with an opportunity to enrich their lives.

## The Indiana University Faculty Endowment Income Matching Program

1. Endowment funds received after December 1, 1995, for the purpose of direct faculty support, especially for Chairs and Professorships, are eligible for this match.

2. The full match, that is 1:1, will consist of a payout equal to 5 percent of the principal on an annual basis and will be available for gifts of at least $1,000,000. If the gift falls between $500,000 and $1,000,000, the match will be based on a ratio of 1:2. Payouts will be in perpetuity. A contractual commitment will be provided to the donor.

3. The match opportunity will be in effect until December 31, 1999. A maximum of $4,000,000 will be allocated during this time. Allocations will be made on a first-come, first-served basis, open to all campuses. Unspent available match funds will not be carried forward.

4. The source of funds for the match will be one-half from University administration and one-half from campus administration. At their option, Chancellors may choose to charge the successful unit for all or part of the campus's portion of the match, or they may distribute all or part of the charges to the entire campus.

5. To take an example, Mary Jones donates $500,000 for endowment for a faculty position in the School of Public and Environmental Affairs at IU Bloomington. Assume that the payment from the endowment is $25,000 per year (that is, 5 percent of $500,00, the current spending policy of the IU Foundation Board of Directors).* The match is 1:2 on this principal amount ($500,000) in perpetuity. Thus, in addition to the $25,000, SPEA receives an additional $12,500 per year for support of this position. Of the $12,500, University administration will provide $6,250. The remaining $6,250 is the responsibility of, in this case, the Bloomington campus.

6. Gifts may be paid over a maximum of five years. The match will be available only if there is a firm, written commitment. However, matching funds will be provided only to the extent that payment has been received (with one exception noted below). So, if there is a gift of $1,000,000 to be paid over four years and $250,000 is received the first year, then the matching funds for the first year are $12,500. Here the match rate is 1:1, and the payout is 5 percent of $250,000.

7. In the case of irrevocable trusts established during the match period with no payout until termination of the trust, one-half of the institutional payout will

---

*The actual payment from an endowment fund is determined by the current spending policy and the investment policy set by the IU Foundation Board of Directors.

begin when the trust is established. The remaining matching funds will become available when the trust terminates, as will, of course, the trust income. Thus, if there is an irrevocable trust of $1,000,000 established during the match timeframe, then the payout from institutional funds (that is, University administration plus the campus) will be $25,000 per year until the trust matures. After that, institutional funds will equal $50,000 per year (at the 1:1 payout ratio) plus the income generated from the trust itself based on its value at maturity.

8. The University President, in consultation with the IU Foundation President, reserves the authority to limit eligibility. In particular, it should not be possible for a single mega-gift to deplete all matching monies. In order to determine the upper limit of a specific gift, a brief written proposal should be submitted to the IU President. The IU Foundation Executive Director, Capital Campaigns will be the initial qualifier of matches under this program.

9. A qualified gift for a 1:1 match may be distributed between more than one endowed faculty program, where each would qualify on its own for a lesser match of 1:2, or no match at all. For example, a $1,000,000 gift will qualify for the 1:1 match regardless of how the gift is distributed among qualified programs. It is the size of the gift that matters, not how it is distributed among qualified programs at IU.

10. Any gift that is eligible for the match must be administered by the IU Foundation or IU and not by an outside trustee.

11. Responsibility for authorizing exceptions to this policy rests with the University President.

## Gift Vehicles Eligible for the Matching Program

*A DONOR MAY USE ANY OF THE FOLLOWING GIFT VEHICLES, IN ANY COMBINATION, IN ORDER TO REACH THE $500,000 MINIMUM REQUIREMENT FOR THE INCOME MATCHING PROGRAM.*

### Outright Gifts (Cash and Securities)

Outright gifts of cash or securities that meet the minimum amount of $500,000 or above are eligible for the matching program. These commitments may be received (between 12/1/95 and 12/31/99) all at once or as a pledge paid over five years. Gifts of securities will be recorded at their fair market value on the date of transfer. Personal property will not qualify for the match.* Other types of funds will be handled on a case-by-case basis.

*Please note: Gifts of personal property will not qualify for the match because personal property held by the Foundation will generate no income, and selling the property may have adverse tax consequences for the donor.

## Charitable Remainder Trusts

Charitable remainder trusts qualify for the match. However, the payout on the match will be based on the face value of the donor's gift to the IU Foundation, even if the remainder value exceeds the face value at the time the trust terminates. For example, if a donor funds a charitable remainder trust during the match period with $1,000,000, and assuming the annual income will be $50,000, the match of a gift at this level by the University will be 50 percent of the annual income, or $25,000. The ultimate payout of the trust to the IU Foundation depends upon the payment rate to the beneficiary(ies) and investment performance. The age of life income beneficiaries will be considered when deciding whether or not to match gifts of trust.

## Charitable Gift Annuities and Pooled Income Funds

The charitable remainder trust criteria (as described above) also apply to charitable gift annuities and the pooled income funds. Because of the irrevocable nature, these gifts qualify for a match from the University based upon the face value of the gift at the time it is initially received by the IU Foundation.

## Charitable Lead Trusts

Since charitable lead trusts pay the income they generate directly to the IU Foundation, they qualify if the income generated by the trust to the IU Foundation meets the minimum amount required to qualify for the match. For example, a charitable lead trust funded with assets that will produce at least $500,000 over a five-year period will qualify for the match. If this payout is received or pledged to IU during the match period, it qualifies in the same way as an outright gift.

## Bequests

Newly established bequest expectancies will qualify as long as they meet the minimum levels, are first documented during the matching period, and represent a legally binding obligation upon the donor's estate at the time of the donor's death. Age guidelines will be considered when deciding whether or not to match individual bequests. One of the following types of documentation on file at the IU Foundation is sufficient: a copy of the will or excerpt from the will, Arbutus Society enrollment, a signed gift agreement, a letter of intent from the donor, or a letter from the donor's attorney or financial adviser.

## Life Insurance

Life insurance qualifies only if the policy is fully paid-up when given to the IU Foundation or will be paid-up within a five-year period after the date of the gift. The donor must make the IU Foundation the irrevocable owner and beneficiary of the policy for the matching fund program to apply. The match will be based on the death benefit of the policy, and it will apply at the time the policy is received by the Foundation. For example, if a donor makes a gift of a life insurance policy with a $500,000 death benefit, when the policy matures, that account will qualify for the match. Age guidelines may be considered when deciding whether or not to match life insurance gifts.

## Remainder Interest in Real Estate

Gifts of real estate will be considered on a case-by-case basis. Each gift of real estate must have a documented value to determine qualifications for, and the amount of, the match.

For further information, contact Curtis R. Simic, President, IU Foundation at (812) 855–6679.

# Questions
# & Answers

The
Endowment
Campaign
*for*
Indiana
University
Bloomington

*"In all of the areas in which IUB has major academic programs, it should be second to none. Indiana University Bloomington has the spirit and the will to succeed. This campaign will provide us with the resources."*

—Myles Brand

Myles Brand
President,
Indiana University

THE ENDOWMENT CAMPAIGN FOR INDIANA UNIVERSITY BLOOMINGTON is the largest fundraising campaign for one campus in the University's history. It includes all components of the Bloomington campus, with the primary purpose of increasing the number of endowed chairs, professorships, fellowships, and scholarships available to the campus. The Campaign goal is $350 million—$150 million for new endowment and $200 million in ongoing support.

The following pages contain Indiana University President Myles Brand's answers to some of the most frequently asked questions about the Endowment Campaign.

### Why is Indiana University Bloomington launching a campaign at this time?

It has become clear that Indiana University's margin of excellence increasingly depends upon the support of friends and alumni. In the past, IU could count on state and federal governments to provide funding for operations and some quality improvement efforts, but that's no longer true. At the state level, other priorities, such as K–12, entitlement programs, and corrections, are absorbing greater portions of public resources. Higher education cannot expect to receive support for anything beyond the basic necessities. At the same time, the federal government, in its attempt to balance the budget, is allocating fewer dollars for research opportunities. There is absolutely no doubt that the continuation of IU Bloomington's tradition of excellence and quality will require the direct support that comes through a campaign.

### What is your vision for the University upon successful completion of this campaign?

My vision is simple and straightforward: In all of the areas in which IUB has major academic programs, it should be second to none. Indiana University Bloomington has the spirit and the will to succeed. This campaign will provide us with the resources.

The single most important characteristic of an excellent university is the quality of its faculty, students, and staff. To attract and retain the world's leading faculty members, we must be able to provide endowed chairs and professorships.

IUB is already one of the great university campuses in the country, indeed the world. Unfortunately, however, we lag behind many Big Ten institutions and other major research universities in the number of endowed chairs and professorships. This is more than a matter of numbers, but speaks to the defining essence of IU.

### How does this campaign differ from the University's usual fundraising efforts?

IU Bloomington, like other major college campuses across the country, seeks funds on an annual basis to support its faculty, students, and physical facilities. A campaign, by contrast, focuses on specific, high-priority goals, and the campus organizes itself, school by school, to reach those goals. The IU Foundation, the deans, the chancellor, and the president also dedicate their energy to achieving campaign goals.

### How was the goal of $350 million established?

We discussed campus needs with the faculty, and the chancellor prioritized them. The Indiana University Foundation then undertook a comprehensive market survey to determine the financial feasibility of a campaign. The goal is the result of determining the financial feasibility and matching it with Bloomington campus priorities.

### What do endowments accomplish that other types of gifts do not?

All gifts are important. What makes endowment gifts especially important is their permanence—they continue giving in perpetuity. Properly managed, they not only continue to provide an annual operating income but also grow to meet the eroding effects of inflation. Endowments are a permanent, stable source of income.

### IU already has an outstanding faculty. Why are more endowments to support faculty a focus for this campaign?

Indiana University does have an outstanding faculty. In fact, other major universities would very much like to have some of these faculty members on their campuses. But to retain them, we must provide resources and honors, such as endowed professorships and chairs. By the same token, when Indiana University competes with other outstanding universities for the world's most accomplished teachers, scholars, and creative artists, it needs endowed chairs and professorships to provide the necessary incentives and competitive edge.

Remember, excellent faculty members can go to any major university they choose. Such faculty members raise the level of the intellectual enterprise and they provide the stimulant for creative and innovative work in all disciplines. It is these faculty members who make the difference between a good and a great university. The intellectual environment that they create affects everything we do, from classroom teaching to laboratory research to recital hall performances. Creating this superior intellectual environment is the desired end of a great university. IU Bloomington needs to retain these highly accomplished individuals and to bring others to the campus.

### What is the University doing to encourage endowments that support faculty?

We have created an endowment matching program for faculty chairs and professorships. Our goal, which is ambitious but eminently achievable, is to generate 100 new chairs and professorships by the end of the Campaign, thereby quadrupling the number of chairs and professorships in existence before the Campaign began. It will be a startling accomplishment, to say the least.

The payout of the endowment for these positions is being matched through dedicated funding,* enabling a donor to significantly enhance the effect of a major gift. Indiana University took this step in order to emphasize the importance of faculty chairs and professorships in the development of the Bloomington campus.

### I understand some donors want to support graduate fellowships. Why is graduate student support so important?

Graduate education is part of the core of IU's mission. Training the next generation of faculty members and providing the best-educated leaders for business and the creative arts is, at a deep level, what we are about.

Additionally, good faculty members prefer to work with good graduate students, and good graduate students seek out opportunities to work with a superior faculty in a supportive environment. To attract these superior graduate students to Indiana University Bloomington, we must find means to support their endeavors. Doing so perpetuates our high-quality intellectual environment.

### The Campaign for _Indiana_ in the 1980s was system wide. Why is this campaign specific to the Bloomington campus?

A large, multi-campus university, such as IU, has two choices when it comes to fundraising. One is the university-wide campaign that includes all campuses and all schools at the same time, such as our successful Campaign for _Indiana_. The other, especially apropos for a mature university, is to conduct sequential

---

*The Indiana University Faculty Endowment Income Matching Program is designed to encourage gifts with the goal of raising endowment for faculty positions. President Brand and the Board of Trustees have set aside $2 million in available matching funds for those gifts qualifying for the match before December 31, 1999. Gifts of $500,000 and above, from a single source, designated for chairs and professorships, and received within five years qualify for the match. All income on gifts is to be matched in perpetuity. (Full details are available upon request.)

campaigns for major areas of the institution, such as the recently completed and very successful three-year fundraising campaign at the IU School of Medicine in Indianapolis. It is now time to focus all our energies on the Bloomington campus. One advantage of this approach is that it enables all University resources, especially those of the IU Foundation, to be singularly directed towards a major goal. A sequential approach enables us to utilize existing staff in key areas and is a more efficient and effective way to proceed. This approach works only when a university has achieved a certain level of expertise and experience in fundraising, as IU has done.

### How are the Bloomington faculty and administration involved in the Campaign effort?

They are involved in many ways. Some are working directly with major gift prospects. Others are out taking the Campaign to our many publics. And our faculty is financially supporting this campaign. An effort is now underway to solicit each member of the faculty for the Campaign. The faculty co-chairs are Norm Overly (Education), Susan Gubar (English), and Gary Hieftje (Chemistry).

### My daughter will be entering IU as a freshman in a couple of years. How will the success of this campaign benefit her?

She can expect to have a richer undergraduate experience, both in terms of the quality of the faculty members she will encounter while here and the quality of her classmates (many of whom are highly competitive students who will choose IU not only because of our academic quality but also because of our ability to successfully compete for them through enhanced scholarship offerings).

### My son graduated from IU last year. Why does a successful campaign make any difference to him?

All IU degrees are well regarded today. This campaign is designed to ensure future quality, as well. As IU stays strong and competitive, so will the value of our degrees and their holders.

### I always make an annual gift to IU. Why is it important for me to contribute to this campaign over and above that?

Annual support is essential, and we deeply appreciate it. But this is a special time when our alumni and friends can ensure their support in perpetuity. This is an effort to ratchet up the margin of excellence for IUB through a special gift to the Endowment Campaign for Indiana University Bloomington.

*I've been supporting a particular program at IU for years. Can I still do that with my campaign contribution?*

Absolutely. Because the entire campus and every discipline is involved in the Campaign, we encourage those who choose to support a particular school or program to follow their own interests.

*I might not be able to make a significant contribution this year. How long will I have an opportunity to give to the Campaign?*

The Campaign will run through June 2000.

*This is your first campaign as president of IU. How do you feel about the way it's going so far?*

I am extraordinarily pleased by the rapid progress we have made on the IU Bloomington campaign. As I speak to many of our friends and alumni, I am pleased by their positive feelings about our University. Many individuals have already risen to the occasion in supporting the IU Bloomington campaign. They understand, as I do, the importance of private support. We are a Hoosier family. I look forward to a very successful campaign as we move into the future together.

*I would like to discuss the Campaign goals and issues further. What is the best way for me to communicate with the University?*

I encourage such communication and invite your comments. Should you have an interest in a particular area, be it Journalism, Business, Athletics, etc., I suggest you contact the development officer for that unit. Should you wish to contact me, my mailing address is Bryan Hall 200, Bloomington, IN 47405–1201, and my email address is pres@indiana.edu. We look forward to hearing from you.

# Volunteer's

# Guide

The
Endowment
Campaign
*for*
Indiana
University
Bloomington

*"To furnish the means of acquiring knowledge is the greatest benefit that can be conferred upon mankind. It prolongs life itself and enlarges the sphere of human existence."*
— John Quincy Adams

THE ENDOWMENT CAMPAIGN FOR INDIANA UNIVERSITY BLOOMINGTON is a significant undertaking. The success of our combined efforts to raise $350 million ($150 million for new endowments and $200 million for ongoing support) hinges primarily upon the success of you—our volunteer solicitors. Your knowledge of the prospect and your experience in approaching the individual make you uniquely qualified to handle your assignments. Only you can best judge the amount of preparation and period of cultivation needed prior to actual solicitation. The following suggestions have been found to be helpful by successful volunteers in major university campaigns. They are offered for your consideration.

### 1. Get to know your prospect.

As a volunteer for the Endowment Campaign for IU Bloomington, knowledge of your prospect and an assessment of the size of gift you want to secure are logical starting points. Both your Campaign chair and the Capital Campaign staff can provide an evaluated level of giving for each prospect. Campaign pledge cards are included with your volunteer's kit. If more information is needed, either the Capital Campaign Office at the IU Foundation or the individual academic units will provide supplementary information.

### 2. Cultivate an interest in Indiana University Bloomington.

With prospect-qualifying information in hand, an initial meeting with your prospect to discuss Indiana University Bloomington, its position in higher education, and the urgent needs of the Endowment Campaign, will help open the door. This meeting should be one of cultivation and exploration, not specifically solicitation, and should permit uninterrupted discussion about IU Bloomington. A private luncheon or dinner meeting, or a meeting in a home often proves successful for this purpose. Throughout this initial meeting, try to pinpoint your prospect's particular field of interest. You may be offered a gift; then again, you may not. A gift suggested at this time usually represents a level of giving below that which the prospective donor will make when more fully appreciative of the University's needs. If offered a gift during your first meeting, suggest that you want your prospect to think over the need, the worthiness of an investment in IU Bloomington, and the extent of participation. Also suggest a meeting at a later date to further discuss an endowment commitment.

### 3. Plan for follow-up.

At the end of your first meeting, you should have learned the prospect's particular interest for participation in the Campaign. If your prospect lacks a discernible specific priority, you may decide to suggest a gift opportunity for your prospect. Preparing your prospect's personalized proposal now becomes a critical consideration, and the Capital Campaign staff will help you develop the proposal for whatever gift rationale you suggest. A written proposal can be prepared and appropriate Endowment Campaign support materials assembled to assist you in matching your prospect's interest with institutional priorities. Your carefully prepared proposal should be delivered with the understanding that you want your prospect to review it. Assure the prospect that you will allow time for consideration of the proposal, and soon will arrange a meeting to discuss a commitment.

### 4. Ask for the gift.

After allowing your prospect time to review the proposal and to learn more about the priorities of the Endowment Campaign, it is time to close the gift. Only you will be able to decide the propitious moment for this final meeting, during which you will ask them to make a specific giving decision. You should come away from this meeting with a letter of intent, a pledge card, or some other firm commitment to the Endowment Campaign. This is your last chance, so help the prospect decide the level of gift, discuss with candor and diplomacy the amount the prospect should consider, and conclude your solicitation. Ask for the gift!

### 5. Review incentives for giving.

Remember, working with every prospect should be treated as a "campaign" in and of itself, and every prospect should be motivated to the point of maximum participation. A number of incentives designed to maximize participation in the Endowment Campaign for Indiana University Bloomington can help you achieve success: spreading the pledge payment over three to five years; the possibility of making a capital gift; tax advantages of various methods of giving; the opportunity to establish a permanent named or memorial fund to honor the donor, a close friend, relative, or loved one; the positive effect a gift will have on raising the sights of others; and the specific advantages of planned giving.

### 6. Use the pledge card wisely.

The pledge card can make the difference between asking your prospect to be a token giver or to be a full participant in the Endowment Campaign for Indiana

University Bloomington. Ask your prospect to study the pledge card with you. Note that the pledge card details the purpose of the Endowment Campaign, offers different commitment options, and requires the prospect to personally write in the total gift amount(s) and designate a specific purpose for the gift(s). The prospect should be reminded that a specific payment plan can be selected to accommodate individual preferences. Be sure your prospect writes in the date of the pledge, for this becomes the date on which the pledge collection system will be based. Clearly point out to your prospect that the pledge is a moral commitment, not a legal contract, so that if circumstances make cancellation a necessity, the donor's wishes will be honored. An official receipt will be mailed to the donor by the University, of course.

### 7. Above all, be flexible.

Flexibility is the key in approaching a prospect. Special situations might call, for example, for a lunch or dinner with IU's president, a dean, or the head of an academic department. Perhaps a tour of the campus could be scheduled. The Capital Campaign Office and the IU Foundation, as well as the individual academic units, will assist in these special situations. Many times the question of an unrestricted gift arises. You should keep in mind that such gifts, to be used at the discretion of the Campaign, are most desirable and appropriate, if your prospect is not committed to a particular area of interest.

### 8. Let us know how you're doing.

A close association among you, your Endowment Campaign chair, and the University's professional development staff is mutually beneficial. Strategic as well as moral support is readily available and can make your voluntary job of solicitation easier. Periodic reports on gift negotiations are helpful and provide invaluable progress information on solicitation assignments.

### 9. Keep your sights high.

Not many people find it easy to ask for large gifts. Remember most prospects are fortified by strong convictions about Indiana University and possess a firm resolve to perpetuate its mission. The prospect (like you) is being asked to represent IUB and to ask others to join them in supporting its goals, so never underestimate your prospect's ability to give. Use your enthusiasm to cultivate enthusiasm in your prospect. Stress the personal satisfaction he or she will enjoy from providing essential and vital support to Indiana University Bloomington.

*10. Be proud of your role.*

You are bringing to your prospect the opportunity to provide support to an institution of the highest quality. You are seeking private investments in one of our most valued human endeavors—education. Your volunteer efforts are the key to the success of the Endowment Campaign for Indiana University Bloomington. What you are doing is important. Be proud of your role. We certainly are!

---

*The Indiana University Foundation is designated by the trustees of Indiana University as the official fundraising agency for the University. A not-for-profit corporation chartered in 1936 under the laws of the State of Indiana, the Foundation raises and receives gifts from the private sector, administers funds, and manages assets to enhance the quality of education at Indiana University.*

# How
# to Close
# the Gift

The
Endowment
Campaign
*for*
Indiana
University
Bloomington

THE ENDOWMENT CAMPAIGN FOR INDIANA UNIVERSITY BLOOMINGTON is a national and international fundraising effort being conducted into the year 2000. This campaign seeks to add at least $150 million to the campus's endowment and to augment annual giving by at least $200 million. The Endowment Campaign is the largest fundraising campaign for a single campus in the University's history. Since it includes all components of the Bloomington campus, gifts to the Endowment Campaign will enrich every aspect of teaching and learning at IU Bloomington.

## Objectives

Each Endowment Campaign volunteer needs to meet three important objectives before beginning solicitation of major gifts:

1. Know the Six Basic Closing Stages.
2. Know How to Handle Objections.
3. Know the Major Errors to Avoid in Solicitation.

## Six Basic Closing Stages

Here are the six stages necessary for soliciting and closing a major gift:

1. Opening
2. Questioning
3. Listening
4. Presenting
5. Overcoming Objections
6. Asking for the Gift

### 1. Opening

In any person-to-person encounter, the opening, to a large extent, will determine the outcome. It does not matter whether you are asking for a luncheon date, talking with a colleague, requesting something from an assistant, or soliciting a major gift, your opening will have a definite effect on the outcome of the conversation.

One of the primary goals you are trying to accomplish in the opening is to light a fire under your prospect. It is critical that you involve the prospect in what you are saying. One of the most effective ways to do this is to talk about the prospect's favorite subject—himself or herself.

Try to get the prospect to talk about himself or herself as soon as possible. Be warm and friendly, carry a smile, and give compliments as honestly as possible, whenever possible. Remember to be as specific and sincere as you can be. Keep in mind that you never talk *to* a prospect, but rather you talk *with* him or her. Ask for responses, listen closely, and reinforce positive statements. By drawing a prospect out, you have a better chance of bringing him or her into a meaningful relationship with IU Bloomington.

The key here, as always, is involvement. Always speak from the prospect's point of view; always ask for reactions; above all, talk about his or her accomplishments. This is true whether you are dealing with an individual major donor, a foundation, or a corporation. Foundations and corporations are people. People make decisions. People carry your proposal to other people.

Make your opening as dynamic and intriguing as you possibly can.

## 2. Questioning

If you have done a good job of getting the prospect's attention in the opening, your task now is to keep that attention and deepen his or her involvement. That can be easily accomplished through questioning.

Questions are wonderful things. They allow you to talk *with* the prospect rather than *to* the prospect. Questions automatically force the prospect into involvement. Good questions fall into a number of categories—questions that call for a feeling response, fact-finding questions that verify your research, or challenging and new questions that help uncover your prospect's motivations and needs.

Be careful not to ask questions that require a yes or no answer. This type of question will give you little information. Ask open-ended questions. Do not ask questions like, "Do you think we need more research in the area of human attitudes and values?" but rather, "How do you think we could improve research in human attitudes and values?"

Oftentimes, you can draw a prospect out by making a statement you have heard from a respected third party, then following that by a question like, "How do you feel about this?" Try to emphasize needs and problems as much as possible.

The biggest mistake you can make at this point is to begin talking about the Campaign. During the questioning stage, it is very important that you make sure the prospect is aware of the needs of Indiana University Bloomington before you show him or her how those needs may be met.

## 3. Listening

Listening is probably the most difficult skill to master; however, if you are going to take advantage of all the questions you ask, you will have to do more listening and less talking. That is not easy. The only way a prospect will invest in your solution is if the prospect thinks you have understood his or her position.

A good listener is a participant who understands communication is both an active and selective process. Most people speak at the rate of 100 to 150 words per minute. You are capable of perceiving approximately 400 words per minute.

This gives you a lead time of between 250 and 300 words. You can use this lead time to evaluate what your prospect is saying—anticipating the points he or she will make, judging what has already been said, and judging the importance of each word and each statement.

The technique of listening ahead gives you an opportunity to be discerning in your listening process. Listen with a purpose. Do not interpret. Ask questions and give feedback to your prospect so that he or she knows you are hearing what is being said. You will notice that as you give feedback, your prospects will have a tendency to reinforce the topics that are most important to him or her.

Be empathic in your listening. Put yourself in your prospect's position. By doing this, you will build respect and therefore have a better chance to achieve your desired results.

Listen with your whole body, not just your ears. Lean forward into the conversation. Listen with your eyes as well; you can pick up a lot of information by watching the body language of your prospect. Your own body language and responses will show your prospect that you are alert and interested in what he or she has to say. Use phrases such as, "Let me be sure I have understood what you said" and "Let me see, do I understand this correctly?" These kinds of questions give evidence that you are listening; they encourage the prospect to listen more actively to what you are saying; they help build a common ground between you and your prospect.

Good listening, then, involves your active and meaningful participation. Your feedback to the prospect's responses helps you to qualify and understand his or her position. Probably the most important benefit of active listening is that it makes the prospect feel good about himself or herself. It makes the prospect feel that he or she has something important to say, and that you are listening intently to what is being said.

Developing good listening skills can help you become a more effective solicitor.

## 4. Presenting

This particular skill may seem like the easiest part of your solicitation effort; however, you must be careful not to fall into the common trap of over-simplification. The natural tendency is to emphasize Indiana University Bloomington and its needs, rather than the benefits IU Bloomington can bring to the prospect's needs. Basically, prospects want four questions answered about the University or a specific program:

1. Is it the best?
2. Will it perform the way you say it will?
3. Will it become or remain the best in the future?
4. How will I be paid back for my investment?

Knowing that your prospect wants these questions answered, you can construct your presentation to answer these questions before they are asked. One of the best ways to do this is to talk about benefits and advantages rather than about the Campaign and its needs.

When discussing the Campaign, always try to use dialogue with the prospect:

- Use people stories.
- Make your language vivid and descriptive.
- Make the benefits for donors seem real enough to touch.

Remember Bell Telephone's marvelous slogan, "Reach out and touch someone." It sells the company's benefits rather than the features of the service. Emphasizing the Campaign's benefits rather than focusing on specific features is what you are trying to do with your prospect. Your objective is to show real people solving real problems through IU Bloomington.

## 5. Overcoming Objections

Most of us become uncomfortable when objections are raised. Remembering that an objection is not an attack, but rather a question, will help you overcome this discomfort.

When answering an objection, always show understanding of your prospect's position. Try to gain your prospect's respect by making statements such as, "I see your point of view" or "I can understand why you would have that concern." Take the objection and turn it into a positive statement such as "Myles Brand, IU's president, feels the same way you do about this particular problem. He has talked to the administration about it and the administration has come up with a number of ideas to overcome this problem."

The main point is to let the prospect know his or her objection is acceptable, that others feel the same way, and that this type of question has helped us find constructive solutions to other problems. You can even turn the objection into the very reason the prospect should support the Campaign.

Never let the objection lead into an argument. Do not make the objection bigger than it is. Respond to it with facts and never make excuses. If the objection is weak, however, pass over it. Ignore it and move on with your proposal. It is perfectly legitimate to compromise on minor objections if, in fact, they will not be a hindrance to reaching your primary goal.

Remember that all objections are really questions, and that the prospect's investment in the Campaign will help overcome the cause of the objection. This will help you to convert the objections into reasons for giving.

### 6. Asking for the Gift

This skill is commonly called "the closing." After you have dealt with all the prospect's questions and concerns, it is time to ask for the gift. Most failure in a face-to-face solicitation is a result of not asking for the gift.

It is important that you know how and when to ask. If you have mastered the five previous skills, you will be able to observe when your prospect is ready for you to ask.

Always give the prospect alternatives. Never ask for a yes or no answer. Keep in mind that many prospects will say no two or three times before they say yes.

It is common practice to ask for a larger gift than is expected. This gives you a stronger negotiating position, and in most cases it helps get the gift needed. The prospect knows that this is no ordinary meeting, but that you are there to discuss serious concerns that interest both him or her and the University.

Mastering these six skills will give you a much better chance of closing major gifts for the Endowment Campaign for IU Bloomington.

## Handling Objections & Closing Techniques for Major Gifts

### 1. Assume you already have the gift.

Do not ask for the gift; act as if you already have it.

### 2. Tell a story.

Use a story you have heard about another prospect who had a similar objection. The prospect in the story should overcome his or her objection and make a major gift to IU Bloomington, a specific program, or an academic unit. Always use the prospect's name in your story. Remember to make the story entertaining.

### 3. Reverse the question.

Have the prospect ask you a yes or no question, and then reverse it into a question that you ask. For example:

*Prospect:* "Will the building be named after me?"
*Solicitor:* "Would you like your name on the donor plaque?"
*Prospect:* "If I can afford the gift to get it there. . . ."

### 4. Close on the major objection.

Use this technique when a prospect offers objection after objection.

a.  Hear out each objection completely.
b.  Restate and put greater emphasis on the major objection.
c.  Ask the prospect if he or she would donate, were it not for the objection.
d.  If no, deal with other minor objections in turn.
e.  If yes, work through the last objection and close.

### 5. Last resort.

If all else fails, you may want to try the last resort.

*Solicitor:* "Mr. Stockwealth, I believe Indiana University has a number of great programs, strong leadership, and real vision. All it needs to continue being one of the country's great universities is more support for its faculty and student endowments. Is there anything I did wrong that kept you from making a gift?"

*Prospect:* (Will bring up an objection.)

*Solicitor:* "Of course, I should have thought of that! Thank you for being so honest with me and clarifying your feelings. I do not know how I forgot to clear that up for you."

Then deal with the objection and close.

### 6. Reconsider.

As you start to leave, ask the prospect, "Won't you reconsider?"

## Overcoming Obstacles

You may run into a number of problems in your solicitation presentation that will keep you from closing. Here are a few suggestions to help you overcome these obstacles:

## Problem #1

*Prospect says, "I have to talk to my spouse."*

*Strategy*

a. Ask, "May we both meet with him/her?"
b. Hypothesize, "Just suppose he/she agreed."
c. Ask, "Are there any other questions to which you think he/she will want the answer?"
d. Do your research—be sure to speak with both spouses on the first visit.
e. Get the spouse involved in the Campaign before you visit.

## Problem #2

*Prospect imposes a time limit on the meeting.*

*Strategy*

a. Condense your presentation.
b. Ask, "Is this the only time we will be able to spend together?"
c. Ask, "How long do you think this will take?"
d. Continue with the presentation.
e. Set new agenda and proceed.
f. Reschedule the meeting for a more convenient time.

## Problem #3

*Prospect offers a gift that is too small.*

*Strategy*

a. Say, "Our expectations are greater."
b. Suggest the offered gift as first payment on a larger one.
c. Check the prospect's financial position.
d. Apologize for misleading him or her about the amount you need.
e. Take the smaller gift and upgrade later.
f. Say, "If you could make four or five gifts this size, look what we could do!"
g. Say, "Before I can accept this gift, I have to check with my Campaign chair."

## Problem #4

*Prospect is a non-talker or silent.*

*Strategy*

a. Ask questions.
b. Use gestures to put the prospect at ease.
c. Look and act interested when prospect does talk, and then ask more questions.

   d. Do not let the silence rest on you.

   e. Get another volunteer to play devil's advocate to stimulate the conversation.

   f. Go golfing, fishing, etc. with the prospect, a situation in which it is not necessary to have a lengthy conversation.

   g. Ask a good friend of the prospect to volunteer information about the prospect. Ask questions the friend knows the prospect is thinking about.

   h. Go into your presentation.

## Problem #5

*Prospect is aggressive or talkative.*

*Strategy*

   a. Let him or her talk until he or she runs down.

   b. Hang tough.

   c. Use a high status volunteer to counter lower status person references.

   d. Do not press. Set up another meeting.

   e. Ask questions to change the focus of the conversation.

   f. Ask why he or she came to the meeting.

   g. Look for a bridge to your presentation.

   h. Ask to meet with prospect's spouse.

   i. Playback.

## Problem #6

*Lack of coordination among team members.*

*Strategy*

   a. Clarify roles in advance.

   b. Set an agenda of questions.

   c. Match complementary personalities and styles.

   d. Role-play and practice in advance.

   e. Be flexible.

   f. Work out signals.

# Major Errors to Avoid in Solicitation

In your presentation, be sure to avoid the 14 critical errors that commonly occur when soliciting major gifts.

   1. Not asking for the gift.

   2. Not asking for a large enough gift.

   3. Not listening/Talking too much.

4. Not asking questions.
5. Not talking about benefits to the prospect.
6. Not being flexible/Not presenting alternatives.
7. Not knowing enough about the prospect before the solicitation.
8. Forgetting to summarize before moving to solicitation.
9. Not practicing with team members before solicitation.
10. Asking for the gift too soon.
11. Speaking, rather than remaining silent, after asking for the gift.
12. Settling on too small a gift.
13. Not cultivating the prospect before soliciting.
14. Not sending out trained solicitors.

## Campaign Contacts

[Names and addresses of the contacts here were deleted to protect privacy.]

---

*The Indiana University Foundation is designated by the trustees of Indiana University as the official fundraising agency for the University. A not-for-profit corporation chartered in 1936 under the laws of the State of Indiana, the Foundation raises and receives gifts from the private sector, administers funds, and manages assets to enhance the quality of education at Indiana University.*

The Endowment Campaign for
Indiana University Bloomington

## Seven Steps to a Major Gift

### Step 1: Identify the Prospect.

*Purpose:* To discover a new or newly qualified prospect.

*Questions:* Does the prospect have the financial capacity to make a major gift? What form of assets might the prospect use to make a gift?

### Step 2: Research and Qualify the Prospect.

*Purpose:* To gather and analyze relevant information about a prospect.

*Questions:* What are the prospect's potential interests and priorities? Does the prospect currently have a relationship with Indiana University? What information is still needed to build a gift strategy? Who is the best potential volunteer?

### Step 3: Strategize with Staff.

*Purpose:* To develop a plan for contact, cultivation, and solicitation.

*Questions:* What is a realistic gift target? Which of the prospect's interests best match the priority goals of the Campaign? What does the prospect need to know, feel, and experience to bring about a major commitment?

### Step 4: Involve the Prospect: Make the First Call.

*Purpose:* To build a bridge between the prospect and Indiana University Bloomington.

*Questions:* What are the prospect's attitudes and concerns about Indiana University Bloomington? Which of the prospect's interests and needs can be satisfied by meaningful participation in the Campaign? How much future involvement/cultivation will be required before the ask?

### Step 5: Make the Ask.

*Purpose:* To invite the prospect to consider an investment in the Endowment Campaign.

*Questions:* What is the prospect's reaction to the ask? What are the crucial objections or concerns? What needs to be done to facilitate an actual gift or pledge commitment?

### Step 6: Make the Close.

*Purpose:* To lead the prospect to a commitment.

*Questions:* What further attitudes and concerns must be addressed? What alterations may be necessary to the original request? What professional help is needed (legal counsel, investment advice, etc.)?

### Step 7: Follow Up.

*Purpose:* To express appreciation and thanks.

*Questions:* What kinds of personal attention can be shown to the donor? Where should ties to Indiana University Bloomington be strengthened? What further interests and needs of the donor may be served by another gift?

## Five Prospect Attitudes and Reactions

1. Agreement—Proceed to the next step.
2. Misunderstanding—Clarify the misunderstanding; gently correct with facts.
3. Indifference—Use "closed-ended" questions to discover needs and interests.
4. Skepticism—Overcome with an "expert witness."
5. "Real Objections"—Use the four-step process:

   a. Clarify the objection to make sure you understand it.
   b. Meet the objection but never beat it. Restate the objection as a question; use further questions to narrow the objection to one specific, manageable issue.
   c. Minimize the impact of the objection; try to emphasize the greater good or bigger picture.
   d. Try to gain a neutral position. Ask if the objection will keep the prospect from joining in the Endowment Campaign. Summarize graciously and move on.

# Guide to Giving

The
Endowment
Campaign
*for*
Indiana
University
Bloomington

THE ENDOWMENT CAMPAIGN FOR INDIANA UNIVERSITY BLOOMINGTON is a national and international fundraising effort being conducted into the year 2000. It is the largest campaign in the University's history and includes all components of the Bloomington campus. The Campaign goal is $350 million—$150 million for new endowment and $200 million in ongoing support. Endowment is one of the most cost-effective and manageable ways to achieve the University's goals and prepare for the future. The primary purpose of this campaign is to increase the number of endowed chairs and professorships, fellowships, and scholarships available to the campus. Gifts to the Endowment Campaign will enrich every aspect of teaching and learning at IUB.

## Contents

---

*The Indiana University Foundation is designated by the trustees of Indiana University as the official fundraising agency for the University. A not-for-profit corporation chartered in 1936 under the laws of the State of Indiana, the Foundation raises and receives gifts from the private sector, administers funds, and manages assets to enhance the quality of education at Indiana University.*

## A Message from Curt Simic

Every year, Indiana University benefits from the generosity of thousands of people. Their reasons for giving vary as widely as their interests and their financial circumstances. What they all have in common is the desire to help make a great university even greater, to enable it to better serve the state and the nation.

You share that desire, and IU is pleased to count you among its supporters. Yet your situation, like everyone else's, is unique; your motivations, your goals, and your available resources combine to make your situation unlike that of any other donor. What may seem to be the most obvious way to make your gift may not be the best way for you.

Fortunately, there are many options for setting up a gift to IU. I am sure one of them will suit your purposes. This booklet is designed to help you become familiar with these choices and, I hope, help you identify the ones that are right for you.

While philanthropic impulses may have prompted your decision to support the University—indeed, few gifts are as personally rewarding as a gift to education—you should also consider the potential tax advantages provided by certain types of gifts. Some arrangements offer you other financial benefits—life income, for instance, or professional management of your assets.

The fundraising professionals at the IU Foundation are here to answer any questions or concerns you or your financial advisers may have. We want you to be confident, right from the start, that you have all the information and informed advice you need. In short, we want you to know that you are choosing the best path.

*Curtis R. Simic*

Curtis R. Simic
President, Indiana University Foundation

## The Basics

You will find a wide variety of giving options in this booklet. Some are simple, others more complex. The general information in this section may be useful to you whichever ones you choose.

### Designating Your Gift

What you choose to support is entirely up to you. You may designate your gift for any purpose that contributes to Indiana University's three-fold mission of teaching, research, and service, and that is acceptable to the trustees of the University or the board of directors of the IU Foundation. Among the most useful gifts, however, are those designated for "wherever the need is greatest." These unrestricted gifts offer much-needed flexibility to an otherwise rigid state-appropriated budget. They allow the University to take advantage of unexpected opportunities and meet challenges that arise after state budgets are set. Donors who make unrestricted gifts can be confident that their gifts will be put to the best possible use.

## Endowed Funds: The Gifts That Keep On Giving

An endowment is an investment in the future. When you use your charitable gift to establish an endowment, the gift is invested with two goals in mind: to make the principal grow faster than inflation, and to provide spendable income for whatever specific purpose you have designated. The principal is never invaded, and any earnings over a certain amount—usually five percent—are channeled back into the fund to keep it healthy and growing. Well-managed endowments can generate income indefinitely. That fact makes them uniquely valuable to the University, and therefore especially attractive to donors who wish to leave a legacy at IU.

## Gift Agreements

Whenever a gift fund is set up, it is wise to create a gift agreement. The agreement sets out your specific criteria for how the University will utilize your gift. It ensures that the gift will always be used exactly as you intend. It also may set out provisions for alternative uses, should it become impossible or impractical for the University to carry out your original intention (as when, for instance, advances in knowledge render a given field of study obsolete). For these reasons, the IU Foundation now requires that all new funds have a written gift agreement on file. The Foundation staff will work with you to draw up the agreement.

## Donor Recognition

Indiana University appreciates its supporters. Regardless of what form your gift to the Indiana University Foundation takes, it may qualify you for one of IU's donor recognition groups. The best reward for your contribution, of course, is the knowledge and satisfaction that you have made a difference in the lives of the individuals your gift touches. Nevertheless, the University wants to publicly thank its major donors and recognize them for their philanthropy. Below are the University-wide recognition groups. In addition, the different schools may have their own donor societies.

***The Presidents Circle.*** The Presidents Circle honors the University's most generous benefactors, those who make irrevocable gifts at leadership levels. Lifetime giving of $100,000 or more qualifies a donor for inclusion in the Presidents Circle. One may also become a member if others donate $100,000 or more in his or her honor.

***The Arbutus Society.*** The Arbutus Society recognizes those individuals who inform the IU Foundation of their intention to invest in the future of Indiana University through planned or deferred gift arrangements.

***The Well House Society.*** The Well House Society is unique among college and university donor recognition groups. Donors make annual gifts that are *unrestricted,* that is, they may be used for whatever purpose Indiana University's president and the IU Foundation's board of directors deem best. Alternatively, Well House Society donors may choose to combine their unrestricted gift with one directed to a school, department, or program of their choice. Because a very small percentage of gifts for the University are unrestricted, the Well House Society gives IU a vital source of flexible funds.

# Outright Gifts

Most gifts to the IU Foundation for the benefit of Indiana University are simple, outright transfers of property. They range from $30 checks for the Annual Fund to multimillion-dollar real estate transactions. Regardless of their size or method, however, all have tax advantages for the donor, with the added appeal that the University can put an outright gift to work immediately.

## Gifts of Cash

The most common type of gift is the gift of cash—and with good reason. It is simple, straightforward, and as easy as writing a check. And, because charitable gifts qualify for federal tax deductions, the real out-of-pocket cost of a cash donation is usually much less than its face value: you save whatever tax you would have owed on the amount of the gift. Likewise, some state tax laws offer additional deductions or credits for gifts to education.

For record purposes, a gift of cash is considered made on the date it is mailed or hand delivered. Please make checks or money orders payable to the Indiana University Foundation, the designated fundraising agency for Indiana University.

*Features & Benefits*

- Simple and quick
- Charitable income tax deduction
- IU can make immediate use of your gift
- Estate tax and probate savings

## Gifts of Appreciated Property

Charitable gifts of appreciated property—whether real estate or capital gain securities—can provide even greater tax benefits than a cash gift of equal value. You may take a charitable deduction for the full fair market value of the property, while avoiding capital gains taxes. The IRS currently allows you to deduct the full fair market value of the property up to 30 percent of your adjusted gross income for the year. Any amount over that ceiling can be carried forward for future deduction, for up to five years, subject to the same percentage limitations.

A gift of appreciated property is considered made on the day the transfer is completed. Please contact the IU Foundation for specific instructions.

*Features & Benefits*

- Opportunity to make a substantial gift to IU
- Charitable income tax deduction
- IU can make immediate use of your gift
- Avoid capital gains tax
- Estate tax and probate savings

## Gifts of Tangible Personal Property

A gift of tangible personal property—such as furniture, art works, jewelry, antiques, books, coin or stamp collections, and so on—is deductible for its full fair market value (up to 30 percent of your adjusted gross income) if it meets two conditions: 1) it must be documented by a legitimate appraisal, and 2) it must satisfy the "related use" standard.

"Related use" means that the University must be able to use the gift in a way that is related to or furthers its educational mission. For example, books donated to the library will meet the standard, as will classroom or office furniture, or computers, or business machines. A painting will meet the standard if it is displayed for viewing, but will not if the University sells it. Property that does not satisfy the "related use" standard may still be deducted, but only for your cost basis in the property, subject to a limit of 50 percent of your adjusted gross income. The five-year carryover rule for the deduction applies in both cases. Please note, however, that in order to protect its tax-exempt status, the University must severely limit the non-related-use gifts that it accepts.

A gift of tangible personal property is considered to be made on the date when ownership or legal title is transferred. To make the formal transfer, you may write up a simple "letter of intent to donate" that identifies the property and includes a signed statement of your intent to transfer it to the Indiana University Foundation.

*Features & Benefits*

- Opportunity to make a unique and substantial gift to IU which may be of significant value to teaching, learning, or research
- Charitable income tax deduction
- IU can make immediate use of your gift
- Avoid capital gains tax
- Estate tax and probate savings

## Bargain Sales

You may have property that has appreciated in value, but you only want to give part of that value to the IU Foundation. You may make a "bargain sale" of the property to the Foundation for less than its fair market value, usually your cost basis. You thereby get cash in hand to recoup your original investment, while getting a charitable deduction for the donated difference. You should note, however, that some of the cash recovered will be treated as a capital gain.

For record purposes, the date of the sale is considered to be the date of the gift. Bargain sales require careful planning. Please consult your tax adviser, legal counsel, or other financial planner, and contact the IU Foundation's Office of Planned Giving Services for further information.

*Features & Benefits*

- Possible recovery of original investment
- Opportunity to make a substantial gift to IU
- Charitable income tax deduction
- Reduction in capital gains tax
- Increased cash flow
- Estate tax and probate savings

### Gifts of Closely Held Stock

If you are a business owner and you contribute closely held stock, you may take a charitable deduction for the stock's appraised fair market value. Besides increasing your cash flow, you also avoid the potential capital gains tax on the appreciated value of the stock. The corporation may buy back the stock, but so long as the IU Foundation is not legally obligated to sell back the stock, you may enjoy significant tax savings.

For record purposes, the date of a gift of closely held stock is considered to be the date the stock is transferred.

*Features & Benefits*

- Opportunity to make a substantial gift to IU
- Charitable income tax deduction
- Avoid capital gains taxes
- Positive impact on cash flow
- Estate tax and probate savings
- Excellent estate planning opportunity for yourself and your heirs

## Life Income Plans

You can make a substantial gift to Indiana University while still earning income from the donated assets. These life income plans are some of the most flexible and fruitful options available to donors. They allow you to provide income for yourself, your heirs, or both; avoid significant capital gains and estate taxes; and satisfy your wish to make a substantial gift to IU.

This is how it works: You fund the trust with a significant, irrevocable gift to the IU Foundation to benefit Indiana University. (The gift must be irrevocable to qualify for the federal charitable deduction.) The Foundation invests the gift, and you or your designee receive income for as long as you choose: for a definite term of not more than 20 years, or for the rest of your life. At the end of that time, the remaining principal benefits the University in whatever way you specify.

You may establish a trust using assets such as real estate, stock, or cash. Funding it with appreciated long-term property enables you to protect your profit or reinvest for a higher yield, while avoiding capital gains taxes. You thereby maximize the value and the benefit of the property, both as income and as a gift.

There are two basic types of life income trusts: annuity trusts and unitrusts. The annuity trust pays a fixed *dollar amount*, while the unitrust pays a fixed *percentage*.

With the annuity trust, your income will be the same each year, regardless of the value of the trust. With the unitrust, your income will go up or down as the value of the trust itself fluctuates.

## Annuity Trusts

A charitable remainder annuity trust pays a fixed amount (at least five percent of the fair market value of the trust assets when the trust is established) to you or your beneficiaries at least once a year. The payout is determined when you set up the trust, based on such factors as your age, the number of beneficiaries, your desired income, and the length of the trust term. If the trust earns more income than the agreed amount, the additional earnings are reinvested. If the earnings are less, withdrawals from the trust's principal make up the difference. Once the annuity trust is created, you may not make additional contributions to it.

You will receive an income tax deduction for the value of the charitable remainder interest in the trust at the time you set it up (calculated from tables based on your age), and you avoid capital gains taxes on the transfer of appreciated long-term assets such as real estate or securities. Because the assets are effectively removed from your estate, you also avoid estate taxes.

*Features & Benefits*

- Opportunity to make a substantial gift to IU while receiving life income
- Fixed payout offers the security of guaranteed income
- Can unlock appreciated assets for diversification or increased yield
- Professional asset management
- Can receive an attractive equivalent rate of return
- Immediate tax deduction
- Avoid capital gains taxes
- Estate tax and probate savings

## Unitrusts

A charitable remainder unitrust differs from an annuity trust by paying a fixed percentage—at least five percent—of the fair market value of the trust's assets each year, rather than a fixed sum. That means the income will fluctuate from year to year as the trust's value fluctuates, but because the long-term market pattern is usually one of growth, you can generally expect payments to increase over time. In this way a unitrust can be an effective hedge against inflation.

Choosing a lower percentage may actually increase your income over time because it allows the principal to grow more quickly. As the principal increases, so will the amount of your payment. The difference can be significant. And the more the principal grows, of course, the larger the ultimate gift to Indiana University will be, and the more completely it fulfills your philanthropic goals. You may also make additional contributions to a unitrust.

Your charitable deduction depends on the fair market value of the initial assets you transfer, the payout percentage you choose, the number and ages of beneficiaries, and other such factors. As with an annuity trust, you effectively remove the funding assets from your estate, and you likewise avoid capital gains taxes.

*Features & Benefits*

- Opportunity to make a substantial gift to IU while receiving life income
- Variable percentage payout may protect against inflation as your trust's assets grow
- Larger gift to IU than might otherwise be possible
- Professional asset management
- Receive an attractive "real" rate of return on your assets
- Can unlock appreciated assets for diversification or increased yield
- Immediate tax deduction
- Avoid capital gains taxes
- Estate tax and probate savings

## Pooled Income Funds

Another kind of trust is called a pooled income fund. It allows separate donors to pool their gifts for investment purposes. Two or more donors must irrevocably transfer property into the trust, contributing the remainder interest in the property to the IU Foundation. The Foundation then acts as trustee, investing the combined fund and distributing the annual proceeds to the donors in direct proportion to the assets each one contributed. The actual dollar amount is not specified: it depends on the amount earned by the fund. You may designate yourself as beneficiary, or anyone else living at the time the fund is created.

Your charitable deduction would be the present value of the remainder interest in the property, as determined by IRS tables, on the day you transfer it. You may add to the fund at any time.

*Features & Benefits*

- Opportunity to make a substantial future gift to IU
- Competitive rate of return

- Professional asset management
- Income for yourself or other beneficiary
- Can unlock appreciated assets for diversification or increased yield
- Immediate tax deduction
- Avoid capital gains taxes
- Estate tax and probate savings

## Charitable Gift Annuities

One of the most common and popular ways to make a planned gift is with a charitable gift annuity. It is a simple contract between you and the IU Foundation. In exchange for an irrevocable gift, the Foundation agrees to pay one or two annuitants a fixed dollar amount each year for life. The amount is based on life expectancy: the older you are at the time of the gift, the greater the amount can be. The payments are guaranteed by the general resources of the Foundation.

Charitable gift annuities can be funded with cash, real estate, or appreciated securities. You receive a tax deduction based on your age, the payout rate, and the federal discount rate. If you use an appreciated asset, a portion of each payout will be capital gain, which is therefore spread out over your lifetime. Likewise, a part of each payment would be a tax-free return of principal, increasing the after-tax value of each payment. And because you have effectively removed the assets from your estate, you avoid estate taxes.

A similar type of annuity is the deferred charitable gift annuity. The arrangement is essentially the same; the difference is that the IU Foundation waits to begin your fixed payout until some specified point in the future (at least one year). In either case, at your death the proceeds of the gift annuity become available for Indiana University to use in whatever way you wished.

A deferred charitable gift annuity can be an excellent way to supplement your retirement income. The Foundation receives the gift today and invests it for years; you receive a current tax deduction, but you don't receive the payments until you retire, when you may be in a lower income tax bracket.

*Features & Benefits*
- Fixed payout offers the security of guaranteed income
- Attractive rate of return
- Can unlock appreciated assets for diversification or increased yield
- Professional asset management
- Opportunity to make a substantial gift to IU
- Favorable income tax position now and at retirement
- Immediate charitable tax deduction
- Estate tax and probate savings

# Other Planned Gift Arrangements

Life income plans are not the only kind of planned gift. Many others exist that offer particular advantages for specific circumstances. The following pages present a sampling of the most popular. If you believe your own situation requires something not described here, a specialist from the Office of Planned Giving Services at the IU Foundation will be happy to discuss other options with you.

## Charitable Lead Trusts

A charitable lead trust is like a charitable remainder trust in reverse. You select the assets used to fund the trust and decide how long it will last, and the IU Foundation receives income from the trust while it exists. There is no minimum payout. When the trust terminates, its assets return to you or your designated beneficiary.

This type of trust can be useful if you want to reduce your current income but wish to retain the assets for your family. A charitable lead trust can be a means to transfer substantial amounts of wealth from generation to generation, free (or largely free) of estate, inheritance, and gift taxes.

A charitable lead trust is a complex giving vehicle with many income, estate, and gift tax consequences. You should discuss your goals with your legal and financial advisers to determine whether a charitable lead trust would suit your plans. You are also encouraged to contact the planned giving professionals at the IU Foundation for more detailed information.

*Features & Benefits*
- Reduces current income while retaining assets
- Can be a low-cost means of transferring property to heirs
- Opportunity to make a substantial current gift to IU
- Potential estate, inheritance, and gift tax savings

## Gifts of Real Property Subject to Life Estate

Your personal residence or farm may be the single most valuable asset you own. If it has appreciated significantly in value, you could owe tremendous capital gains taxes if you or your heirs sold the property. An alternative is to give the property to the IU Foundation subject to life estate, which simply means that you or your designees retain the use of the property for life.

You gain an immediate tax deduction for the remainder interest in the property, and you escape the potential capital gains taxes. Best of all, you get to make a substantial gift for Indiana University without disrupting your lifestyle.

Gifts of this kind require detailed language tailored to your specific situation and needs, and the advantages and benefits vary accordingly. The Foundation's planned giving staff will be happy to work with you and your advisers to help you arrange the best plan for you.

*Features & Benefits*

- Opportunity to make a substantial gift to IU while retaining lifetime use
- Immediate tax deduction
- Avoid capital gains taxes
- Estate tax and probate savings
- Can provide a favorable income tax position

## Wealth Replacement with Life Insurance

When you make a gift to the Indiana University Foundation for the benefit of Indiana University, you may use a life insurance trust to replace the value of the donated assets. In this way, you can protect the interests of your heirs while still fulfilling your philanthropic goals. The life insurance provides the dollar amount, and the trust, provided it is irrevocable, removes the proceeds from your estate for tax purposes.

In this arrangement, you create a trust to buy insurance on your life, with your children as beneficiaries. You can use the tax savings from your charitable gift, or the payout from a life income arrangement, to cover the premiums. After your death, the proceeds from the policy pass to the trust free of estate taxes, thereby replacing the value of the original charitable gift.

Wealth replacement life insurance trusts can be set up in several different ways, and all have strict technical requirements. You should discuss them with your financial and legal advisers before deciding to pursue this option. The Foundation's planned giving staff will be happy to answer your questions.

*Features & Benefits*

- Restores asset value to your estate at relatively low cost
- Opportunity to make a substantial gift to IU without consequence to your heirs
- Estate tax and probate savings

## Wills and Estate Plans

A carefully prepared will or estate plan is the best way to ensure that your loved ones are provided for after your death, and that your preferred charities are supported as you intend. They allow you to retain full use of your assets during your lifetime and still make a significant gift for Indiana University. They are technical documents that should therefore be drafted by an attorney, but they may be revised and updated whenever you like, as your wishes and circumstances change.

## Types of Gifts

By far the most common means of making a charitable gift is through a personal trust or will. It's no wonder: such gifts allow you to contribute to Indiana University at a level you might never have managed during your lifetime.

Your bequest can take a variety of forms. Here are a few samples for you to consider.

*Specific Bequest.* The most popular type of charitable bequest, a specific bequest provides that the IU Foundation receive a specific dollar amount, percentage of your estate, or piece of property.

*Residuary Bequest.* A residuary bequest provides that the IU Foundation receive all or a stated portion of your estate after all other bequests, debts, taxes, and expenses have been distributed.

*Contingent Bequest.* A contingent bequest can ensure that if circumstances make it impossible to carry out your primary provisions (as when your spouse or other heirs do not survive you), your assets will then pass to the IU Foundation for Indiana University rather than to unintended beneficiaries.

*Trust Under Will.* You can bequeath a portion of your estate to be held in trust for a specified purpose, as stated in your will.

## Bequest Language

Because the Indiana University Foundation has been designated by the trustees of Indiana University as the official entity for receiving and administering gifts for IU, please incorporate the following language into your will:

*"I give, devise, and bequeath the (sum of/percentage of/residue of my estate) to Indiana University Foundation, a not-for-profit corporation with principal offices located in Bloomington, Indiana, to be utilized for the benefit of Indiana University as specified in a gift agreement on file at said Foundation."*

## Appreciation and Recognition

If you decide to include a gift to Indiana University Foundation for the benefit of IU in your will, we invite and encourage you to let the Foundation know about your decision ahead of time, for several reasons. First, so you can complete a gift agreement and ensure that there will be no question as to how your gift will be used. Second, so that IU and the Foundation can make note of the gift as they plan for the future. And finally, so that we may recognize your generosity and show our appreciation, if you so desire, by including you in the roster of major donors to Indiana University.

# Commemorative

# Gift

# Opportunities

The
Endowment
Campaign
*for*
Indiana
University
Bloomington

THE ENDOWMENT CAMPAIGN FOR INDIANA UNIVERSITY BLOOMINGTON is a national and international fundraising effort being conducted into the year 2000. This campaign seeks to add at least $150 million to the campus's endowment and to augment annual giving by at least $200 million. The Endowment Campaign is the largest fundraising campaign for a single campus in the University's history. Since it includes all components of the Bloomington campus, gifts to the Endowment Campaign will enrich every aspect of teaching and learning at IU Bloomington.

# Commemorative Gift Opportunities

Commemorative gift opportunities available through the Endowment Campaign for Indiana University Bloomington offer alumni, parents, friends, foundations, and corporations numerous ways to provide memorials and testimonials to family, friends, organizations, or other individuals. These gifts can embody their donor's ideals and provide essential support to ensure a strong future for IU Bloomington.

Each commemorative gift provides a naming opportunity for the donor according to his or her wishes, and appropriate recognition will be given. Methods of making commemorative gifts include outright gifts of cash, gifts of securities, gifts of real property, gifts of life insurance, planned gifts which can take many forms, and gifts through a will.

An IU Foundation representative will be happy to work with anyone desiring to make a commemorative gift and explore the options through which that gift may be given. For details on these and other named and memorial gift opportunities, see the *Guide to Giving* or contact the Indiana University Foundation Office of Planned Giving Services at (800) 558–8311 or (812) 855–8311.

# Guidelines for Naming Opportunities and Endowed Funds

The monetary amounts listed are University thresholds. Each unit may establish higher minimums for certain endowments based on unique requirements of the individual unit, the discipline involved, and the scope of the program relative to budget and other factors.

## Support for Faculty*

*Deanship.* To endow the deanship of a school requires a gift of $3 million or more.

*Directorship or Departmental Chair.* To establish a directorship or departmental chair requires a gift of $2 million or more.

*Faculty Chair.* To establish a faculty chair requires a minimum gift of $1 million.

*Professorship.* To establish an endowed professorship requires a minimum gift of $500,000.

*Faculty Research Fund.* To establish a faculty research fund requires a minimum gift of $250,000.

*Visiting Professorship.* To establish an endowed visiting professorship requires a minimum gift of $250,000. The annual proceeds will be used to invite a distinguished scholar to campus for a finite period of time.

*Lectureship.* To establish an endowed lectureship requires a minimum gift commitment of $100,000. The annual proceeds from this endowment will be used to pay for honoraria, publicity, and the expenses of a member of the faculty or a visiting lecturer from another institution or organization on the campus.

*The position, not the person, is endowed.

*The Indiana University Faculty Endowment Income Matching Program has been designed to encourage gifts with the goal of raising endowment for faculty positions. President Brand and the Board of Trustees have set aside $2 million in available matching funds for those gifts qualifying for the match before December 31, 1999. Gifts of $500,000 and above, from a single source, designated for chairs and professorships, and received within five years, qualify for the match. All income on gifts is to be matched in perpetuity. (Full details are available upon request.)*

## Support for Students

*Graduate Student Fellowship.* Establishment of an endowed graduate student fellowship requires a minimum gift of $200,000. A fellowship is ordinarily awarded to a student who is working toward an advanced degree in any of the graduate fields. An endowed fellowship should provide support for the majority of the recipient's expenses.

*Herman B Wells Scholarship.* A scholarship in the Herman B Wells Scholarship Program can be established with a minimum gift of $150,000.

*Undergraduate Scholarship.* To establish a full-tuition undergraduate endowed scholarship requires a minimum gift of $25,000.

## Support for Programs and Facilities

**School.** Opportunities exist to name several of the schools and the main library on the campus, by providing a gift for the general endowment to benefit the unit. The minimum gift commitment required to do so varies with the respective schools, but the minimum gift to name a school is $10 million.

**New or Renovated Building.** To name new or renovated buildings generally requires a gift of one-half of the construction cost of the capital project.

**Research Center, Institute, or Academic Program.** To name a research center, institute, or an academic program requires a gift commitment of $1 million or more; the size of the gift is to be determined by the specific center, institute, or program to be named.

**Campus Library.** To establish a campus library, a gift commitment of $1 million or more (depending on the size of the library) is required. Endowment income will benefit the collections, service, and technology needs of the particular library.

**Laboratory.** To establish an endowed laboratory requires a minimum gift commitment of $1 million. The annual earnings from the endowment will be used for equipment, technology, enhancements, and research.

**Classroom.** To establish an endowed classroom requires a minimum gift commitment of $500,000. The annual earnings will be used for equipment, technology, enhancements, refurbishment, and modernization.

**Collection Fund.** To establish an endowed collection fund requires a minimum gift of $250,000. The income from an endowed collection fund may be used for the purchase of books or other materials in a specific field and, to the extent not needed for purchases, for the preservation of books. The income may also be used for book repair, cataloguing, or other expenses of the library.

NOTES

*Five-year pledges can be made to create these endowments.*

*    The Indiana University Faculty Endowment Income Matching Program has been designed to encourage gifts with the goal of raising endowment for faculty positions. President Brand and the Board of Trustees have set aside $2 million in available matching funds for those gifts qualifying for the match before December 31, 1999. Gifts of $500,000 and above, from a single source, designated for chairs and professorships, and received within five years, qualify for the match. All income on gifts is to be matched in perpetuity. (Full details are available upon request.)*

*All gifts to the Endowment Campaign for Indiana University Bloomington are tax deductible within the regulations of the Internal Revenue Service. Prospective donors to the Endowment Campaign may wish to consult their attorney or tax advisor to determine which gifts are most appropriate to their financial situation.*

*The Bloomington campus chancellor, or his designee, has the latitude to approve the establishment of named funds in amounts less than those stated above, provided that it is understood that, within a reasonable period of time from the establishment of the fund, the principal of the fund, excluding interest income, will equal the stated minimum.*

*It is the general policy of Indiana University that the University President shall approve the establishment and activation of named funds upon receipt of the gifts by the IU Foundation. The president of the University, in consultation with the Bloomington chancellor and deans and the IU Foundation president, sets minimum gift level amounts and establishes guidelines for gift-naming opportunities as approved by the IU Board of Trustees. Approval cannot be granted until the donor's name is known or until the name or names of the person or persons being memorialized are known.*

# Commemorative Gift Opportunities for Individual Units

Selected gift opportunities have been established for all academic units participating in the Campaign. For details on a unit's specific needs and objectives, please refer to its individual case statement or contact the unit's chief development officer.

## IU Art Museum

| | |
|---|---|
| Name the Museum | $10 million |
| Name the Director's Chair | $2 million |
| Name the Education Chair | $1 million |
| Name the Curatorship for African Art, Oceania, and the Americas | Reserved |
| Name the Curatorship for Ancient Art | Reserved |
| Name the Curatorship for Western Art through the 18th Century | $1 million |
| Name the Curatorship for 19th and 20th Century Art | $1 million |
| Name the Curatorship for Works on Paper | $1 million |
| Name the Curatorship for Asian Art | $1 million |
| Name the Conservatorship of Objects | $750,000 |
| Name the Conservatorship of Paintings | $500,000 |
| Name the Conservatorship of Works on Paper | $500,000 |
| Endow a Graduate Fellowship | $300,000 |

## College of Arts & Sciences

Name the College of Arts & Sciences . . . . . . . . . . . . . . . . . $25 million

Name the College Honors Program . . . . . . . . . . . . . . . . . . $5 million

Name the Liberal Arts Management Program . . . . . . . . . . . $3 million

Name the Women's Studies Program . . . . . . . . . . . . . . . . . $3 million

Endow the Dean's Chair . . . . . . . . . . . . . . . . . . . . . . . . . . . $3 million

Endow a Departmental Chair . . . . . . . . . . . . . . . . . . . . . . . $2 million

Endow a Science, Social Science, or Humanities Chair . . . . $1 million

Endow a Laboratory . . . . . . . . . . . . . . . . . . . . . . . . . . . . . . $1 million

Endow a Professorship in Science,
Social Science, or Humanities . . . . . . . . . . . . . . . . . . . . . . . $500,000

Endow a Classroom . . . . . . . . . . . . . . . . . . . . . . . . . . . . . . . $500,000

Endow a Graduate Fellowship . . . . . . . . . . . . . . . . . . . . . . . $400,000

Endow a Visiting Professorship . . . . . . . . . . . . . . . . . . . . . . $250,000

Endow a Faculty Research Fund . . . . . . . . . . . . . . . . . . . . . $250,000

Endow a Dean's Scholar . . . . . . . . . . . . . . . . . . . . . . . . . . . $200,000

Endow an Undergraduate Scholarship . . . . . . . . . . . $25,000–200,000

Endow a Lectureship . . . . . . . . . . . . . . . . . . . . . . . . . . . . . . $100,000

Endow a Summer Fellowship . . . . . . . . . . . . . . . . . . . . . . . $100,000

Endow a Teaching Award . . . . . . . . . . . . . . . . . . . . . . . . . . . $40,000

Endow a Book Fund . . . . . . . . . . . . . . . . . . . . . . . . . . . . . . . $25,000

## Athletics

Endow the Academic Counseling Office for IU Athletes . . . $2 million

Endow the Marching Hundred Band . . . . . . . . . . . . . . . . . . $2 million

Endow Computer Labs for Athletes . . . . . . . . . . . . . . . . . . $1 million

Endow the Student Athletic Board . . . . . . . . . . . . . . . . . . . $1 million

Endow the University Softball Complex . . . . . . . . . . . . . . . $1 million

Endow the University Cheerleading Squad . . . . . . . . . . . . . $1 million

Endow an Undergraduate Scholarship for an IU Athlete* . . . $250,000

Name an Undergraduate Scholarship for an IU Athlete* . . . . $100,000

Create a Sustaining Endowment Fund
to Support IU Athletics . . . . . . . . . . . . . . . . . . . . . . . . . . . . . $25,000

*Donors may designate these gifts to particular varsity sports, including the following: men's and women's basketball, men's and women's cross country, men's and women's golf, men's and women's soccer, men's and women's swimming and diving, men's and women's tennis, men's and women's track and field (indoor and outdoor), football, baseball, wrestling, volleyball, softball, and water polo.

## School of Business

Name the School of Business . . . . . . . . . . . . . . . . . . . . . . . . Reserved

Name the Corporate and Graduate Center . . . . . . . . . . . . $9 million

Name the Existing School of Business Building . . . . . . . . . $9 million

Endow the Deanship . . . . . . . . . . . . . . . . . . . . . . . . . . . . . $3 million

Establish Named Directorships or Departmental Chairs . . . $2 million

Name the Business Library . . . . . . . . . . . . . . . . . . . . . . . . . $2 million

Endow a Faculty Chair . . . . . . . . . . . . . . . . . . . . . . . . . . . . $1 million

Endow a Professorship . . . . . . . . . . . . . . . . . . . . . . . . . . . . $500,000

Endow a Visiting Lectureship . . . . . . . . . . . . . . . . . . . . . . . $250,000

Endow a Faculty Research Fund . . . . . . . . . . . . . . . . . . . . . $250,000

Endow a Graduate Fellowship . . . . . . . . . . . . . . . . . . . . . . $200,000

Endow an Undergraduate Scholarship . . . . . . . . . . . . . . . . . $50,000

## School of Continuing Studies

Endow a Professorship in Labor Studies . . . . . . . . . . . . . . . $500,000

Endow an Undergraduate Scholarship . . . . . . . . . . . . . . . . . $25,000

## University Libraries

Name the Main Library . . . . . . . . . . . . . . . . . . . . . . . . . . . $20 million

Name the Main Library East Tower . . . . . . . . . . . . . . . . . . . $5 million

Name the Main Library West Tower .................. $5 million

Name a Campus Library .......................... $1 million

Endow Librarian Positions

    Dean of the University Libraries ................ $2 million

    Head of the Lilly Library or a Campus Library ..... $1 million

    Head of Preservation, Reference,
    or Manuscript Curator .......................... $750,000

Name the Preservation Laboratory .................... $500,000

Endow Collections ........................ $10,000 and above

[*Note:* For space considerations, some of the schools were omitted from this section.]

# Campaign Contacts

For more information on the Endowment Campaign or questions or concerns you may have, please contact any of the following individuals at Indiana University Bloomington or the IU Foundation. To discuss options for giving to the school or program of your choice, contact the chief development officer for the specific school on the Bloomington campus.

MYLES BRAND

*President*
Indiana University
Bryan Hall 200
Bloomington, IN 47405
Phone: (812) 855–4613
pres@indiana.edu

CURTIS R. SIMIC

*President*
IU Foundation
State Road 46 By-Pass,
Showalter House
P.O. Box 500
Bloomington, IN 47402
Phone: (800) 558–8311
or (812) 855–6679
crsimic@indiana.edu

KENT E. DOVE

*Executive Director, Capital Campaigns*
IU Foundation
State Road 46 By-Pass,
Showalter House
P.O. Box 500
Bloomington, IN 47402
Phone: (800) 558–8311
or (812) 855–1293
kedove@indiana.edu

*Unless otherwise specified, all campus addresses listed below can be completed by adding Indiana University, Bloomington, IN 47405.*

### IU ART MUSEUM

Eileen E. Savage
*Associate Director for Development*
IU Art Museum
(812) 855–1031
eisavage@indiana.edu

### COLLEGE OF ARTS & SCIENCES

Susan Green
*Executive Director of Development
and Alumni Programs*
Kirkwood 208
(812) 855–7934
greens@indiana.edu

### ATHLETICS

W. David Martin
*Associate Athletic Director
for External Affairs
Executive Director, Varsity Club*
Assembly Hall, 47408–1590
(812) 855–0866
kmtaylor@indiana.edu

### SCHOOL OF BUSINESS

Rick Dupree
*Executive Director of Development*
Business 749
(812) 855–9000
rdupree@indiana.edu

### SCHOOL OF CONTINUING STUDIES

Judy Wertheim
*Executive Associate Dean*
Owen Hall 205
(812) 855–8995
jwerthei@indiana.edu

### SCHOOL OF EDUCATION

Sarah Baumgart
*Director of External Relations*
Wright Education Building 4115
(812) 856–805
baumgar@indiana.edu

### SCHOOL OF HEALTH, PHYSICAL EDUCATION, & RECREATION

Susie Bair
*Director of Development
and External Affairs*
HPER 146
(812) 855–3096
sbair@indiana.edu

### SCHOOL OF JOURNALISM

Kathy Parker
*Director of Development
and Alumni Affairs*
Ernie Pyle 201
(812) 855–6317
kaparker@indiana.edu

### SCHOOL OF LAW

Angela Lieurance
*Assistant Dean for Development
and Alumni Relations*
Law 200
(812) 855–9953
angelalieurance@law.indiana.edu

### UNIVERSITY LIBRARIES

Cameron McGuire
*Director of Development*
Library Administration C-2
(812) 855–3403
mcguire@indiana.edu

SCHOOL OF LIBRARY &
INFORMATION SCIENCE

Tony Sloan
*Development Director*
SLIS 011C
(812) 855–5530
tosloan@indiana.edu

SCHOOL OF MUSIC

Barbara Monahan
*Director of Development*
MAC 426
(812) 855–4737
bmonahan@indiana.edu

SCHOOL OF OPTOMETRY

Julie Walsh Seiler
*Senior Development Director*
IU Foundation
P.O. Box 500
Bloomington, IN 47402
(812) 855–1367
jwseiler@indiana.edu

SCHOOL OF PUBLIC &
ENVIRONMENTAL AFFAIRS

Tony Sloan
*Development Director*
SPEA 316
(812) 856–4868
tosloan@indiana.edu

The Endowment Campaign for Indiana University Bloomington

# Standards of Giving

A fundamental of fundraising for the Endowment Campaign for Indiana University Bloomington is the identification, correct evaluation, and thoughtful solicitation approach to alumni and friends of IU Bloomington. It is important for volunteers and prospective donors to be aware of the caliber of gifts required. A better solicitation effort and more meaningful response will result when each discussion is undertaken with this information in hand.

To maximize this awareness, the following table offers specific standards of giving necessary to ensure the success of the Endowment Campaign and suggests to our volunteer workers and prospective donors the levels of support which must be achieved.

*Curtis R. Simic*

Curtis R. Simic
President, Indiana University Foundation

## ENDOWMENT GOAL: $150,000,000

| Gift Amounts | Number of Gifts Needed | Total |
|---|---|---|
| $15,000,000+ | 1 | $15,000,000 |
| $10,000,000–14,999,999 | 2 | $20,000,000 |
| $5,000,000–9,999,999 | 3 | $15,000,000 |
| $2,500,000–$4,999,999 | 6 | $15,000,000 |
| $1,000,000–2,499,999 | 17 | $17,000,000 |
| $750,000–999,999 | 20 | $15,000,000 |
| $500,000–749,999 | 30 | $15,000,000 |
| $250,000–499,999 | 50 | $12,500,000 |
| $100,000–249,999 | 100 | $10,000,000 |
| $25,000–99,999 | 400 | $10,000,000 |
| Under $25,000 | Many | $ 5,500,000 |
| Total | | $150,000,000 |

**The Endowment Campaign
for Indiana University Bloomington**

Curtis R. Simic
President
Indiana University Foundation
P.O. Box 500
Bloomington, IN 47402

Dear Curt:

   To assist Indiana University Bloomington in fulfilling its important responsibilities and in consideration of the gifts of others, I intend and expect to contribute the sum of $ _____ to the Indiana University Foundation for The Endowment Campaign for Indiana University Bloomington.

   My gift is:

   ❑ Designated for the following purpose(s):

   _____

                                           or

   ❑ To be used at the discretion of the Board of Directors of the Indiana University Foundation.

   I expect to make this gift over a period of _____ years, as follows:

   $ _____ Herewith

   $ _____ on or before _____

   $ _____ on or before _____

                                           or

   _____

   _____

   This statement of intention and expectation shall not constitute a legal obligation and shall not be legally binding in any way on me or my estate. While I consider that I have a moral obligation to make this gift, I reserve the right to adjust or to cancel it in the event of unforeseen circumstances.

                                   Sincerely yours,

                                   _____

                                   (Signature)

                                   _____

                                   Name (please print)

                                   _____

                                   (Date)

INDIANA UNIVERSITY FOUNDATION • SHOWALTER HOUSE, P.O. BOX 500 • BLOOMINGTON, INDIANA 47402
*Phone:* (800) 558–8311     (812) 855–8311     *Fax:* (812) 855–6956

## Contents

| Appointed by the Governor | Term Expires |
|---|---|
| John D. Walda, President | 1999 |
| Frederick F. Eichhorn Jr., Vice President | 1999 |
| P. A. Mack Jr., Vice President | 1998 |
| William A. Cook | 1998 |
| Rose E. Gallagher* | 1999 |
| Robert H. McKinney | 1998 |

*Appointment is made from the Indiana University student body.

### Elected by Indiana University Alumni

| | |
|---|---|
| Cora Smith Breckenridge | 2000 |
| Ray Richardson | 1998 |
| James T. Morris | 1999 |

ADDITIONAL OFFICERS,
APPOINTED BY THE TRUSTEES

Steven A. Miller, Treasurer

James P. Perin, Assistant Treasurer

J. Susan Parrish, Secretary

Dorothy J. Frapwell, Assistant Secretary

## Alumni Association

Indiana University's more than 400,000 alumni live in all 50 states and in 143 international locations and are organized in 100 alumni clubs. During the first year of the "Pride of Indiana" membership campaign, IUAA has grown to more than 73,000 members, making it the sixth largest association in the country.

The goal is to have 100,000 members by the year 2000. The association sponsors a variety of programs. Among them are Mini University each summer on the Bloomington campus; family camping at Elkhart Lake, Wisconsin; a worldwide educational travel program; the Good Friends volunteer program for students in grades K–12; and the Alumni Student Recruiters program. More than 21,000 Hoosiers are driving cars with IU license plates. Alumni Publications puts out a magazine for members six times a year, a mini-magazine for nonmembers twice a year, more than 50 constituent publications, and a dozen club newsletters.

IU's alumni have a new home on the Bloomington campus. The successful completion of the Virgil T. DeVault Alumni Center campaign was celebrated during Cream and Crimson Weekend with a grand opening attended by more than 1,200 persons. More than 7,000 alumni and friends contributed $5.3 million to renovate an existing university building. Six meeting rooms are available for university and association meetings and events. All offices of the IUAA are located in the building. More than 600 personalized bricks have been sold for $1,000 and are laid on the Haugh Plaza just outside the Kelley Dining Room. The sale of bricks will continue to build an endowment for maintenance and future expansion.

Jerry Tardy is the university director of alumni affairs and executive director of the alumni association; John D. Hobson and Janet C. Shirley are associate executive directors.

Alumni directors across the state:

Stefan Davis, *Indianapolis*

Bette Davenport, *Richmond*

Jennifer Bosk, *Fort Wayne*

Suzanne Wallace, *Kokomo (Interim)*

Thomas Higgins, *Gary*

Joann Phillips, *South Bend*

Deborah Baird, *New Albany (Interim)*

## University Traditions

*School Colors:* Cream and crimson were chosen by the class of 1888 as the Indiana University colors.

*School Song:* "Hail to Old I.U." is the alma mater song of Indiana University. It was composed in 1892 by J. T. Giles, class of 1894. Hoagy Carmichael's "Chimes of Indiana," written and dedicated to the university in 1935, is also part of IU's heritage.

*School Flower:* The trailing arbutus, found by Professor Herman B. Boisen on a hill east of Bloomington in 1877, is the Indiana University flower. The school yearbook carries its name.

*Well House:* The T. F. Rose Well House was presented to the university in 1908 by IU trustee Theodore F. Rose. Its stone arches originally were the portals of the "Old College Building" erected on

Seminary Square in 1855. In earlier times, tradition held that a female student attained coed status by being kissed in the Well House during the 12 strokes of midnight on the Student Building clock.

*Chimes:* The classes of 1899 through 1902 raised the funds to install an 11–bell chime in the tower of the Student Building in 1906. The bells were destroyed by a fire in late 1990 and were replaced by 14 new bells in 1991.

*Old Oaken Bucket:* This trophy, a symbol of the football rivalry between Indiana and Purdue, was donated in 1925 by the IU and Purdue alumni of Chicago. It resides for a year with the winning team, or in the event of a tie, for six months with each school.

*Little 500:* Beginning in 1951 as a one-day 50–mile men's bicycle race, the Little 500 now consists of several events including the Mini tricycle race. A women's bicycle race was added in 1988.

*Founders Day:* Although the university was established on January 20, 1820, its anniversary is celebrated in March on Founders Day (called Foundation Day before 1950). Students are recognized for scholastic achievement and faculty members for outstanding teaching during Founders Day ceremonies.

*Note:* Certain sections of this booklet were omitted for the sake of brevity.

# YOUR GIFT TO THE ENDOWMENT CAMPAIGN FOR INDIANA UNIVERSITY BLOOMINGTON

*The Endowment Campaign* is the largest in the University's history and includes all the components of the Bloomington campus. The Campaign goal is $350 million–$150 million for new endowment, and $200 million in ongoing support.

*Endowment* is one of the most cost-effective and manageable ways to achieve the University's goals and prepare for the future. The primary purpose of the Campaign is to increase the number of endowed chairs and professorships, fellowships, and scholarships available to the campus. Gifts to the Endowment Campaign will enrich every aspect of teaching and learning at IU.

The Indiana University Foundation is designated by the trustees of Indiana University as the official fundraising agency for the University. A not-for-profit corporation chartered in 1936 under the laws of the State of Indiana, the Foundation raises and receives gifts from the private sector, administers funds, and manages assets to enhance the quality of education at Indiana University.

800 558-8311 or 812 855-8311
Bloomington, IN 47402
P.O. Box 500
Indiana University Foundation
Capital Campaign Office

INDIANA UNIVERSITY BLOOMINGTON
*for*
THE ENDOWMENT CAMPAIGN

THE ENDOWMENT CAMPAIGN
*for*
INDIANA UNIVERSITY BLOOMINGTON

# INVESTING IN THE FUTURE OF INDIANA UNIVERSITY BLOOMINGTON

*This is my/our commitment to The Endowment Campaign for Indiana University Bloomington*

Name _____

Home Address _____

_____

Business Address _____

_____

Home Phone _____

Business Phone _____

Preferred mailing address (check one): ☐ Home ☐ Business

Is this gift from you and your spouse? ☐ Yes ☐ No

If so, spouse's name: _____

_____

_____

I/we pledge and invest $_____ in the future of Indiana University Bloomington.

Please send me courtesy reminders for gifts of $_____ to be contributed:

☐ annually ☐ semi-annually ☐ quarterly ☐ other_____

beginning _____ / _____ and ending _____ / _____
         (mo)  (yr)        (mo)  (yr)

*My/our gift will be matched with $_____

from _____ (Matching Company Name),

making the total commitment $_____.

*Note: Your company requires that each subsequent pledge payment must be accompanied by a complete matching gift form.*

*Please distribute each gift as follows:*

Amount:               Program

$ _____   _____

$ _____   _____

$ _____   _____

I/we wish to make my/our gift or initial pledge amount by (please check one): ☐ Mastercard ☐ Visa ☐ Check enclosed

Credit Card Number _____

Expiration Date _____

Signature _____

☐ I/we prefer this gift remain anonymous.

☐ Please send information about giving through wills and trusts.

Special Notes _____

_____

_____

_____

_____

_____

Donor Signature _____

Date _____ / _____ / _____

Donor Signature _____

Date _____ / _____ / _____

IU Representative _____

## THANK YOU FOR YOUR VALUABLE INVESTMENT IN THE FUTURE

## SAMPLE CASE STATEMENT

# Making a World of Difference

◆

## The St. Louis YMCA

The mission of the St. Louis YMCA is to provide quality programs in fitness, family activities and positive personal values for youth—all at a price to encourage participation across the broadest possible spectrum of economic levels of our society.

The YMCA of Greater St. Louis is serving people—all kinds of people—children of all ages, teens, adults, seniors, and handicapped, every race and religion, every income level, male and female alike. As we seek to improve and expand our considerable array of programs for youth and adults, our basic goal remains ever-constant ". . . to assist each individual to grow in body, mind and spirit."

This is the YMCA of Greater St. Louis.

# Milestones Along the Way

1853     October 20, 1853. Referring to the founding of the St. Louis YMCA, the Missouri Republican says, "It is our privilege to record the beginnings of an enterprise, which contains in it the germs of more good to St. Louis than any undertaking which has ever been entered upon here."

1877     Supported by community business firms, the YMCA organizes to find jobs for the unemployed.

1905     The YMCA initiates the first resident summer camp for St. Louis area youth.

1926     The St. Louis YMCA begins the national movement of Y Indian Guides, a program directed to cement father/son relationships.

1964     Amid the turmoil of the civil rights movement, the St. Louis Y pioneers a detached street worker program for inner-city youth.

1967     To meet the exercise needs of a growing office-bound workforce, the YMCA emphasizes cardio-vascular fitness as a way to prolong active, productive lives.

1977     The St. Louis YMCA successfully completes a major capital campaign for needed expansion.

1983     Resulting from the dramatic rise in both single-parent families and homes with two working parents, the St. Louis YMCA becomes the leader in before-and-after-school child care based in elementary school facilities.

# The Path of Progress

In 1953, the St. Louis YMCA consisted of a couple dozen men in a city of 74,000 people. Today, the metropolitan area contains over two million people and the Y serves nearly 150,000 women, men, girls and boys.

In 1977, the City of St. Louis launched a vigorous program of growth and development. That same year, catapulted by a ten million dollar capital campaign adding three new Program centers, the YMCA of Greater St. Louis entered a period of unparalleled growth.

- Total attendance has nearly doubled. The St. Louis Y ranks third in attendance in a comparison of St. Louis leisure time organizations.

| | |
|---|---|
| ARCH | 6,369,640 |
| CARDINALS (baseball) | 2,559,709 |
| YMCA | 1,986,143 |
| ZOO | 1,903,000 |
| BLUES | 596,000 |
| BOTANICAL GARDEN | 550,000 |
| GRANT'S FARM | 515,298 |
| ART MUSEUM | 500,000 |
| THE MUNY | 387,826 |
| SYMPHONY ORCHESTRA | 336,330 |
| STEAMERS | 335,805 |
| CARDINALS (football) | 309,612 |

- Y participants represent one-sixth of the people served by United Way agencies.
- 48.7 percent of YMCA memberships are women and girls.
- There are more youth involved in YMCA programs than are enrolled in the St. Louis City Schools.
- A 160 percent increase in participant-generated income has created greater self-reliance and financial stability.

## The YMCA of Greater St. Louis . . . Today

| | |
|---|---|
| Visible | Twelve neighborhood program centers, a branch serving Washington University students and a youth and family camp. |
| "Of" the Community | 475 civic and business leaders serve on YMCA Corporate and Branch Boards of Directors. |
| Well-attended | 149,118 individuals actively participate in Y programs and services annually. |

## Current Programs

### Fitness

The YMCA provides much more than quality fitness facilities. Fitness testing, nutritional counseling and many other services support the Y's entire approach to physical conditioning and good health. Over 65 St. Louis corporations recognize the important relationship between physical health and employee productivity. These employers look to the Y to deliver fitness programming to their people. Reduced health costs, lowered absenteeism and employee satisfaction are the valuable by-products of corporate fitness.

### Aquatics

The YMCA teaches more people to swim than any other organization in our community. Aquatic enrollments total 39,968.

### Youth Sports

Nearly 21,000 girls and boys learn the fundamentals of basketball, gymnastics, T-ball, soccer, hockey and other sports in the YMCA Y-Winners program. Although winning is fun, Y-Winners emphasizes learning the game and giving every kid the chance to participate. Parents are developed as coaches. Kids have fun. Everyone becomes a winner.

### Camp Lakewood: Resident Summer Camp

Values development, new experiences and recreation . . . this is a summer camp for over a thousand girls and boys at Camp Lakewood. Building self-reliance and responsibility in children requires a variety of learning experiences. Swimming, canoeing, nature exploration, horseback riding, crafts, campouts and many other activities allow kids to lead, to work independently and to test their abilities. Scholarships are available for children unable to pay full fee.

## Trout Lodge

Occupying the same grounds as Camp Lakewood, Trout Lodge offers nearly 14,000 people a beautiful setting for family retreats and outdoor educational experiences. Religious, educational and business groups are booked throughout the year. Trout Lodge is a nationally approved site for Elderhostel and offers seniors a variety of non-traditional educational programs.

## Child Care and Development

Over 9,000 children and their parents realize the benefits of YMCA preschools, day care centers, latchkey programs, day camps and summer fun clubs. Far from a baby-sitting service, Y programs instruct, nurture and enhance child development through positive learning experiences.

## Leadership Development

782 teenagers develop leadership skills and enjoy responsible involvement in Youth In Government, Camp Lakewood's Counselor-In-Training program and in a variety of Branch volunteer activities.

## Adult Sports

19,801 adults enroll in league team sports.

## Handicapped Classes

553 handicapped individuals utilize Y facilities for physical therapy, group exercise classes and swim classes.

## Youth Employment

In partnership with the business community, the YMCA employs over 2,000 young people, ages 16 to 21.

## A Plan for the Future

The YMCA has always followed the philosophy that as long as its core programs meet high standards and attract sufficient volume, they remain. However, new approaches and new programs are being continuously developed in response to constantly emerging needs in an ever-changing society. That is why, after six years of rapid growth, the Y instituted an intensive planning process:

1. The Department of Urban Affairs at St. Louis University provided information on the changing demographic nature of Branch service areas.

2. Y officials interviewed six or more "community knowledgeables" in each of the 12 geographic areas in which YMCA program units are situated asking each person to comment on how changes are impacting lives and how the "Y" might best respond. Y workers were particularly interested in the ramifications of factors affecting family life, the value-developing needs of youth, and the degree to which Y fitness programs meet modern needs.

3. Based on this data plus questionnaire results from members, YMCA staff and board members:

   a. Examined current programs for relevance and projected program design changes appropriate to the findings.

   b. Projected participation levels of redesigned programs in five year and ten year intervals.

   c. Determined the personnel, facility and operating revenue changes required in order to achieve projected program levels.

4. A planning committee commissioned by the Metropolitan Board conducted extensive review meetings to determine the validity of the conclusions each contained.

5. In November 1984, the YMCA's Metropolitan Board adopted the master plan, established general priorities for facility development and engaged the national Y's Buildings and Furnishings Service to provide construction cost estimates.

## Points in Planning

Some major demographic and lifestyle changes that influenced program and facility decisions were:

- Married couples' share of all households plunged sharply in the '70s, indicating that families will face increasing disruptions and breakdowns.
- The rapid rise of women in the workforce (approaching 50 percent) signals a continuing rate of growth of female participation in the YMCA (now at 48.7 percent). Other "Y" programs that will be in increased demand as a result are after-school youth programs, day care, and teen-age and grade school-age programs with a strong values component.
- The "baby boom" generation has reached child-bearing age increasing the need for activities for young families, fitness and recreation facilities designed for family use, and the expansion of facilities and programs for pre-schoolers.
- Those constituting the "empty nest" family cycle and senior citizens make up an increasing proportion of the population. For most St. Louisans, one-third of life will occur after the eldest child leaves home. Greater need for active and vigorous lifestyles means added pressure on the YMCA to respond with programs and facilities tailored to that age. Adult fitness, camping and social activities are but a few Y programs already experiencing this demand.
- The increase in disadvantaged persons—the physically and culturally handicapped and the economically deprived—calls for creative approaches to the needs of these special populations.

## The YMCA Responds

The dramatic expansion of YMCA programs brought about by the highly successful "Path of Progress" capital development program of 1977 is poignant testimony to the impact the YMCA can have on the quality of life in St. Louis given the needed tools. Recent experience indicates that an equally dramatic growth rate will be achieved in the decade ahead with the commitment of all top community leaders. The payoff in enriched lives will be as significant as in any project in recent memory.

## YMCA Objectives

### Fitness for Living

Expand enrollment in fitness activities from 92,701 youth and adults to 154,000—a 66 percent increase in participation in sports and cardio-vascular programs! New levels will be accomplished through the development of a new fitness center in West County, a leased fitness facility for working youth adults in Downtown St. Louis, and expansion of fitness facilities in several existing centers.

## Family Programs

Mount a concerted effort to increase enrollments in family-related activities from 19,848 to 36,000. In order to provide values education and family enrichment experiences to greater numbers of people, a comprehensive new building designed to serve all ages will be built. Extensive family camping facilities are planned at the YMCA of the Ozarks.

## Aquatic and Water Safety

A new pool and expanded locker room that will increase the number who can use existing pools will result in a broadening of aquatic and water safety services from 31,850 to 41,000 further strengthening the Y's title as "swim teacher for St. Louis."

## Combined Impact

What is planned is a quantum leap in the positive impact of YMCA programs on the lives of St. Louisans. By combining the upgrading and expansion of existing facilities with new construction, limited only in areas in which no YMCA buildings now exist, significant growth will be accomplished at a considerable saving over other alternatives. Participation in YMCA activities will increase an impressive 66 percent.

# New and Improved Facilities

To achieve planned objectives, YMCA and community leaders must act now to establish new Y facilities and renovate others.

WEST COUNTY CENTER                                    $4,000,000

Construct a new family program and fitness center accessible to the youth and families of the Parkway and Rockwood school districts.

YMCA OF THE OZARKS                                    5,000,000

Build a new lodge and family program center, remodel youth camp cabins and build new program areas for resident camping at Sunnen Lake.

NORTH COUNTY CENTER                                   1,050,000

Completion of the Emerson Fitness Center will expand fitness programs for all ages. The addition will include a gymnasium, indoor track and expanded locker rooms.

DOWNTOWN FITNESS CENTERS                                           2,600,000

This includes two projects: major renovation of the existing Downtown Y which was constructed in 1962 and the leasing and remodelling of space for a 2nd cardio-vascular fitness center for men and women located closer to the River.

MID-COUNTY FITNESS AND FAMILY CENTER                              2,000,000

Renovate and upgrade locker rooms, the gymnasium, the pool, exercise areas, and public use areas to expand capacity and increase service to Brentwood and to those employed in the Clayton Area.

KIRKWOOD/WEBSTER GROVES                                           1,050,000

Replace older portions of the Kirkwood building to house a gymnasium, indoor track, expanded locker rooms and exercise areas.

SOUTHSIDE & CARONDELET CENTERS                                      654,000

Renovate these two old but busy buildings in order to extend their useful lives by ten years or longer. Both facilities serve areas whose stability and gradual revitalization are crucial to the further renaissance of the City. Replacement now would cost many times the planned expenditures.

MONSANTO                                                           250,000

This program center was built in 1980 and has far exceeded planned participation levels. It is so successful that it has become a national model of what can be done by non-profit organizations to address the family recreation needs of the inner city. Additional space is needed for more fitness areas and for day care facilities.

JEFFERSON COUNTY AND WEST ST. CHARLES COUNTY       700,000

Property acquisition and outreach facilities are needed in these two remaining major population growth areas. Modest facilities are planned to serve day care needs and provide a command post for community-based Y programs.

WESTPORT FITNESS CENTER                                            500,000

Plans involve leasing and renovating existing space for a cardio-vascular fitness center for the apartment dwellers and the young adults working in the Westport Area.

WASHINGTON UNIVERSITY—CAMPUS Y                                      90,000

This Branch addresses the needs of college students to develop socially and to relate meaningfully to the larger community through service projects. An expanded endowment will supplement a budget that is modest in comparison to the impact on values and the broad community service this Center provides.

TOTAL IMMEDIATE PROJECTS:                                       $17,894,000

## A Call for Action

The need is now at hand to build upon an earlier investment and a rich legacy, to build for today's needs and for tomorrow's. The goal is challenging but not unreasonably so. Eight years ago, the task of achieving a smaller goal must have seemed much more formidable. Yet, the goal was reached.

While much has been achieved, much remains to be done. Large concentrations of St. Louis families who need and would respond to YMCA programs live too far from existing facilities to participate regularly. Several YMCA buildings reflect heavy use over long periods of time. The quality-seeking people of modern society are not attracted to institutions with buildings that have seen better days and call into question the leadership's ability to either understand the present or anticipate the future. Other YMCA buildings are incomplete due to phased construction and now are ready for completion as earlier planned.

This important bridge on the YMCA's and St. Louis' continuing path of progress needs the generous support of all those who see in the programs of The YMCA of Greater St. Louis an enduring asset in the ongoing life of this community and its people.

# SAMPLE CASE STATEMENT WITH COMPANION PIECES

Case Statement 360

The Case for Aliber Hall Booklet 376

The Plough Pharmacy Scholarship Fund Booklet 380

**Second Century Fund**

DRAKE UNIVERSITY•DES MOINES, IOWA

# BUILDING
## for the
# FUTURE

This document has one purpose.

That purpose is to answer the question: "Why is it necessary to seek at least $25 million in gifts and grants for Drake University's Second Century Fund?"

Do not be misled by the apparent simplicity of our purpose. The question is a complex one. It focuses attention on the growth and the aspirations of Drake University as it completes 100 years of service to a constituency which includes not only the City of Des Moines and the State of Iowa, but the Midwest and the nation as well.

Since its founding in 1881, Drake University has been successful because it has been more than an educational institution. From the beginning the University established itself as a community. First, Chancellor George Carpenter and the faculty recognized that education involved not only classroom activity and study but also work, play, worship, and community life. They believed that a liberal education must develop a student's ability to integrate all of life's experiences.

Even the name of the University's first building, The Students' Home, is emblematic of the kind of education which Drake University espoused in 1881 and continues to offer today. The Students' Home was a place where students and faculty lived and worked together, where education was value oriented, and where learning occurred as much through social process and close interpersonal relationships as through diligent study.

The truly liberal education which Drake has since offered demands a special type of faculty. They are committed to teaching, but more than that they are scholars—people who believe that education is a lifelong process. They are community-minded individuals who participate in campus life and involve themselves with Drake students as counselors and advisors. They are active in the Des Moines community as well because they know that an educated person has the duty to contribute conscientiously to community life.

"If the traditions and values are to be preserved, the University must build for the future."

In the century since The Students' Home was hastily constructed in the brief span of one summer to encompass a dormitory, classrooms, dining room, chapel, and offices, the school in the countryside has become a distinguished urban institution. The campus facilities have grown to include 128 acres and 40 buildings. Within the past ten years alone, a computer sciences center, law school building, health center, fine arts center, biological science building, student and university center, and health and recreation center have been constructed. The undergraduate student body numbers 4,500 in six colleges, with another 2,000 students enrolled in the Law School, graduate programs and the College for Continuing Education. The current student body comes from nearly every state and several foreign countries. Drake enjoys a national reputation based upon the performance of its graduates.

Drake University must not abandon the principles it has spent 100 years developing, but if the traditions and values are to be preserved, the University must build for the future. Scholarship funds must be increased so that the University can continue to help the kinds of students who will benefit from a Drake education. The endowment must be increased so that the University can reward and retain outstanding faculty. A badly-needed building to house the College of Business Administration must be constructed, the campus modernized, equipment brought up to date, and the library endowed so that Drake students of the future can be educated with the same care as their predecessors.

What Drake has been, is now, and will be in the future all come together in this Second Century Fund campaign. Drake's distinctive 100-year contribution to educational excellence, achieved through the growth and quality of students, faculty, and physical surroundings, must be preserved and passed on to future generations. It is the responsibility of all of us who have concern for this University to see that this takes place.

Wilbur C. Miller
*President*

| | |
|---|---|
| **Endowment** | **$13,000,000** |
| Faculty Development Endowment | 5,000,000 |
| General Purpose Endowment | 3,500,000 |
| Library Development Endowment | 1,000,000 |
| Scholarship-Fellowship Endowment | 3,500,000 |
| **One-Time Projects** | **$12,000,000** |
| Aliber Hall—College of Business Administration | 5,000,000 |
| Campus Modernization | 4,250,000 |
| Equipment Modernization | 750,000 |
| Operational Expenses | 2,000,000 |
| **Total** | **$25,000,000** |

For one of the few times in its 100-year history, Drake University is undertaking a national campaign to raise a very substantial sum of money—$25 million—from private donors for the comprehensive benefit of the University.

The campaign has evolved over a period of four years. An intensive institutional self-study pinpointed high priority programs and projects for which customary funding is not available and, more importantly, demonstrated that the campaign is needed and justified.

An independent study to examine the financial feasibility of such a campaign followed and was completed during the Summer of 1980. Results of this study revealed an unusually strong interest in Drake University among corporate, professional, foundation, and civic leaders in Iowa and elsewhere. The study indicated that Drake has a legion of supporters whose commitment to the University is sufficiently strong that they will meet its needs if so requested.

Guided by these findings, the Drake University Board of Trustees unanimously approved on October 31, 1980, a $25 million Second Century Fund campaign. This campaign is intended to continue Drake's 100-year tradition of educational excellence, and to build for the University's future.

As Chairman of the Development Committee of the Board of Trustees, I have accepted the privileged position of chairing the Second Century Fund campaign. In this capacity, I will be working with the campaign steering committee, other members of the Board, and volunteer leaders around the country who are as dedicated as I am to the success of Drake University.

Briefly, we are undertaking a three-year campaign to raise $25 million for Drake. The $25 million goal takes into account annual fund support normally to be anticipated during the period of Second Century Fund activities.

Today, in spite of sound financial management, Drake University stands at a crossroads. New channels through which will flow added sources of strength to nurture and revitalize the superiority of our University must be developed. There is no doubt that Drake's alumni and friends have the capacity to see that these needs are met. Our campaign is one that can and will be successful.

While strong volunteer leadership is essential in such a campaign, its success will be reflected in the attitudes of prospective donors who recognize that the strength and betterment of the University are worthy of their philanthropic investments. Here is an opportunity for every friend of Drake to establish a lasting legacy for the advancement of human welfare. Join in this exciting adventure—Drake University's Second Century Fund.

R. N. Houser
*National Chairman*

# Building an Endowment for the Future

The major portion of the Second Century Fund will go into Drake University's endowment—those funds which are invested to provide the University with a permanent source of guaranteed income. An endowment is not extra money, something to fall back upon when times demand it. To the contrary, a quality university of national standing can be expected to maintain its position only if its endowment assets are of dimensions similar to those of comparable institutions. Nationally, institutions like Drake consider the endowment base adequate if it is approximately twice the annual operating budget. Currently, Drake's endowment is only about one-third the size of its operating budget. Only by increasing endowment can Drake continue to meet the challenge of providing a superior education to talented and deserving students. The Second Century Fund goal represents a vital and important first step toward the fulfillment of Drake's endowment needs, and clearly signals the path to be pursued in the future.

## Faculty Development Endowment: $5,000,000

The heart of any university is its faculty. Drake has traditionally attracted dedicated faculty with the skills to inspire students to achieve their full academic potential while instilling in them a respect for moral and ethical values. It is a faculty well-equipped to provide education for leadership.

Quality faculty come to Drake University because of the extraordinary opportunities to develop a career in an educational climate that fosters innovation and a total commitment to educational excellence. A faculty development endowment will allow the University to continue to attract and retain faculty of high caliber.

***Endowed Professorial Chair: $750,000 Endowment for Each Chair.*** Annual income resulting from an endowed professorship will provide salary, personnel, and program incentives to place an educator of superior qualifications in a college of the University where that person can have a profound effect on the curriculum and on the college's efforts to recruit both excellent faculty and superior students. Colleges for which an endowed chair would be of immediate benefit include the College of Business Administration, the College of Education, the College of Fine Arts, the School of Journalism and Mass Communication, the Law School, the College of Liberal Arts, and the College of Pharmacy.

***Professional-Curricular Enhancement.*** Universities, businesses, industries, and professions face the common challenge of keeping pace with progress by providing the opportunities for those in responsible positions to develop further their skills and knowledge. At Drake, there has been an awareness of this challenge from the time the University was founded. However, funding for faculty development has been implemented only to the extent that the operating budget permits. In recent years, these funds have averaged only $25,000 annually.

Endowment support for professional—curricular enhancement is intended to increase these funds at least seven-fold and make possible the following:

1. Named professorships: Merit awards for outstanding faculty work in enriching curricula, strengthening student achievement, augmenting professional knowledge, and providing public service.
2. Continuing professional educational opportunities:
   a. Supplementary study for faculty to update professional expertise or to convert their knowledge and skills to related disciplines.
   b. Leave time for special study or professional activities.
   c. Participation in key professional meetings and events.
3. Special project funding for:
   a. Assembling specialized materials and equipment.
   b. Additional programs designed to encourage faculty to develop programs of special interest for the community.

## General Purpose Endowment: $3,500,000

Endowment for general purposes must be sufficient to assure the continuity of Drake's present level and quality of education and service. The University must be in a position to furnish the support to ensure that each academic discipline and department can adapt to changing needs and rise to its own level of excellence to continue providing students with the quality education they have a right to expect. As the continuity of its programs is assured, Drake's certain of retaining its position of educational leadership is ensured.

## Library Development Endowment: $1,000,000

Unprecedented increases in the cost of books, periodicals and materials, have made library development a serious concern of universities today from coast to coast. Drake University is no exception. An escalating inflation rate has made it increasingly difficult for Cowles Library to carry on an aggressive program of acquisitions. In 1973, the library purchased 16,175 books for $180,000. In 1979, over $200,000 was spent to purchase 10,310 books. While its purchase of serials has remained constant at 2,000 per year, the library's budget for that purpose has increased by 76 percent since 1973 and now stands at $180,000. An endowment that would provide an annual base which the University could use to purchase books will lessen the effects of this inflation on the operating budget.

## Scholarship-Fellowship Endowment: $3,500,000

Recognizing the importance of helping deserving students finance a college education, Drake University spent $3,951,573 on student financial aid in 1979–80. This represented 27.5 percent of the $14,354,599 which Drake students received from federal, state, and private scholarship aid to attend the University. The need to budget even more money for financial aid is essential for three reasons:

1. Drake University is dedicated to the ideal that students who have the potential deserve an education. Economic class must not prevent a student from receiving an education at Drake.
2. Federal programs are being tightened so that less federal aid will be available to students.
3. The financial needs of students are becoming more difficult for their families to meet because of the effects of inflation on personal incomes.

While there is a great urgency for scholarships based on need, Drake University also is intent upon attracting the brightest and most gifted students with merit scholarships which recognize academic and leadership qualities. Responses to the Drake National Alumni Scholarship program each year prove how heavily financial incentives are weighed by good students. Hundreds of high school graduates in the upper 10 percent of their classes—many valedictorians and salutatorians—compete for these awards, which cover four years' tuition, lodging, board, and fees.

It is the purpose of the substantial scholarship-fellowship endowment to supplement by at least $250,000 annually the funding now provided for need, merit, and combined need-merit scholarships and fellowships at Drake University.

# Building and Modernizing for the Future

## Aliber Hall, College of Business Administration: $5,000,000

A growing College of Business Administration now enrolling over 1,200 students must be provided with the environment and space necessary for it to function in a manner which befits its stature. This goal will be realized with the construction of a new business administration building which will be named Aliber Hall in recognition of gifts from the Aliber Foundation, the late Robert Aliber, and other members of the Aliber family.

Aliber Hall will be a concrete and masonry structure designed to harmonize with existing campus architecture. The building will be strategically situated near Olmsted Center and Meredith Hall. This will facilitate the College's development of conferences, institutes, and short courses.

"The University must . . . continue providing students with
the quality education they have a right to expect."

Some of the major features planned for the new building include an insurance center, a business development and research center, and a large computer facility which will be connected with the University's Dial Center for Computer Sciences.

Aliber Hall also will provide the College of Business Administration with versatile classroom space. In addition to a seminar room, a 50-seat classroom, and a 160-seat lecture hall, the new building will have two case study rooms with the capacity to serve as a behavioral studies laboratory. There will also be three accounting laboratories, two of which will be partitioned so they can be merged into a large, tabled classroom accommodating 40 students.

One of its important attributes will be office space not only for faculty and administration, but also for student organizations as well. The building will contain offices which will house faculty members from the College of Business Administration and from the Economics Department of the College of Liberal Arts. In addition to departmental offices and seven clerical offices, the new building will contain all of the administrative offices for the College, a conference room, reception area, staff lounge, and secretarial work area. Space for students will include a student reading room and student organizations' headquarters.

The $5 million estimate includes cost of construction, site preparation, fixed and movable equipment furnishings, heating, cooling, and utilities installation.

## Campus Modernization: $4,250,000

Drake's 128-acre campus and 40 buildings are located within Iowa's largest community and capital city. The University is a harmonious blend of historically significant buildings sheltered by oak and maple trees older than the University itself and a more modern campus designed by America's leading architects and constructed since the end of World War II. Although much is done each year to keep the campus in a state of repair and emergencies are dealt with expeditiously, the budget has not permitted a comprehensive refurbishment and renovation of those buildings and areas of campus which are beginning to show a century of wear. Economically, renovation is far more cost efficient than beginning anew. Moreover, in every case the older buildings are structurally sound, although they are not use or energy efficient by today's standards. Of even more importance is the traditional and historical value of these buildings, especially the venerable old buildings of the inner campus. In order to meet its educational objectives, Drake University must have a campus which matches in quality the academic programs it offers and which retains the traditional appearance alumni and friends remember and cherish.

The Second Century Fund will ensure that an integrated program of campus modernization will take place.

The general effects of this program will be:

1. The redesigning and rebuilding of areas which need improved access for the handicapped and elderly.
2. Structural and equipment changes which are needed to conserve energy and conform to accepted safety standards.
3. General refurbishment of buildings throughout the campus.
4. Modernization and enlargement of the physical plant administrative center.
5. A number of projects designed to increase the beauty of the campus and its functional capabilities. Among these projects are replacing outdated lighting equipment for greater campus safety and security, establishing new parking areas, acquiring properties surrounding the campus, and landscaping certain campus areas to highlight and enhance the architecture.

In addition to the updated physical plant administrative facilities and the grounds improvements, specific projects in the campus modernization program include:

1. *Cole Hall:* Dedicated in 1904 as the original Law School building, Cole Hall must be remodeled to fit the needs of the departments which will occupy it when the College of Business Administration moves to the new Aliber Hall.
2. *Cowles Library:* In addition to renovating the research and general circulation centers, the University must provide a periodical center and a microfilm reading and storage area for the library.
3. *Harvey Ingham Hall of Science:* Laboratories, installed when the building was erected 31 years ago, must be replaced on all three floors.
4. *Howard Hall:* Completed in 1903 as a Conservatory of Music, the second oldest building on campus needs extensive interior and exterior remodeling in addition to an air-conditioning system.
5. *Memorial Hall:* Constructed in 1905 as the Bible College, the building now houses the College of Education and needs considerable renovation of administrative and classroom areas plus a new air-conditioning unit.
6. *Old Main:* The symbol of Drake University since its dedication on September 18, 1883, Old Main is now the administrative headquarters of the University. As such, its office complexes on each floor must be redesigned to accommodate up-to-date administrative functions.
7. *Old Main Auditorium:* Completed in 1900 as an addition to Old Main, this elegant and venerable structure must be completely restored before it can once again be returned to use. Plans call for the replacement of old seating, the outdated public address system, and the obsolete plumbing. In addition, the stage, green room, auditorium ceiling, walls, and entrance ways must be completely rebuilt. A fire protection system and access ramps for the handicapped and elderly also must be installed.

### Equipment Modernization: $750,000

In virtually every field of industry, business, and government, as well as in education, obsolescence of equipment sets in earlier today than ever before. The continued rapid development of technology makes early obsolescence an ever-present fact of modern living.

Equipment modernization needs include: increased computer capabilities, up-to-date laboratory and classroom equipment, new printed and audio-visual aids, added audio-visual equipment, electronic and print media equipment, new musical instruments, new visual arts and performing arts equipment, and up-to-date office equipment.

### Support to Help Meet Operational Expenses: $2,000,000

Day-to-day operational expenses also must be taken into consideration. In University financing, no matter how astute the planner or careful the planning, the *present* too often intrudes upon and eventually overshadows the *future*. The Second Century Fund will provide additional revenue to help the University meet these expenses. It also is designed to provide a cushion against inflation so that Drake University can better plan and build for the future without fear of being constantly overwhelmed by the present.

## Commemorative Gift Opportunities

Commemorative gift opportunities offer alumni, parents, friends, foundations, and corporations numerous ways to establish named gifts as memorials and testimonials to family, friends, organizations, or other individuals. These gifts embody the donor's ideals and provide essential support to ensure a strong future for Drake.

A University representative will be glad to work with anyone desiring to make a commemorative gift, and explore a number of options through which such a gift may be developed. A few of the more traditional categories are listed below.

### Professorships

A named endowed professorship may be established for an existing professorship or a new professorship in a school or a field of study. Such an endowment fund may be established with a gift or gifts to total $750,000.

### Lectureships

A named endowment fund to provide a lecture program (that is, one which may be used for the honorarium and expenses of a special guest lecturer) may be established with a fund of not less than $10,000.

## Scholarships

A named endowment scholarship may be established with a fund of not less than $25,000 or a guarantee of annual support for one or more recipients totaling at least $1,200.

## Fellowships

A named endowed fellowship may be established with a fund of not less than $100,000 or a guarantee of annual support for one or more recipients totaling at least $5,000 but with no award being made which is less than $1,000 to a recipient.

## Prize Funds

A named financial award for outstanding accomplishment may be provided through the establishment of a prize fund with an endowment of not less than $5,000 to furnish awards of approximately $200 or more to one or more students each year.

## Book Funds

The earnings from an endowed book fund may be used for the purchase of books or other materials in a particular field or library and also may be used as specified by the donor for other expenses of the library. Such a fund may be established with not less than $5,000.

## Funds for Student Activities

Gifts and funds will be accepted for the support of recognized student activities if such activities have the approval of the Vice President for Student Life.

For further information regarding these or other named and memorial gift opportunities contact:

Office of Institutional Development
Drake University
319 Old Main
Des Moines, Iowa 50311
Telephone (515) 271–3154

# Methods of Giving

Certainly, the tax rewards alone should not motivate one to give—they are not the starting point. The desire to help Drake University comes first, and those who make gifts to Drake are generously rewarded by tax laws.

Some methods of giving include: outright gift of cash, gift of securities, gift of real property, gift of life insurance, deferred gifts which can take many forms, and gifts through a will.

One or a combination of these methods may have a particular appeal in planning one's gift. Drake University provides estate planning and tax advice to donors; however, it is suggested that professional tax or legal advice be obtained in order to realize the maximum tax benefits from such gifts.

## SECOND CENTURY FUND SUMMARY.

**Endowment**

| | | |
|---|---|---|
| Faculty Development Endowment | $5,000,000 | |
| Named Endowed Chairs | | |
| Professional-Curricular Enhancement | | |
| General Purpose Endowment | 3,500,000 | |
| Library Development Endowment | 1,000,000 | |
| Scholarship-Fellowship Endowment | 3,500,000 | |
| Second Century Fund Minimum Endowment Goal | | $13,000,000 |

**One-Time Projects**

| | | |
|---|---|---|
| Aliber Hall, College of Business Administration | $5,000,000 | |
| Campus Modernization | 4,250,000 | |
| Projects in Cole Hall, Cowles Library, Harvey Ingham Hall of Science, Howard Hall, Memorial Hall, Old Main, Old Main Auditorium | | |
| Grounds modernization, beautification and expansion | | |
| Expansion of Physical Plant Administrative Facilities | | |
| Equipment Modernization | 750,000 | |
| Support to help meet Operational Requirements | 2,000,000 | |
| Second Century Fund Minimum One-Time Projects and Operational Support Goal | | $12,000,000 |
| Second Century Fund Goal | | $25,000,000 |

On the preceding pages you have read about an exciting program designed to build for the future of Drake University. On the following pages are the names of those who endorse and support the Second Century Fund and who have accepted the challenge of its leadership.

This is more than a campaign designed simply to raise $25 million, or a campaign to build and renovate buildings, to increase endowment, or to generate operating revenues alone. These are mere symbols which represent in concrete terms our real mission—namely, to ensure through thoughtful building the educational quality of Drake University and to keep the promise of our future. This campaign will assure that teaching and learning will continue at Drake in an environment conducive to producing the best possible graduates, to conducting the best possible research, and to providing the best possible service.

Our campaign goal is an ambitious one which cannot be achieved through the contributions of a few prominent individuals or a select group of businesses, corporations and foundations alone. In order to meet the challenge of our program, everyone will need to give generously. As you are asked to join our effort, I am confident you will respond in a manner which befits the magnitude of the undertaking and with the knowledge that the future of Drake University promises to be as distinguished as its past. All of us united in this common cause embodied in the Second Century Fund can make that promise a reality.

Robb B. Kelley
*Chairman,*
*Drake Board of Trustees*

# Second Century Fund

DRAKE UNIVERSITY•DES MOINES, IOWA

## The Case for Aliber Hall

## Aliber Hall Fulfills a Need

At Drake University, education for business is not an ancillary program—it is a core educational component. However, the physical environment in which the University fulfilled this accepted responsibility had become outmoded and could no longer provide the educational and administrative quarters to support the programs offered.

The College of Business Administration, now enrolling over 1,500 students, required the educational environment and space necessary for it to function efficiently. Physical improvements were needed to provide specialized instruction, to centralize faculty and administration of the College and to improve student services.

Today, the College of Business Administration's student population of more than 1,500 exceeds one-fifth of Drake's total enrollment and is the second largest college of the University. With the new technologies of the 1980s, expanded use of computer information systems in business and government, and with more women and minorities seeking managerial careers, growth prospects for the College look excellent.

For these reasons, Drake's Board of Trustees realistically recognized the need for a more suitable business education environment and authorized the construction of a $5 million building, housing the College of Business Administration. The project is a major part of Drake's Second Century Fund, a national voluntary fundraising effort designed to raise $25 million for increased endowment and several one-time projects.

## Educational Center for Business

Completed this fall, Aliber Hall adds a new dimension to the College of Business Administration. It not only provides resources to improve traditional education areas, it also houses specialized instructional centers and makes possible centralization of the College's faculty and administration.

The new building, located just south of Drake's Olmsted Center, harmonizes in appearance with existing University structures. It contains 47,300 square feet of space on three stories above grade and a lower level. Each level of the facility has been designed to produce a functionally efficient and aesthetically stimulating learning environment.

The main administrative area is situated on the second floor and is equipped with a reception area, conference rooms and a staff lounge. Faculty offices exclusively occupy the third floor. Classrooms, seminar and conference rooms; a computer room and laboratory; a case study room; accounting laboratories; and specialized instructional centers in business development and research, insurance and executive development are located on the lower level as well as the first and second floors.

Structural features include a north arcade, entry ways from both the north and south to accommodate campus traffic and public access from University Avenue and a 148–seat lecture hall with access from the first floor. A focal point of the building is the spiral staircase to the upper levels of the structure. A primary siting consideration was the preservation of the "north-south" green mall-type area through the center of campus.

## Commemorative Gift Opportunities

Aliber Hall is providing a suitable environment to ensure the continued growth and distinguished reputation of Drake's College of Business Administration. However, the completion of financing for Aliber Hall remains a challenge. The generosity of The Aliber Foundation and the Robert Aliber family provides impetus for encouraging the commitment of substantive support from alumni and friends of Drake University.

Aliber Hall is a showcase for Drake University. For this reason, we are offering numerous gift opportunities for individual office and room facilities within the Hall. Each area provides a naming or memorial opportunity according to the donor's wishes, and appropriate recognition will be placed in each area so named.

You are invited to share in these naming opportunities and to help complete financing of Drake's new College of Business Administration, Aliber Hall.

The Second Century Fund offers alumni, parents, friends, foundations and corporations numerous ways to provide memorials and testimonials to family, friends, organizations or other individuals. Your commemorative gift can embody the donor's ideals and provide essential support to ensure a strong future for Drake University.

To participate or get further information, call or write Drake University, Second Century Fund, Des Moines, IA 50311. Our telephone number is (515) 271–3154. Your inquiry will receive prompt and courteous attention.

## ALIBER HALL: GIFT OPPORTUNITIES.

| Building | (Reserved) |
|---|---|
| Floor (4) | $1,000,000 |
| Lecture Hall | 500,000 |
| Dean's Suite | 250,000 |
| Conference Room | $75,000 |
| Dean's Office | (Reserved) |
| Computer Suite | 250,000 |
| Computer Classroom | $100,000 |
| Computer Laboratory | 50,000 |
| Insurance Center Suite | 200,000 |
| Director's Office | (Reserved) |
| Business Development/Research Center Suite | 150,000 |
| Executive Development Room | 150,000 |
| Student Administration Suite | 100,000 |
| Case Room | 100,000 |
| Accounting Laboratory (1st Floor) | 100,000 |
| Research Library | 75,000 |
| Accounting Laboratory (3) (Lower Level) | 75,000 |
| Student Reading Room (Lower Level) | 75,000 |
| Staff Lounge (Second Floor) | 75,000 |
| Seminar Room (First Floor) | (Reserved) |
| Student Organization Room | 40,000 |
| Conference Room (2) (First Floor) | 40,000 |
| Conference Room (2) (Second Floor) | 25,000 |
| Faculty Offices (53) (Third Floor) | 10,000 |

**Second Century Fund**

The Drake University Second Century Fund is a national voluntary fund raising effort designed to raise $25 million. In order to maintain and improve its position in higher education, Drake University must address itself to a number of urgent needs for which customary funding is not available. There are two major categories of needs: increased endowment, including faculty development, general purpose, library development and scholarship-fellowship totaling $13,000,000; and one-time projects, including Aliber Hall (College of Business Administration), campus and equipment modernization and support to help meet operational requirements totaling $12,000,000.

Drake University admits students without regard to sex, race, color, national or ethnic origin or handicap.

# Second Century Fund

DRAKE UNIVERSITY•DES MOINES, IOWA

# The Plough Pharmacy Scholarship Fund

Drake University has been honored as the first private educational institution in the country to be awarded a $500,000 gift from the Plough Foundation for the purpose of establishing a scholarship program for Drake's College of Pharmacy.

## The Plough Story

Abe Plough, founder of Plough, Inc., a pharmaceutical company, and the Plough Foundation, based in Memphis, Tennessee, established the Plough Pharmacy Scholarship Fund as an expression of gratitude for the support of retail pharmacists who over the years enabled Plough, Inc. to grow and prosper. It is their commitment to today's youth who will be tomorrow's pharmacy professionals.

## The Scholarship Fund

Drake University is only one of nine schools nationally that now participate in the Plough Pharmacy Scholarship Fund. This scholarship will provide financial assistance of up to $1,000 per year to selected Drake full-time undergraduate pharmacy students. Dollar awards to Plough Scholars may be increased in subsequent years.

## The Challenge

An important element of this generous gift is that Drake University, over the next eleven years, must match the gift with a $500,000 advance to the Plough Scholarship Fund. Beginning in 1998, the Fund will begin to return the $500,000 to Drake until finally in the year 2008, the University will have received all of the money invested plus more than $2,000,000 in endowment.

## Help Meet the Challenge

You are invited to help Drake meet the challenge presented by the Plough Foundation. Your generous support of this scholarship fund will ensure that many eligible students will receive their pharmacy education through Drake's College of Pharmacy. Together, we can make a long-term commitment that will help Drake University continue its program of training qualified pharmacy professionals.

To participate or get further information, call or write Drake University, Plough Pharmacy Scholarship Fund, Des Moines, IA 50311. Our telephone number is (515) 271-3154. Your inquiry will receive prompt and courteous attention.

## PLOUGH PHARMACY SCHOLARSHIP FUND.

| Year | Drake Contribution | Plough Contribution | 1/2 of Int. Add to Principal | Total Principal | Total Interest @ 12 percent | 1/2 of Int. Available for Schol. |
|------|------|------|------|------|------|------|
| 1 | 50,000 | 50,000 | 100,000 | 12,000 | 6,000 | |
| 2 | 45,000 | 45,000 | 6,000 | 196,000 | 23,520 | 11,760 |
| 3 | 45,000 | 45,000 | 11,760 | 297,760 | 35,731 | 17,865 |
| 4 | 45,000 | 45,000 | 17,865 | 405,625 | 48,675 | 24,337 |
| 5 | 45,000 | 45,000 | 24,337 | 519,962 | 62,395 | 31,198 |
| 6 | 45,000 | 45,000 | 31,198 | 641,160 | 76,939 | 38,470 |
| 7 | 45,000 | 45,000 | 38,470 | 769,630 | 92,356 | 46,178 |
| 8 | 45,000 | 45,000 | 46,178 | 905,808 | 108,697 | 54,348 |
| 9 | 45,000 | 45,000 | 54,348 | 1,050,156 | 126,018 | 63,009 |
| 10 | 45,000 | 45,000 | 63,009 | 1,203,165 | 144,380 | 72,190 |
| 11 | 45,000 | 45,000 | 72,190 | 1,365,355 | 163,842 | 81,921 |
| 12 | — | — | 81,921 | 1,447,276 | 173,673 | 86,837 |
| 13 | — | — | 86,837 | 1,534,113 | 184,093 | 92,047 |
| 14 | — | — | 92,047 | 1,626,160 | 195,139 | 97,570 |
| 15 | — | — | 97,570 | 1,723,730 | 206,848 | 103,424 |
| 16 | (50,000) | | 103,424 | 1,777,154 | 213,258 | 106,629 |
| 17 | (45,000) | | 106,629 | 1,838,783 | 220,653 | 110,327 |
| 18 | (45,000) | | 110,327 | 1,904,110 | 228,492 | 114,246 |
| 19 | (45,000) | | 114,246 | 1,973,356 | 236,802 | 118,401 |
| 20 | (45,000) | | 118,401 | 2,06,757 | 245,610 | 122,805 |
| 21 | (45,000) | | 122,803 | 2,124,562 | 254,948 | 127,474 |
| 22 | (45,000) | | 127,474 | 2,207,036 | 264,844 | 132,422 |
| 23 | (45,000) | | 132,422 | 2,294,458 | 275,335 | 137,667 |
| 24 | (45,000) | | 137,667 | 2,387,125 | 286,455 | 143,228 |
| 25 | (45,000) | | 143,228 | 2,485,353 | 298,242 | 149,121 |
| 26 | (45,000) | | 149,121 | 2,589,474 | 310,736 | |
| | — 0 — | 500,000 | 2,089,474 | | | 2,089,474 |

**Second Century Fund**

Explanation of columns:
1) Drake share
2) Plough share
3) 1/2 of interest added to principal
4) Accumulated principal
5) Total annual interest based on estimated 12—NET
6) 1/2 of interest available for scholarship

The Drake University Second Century Fund is a national voluntary fund raising effort designed to raise $25 million. In order to maintain and improve its position in higher education, Drake University must address itself to a number of urgent needs for which customary funding is not available. There are two major categories of needs: increased endowment, including faculty development, general purpose, library development and scholarship-fellowship totaling $13,000,000; and one-time projects, including Aliber Hall (College of Business Administration), campus and equipment modernization and support to help meet operational requirements totaling $12,000,000.

Drake University admits students without regard to sex, race, color, national or ethnic origin or handicap.

## SAMPLE PROGRAM BROCHURE

**EXCELLENCE WITH CARING**

La Crosse Lutheran Hospital Capital Improvement Program

Lutheran Hospital Foundation
1910 South Avenue
La Crosse, Wisconsin 54601–5467
(608) 785–0530 ext. 3045

Dear Friends:

In the 85 years since it was founded, La Crosse Lutheran Hospital has touched, in some way, so many families in the Tri-State Region. At times of medical crisis, we almost take for granted this outstanding center of health care excellence—it was here when we arrived and we expect it always will be. We expect, too, that it will be equipped and staffed to provide the very latest and most complete medical care available anywhere.

Our expectations of La Crosse Lutheran are based on past performance and on a record of constant planning for the future medical needs of our communities. This unceasing effort to keep abreast of ever changing medical knowledge and technology is achieved, of course, by the devotion and dedication of people.

We all recognize the contributions of the medical staff and hospital and clinic personnel, but let me emphasize the voluntary contributions made by the people of the Tri-State Region. From its founding in 1899, volunteers have served La Crosse Lutheran Hospital with their time and resources—without this abiding community support, the record of our hospital's performance would be limited indeed.

Now, this year, we are needed to give our tangible support to La Crosse Lutheran Hospital by pledging to the capital improvement campaign. It's our turn to help this center for health care excellence meet our expectations, to be here when we need it, to be equipped and staffed to provide Excellence With Caring.

Your thoughtful consideration of our program and request for support is sincerely appreciated.

*James O. Ash*

James O. Ash
General Chairman

## The Challenge

Our challenge at La Crosse Lutheran Hospital for over 85 years has been the challenge of medicine—to provide superior, cost-effective medical care to our patients while keeping pace with rapidly advancing medical knowledge and technology. Together with Gundersen Clinic, Lutheran maintains its leadership role in providing consistently excellent care without compromise.

While the horizon of medicine is infinite, those practicing medicine want to be sure that quality health care is not jeopardized by cost containment guidelines.

At La Crosse Lutheran, like hospitals everywhere, we are acutely aware of quality vs. cost. Our hospital's Board of Trustees and management continuously address this issue.

"Quality health care requires investment—time, effort, and money—by all of us. This project helps ensure continued health care quality."

—John H. Shuey

The average patient bill at Lutheran is about $350 less than at other similar Wisconsin hospitals. This results in a savings to our community of more than $5 million a year.

In 1977 Lutheran was the first hospital in the community to offer a structured Same-Day Surgery service. Today, Same-Day Surgery accounts for 25 percent of all surgeries performed here, and a 30 to 50 percent savings on our patients' hospital surgical bills.

And our innovative 21-day residential treatment program for chemical dependency, charging $1,300 per client treated as compared to traditional hospital inpatient 21-day programs that cost $4,000 to $6,000, has saved our government, our insurance carriers and our patients nearly $3 million over the last three years.

Through energy conservation programs, $110,000 is saved each year. Group purchasing of supplies through Shared Health Services has saved another $154,000 during the past year.

These cost containment policies and philosophies of La Crosse Lutheran make it a leader among hospitals.

Our commitment is real. Commitment not only to do our part to keep health care costs under control, but to maintain a modern medical facility committed to Excellence With Caring.

## Commitment to the Future

It is in this same spirit that we confront the next challenge facing La Crosse Lutheran Hospital. In providing the most efficient and effective medical care, the time is right for us to further our commitment to the future and to Excellence with Caring. This takes the form of a $25.35 million Capital Improvement Project. Selected from 35 alternative proposals—assessed, evaluated, and approved under the closest scrutiny—the project is designed with cost containment, increased efficiency, and the latest patient care advances in mind. It will position La Crosse Lutheran, patients and staff alike, to greet the 1990s, and beyond, with confidence.

"Dramatic changes are occurring in the delivery of health care in this country. With this project, the La Crosse Lutheran Hospital and Gundersen Clinic will be better equipped to supply the needs of this area for the demands on the health care system of the future."

—Sigurd B. Gundersen, Jr., M.D.

Focusing primarily on medical programs and services, building improvements are concentrated in four distinct areas within the hospital.

## Replacing Aging Facilities and Saving Beds

La Crosse Lutheran Hospital's new construction will add three additional floors to the 1979 and 1973 wings. Designed to replace the obstetrics, cardiology and laboratory services, this new construction will reduce the hospital's overall capacity by 67 beds. In addition, it will bring greater space efficiencies, permitting the aging south wings to be used for a number of the hospital's growing support and ancillary services. These units, almost 60 years old, cannot continue to meet the space, safety and comfort needs of our patients and modern medical practices.

In spite of this inpatient bed reduction, La Crosse Lutheran remains the largest hospital and maintains the highest occupancy rate in the Tri-State Region. By reducing the bed count and encouraging shorter hospital stays, we continue the trend toward maximum efficiency.

> "With a 'kick-off' pledge of $300,000 by the La Crosse Lutheran Hospital Auxiliary, how can the campaign not succeed."
> —Robert T. Frise

An added benefit of the new construction is the reconfiguration of the main lobby area into a highly efficient area designed to expedite the patient admitting process. To accommodate our growing outpatient services, the registration department for these patients will be expanded and located conveniently near the Trauma & Emergency Center and the main lobby. Relocation of the Auxiliary Gift Shop and Flower Mart, will provide for expansion of the Outpatient Physical Therapy Department.

## Obstetrics: The New Life Family Center

All obstetrical services at La Crosse Lutheran Hospital and Gundersen Clinic, Ltd., are collectively grouped under the New Life Family Center. This collection truly makes Lutheran and Gundersen leaders in providing maternity care that meets the needs and desires of mothers and their families.

Acknowledging the tremendous growth in the number of births at Lutheran (over 350 percent in the last 20 years) and the changing demands for delivery alternatives, the building project will provide the special environment essential to outstanding family-centered maternal and newborn care. The new obstetrical unit will have six attractively decorated, homelike "birthing rooms" which enable the family to stay in one room throughout the birth experience. One of the birthing rooms is designed as a high-risk labor, delivery and recovery room. In addition, there will

> "La Crosse Lutheran Hospital and Gundersen Clinic can always be proud of the service that they provide to the mother and her newborn. With the facilities planned for the new addition, the finest service and caring for families will be available in the Tri-State Region."
> —Thomas N. Roberts, M.D.

be two delivery rooms for Caesarean births associated with a high-risk labor room and two-bed recovery room.

Besides providing additional and more efficient space for labor and delivery, the new obstetrical unit will include a special area for patient and family education.

Critical to the care of the high-risk infant, the neonatal intensive care unit and a four-bed pediatric special care unit, now located on two different floors of the hospital, are scheduled for relocation adjacent to the new obstetrical unit. La Crosse Lutheran's New Life Family Center provides this region with two neonatologists and one of Wisconsin's few perinatologists. This specialized obstetrical care makes it possible for mother and infant to remain together during their hospital stay.

This area's only pediatric cardiac surgery and infant neurosurgery is also available at La Crosse Lutheran Hospital.

## Heart Care: The Wisconsin Heart Institute

The Wisconsin Heart Institute was organized just two years ago but our commitment to heart care began over 20 years ago with one cardiologist and one cardiac surgeon. The Institute consolidated community cardiology services with those of Gundersen Clinic and La Crosse Lutheran Hospital and, today, offers sophisticated and comprehensive heart care.

"The Excellence with Caring campaign is vital to adequately provide the needed facilities to respond to future demands in the health care field for La Crosse Lutheran Hospital's service area."

—Elaine Bakken

The number of heart disease deaths in this country is greater than auto accident and cancer deaths. In addition to being America's number one killer, heart disease can have disabling effects on the individual's, as well as the family's, quality of life.

However, the first symptom of heart disease does not have to be a person's last. Over 60 percent of heart disease is preventable. And surgery is one of the last options considered for a patient. In fact, through efforts of prevention, diagnosis, and treatment, actual open heart surgeries declined slightly last year.

In 1978, 879 patients were treated in our Coronary Care Unit; a brief five years later, 1,294 patients were treated. These statistics continue to climb because of the hospital-clinic commitment to the prompt care of all cardiac conditions using the most modern techniques and equipment available. There has been dramatic growth in the treatment of patients utilizing angioplasty, electrophysiology, nuclear cardiology, and graded exercise testing (GXT).

The building project will consolidate the Institute services on one floor and create a new "intermediate care area"—a much-needed transfer point for patients from the Coronary Care Unit and the Cardiac Rehabilitation Unit as well as for other medical/surgical patients requiring intermediate care services.

## The Laboratory: The Critical Consolidation

The requests for tests critical in diagnosing and treating patients continue to increase, resulting in over 355,000 tests performed in 1983 alone. We voluntarily postponed the laboratory services expansion, approved by the State of Wisconsin three years ago, so that it could become a part of the current proposal and be built as a centralized unit on one floor instead of multiple laboratories on three floors.

The new laboratory, containing less square feet than the existing quarters, will bring histology, pathology, bacteriology, blood bank, immunology and all laboratory offices into one consolidated efficient area. La Crosse Lutheran Hospital's modern, new laboratory, located closer to patient care areas, will perform its vital role in the consistent provision of quality, cost-effective patient care.

### LABORATORY FLOOR PLAN.

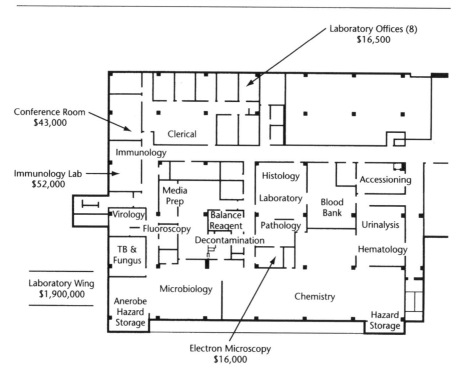

## Fourth Floor Needs

*Stationary Equipment*

Pass-Through Sterilizer—$10,000

ROS Water Still (2)—$6,000

6' Fume Hood—$5,000

RO Still—$5,000

5' Hood w/sink—$5,000

5' Hood w/gas—$4,500

4' Fume Hood—$4,000

Microscope Table—$500

*Portable Equipment*

Tissue Processor—$15,000

Double Door Refrigerator—$6,500

Steam Autoclave—$3,000

Crash Cart—$1,500

Refrigerator/Freezer—$750

Recliners (8)—$350

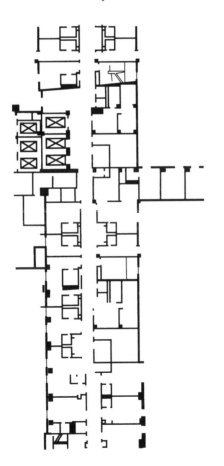

## Meeting the Challenge: The Tri-State Area

La Crosse Lutheran is the largest hospital in the Tri-State Region. Most of the 17,000 inpatients served each year come from an 18-county area. While 36 percent (6,300) of all patients are from La Crosse County, another 6,000 patients annually come from other Wisconsin counties surrounding La Crosse; 2,500 come from the Minnesota counties of Winona, Fillmore and Houston; and more than 2,000 come from Iowa counties.

In addition to our commitment to Excellence With Caring for the patients who come to La Crosse Lutheran Hospital, our commitment to technology, information and treatment support for the Tri-State Region's hospitals with fewer beds, physicians and their patients is strong.

"The needs have been identified. We now must marshal our resources to meet these needs. This capital campaign, to me, represents a commitment to quality, a commitment to community, and a commitment to caring."

—Dorothy Dedo

## THE TRI-STATE REGION.

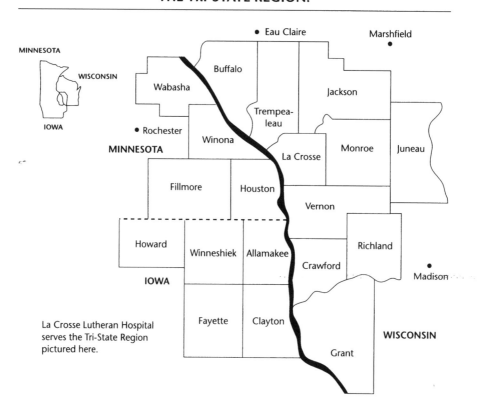

La Crosse Lutheran Hospital serves the Tri-State Region pictured here.

## Health Care: Containing the Costs

In 1984, the average increase in U.S. hospital prices was six percent. La Crosse Lutheran Hospital prices increased by only five percent. Included in this increase was $1 million to help reduce our future borrowing for this building project, making our actual price increase only about three percent.

> "At Lutheran we are very aware of the public concern about the cost of health care. Our commitment is to optimize the use of resources available and to constantly look for less costly ways to provide quality service."
>
> —Jack Schwem

Traditionally, Lutheran's capital and equipment costs have comprised only a small percentage of our total financial requirements, even during periods of major construction. We are committed to this cost-containment philosophy once again.

We have initiated an extensive fund raising campaign in an attempt to further reduce the need for borrowing. Each dollar contributed during the campaign will result in a savings of $4.50 in future debt expense.

La Crosse Lutheran believes that this unique building project addresses identified services and technological needs within the cost-containment commitment of the hospital.

Personal and community support will assure us that the quality of care we receive today will be available for our children and our children's children.

## Campaign Leadership

James O. Ash
GENERAL CHAIRMAN

Terry Gillette
CHAIRMAN, BUSINESS AND
PROFESSIONAL DIVISION

Roland L. Solberg
CHAIRMAN, INDIVIDUALS AND
FOUNDATIONS DIVISION

Kenneth O. Blanchard
CHAIRMAN, TRI-STATE DIVISION

Stefan T. Guttormsson
CHAIRMAN, STEERING COMMITTEE

Sigurd B. Gundersen, Jr., M.D.
CHAIRMAN, MEDICAL STAFF DIVISION

Peter Koukola
CHAIRMAN, EMPLOYEE DIVISION

Walter F. Baltz, Jr.
VICE CHAIRMAN

Jack Glendenning
VICE CHAIRMAN

A. Erik Gundersen, M.D.
VICE CHAIRMAN

Adolf Gundersen, M.D.
VICE CHAIRMAN

Richard T. Lommen
VICE CHAIRMAN

Donald Zietlow
VICE CHAIRMAN

James O. Heinecke
TREASURER, FIDUCIARY COMMITTEE

Edward Carlsson, Ph.D.
FIDUCIARY COMMITTEE

Grace Hanson
IMMEDIATE PAST PRESIDENT,
LA CROSSE LUTHERAN HOSPITAL AUXILIARY

John H. Shuey
PRESIDENT,
LUTHERAN HOSPITAL FOUNDATION

Robert T. Frise
CHAIRMAN OF BOARD,
LA CROSSE LUTHERAN HOSPITAL

Jack Schwem
PRESIDENT,
LA CROSSE LUTHERAN HOSPITAL

Nora A. Starcher, CFRE
EXECUTIVE DIRECTOR,
LUTHERAN HOSPITAL FOUNDATION

EXCELLENCE
WITH
CARING

## How You Can Help

Excellence With Caring is a shared responsibility beginning with each and every one of us. Personal and community support is vital to the success of the capital fund drive for La Crosse Lutheran Hospital. We ask you to consider financial support of this project, sharing in the hospital's investment to assure continued quality health care for you and your neighbors.

"As visitor and patient at La Crosse Lutheran Hospital, I am always impressed with the high quality medical care and the warmth and compassion of the staff."

—Barbara Frank

There are several opportunities available to you to help Lutheran while gaining tax and income benefits for yourself. To make your gift effective, carefully consider one of the following:

*Cash:* Cash gifts are the most common campaign gifts and may be pledged over a three- to five-year period. A pledge often enables you, as a donor, to contribute a larger gift if it is spread over a longer period of time.

*Stocks and Bonds:* Stocks, bonds, or other forms of securities which have appreciated in value are the next most common form of gift. The tax advantages to the individual make them highly attractive. Money market funds also make excellent gifts.

*Real Estate:* A gift of real estate is another convenient way to contribute. If you are hesitating to sell some real estate due to potential large capital gains taxes, you may transfer the property to Lutheran Hospital Foundation and derive substantial benefits.

*Life Insurance:* This may provide an easy way to make a substantial gift. You may be one of the fortunate people whose life insurance policy has outlived its original purpose. A policy can be assigned to Lutheran Hospital Foundation whether it is paid up, partially paid up, or is a new policy.

*Gifts Through Your Will:* While current gifts are needed, you are not limited to this form of giving. By making a bequest to the Foundation in your Will you can help ensure the future of quality health care at Lutheran Hospital. Or, you may consider leaving your assets in Trust, assigning the income to one or two beneficiaries and the Trust principal to Lutheran Hospital Foundation.

*Other Forms of Giving:* These include life income plans and trusts, family business gifts, and commemorative or memorial gifts. There are a variety of plans which can bring immediate benefits to you. We urge you to consult your own legal or financial counsel to determine which plan is best for you. Appropriately, you'll be able to receive the maximum benefit for your objectives, while supporting La Crosse Lutheran Hospital at the same time.

# Time Enough to Give Enough

"I heartily endorse financial support of the Lutheran Hospital's 'Excellence with Caring' campaign. It is extremely comforting to me to know that my family has excellent medical service available and that it is easily accessible and convenient."

—J. O. Heinecke

EXCELLENCE
WITH
CARING

Systematic giving over three to five years makes possible substantial gifts. Depending on the donor's tax bracket, the net cost to the donor can be substantially decreased. Seemingly small amounts paid regularly over 36 months add up to a significant total:

| Three-Year Pledge | Monthly | Quarterly | Semi-Annually | Annually |
|---|---|---|---|---|
| $1,000.00 | 27.78 | 83.33 | 166.67 | 333.33 |
| $1,800.00 | 50.00 | 150.00 | 300.00 | 600.00 |
| $3,000.00 | 83.33 | 250.00 | 500.00 | 1,000.00 |
| $3,600.00 | 100.00 | 300.00 | 600.00 | 1,200.00 |
| $5,000.00 | 138.89 | 416.67 | 833.34 | 1,666.67 |
| $7,500.00 | 208.33 | 625.00 | 1,250.00 | 2,500.00 |
| $9,000.00 | 250.00 | 750.00 | 1,500.00 | 3,000.00 |
| $10,000.00 | 277.78 | 833.34 | 1,666.67 | 3,333.33 |
| $15,000.00 | 416.67 | 1,250.00 | 2,500.00 | 5,000.00 |
| $25,000.00 | 694.44 | 2,083.34 | 4,166.67 | 8,333.33 |
| $36,000.00 | 1,000.00 | 3,000.00 | 6,000.00 | 12,000.00 |

## SAMPLE CAMPAIGN PLAN

# The Academic Endowment Campaign

◆

## Indiana University–Bloomington Campaign Plan

## September 22, 1995

# Table Of Contents

◆

# Introduction

Indiana University–Bloomington (IU-B) is engaged in a planning process and advanced gift program to prepare for a large and comprehensive capital fundraising campaign focusing on the need for endowment. With the authorization of the Trustees of the University for most of the major components of the campaign, and operating under the aegis of the Board of Directors of the Indiana University Foundation (IUF), the Campaign's intensive planning phase began in 1994; the advance gift phase began July 1, 1994; and the public phase of the Campaign is expected to begin by 1998. Before the public phase of the Campaign begins, the Trustees of the University will be asked to formally approve the full Campaign program and plan, which will be specified in two detailed Campaign documents:

1. The *Case Statement* will specify the objectives for which funds are to be sought.
2. The *Campaign Plan* will map out the course of action by which these funds are to be raised.

THIS DOCUMENT IS THE *CAMPAIGN PLAN.* It has been prepared to accomplish several objectives:

1. To establish the basic fundraising principles on which a campus-wide capital funding program can be developed.
2. To outline the overall or "core" plan for the Campaign including the organizational structure, both volunteer and professional, which will be required.
3. To define and describe the relationships implicit on such an effort:
   a. Academic planning and participation
   b. Prospect identification, management and research
   c. Formation of the Nucleus Fund
   d. Major gifts phase
   e. Annual giving and its relationship to the Capital Campaign
   f. Goal setting
   g. Cultivation and involvement of prospects and leadership
4. To establish a timetable for key activities required for the Campaign.
5. To suggest the main elements of supporting publications, public communications and cultivation programs.

Upon approval of this Campaign plan, the University will have a unifying master blueprint for all operations of the campus' development program for 1995 through 2000.

## Premises of the Campaign Plan

The Campaign Plan is based on the following assumptions:

1. The Campaign will be authorized by the Trustees of Indiana University and conducted under the aegis of the Board of Directors of the IUF as an exercise of their chartered responsibility as the official fundraising agency of Indiana University.

2. The period of intensive fundraising will be from July 1, 1994 through December 31, 2000, or that academic year.

3. The goal will be large—in the $150 million range for endowment and $350 million overall.

4. The personal solicitation of prospects will be concentrated on those believed to be able to contribute $25,000 or more.

5. The Campaign will have its own identity, but it will be managed in conjunction with other ongoing fundraising activities. It will be carefully coordinated with the University's various annual fund programs and continuing promotional and event schedules. Every major officer of the campus will have a role.

6. The structure and scope of the Campaign will reflect both the campus' evolving emphases and its internal operating structure. This will be a campus-wide Campaign, but development efforts on behalf of particular schools or other units that have their own constituency may occur as campaign components within the overall program.

7. Ongoing support programs will be treated as an "operating component" of the Campaign and all alumni, whether or not they are capital prospects, will be asked to participate in annual giving and other ongoing development programs. Thus, the specific capital fundraising targets of the campaign will be presented as an enhancement to—rather than in place of—ongoing private support.

8. Gifts will be sought in all forms, including cash and securities, real and personal property, trusts, life income agreements, pledges in the form of bequests and any combination of these. Commitments may be paid over three to five years, or longer in the case of special circumstances.

9. Funds raised for the University through the efforts of this Campaign will supplement, but in no way supplant, the operating and capital support for the campus from the State of Indiana.

10. The projected effects of inflation will be taken into account in calculating the amounts needed to fund Campaign objectives.

11. The condition of the stock market and the nation's economy over the next five years will be a variable factor in the giving capacity of many prospects.

12. Tax laws affecting charitable contributions are subject to change; any dele-terious changes during the Campaign will require new strategies or adjust-ments in the Campaign Plan.

13. Corporate and foundation giving is increasingly oriented toward specific pro-grams with well-defined goals. This implies a need for an imaginative pack-aging of existing and proposed programs based on detailed descriptions and renderings as applicable for these programs.

14. The readiness of various component units of the Campaign may vary and influence the timetable of the public phase of the Campaign. For example, if one of the major components is not ready to proceed at the target date of the Campaign kickoff, inhibiting the Campaign's ability to conduct the advance gift phase for that program on a timely basis, the public announce-ment of the overall Campaign may necessarily be delayed.

# Perspective

This plan encompasses the basic requirements for organizing and seeking con-tributions to the "Academic Endowment Campaign." The Campaign is designed to appeal to graduates of the University, other special friends, foundations, cor-porations, corporate foundations and businesses located and headquartered both within and outside the State of Indiana. The Campaign will seek a total of $350 million during the period from July 1, 1994, through December 31, 2000, or the conclusion of that academic year, to enhance the endowment and supplement on-going programs.

The total Campaign goal is comprised of two major elements: 1) Ongoing support accounts for $200 million of the overall goal; 2) Endowment goals amount to $150 million. During the past four years, private support to Bloom-ington's various programs including schools with joint programs on the Indi-anapolis campus, has averaged $33 million, of which about $15 million each year has been designated for endowment purposes. A portion of those funds has been contributed for purposes which will be "featured objectives" in the "Academic Endowment Campaign"—faculty and student support. As the Campaign begins, of course, those gifts must not be counted twice, so they will be included in the appropriate category of Campaign objectives.

However, continuing the support of programs outside those objectives is criti-cal to the well being of the campus. As a result, the total Campaign goal is a com-bination of ongoing support added to the Campaign's "featured objectives." It is our expectation that increases in ongoing support will increase 30 percent to 50 per-cent during the campaign time period as a consequence of the publicity, increased cultivation activities and a deepening awareness of IU's need for private support.

The endowment goal of $150 million, includes funds for those academic endowments which have been assigned the highest priority by the Bloomington Chancellor. Campaign efforts to raise this $150 million that is above and beyond ongoing support programs will focus on major gifts of $25,000 or more. Pace-setting gifts of $100,000 or more will be sought during the Nucleus Fund phase to stimulate the Campaign toward a quick and successful completion. (See Standards of Giving Table below.)

The primary requisite governing this entire undertaking is that the Academic Endowment Campaign will seek to fulfill documented needs of the campus.

Planning for this capital venture is being undertaken with great care and deliberation. The plan which follows documents steps which must be taken to ensure success in the *initial* phases of the Campaign. Except for brief discussions of public relations and campaign policy, the plan which follows deals almost exclusively with the preparatory phases—Advanced and Major Gifts—of the Campaign. Plans for subsequent phases—Special and General—will be developed at the appropriate times in the campaign schedule.

# Plan for the Advance/Major Gifts Phase

## A. Advance/Major Gifts: The Critical Factors

The Advance/Major Gifts phase of the Campaign is the all-important phase. For this reason, it is urged that, in the initial stages of the campaign organization, all planning and action be directed primarily toward gifts of $100,000 or more (except in relation to the necessarily smaller gifts of a few members of the IUF Board of Directors and the Advanced/Major Gifts Committee). The following figures are targets and illustrate the pattern in which gifts should be sought to achieve the Campaign goal.

### TABLE OF GIFTS NEEDED TO RAISE $150 MILLION.

| Gift Amount | Number of Gifts Needed | Total in Range |
|---|---|---|
| $15,000,000+ | 1 | $15,000,000 |
| 10,000,000–14,999,999 | 2 | 20,000,000 |
| 5,000,000–9,999,999 | 3 | 15,000,000 |
| 2,500,000–4,999,999 | 5 | 12,500,000 |
| 1,000,000–2,499,999 | 20 | 20,000,000 |
| 750,000–999,999 | 20 | 15,000,000 |
| 500,000–749,999 | 40 | 20,000,000 |
| 250,000–499,999 | 50 | 12,500,000 |
| 100,000–249,999 | 100 | 10,000,000 |
| 25,000–99,999 | 400 | 10,000,000 |
| Totals | 641 | $150,000,000 |

A table of standards of giving is a sobering thing, and rightly so. It says, in effect, that without gifts of the order of magnitude indicated, the entire effort has little, if any, chance of succeeding. In a mood of urgency created by this awareness, Endowment Campaign leaders are better prepared to offer specific suggestions to prospective donors.

Large amounts of money are not raised by casually saying, "Anything you can spare will be quite all right." In advance of any asking, the Campaign leadership must know what standards of giving are necessary to succeed. When so informed, they can and must communicate a sense of these standards to the entire constituency of workers and prospective donors.

A fundamental of fundraising—one which we must practice throughout the Campaign—is the identification, correct evaluation and thoughtful approach to alumni and friends of IU. The volunteer is better able to do a good job when he/she: 1) proceeds with an awareness of the caliber of gifts required for success; and 2) makes each major gift approach fortified by a specific evaluation of the prospect's capacity to give.

·

## B. Nucleus Fund

The Advance Gifts phase of the Campaign will develop and gain its momentum from the pace-setting gifts of Directors of the IU Foundation, board members of academic unit advisory committees, and 50 to 100 other donors. The success of the Nucleus Fund depends, to a large degree, on securing 100 percent participation from these groups. Once their commitments are made, these leaders are in position to help secure the additional gifts and pledges needed to fulfill the Nucleus Fund goal. A total of approximately 40 percent of the Campaign endowment goal—that is at least $60 million—should be secured before public announcement of the Campaign in 1998.

We realize that some of the gifts from various Board members may be modest; however, sufficient giving ability exists within the present Boards to help make the Nucleus Fund figure an impressive demonstration of tangible leadership. The Nucleus Fund when completed will offer the following advantages:

1. It will give the Boards an opportunity to set an example which will show the way for all the University's constituencies.
2. It will demonstrate that the University has been realistic in setting the objectives for the capital components of the Campaign at $150 million, over and above the $200 million goal for ongoing support.
3. It will set the tone for the remaining major gifts effort, and thus, for the Campaign.
4. It will inspire every major gift prospect subsequently solicited.

The building of a Nucleus Fund (screening, rating and formation of the Campaign committee structure) will occur under the general direction of the President of the IUF and under the specific direction of the Nucleus Fund/Executive Committee. The organizational chart included in Appendix I illustrates the Nucleus Fund organization, which also forms the framework for the overall Campaign leadership structure that will emerge during the Nucleus Fund/Advance Gift phase of the Campaign.

### C. Organizing for the Advance Gifts Phase

The chart included in Appendix II presents the Major Gifts leadership structure for the Endowment Campaign. Listed below is a brief description of each component of the Campaign and the summary of the responsibilities and objectives to be assumed by each committee chairperson.

# Campaign Committees

[Some material was omitted from this section for the sake of brevity.]

It is proposed that the Academic Endowment Campaign be operated under the direction of a national chairperson or persons.

The duties of the chairperson(s) are as follows:

1. Serve as the Campaign Chief Executive Officer
2. Enlist chairpersons and other top volunteer leaders for the principal functioning units of the Campaign organization
3. Make a significant gift to the Campaign commensurate with his/her own ability
4. Spearhead and/or accompany President Brand in cultivation and solicitation visits with top-level prospects
5. Assume specific responsibility for the personal and/or corporate commitments for members of the nucleus fund-executive committee and of appropriate principal component chairpersons
6. Preside at executive committee meetings
7. Act as primary spokesman, with President Brand, for Campaign goals, themes, objectives and strategies
8. Serve as keynote speaker at Campaign kickoff and other critical Campaign functions and cultivation affairs
9. Provide inspiration and motivation for volunteer leaders to fulfill Campaign commitments
10. Review and approve all major strategy and marketing plans for the Campaign

The campaign committees are as follows:

1. The Nucleus Fund Committee*
2. Endowment Campaign Executive Committee
3. Academic Unit Campaign Committees
4. Other Campaign Committees

> Faculty-Staff Committee
>
> Public Relations Committee

# Role of Chairpersons of Academic Unit Component Committees

The Academic Unit Committee chairpersons perform the most important roles in the Campaign organization. It will be the chairperson's responsibility to put together the respective committees just described, to persuade committee members to accept appropriate assignments, and to keep them on a steady and productive pursuit of their prospects. The chairperson should, if possible, be a resident of the state and/or very knowledgeable about Indiana University, be capable of making major personal gifts, be active in business with considerable influence and should not be hesitant to ask for large gifts. In brief, the tasks of the Academic Unit Campaign chairpersons are as follows:

1. To put together strong committees willing to seek gifts in the $25,000 and up range from individuals and their personal and family foundations
2. To work closely with the National Campaign Chairperson in all matters affecting the committee's responsibility
3. To make a significant personal gift commensurate with his/her own ability.
4. To ask personally for certain major gifts
5. To hold meetings of the committees regularly in which its members can screen and rate new prospects, take additional assignments and report on progress
6. To follow up periodically with members of the committee and make regular reports to the Executive Committee on the progress of the unit campaign
7. To see that members of the committee are fully informed about the Campaign and then to see that each member of the committee has made a personal commitment in accordance with his or her ability
8. To participate in cultivation events as desirable

*The "Nucleus Fund" designation will cease being used once the $60 million Nucleus Fund is achieved and the public phase begins.

## The Campaign Timetable: Broad Outlines of Activity, July 1, 1994–December 31, 2000

*I. Planning Phase*

    Draft Preliminary Timetable

    Draft Initial Statement of Campaign Goals

    Conduct Market Survey of Leading Alumni and Donors

    Build Major Gift Prospect Lists, Research IU Relationships

    Develop Communications and Marketing Plans

    Begin Case Stating Process

    Develop Staff Organization Plan and Campaign Budget

    Present Preliminary Plans to Trustees and Directors

    Recruit and Hire Campaign Staff As Needed

    Refocus Existing Staff On Major Gifts

    Begin Corporate and Foundation Advance Gifts Efforts

    Begin Soliciting Major Leadership Gifts

*II. Advance Gifts and Leadership Recruitment*

    Conduct Prospect Screening and Rating Programs

    Enlist Nucleus Fund Chair

    Begin Solicitation of Board of Directors

    Identify, Enlist and Educate Campaign Chair(s)

    Identify, Enlist and Educate Academic Unit Chairs

    Produce Pre-Campaign Literature and Case Statement

    Obtain Approval of Full Campaign by Trustees of IU
and Directors of the IUF

    Solicit Campaign Committees and Others for Nucleus Fund

*JUNE 30, 1998: DEADLINE FOR COMPLETION OF NUCLEUS FUND GOAL*

*III. Public Phase of Campaign*

    Public Kickoff Event—Fall 1998

    Continue Activity of Academic Unit Campaigns

Continue Adding Names to Major Gifts Prospect List

Continue Prospective Donor Contact and Cultivation as Required

Continue Major Gifts Solicitations

Continue Distribution of Campaign Information to News Media and Prospects

Continue to Enlist, Organize and Train Volunteer Leadership

Ongoing Recognition of Donors of Major Gifts

Campaign Victory Celebration

*DECEMBER 31, 2000: DEADLINE FOR*
*100 PERCENT OF CAMPAIGN DOLLAR OBJECTIVE*

## Public Relations and Public Information

The results of the Campaign market survey indicate a need to develop a strong communications program for the Bloomington campus to address identity and image concerns uncovered during the survey. This effort should begin in earnest immediately and parallel and complement campaign communication efforts.

A vigorous effort will be made to interpret the Campaign through various written and audio-visual materials, public events and special events for Campaign leaders and volunteers. Eventually, a Campaign newsletter may be published to keep volunteer leaders and donors informed of the progress of the Campaign. Through the IU News Bureau, the campus will also seek to keep the general public informed of the Campaign and the importance of the program to the future of the University through various forms of printed and electronic media as may be appropriate.

## Staffing

The IUF is responsible for providing the following:

1. Liaison with the President, Chancellor and Board of Directors of the IUF Board
2. Under the coordination of the President of the IUF, assistance in the development of the Nucleus Fund
3. Assistance in the formation of the Academic Unit Campaign Committees
4. Coordination of ongoing development activities with the Campaign

5.  Liaison for the Campaign with annual fundraising programs
6.  Maintenance of the President's, Chancellor's and the Chair of the Campaign's schedule
7.  Research on major gift prospects by phases in the Campaign
8.  Service to Campaign solicitation activities, e.g., corporate, faculty-staff, annual fund, planned giving, etc
9.  Handling of gifts, gift records and acknowledgments
10. Production of campaign status reports in compliance with approved guidelines.
11. Supervision of budget and control of expenses
12. Development and production of a publication supporting the case for all components of the Campaign
13. Assistance in the development of specific component case statements to ensure thematic and design consistency
14. Production of written proposals for major gift solicitations
15. Prospect management and maintenance of the Campaign prospect files

# Staff Organization

In large measure, the effectiveness of the Campaign will depend upon staffing. The leadership and chairpersons of all of the operating divisions of the Academic Endowment Campaign will need to have the full-time assistance of the most experienced and able staff available.

Many if not all of the present officers in the University will be involved in the operation of the Campaign in one way or another. Among the officers who will have key responsibilities are the following:

*IU President*—It has been pointed out before that the role of the President in the Campaign is crucial. Dr. Brand is among the University's most persuasive representatives, and it will be essential for him to be available to undertake certain key negotiations in the early stages of the Campaign and for closing on some prospect solicitations as the Campaign moves through its various phases.

*IU Vice President and Chancellor*—As one of the campus' most articulate spokespersons, Dr. Gros Louis must play a key role in interpreting the case for support to various constituencies and conveying the positive impact of the campaign to donors. He must also play a key role in working with the Deans of the campus on all campaign related matters.

*IUF President*—Mr. Simic will advise Campaign leadership and Campaign staff in matters which affect the University. He will play a major role in meetings of the

Executive Committee and will be the University's principal liaison with the Campaign. He will also play a key role in numerous nucleus fund solicitations.

*IU Vice Presidents*—All must be available for advice and counsel on Campaign matters as they relate to their areas.

*Deans*—All must be available for advice and counsel on Campaign matters as they relate to their counterparts. Active leadership in each academic unit campaign will be required as well as participation in the solicitation of lead gifts for the unit.

*IUF Senior Vice President-Development*—Mr. Kirsch is responsible for directing the activity of all Foundation staff involved with the campaign and assisting the campaign management team in strategic and operational aspects of the campaign.

*Campaign Director*—As director of the Campaign, Mr. Dove will serve as chief campaign strategist. He will have jurisdiction in all important aspects of the Campaign. He will play a key role in ensuring that all elements of the campaign plan are executed in proper sequence and on schedule.

*Campaign Development Staff*—The Campaign development staff will be organized with regional responsibilities carefully coordinated with component project responsibilities. This will require constant communication and cooperation between Foundation staff and directors of academic unit campaigns.

- *Executive Director of Development*—The Executive Director of Development will participate in directing specified Foundation staff and certain constituent units involved with the Campaign and provide leadership for annual support initiatives within the Foundation and on the Bloomington campus.
- *Associate Director of the Campaign*—An Associate Director may be appointed to work with constituent unit programs and to manage certain operational aspects of the Campaign as designated by the Director. The Associate Director will also provide staff support to the Campaign Executive Committee.
- *Academic Unit Campaign Directors*—The Academic Unit Campaign Directors, namely the chief development officer of each unit, are responsible for staffing the members of their various campaign committees and are responsible for directing the component campaigns assigned them within the parameters set forth in the Campaign Plan. Accordingly, each unit campaign director will be asked to submit to the Campaign Director by November 15, 1995, a campaign plan for their respective unit.

- *Director of Planned Giving*—The Director and staff are responsible for identifying, cultivating and soliciting planned gifts—anticipated to be a major component of the campaign—and for providing service to the academic units in this area.
- *Director of Corporate and Foundations Relations*—The Director is responsible for that portion of the Campaign relying on corporate and foundation support, as well as for other ongoing campus, corporate and foundation relations programs.
- *Senior Development Directors*—These individuals are responsible for the identification, cultivation and solicitation of major prospects in their assigned territories. They are also responsible for the training and staffing of any regional Campaign volunteers.
- *Staff Reporting Expectations*—Beginning December 1, 1995, every IUF and academic unit development officer with Campaign responsibilities will be expected to complete a monthly activity report to be shared with the Dean/Director and with the Campaign Director. The format for such a report is included in Appendix III.

Additionally, on a monthly basis, all individuals with campaign solicitation responsibility will be asked to submit to the campaign director's office a report to include new solicitations, the status of outstanding solicitations and the closure on any solicitations. A form is attached as Appendix IV.

Development officers will be expected to perform under the guidelines established by and for major gift officers in the summer of 1994 subsequent to the development program review conducted by Grenzebach and Associates. These expectations are attached as Appendix V.

## Annual Giving During the Endowment Campaign

It is recommended that during the life of the campaign, the IUF assume responsibility for annual giving programs on the campus, thereby enabling development officers to meet the new responsibilities and expectations imposed by the campaign through devoting a maximum amount of time to major gift fundraising. A brief plan for this approach is included as Appendix VI.

## Budget

The Campaign is budgeted at 5 percent of the endowment goal. The proposed campaign budget is attached as Appendix VII.

## Campaign Operations

There are many keys to success in a fundraising enterprise. The following, however, cannot be overlooked.

## A. Board Participation

We have stressed the importance of the Nucleus Fund and Director support. We look to these Boards, as well as to leadership from academic unit campaign committees, to provide vigorous leadership in the enlistment of committee members and in the actual solicitation of funds from prospects for significant gifts.

## B. A Voluntary Effort

Major gift solicitation should be undertaken principally by volunteers except in special cases of the involvement by the President and members of the University's administration and faculty. The principle of voluntary participation in Advance and Major Gift solicitation also applies straight down the line in the whole Campaign organization. The effectiveness of workers comes as much from their readiness to commit their own time, energy and money as from their persuasiveness in selling the campus' case for support.

## C. Solid Prospecting

Major gift prospecting is a "sights-raising" search for giving potential. Potential is an indication of a person's capacity to give, not to be confused with propensity, which is a factor of interest and our ability to cultivate and to sell the program.

At the moment there are about 400 prospects identified with significant gift potential. Experience would indicate that this number of prospects is inadequate to achieve the gift tables as indicated in a previous section of this plan. Peer screenings and ratings will bear this out. The approximate number of solid prospects needed in each of the major gift categories are indicated as follows:

### NUMBER OF PROSPECTS NEEDED TO RAISE $150 MILLION.

| Gift Amount | Number of Gifts Needed | Total in Range | Number of Prospects Needed |
|---|---|---|---|
| $15,000,000+ | 1 | $15,000,000 | 4 |
| 10,000,000–14,999,999 | 2 | 20,000,000 | 8 |
| 5,000,000–9,999,999 | 3 | 15,000,000 | 12 |
| 2,500,000–4,999,999 | 5 | 12,500,000 | 20 |
| 1,000,000–2,499,999 | 20 | 20,000,000 | 80 |
| 750,000–999,999 | 20 | 15,000,000 | 60 |
| 500,000–749,999 | 40 | 20,000,000 | 120 |
| 250,000–499,999 | 50 | 12,500,000 | 150 |
| 100,000–249,999 | 100 | 10,000,000 | 300 |
| 25,000–99,999 | 400 | 10,000,000 | 1,000 |
| Totals | 641 | $150,000,000 | 1,754 |

## D. Pledges

Pledges over a period of several years are a necessary factor in making possible on every level the size of gifts essential to success in a capital campaign. The standard provided for payment of pledges to the Campaign should be up to five years. Provision should be made for extending the payments beyond that in special cases.

## E. Prospect Identification and Rating

Because the number of prospects needed is not sufficient, prospect identification and rating will be vital to the success of the campaign. In particular, intensive efforts on the part of all campaign development officers need to be undertaken immediately and extend through the pre-public phase. An explanation of the rating process is offered in Appendix VIII. It is recommended that of the various methods proposed for rating, the individual one-on-one method be used predominantly. IUF will offer training sessions and track results.

## F. Gift Credits

All pledges and gifts will be counted in accordance with the guidelines published by the Council for Advancement and Support of Education (CASE). A summary of those guidelines is attached as Appendix IX.

## G. Naming Opportunities

Named and memorial gift opportunities are available to donors to encourage and recognize support. The University guidelines are outlined in Appendix X.

## H. Prospect Management

Management of prospects will be accomplished under the established terms of the University's prospect management system. These are outlined in Appendix XI. Priority in all cases will be given to the Campaign in prospect assignment.

## I. Matching Funds

The Indiana University Board of Trustees has approved a program to match the endowment income on certain gifts throughout the University. This program will be available for certain gifts made to the Bloomington campaign. The general guidelines are outlined below.

# Endowment Matching Program

1. Endowment funds received after December 1, 1995, for the purpose of direct Faculty support, especially for Chairs and Professorships, are eligible for this match.

2. The full match, that is 1:1, will consist of a payout equal to 5 percent of the principle on annual basis and will be available for gifts of at least $1,000,000. If the gift falls between $500,000 and $1,000,000, the match will be based on a ratio of 1:2. Payouts will be in perpetuity. A contractual commitment will be provided to the donor.

3. The match opportunity will be in effect until December 31, 1997. A maximum of $500,000 will be allocated each year during this time for a total of $1,000,000. Allocations will be made on a first-come, first-served basis, open to all campuses. Unspent available match funds will not be carried forward.

4. The source of funds for the match will be one-half from University administration and one-half from campus administration. At their option, Chancellors may choose to charge the successful unit for all or part of the campus' portion of the match, or they may distribute all or part of the charges to the entire campus.

5. To take an example, Mary Jones donates $500,000 for endowment for a faculty position in SPEA at IUB. Assume that the payment by the IUF is $25,000 per year (that is, 5 percent of 500k). The match is 1:2 on this amount. Thus, in addition to the $25,000, SPEA receives an additional $12,500 per year for support of this position. Of the $12,500, University administration will provide $6,250. The remaining $6,250 is the responsibility of IUB.

6. Gifts may be paid over a maximum of five years. The match will be available only if there is a firm, written commitment. However, matching funds will be provided only to the extent that payment has been received (with one exception noted below). So, if there is a gift of $1,000,000 to be paid over four years and $250,000 is received the first year, then the matching funds for the first year are $12,500. Here the match rate is 1:1, and the payout is 5 percent of $250,000.

7. In the case of irrevocable trusts established during the match period with no payout until termination of the trust, one-half the institutional payout will begin when the trust is established. The remaining matching funds will become available when the trust terminates, as will, of course, the trust income. Thus, if there is an irrevocable trust of $1,000,000 established during the match timeframe, then the payout from institutional funds (that is, University administration plus the campus) will be $25,000 per year until the trust matures. After that, institutional funds will equal $50,000 per year (at the 1:1 payout ratio) plus $50,000 from the trust itself.

8. The President, in consultation with the IUF President, reserves the authority to limit eligibility. In particular, it should not be possible for a single megagift to deplete all matching monies. In order to determine the upper limit of a specific gift, a brief written proposal should be submitted to the President.

9. Appendix XII details the various gift vehicles eligible for this match and payout qualifications for each vehicle.

## Appendix I

## NUCLEUS FUND ORGANIZATION.

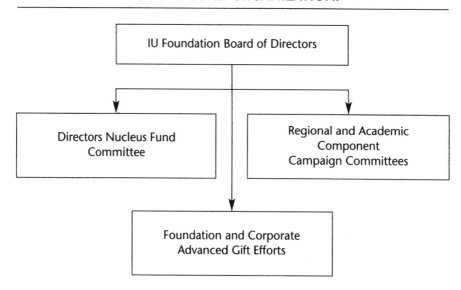

**Appendix II**

## ENDOWMENT CAMPAIGN LEADERSHIP STRUCTURE.

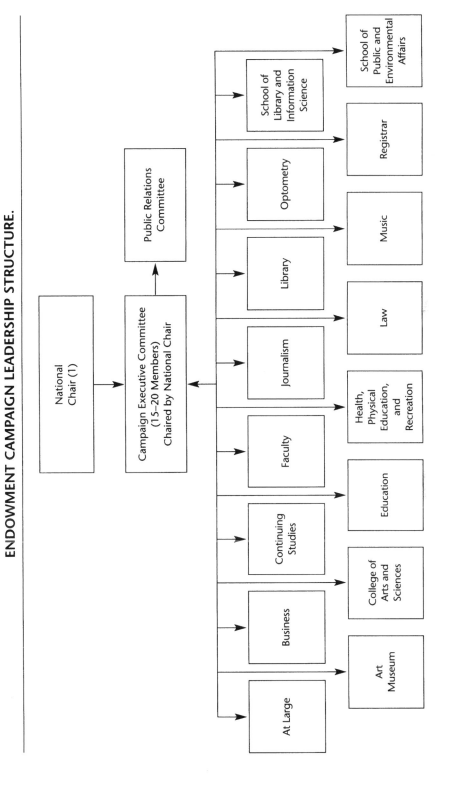

## Appendix III

## ACTIVITY REPORT.

Development Officer:

Today's Date:                                              Covers (    ) Working Days

1. Prospect/Volunteer Contacts {(*) first time contact; (#) prospect rating/screening session}:

2. Solicitations: A) Proposals Submitted B) Gifts Closed (list name/amount/purpose):
   A) Proposals Submitted

   B) Gifts Closed

3. New Volunteers Recruited:

4. Important Campus Meetings/Contacts:

5. Major Activity/Meetings Scheduled for Next Two Weeks:

Appendix IV

## BY PROJECT: INDIANA UNIVERSITY FOUNDATION MAJOR GIFT PROPOSAL UPDATE.

Month

| Staff/Vol. | Project | Prospect | Date of Solicitation | Amount of Solicitation | Written Verbal | Last Report Status | Current Status |
|------------|---------|----------|----------------------|------------------------|----------------|--------------------|----------------|

# Major Gifts Fundraising Guidelines

Indiana University implemented a constituency-based development program in 1983, delegating a major part of the responsibility for fundraising to campuses throughout the University system and to constituent schools, colleges, and departments on all campuses. The constituency-based development program:

- allows Foundation staff to work in cooperation with the development officer(s) of each constituent fundraising unit on behalf of University-wide priorities;
- is successful because it is conducted by and for the former academic homes of alumni and allows for a broad range of giving opportunities to the University (more than 95 percent of gifts received from donors are restricted to specific units or programs);
- provides an opportunity for administrators and faculty, system-wide, to be involved in development programs which identify academic needs and priorities through the University administrative structure.

Major gifts are an integral part of the total development program. Each year approximately 50 percent of the total voluntary support to Indiana University through Indiana University Foundation comes from gifts of $50,000 or greater. Individuals who are responsible for major gifts acquisition include faculty members and administrative staff. There are significant differences in the amount of time units and individuals allocate to major gifts, ranging from full time to a small percentage of time due to other responsibilities.

In order to place appropriate emphasis on major gifts, the Committee on Standards, Expectations and Measurement of Major Gifts recommends that the following guidelines be adopted as a set of general expectations for professional development personnel. These expectations are offered as general guidelines for a *full time* major gift officer. They may be altered by a variety of circumstances identified in the guidelines or as agreed upon by the fundraiser and her/his supervisor.

I. The major gifts threshold is currently defined as an outright or deferred gift of a minimum of $25,000 over a five-year period or a single year commitment of $5,000 or greater. This definition may be modified for a given unit upon consultation with the unit head and the Indiana University Foundation. Some units which have a more mature development program or are involved in a capital campaign may adopt a higher base. Gifts at levels below those described above, while possibly significant to a particular program, are typically not characterized as major gifts or produced with the methodology or intensity of efforts desired or described in this document.

II. Guidelines for Annual Expectations of a Full-Time Major Gifts Officer:
   A. Manage a pool of approximately 150 individuals. This pool should represent a balance of individuals at various stages in the development continuum. As a guideline the following distribution is recommended: (the mix might change based on the status of a campaign or project)

   | | | |
   |---|---|---|
   | Cultivation | 65 | 43 percent |
   | Solicitation | 35 | 24 percent |
   | Stewardship | 50 | 33 percent |

   It is assumed that most or all volunteers will fall into one of these categories. Everyone in the pool should receive *at least* one meaningful contact each year. Individuals in the solicitation stage require several substantive personal contacts yearly, with particular attention paid to the value of the contact in moving the prospect towards closure of a gift.
   B. Make or cause to be made an average of 180 meaningful calls per year. Based on past experience, a full time major gifts officer can be expected to make 180 face to face personal calls per year. However, other forms of meaningful contacts may be included, as well as those defined by each unit head, dean or director in consultation with the development officer. Each meaningful contact should be reported through the prospect management system.
   C. Make or cause to be made a minimum of 30 major gift solicitations per year. This should produce 15–20 gifts.
   D. Identify 15–25 new prospects to be managed through the prospect management system who have the inclination and capability which qualify them as major gift prospects. In general, 50 individual contacts will be made to identify and qualify 15–20 new prospects and these prospects will replace individuals who have been removed from the prospect pool.
   E. Make or cause to be made stewardship calls on all donors in the pool. Using the proposed pool distribution, this could require 50 individual contacts. The nature of stewardship contacts may take a variety of forms ranging from individual meetings to invitations to special events. As the major gifts officer expands their donor base it will be essential to rely on a variety of institutional contacts to accomplish the stewardship function.
   *Summary.* Given the capacity of 180 face to face personal calls for a full time major gifts officer and the need to make calls in all areas—solicitations (30–35), cultivation (65), stewardship (50), and prospect identification (50), it is clear that the number of calls may exceed the capacity of a staff member. Solicitation calls should receive the highest priority, with cultivation calls and new prospect identification secondary. Stewardship

calls, although critical, may require the use of other institutional contacts to accomplish the stewardship function in some cases.

III. The comprehensive nature of these guidelines is designed to assist Indiana University in maintaining and coordinating the solicitation of major gifts. These guidelines will be helpful in setting goals and measuring the performance of major gift development officers. Considerations which may affect the prospect pool each staff member is expected to maintain includes the following:

A. Percentage of time spent in major gifts solicitation
B. Geographic proximity to prospects
C. Complexity/size of gifts being sought
D. Campaign/noncampaign mode
E. General experience as a development officer
F. Nature of constituency

IV. The importance of major gift acquisition should be part of the strategic plan of every unit. The President, deans, directors, and unit heads should have a defined role in major gift fund raising. As part of the planning process, it is essential that support be provided within each unit for the acquisition of major gifts. This support includes:

A. Budget
  1. Travel
  2. Special Events
B. Provision for administrative support
  1. Clerical
  2. Writing Services
  3. Research
  4. Equipment—access to the IUF database
C. It is assumed that the IUF will continue to make available support services including, but not limited to, consultation for legal questions, planned giving, and corporation and foundation relations, as well as prospect management, research services, donor records, and proposal writing.

In carrying out the duties of major gift fundraising, it is expected that each representative of Indiana University will observe the highest standards of personal and professional conduct. Accordingly, major gift officers are expected to carry out their duties in a manner which inspires and assures the confidence of fellow major gift and development officers, donors, alumni and friends of the University as directed in the IUF code of ethics.

It is also expected that each major gift fundraiser will meet with his/her supervisor throughout the year to discuss and adjust these goals as appropriate to each individual position.

**Appendix VI**

---

# Annual Giving Program During the Endowment Campaign

## Background

Currently, the Indiana University Foundation's Annual Giving Office produces three major mailings each year and provides Telefund services which are used extensively by the academic units. Additionally, each academic unit, and many departments within some units, make multiple mailings each year. Combined, it is estimated that more than 140 mailings and over 565,000 pieces of mail are sent each year. The actual number is unknown and is likely much higher. At the present time there is no reliable mechanism in place to track this information.

The system has become increasingly cumbersome and too complex to effectively coordinate. This lack of coordination has resulted in duplication, higher printing costs, increased staff, and confusion and sometimes ill-will on the part of alumni who receive overlapping fundraising letters and phone calls.

The Annual Fund is the cornerstone of a comprehensive fundraising program. However, it is expensive based upon cost per dollar raised, and labor intensive. Staff resources dedicated to direct mail and telefund programs are resources lost for the Endowment Campaign. A central annual giving program will result in efficiencies which will allow more time for unit development officers to focus on major gifts for the campaign and other unit priorities.

## Advantages

A centralized annual giving program has many advantages:

1. It will reduce work loads within the various units, allowing development officers to make additional major gift contacts for the upcoming endowment campaign.
2. Economies of scale would be an option for the first time. By centralizing the annual giving program, large mailings will help to reduce the overall costs.
3. It will provide a coordinated annual giving calendar, which does not currently exist. This calendar will maximize everyone's efforts, and avoid our current problem of "oversoliciting" our alumni.
4. It will allow for a specific identity to be created for the Annual Fund with a campus-wide theme. Penn State University is just one example of how this approach has reaped significant rewards. *For instance, their alumni participation increased from 16 percent to 20.5 percent after centralization, and net income on mailings alone went up 29 percent.*

## Technology

Technologies associated with direct mail have eliminated the problems involved with personalizing individual mailings. Today, even with a campus-wide unified mailing, the mailing can be tailored to represent a specific unit. While costs might dictate that donor acquisition and lapsed retrieval mailings remain somewhat generic, donor renewal mailings would include significant personalization.

Telefund automation, the next logical enhancement of our annual giving program, will allow for an increased number of calls to be made each year and for a corresponding increase in income. While the Telefund has seen steady growth in dollars pledged, from $2,190,566 in 1990–91 to $3,221,309 in 1994–95, automation would increase dollars pledged to as much as $4,266,000 over a twelve month period. It will also allow additional personalization by providing more data about our donors both before and after phone contact is made. Automation will also allow for more contacts to be made, further enhancing the ability to speak with IU's alumni on a personal basis.

## Summary

Overall, the centralization of the annual giving program is the next logical step in the evolution of fundraising on the Bloomington campus, particularly as we prepare for the campaign. A centralized annual giving program should allow unit development officers to concentrate on major gifts, reduce costs, increase gifts, and foster goodwill with our alumni. These outcomes will benefit the university not only during the campaign but for many years thereafter. Centralization could be accomplished after the successful automation of the Telefund.

The differences between the current and proposed systems are summarized below:

| *CURRENT SYSTEM:* | *PROPOSED SYSTEM:* |
| --- | --- |
| Focus on Annual Giving in most constituent programs | Focus on major gifts in all constituent programs |
| Level or modest growth in donors and gift income | Significant increases in donors and gift income |
| Multiple, overlapping solicitations leading to confusion and sometimes ill-will toward IU | Reduced mailings and fewer overlapping solicitations |
| High printing costs due to a number of small mailings | Lower printing costs due to volume discounts |
| No effective campus coordination of mailings or direct mail tracking system | One comprehensive solicitation calendar managed by the Foundation |

## Appendix VII

# Memorandum

TO:     Rod Kirsch
FROM:   Kent Dove
RE:     Budgeting the Academic Endowment Campaign
DATE:   December 19, 1994

For the purpose of initiating discussion, I write to make recommendations as to how the additional funds that will be needed to underwrite the Academic Endowment Campaign might be generated. The underlying premise here is that it costs money to raise money and that the University and the Foundation both should share in assuming these costs.

My view of the needs of the campus and who should pay these costs are:

## Major Gifts Officers

Two academic areas, Business and the College of Arts and Sciences, will need to add a full-time major gifts officer. Both currently have already budgeted positions open. Given appropriate job descriptions and corresponding selection, these new hires could meet the campaign's needs. I recommend that these respective academic units be responsible for their costs plus the support help that will be needed. In the first year, I have budgeted each of the major gift officers at $65,000 plus 25 percent benefits for a total of $81,250 per position. Support staff, one for each major gift officer, is projected at $18,000 plus benefits for a total of $22,500 each. I recommend that these persons be housed in the academic units.

Two other academic areas, Education and the School of Public and Environmental Affairs, could share a major gifts officer. The costs are the same as above. I recommend that the University assume these costs and that these people be housed in the IU Foundation.

Next, there is a grouping of units, all of which will require attention, but only on a part-time basis: Music*, School of Health, Physical Education & Recreation, Art Museum, University Libraries, School of Library & Information Science, Optometry, Continuing Studies and Journalism. I recommend two major gifts officers and one support staff to service all these areas to be paid for by the University and to be housed in the Foundation.

One unit, Law, is sufficiently staffed and will require only advisory assistance from the Executive Director of the Campaign.

## Planned Gifts Officers

Additionally, I recommend that three planned gifts officers be added to the staff to serve the entire campus during the campaign and that the University provide for these positions which should be housed in the Foundation.

## Campaign Administration

The IU Foundation should provide for the campaign administration officer, the Executive Director of Capital Campaigns and his assistant.

## Operating Costs

It is further recommended that the other direct costs of the campaign, communications, training (volunteer and staff), office supplies and printing, telephones, representation, etc., be paid out of unrestricted gifts to the campaign and/or that costs be recovered from the units on their gift income from the campaign.

*Staffing needs may be met by a new person when hired in early 1995.

attachments

## DRAFT IU ENDOWMENT CAMPAIGN BUDGET.

| | 1994–95 | 1995–96 | 1996–97 | 1997–98 | 1998–99 | 1999–2000 |
|---|---|---|---|---|---|---|
| Salaries & Benefits | | | | | | |
| Professional | | $731,250.00(a)* | $767,812.00(a)* | $806,203.00(a)* | $846,513.00(a)* | $888,839.00(a)* |
| Secretarial/Clerical | | $161,875.00(a) | $169,969.00(a) | $178,467.00(a) | $187,390.00(a) | $196,760.00(a) |
| Administration | $166,250.00 | $174,563.00(a) | $183,291.00(a) | $192,456.00(a) | $202,079.00(a) | $212,183.00(a) |
| Fees for Consultants | | $50,000.00 | $50,000.00 | $50,000.00 | $50,000.00 | $50,000.00 |
| Market Survey | $60,000.00 | | | | | |
| Office Supplies & Printing | | $25,000.00 | $25,000.00 | $22,500.00 | $20,000.00 | $15,000.00 |
| Telephone & Other Communication Networks | | $25,000.00 | $25,000.00 | $25,000.00 | $25,000.00 | $25,000.00 |
| Publications/Print & AV Materials | | $300,000.00 | $30,000.00 | $18,500.00 | $10,000.00 | $10,000.00 |
| Public Announcement Event | | $40,000.00 | | | | |
| Representation | | $12,000.00 | $20,000.00 | $20,000.00 | $20,000.00 | $15,000.00 |
| Travel | | $20,000.00 | $50,000.00 | $60,000.00 | $40,000.00 | $40,000.00 |
| Special Events/Leadership Training | | $15,000.00 | $25,000.00 | $15,000.00 | $10,000.00 | $10,000.00 |
| Space & Office Furnishings | | | | To Be Determined | | |
| Campaign Victory Celebration | | | | | | $35,000.00 |
| Undistributed | | $20,000.00 | $40,000.00 | $30,000.00 | $20,000.00 | $15,000.00 |
| Totals | $226,250.00 | $1,574,688.00 | $1,386,072.00 | $1,418,126.00 | $1,430,982.00 | $1,512,782.00 |

Notes by line item:

Professional: Six major gift officers at $65,000 a year; 3 planned giving officers, two at $70,000 a year, one at $55,000 a year, plus 25 percent benefits for all nine.

Secretarial/Clerical: Seven support staff at $18,000, plus 25 percent benefits.

Administration: Executive Director, Capital Campaign and Assistant to Executive Director of the Capital Campaign.

Fees for Consultants: Contingency funds to be used if outside assistance is desirable, i.e., audio visual needs, case statement, planned giving.

Market Survey: See attached outline

(a) Includes 5 percent annual adjustment.

*The Foundation does not necessarily have to assume all personnel costs. They may be shared with the academic units.

## FUNDING THE ACADEMIC ENDOWMENT CAMPAIGN.

| Position | Personnel Cost* | Travel Budget | Funded by | Housed by |
|---|---|---|---|---|
| Major Gifts Officer, Business | $81,250 | $5,000 | Academic Unit | Academic Unit |
| Support Staff, Business | 22,500 | | Academic Unit | Academic Unit |
| Major Gifts Officer, COAS | 81,250 | 5,000 | Academic Unit | Academic Unit |
| Support Staff, COAS | 22,500 | | Academic Unit | Academic Unit |
| Major Gifts Officer, Education & SPEA | 81,250 | 5,000 | Indiana University | IU Foundation |
| Support Staff, Education & SPEA | 22,500 | | Indiana University | IU Foundation |
| Major Gifts Officers, Group | 162,500 | 7,500 | Indiana University | IU Foundation |
| Support Staff, Group | 22,500 | | Indiana University | IU Foundation |
| Planned Giving Officers | 243,750 | 12,500 | Indiana University | IU Foundation |
| Support Staff, Planned Giving | 45,000 | | Indiana University | IU Foundation |
| Campaign Administration | 175,000 | 3,000 | IU Foundation | IU Foundation |
| Support Staff, Administration | 22,500 | | IU Foundation | IU Foundation |

| Costs Allocated to: | Personnel | Travel | | |
|---|---|---|---|---|
| Academic Units | $207,500 | $10,000 | | |
| Indiana University | 581,250 | 25,000 | | |
| IU Foundation | 197,500 | 3,000 | | |

*First year only. Campaign to be budgeted for five years. Totals include salary plus benefits.

# Summary of Professional Staffing Needs

*Need Full-Time Position*

College of Arts and Sciences

Business

*Need Split Position*

Education

School of Public and Environmental Affairs

*Need Share Positions*

Health, Physical Education, and Recreation

University Libraries

Journalism

School of Library and Information Science

Optometry

Continuing Studies

Art Museum

Music*

*Adequately Staffed*

Law

Music*

*Depending upon person hired early in 1995.

## Appendix VIII

# Prospect Rating Sessions and Techniques

The purpose of prospect rating is to determine accurately within a range an individual's ability to give. The evaluator should not be concerned with what the individual might give—or even that he/she will give. Further research subsequent to the evaluation will address these questions. The sole criteria during the evaluation should be to establish what a donor can do given his/her personal circumstances.

The purpose of the rating session *is not* to have the professional staff member offer evaluations. The staff member should not participate in the evaluation other than to explain the purpose of the session, to keep the session moving and to clarify and answer questions as to form and procedure. The professional staff member should make no comments to the evaluator which could influence a rating. Pertinent information on the prospect held by the professional staff member should be noted and conveyed directly to file.

*Small Group Discussion:* In this procedure the leader calls out the name of the prospect and a roundtable discussion ensues. A rating is agreed to. Pertinent comments are recorded by the professional staff member. This is the best method of evaluation, but its success is dependent on the group leader's ability to initiate discussion and the group's willingness to participate in an open and forthright fashion.

*Group Individual Rating:* In this procedure each member of the group is given a rating book and works individually without discussion to rate the prospects and offer appropriate written comments. The professional staff member collects the evaluations and tabulates the information after the meeting. The major disadvantage here is that there is no exchange of ideas or information within the group. The advantage is that there is the feeling on the part of the evaluator that he/she has more confidentiality; hence, the possibility of a more realistic evaluation and more pointed and useful comments.

*Individual One-On-One:* In this procedure the professional staff member meets individually with the evaluator and verbally goes through the list recording on the evaluation form pertinent comments. The advantage of this process is that the evaluator can feel he/she has complete assurance of confidentiality. No one else will hear the comments or know his/her personal feelings about the prospect. The disadvantage is that the validity of the evaluation is limited to the extent of the evaluator's knowledge. There is no second and third opinion. And, the single evaluator may not know a number of the prospects well enough to rate them thus necessitating additional rating sessions involving other evaluators.

*Individual Solitary:* In this process the evaluator is given or mailed a list of prospects and rating instructions and then is left on his/her own. The evaluation is either picked up or mailed back on or before a mutually agreed upon date. This procedure should be used only in special instances. Its advantage is that it gives the evaluator time to reflect and to substantially consider his/her rating and comments. It leads, generally, to a very thoughtful, thorough evaluation when done properly. The disadvantage is that often the individual will put off doing the evaluation thereby frustrating the process.

The evaluation should be done by knowledgeable individuals. Secondhand and hearsay information is of little or no value. Speculation is just that. Bankers, lawyers, investment counselors, insurance executives, the socially prominent and those actively involved in organized philanthropy in communities with organized efforts make the best evaluators.

# General Guidelines for Recognizing and Counting Gifts to the Endowment Campaign

All gifts and pledges to Indiana University-Bloomington during the campaign period July 1, 1994, through December 31, 2000, or the end of that academic year, will be counted toward the total campaign goal in accordance with the following guidelines. (The guidelines described below in summary form generally conform to the CASE Campaign Standards issued in April of 1994.)

1.  All *outright gifts* in the form of cash, marketable securities, closely held stock, real property and gifts of tangible personal property.
2.  All *pledges* of five (5) years or less which are initiated between July 1, 1994 and the conclusion of the campaign and documented in writing by the donor(s).
3.  All gifts for *ongoing support* received during the campaign period.
4.  The face value of all *realized bequests* received during the campaign period.
5.  *Future bequest commitments* from donors, if properly documented, will be reported in campaign totals at face value and recorded at discounted present value for internal purposes.
6.  *Charitable remainder trusts* held by the Foundation or another trustee and *pooled income funds* will be reported in campaign totals at their face value and will also be recorded at discounted present value for internal purposes.
7.  The face value of the income interest received or pledged during the campaign time period from *charitable lead trusts* on trusts held by the Foundation or another trustee.
8.  The face value of *charitable gift annuities* will be reported in campaign totals; the present value also will be recorded for internal purposes.
9.  *Matching gifts* awarded in support of the campaign.
10. Gifts of *life insurance* will be recognized as provided in the CASE Campaign Standards based on the nature of the policy, i.e, paid-up; existing, but not fully paid-up; new policy.
11. The following types of gifts or intentions will not be recognized in campaign totals: oral pledges, gifts previously counted in the Campaign for Indiana, earnings on gifts, governmental funds, contracted research revenue.
12. *Exceptions* to the foregoing may be made for good cause on a case-by-case basis. Such exceptions shall be approved by the Executive Committee of the Bloomington Endowment Campaign.

**Appendix X**

# Guidelines for Naming Opportunities and Endowed Funds for the Bloomington Campus Campaign

## General Policy

It is the general policy of Indiana University that the University President approve the establishment and activation of named funds upon the receipt of gifts by the IU Foundation as described below.

The President of the University in consultation with campus Chancellors, Deans and the IU Foundation President sets minimum gift level amounts and establishes approved guidelines for gift naming opportunities.

The Board of Trustees, in all gift naming opportunities, reserves the final right of approval for the name or names designated for any of the gift naming opportunities which follow. Approval cannot be granted until the donor's name is known or until the name or names of the person or persons being memorialized are known.

The gift levels described below are intended as minimum amounts needed to name the respective opportunity. In most cases, gifts may be made outright over a multi-year pledge period, through a trust or similar irrevocable instrument. The selection of holders of all endowed positions is the responsibility of the cognizant deans in consultation with the affected department and the campus Chancellor.

## Specific Gift Naming Opportunities

The monetary requirements cited in the paragraphs below are University minimums. In each category both numbers represent the minimum amounts needed for endowments in various sized programs. The larger number is not a cap; it is a minimum figure for a larger or more comprehensive program. Each school or college may establish higher minimums for certain endowments based on unique requirements of the individual unit, the discipline involved and the scope of the program relative to budget and other factors.

1. The opportunity exists to name several of the schools on the campus by providing a gift for the general endowment to benefit the unit. The minimum gift commitment required to do so varies with each respective unit.
2. To name a *research center, institute* or *academic program* requires a minimum gift commitment of $1 to $3 million for endowment.

3. To name a *branch library,* a minimum gift commitment of $1 million is required. Endowment income will benefit the collections, service and technology needs of the particular library.

4. To establish a *deanship,* $3 million or more is necessary. In such cases, the position—not the person—is endowed.

5. To establish *directorships* or *departmental chairs,* gifts of $2 million or more are necessary. The position, not the person, is endowed.

6. To establish an *endowed faculty chair* requires a minimum endowment of $1 million.

7. To establish an *endowed professorship,* a minimum gift of $500,000 is required.

8. To establish an *endowed visiting professorship* requires a minimum gift of $250,000. The annual proceeds will be used to invite a distinguished scholar to campus for a finite period of time.

9. To establish an *endowed lectureship* requires a minimum gift commitment of $100,000. The annual proceeds from this endowment will be used to pay for honoraria, publicity and the expenses of a member of the faculty or a visiting lecturer from another insitution or organization to present a lecture on the campus.

10. To establish an *endowed laboratory* requires a minimum gift commitment of $1,000,000. The annual earnings from the endowment will be used for equipment, technology enhancements and research.

11. To establish an *endowed classroom* requires a minimum gift commitment of $500,000. The annual earnings will be used for equipment, technology enhancement, refurbishment and modernization.

12. To establish an *endowed faculty research fund* requires a minimum gift of $250,000.

13. To establish an *endowed graduate student fellowship* requires a minimum gift of $200,000. A fellowship is ordinarily awarded to a student who is working toward an advanced degree in any of the graduate fields. An endowed fellowship should provide support for the majority of the recipient's expenses.

14. To establish a scholarship in the *Herman B Wells Scholarship Program* requires a minimum gift of $150,000 for endowment.

15. To establish an *undergraduate endowed scholarship* requires a minimum gift of $25,000.

16. To establish an *endowed book fund* requires a minimum gift of $25,000 for endowment. The income from an endowed book fund may be used for the purchase of books or other materials in a specified field. It may also be used, to the extent not needed for purchases, for preservation of books. It may also be used for repair, cataloging and other expenses of the library.

17. To name new or renovated buildings and facilities generally requires one-half the construction cost of the capital project.

## Exceptions for Endowments and Funds

The campus Chancellor, or his/her designee, shall have the latitude to approve the establishment of named funds in amounts less than those stated above, provided that it is understood that, within a reasonable period of time from the establishment of the fund, the principal thereof, including interest income and additional gifts, shall equal the stated minimum. If the stated minimum is not achieved, then the fund may be terminated and the funds expended for the college, school or department originally designated by the donor. The annual income from a fund established hereinunder and not terminated as provided shall continue to be accrued to the principal until the minimum endowment level is reached.

**Appendix XI**

---

# Indiana University and Indiana University Foundation Prospect Management Program

## Policies and Procedures

(Draft 4/5/94, Jim Smith) (Revised 8/4/95, Kathy Wilson)

## INTRODUCTION

### Mission

The prospect management program (PMP) is designed to provide effective management of cultivation, solicitation and stewardship activities with individuals, corporations, foundations and other prospects determined as having the interest and capability of making a major gift to Indiana University.

### Means

PMP fulfills its mission by: 1) creating and maintaining a database that includes major gift prospects, the staff and volunteers assigned to those prospects, documentation of significant contacts and "moves" with prospects, and background research information; 2) regularly convening a prospect assignment committee to act on requests for assignment and to address other issues; and 3) periodically conducting prospect review sessions to ensure effective and coordinated management of top-level prospects.

### Role of Development Professionals

PMP functions at its optimum level when development staff contribute in the following areas: 1) Communication—staff who are co-assigned to a prospect utilize a team approach and proactively share plans, activity and information with each other; 2) Documentation—documenting significant contacts and "moves" in the Benefactor major prospects module, and share that documentation with all appropriate staff.

### Prospect Management Program Authority and Administration

The Prospect Management Program is managed on behalf of Indiana University by the Indiana University Foundation, in accordance with its designation by the Indiana University Board of Trustees as the officially designated fundraising agency for Indiana University. The Senior Vice-president for Development of the IU Foundation, in consultation with the President of the IU Foundation, has ultimate administrative authority for the program, including formulation and revisions of the policies and procedures governing the program.

## POLICIES AND PROCEDURES

### 1. Prospect Assignment

*Policy.* Prospects submitted for assignment in PMP should, through prior activity or research, have been determined to: 1) be capable of fulfilling a commitment of at least $25,000 over 5 years or $5,000 in 1 year; and 2) have a demonstrated interest in supporting the University and the specific program or project for which support is being sought. In particular, evidence of linkage with the prospect should include personal contact leading to qualification between the prospect and the staff or unit requesting assignment.

*Procedures.*

1.1 *Request for Assignment*—Development staff may request assignment to a prospect by completing and submitting a "Request for Prospect Assignment" form to the Director of Research at IUF.

1.2 *Assignment Committee Action*—The prospect assignment committee meets on alternate Mondays. All requests received by the Wednesday prior to the meeting will be considered.

1.3 *Clearance Levels*—The prospect assignment committee will assign a clearance level of cultivation, solicitation or stewardship. The request may be denied, in which case the committee will provide a written explanation of its decision.

1.4 *Deferred Action*—The prospect assignment committee may defer action on a request when: 1) the request form is not complete, i.e., a rating is not provided or there is no evidence of personal contact, in which case the form will be returned to the requester; 2) clarification or further information is needed from other parties, in which case such information may be sought by committee members, or the requester may be instructed to secure the information and forward it to the committee.

1.5 *Primary Manager*—The prospect assignment committee will act upon requests for assignment as primary manager and will make final decisions in instances where more than one individual has requested primary manager status.

1.6 *Appeals of Assignment Committee Decisions*—Decisions made by the prospect assignment committee may be appealed in writing to the IUF Senior Vice-President of Development within 20 working days after the committee decision is received.

1.7 *Length of Assignment and Clearance*—Assignment for cultivation and stewardship clearance levels will be for up to one year, at which time the assignment must be renewed with a written justification. Clearance for solicitation will be for a six-month period, and may be renewed and justified as already described. If there is a lack or absence of documented contact between the assigned staff and moving the prospect to closure, requests for reassignment may be denied.

1.8 *Rating of Prospects*—All prospects in PMP must have a rating assigned to them at the time the request is made.

1.9 *Committee Members*—The prospect assignment committee consists of the following: Sr. Vice-President Development, Vice-President Indianapolis, all IUF Sr. Development Directors, Director of Corporations, Exec. Director of Development, Director of Development Services, and Director of Research who chairs the committee. One representative from each of the Bloomington and Indianapolis Development Councils will be selected to serve a one-year term on the committee for the period September–August.

## 2. Documentation

**Policy.** All relevant prospect contacts must be documented on a "Contact Report" and on the prospect's Benefactor record in the Major Prospects module. Further, this information is to be shared with all co-assigned staff and, if applicable, with the unit development officer from the prospect's academic home and with the IUF staff assigned to the geographic area in which the prospect resides. Written documentation should NOT preclude verbal communication among co-assigned staff.

**Procedures.**

2.1 *Documentation of Contacts*—Within twenty (20) working days after the contact, the IUF development officer should arrange for summary information about the contact to be entered into the Benefactor database. The unit development officers should send their contacts to the Director of Research at IUF to arrange for that information to be entered into the Benefactor database. Every development officer should complete a contact report and send it to the Director of Research at IUF, indicating the appropriate IUF staff, co-assigned staff and unit development officers who should receive copies. Also, the development officer should note on the form whether this contact is to be considered as "meaningful."

2.2 *Distribution of Contact Reports*—Each development officer will be responsible for distributing their own contact reports to individuals requiring copies. Individuals requiring copies are: 1) Senior Vice President of Development; 2) Director of Research; 3) all development officers assigned to the prospect; 4) development officer(s) where prospect holds degree(s); and, 5) to those development officers with geographic responsibility where the prospect resides.

2.3 *Documentation Standards and Conventions*—Information entered into the Benefactor Major Prospects Module must be in accordance with the conventions established to ensure consistency of data stored in that module. Special care should be taken in entering information that does not directly impact the cultivation, solicitation or stewardship strategy for an individual, or may be sensitive in nature.

## 3. Prospect Review

*Policy.* On an as needed basis, the Director of Research will convene a meeting for the purpose of reviewing current activities with selected major gift prospects and determining how to maximize support from each prospect. Such meetings will be held on a regularly scheduled basis during large capital campaigns.

### *Procedures.*

3.1 *Selection of Prospects for Review*—Prospects may be selected for review on the basis of their rating, their status as a prospect for a specific project, or other reasons specified by the Senior Vice-President for Development.

3.2 *Notification of Development Staff*—Notification of all staff assigned to a prospect to be reviewed will be sent at least 15 working days prior to the scheduled review session. Included in this notification will be the names of those prospects to be reviewed.

3.3 *Attendance*—All staff assigned to prospects being reviewed are expected to attend and be prepared to discuss current strategy with each prospect. If attendance is impossible, written comments on each prospect should be sent to the Director of Research at least seven working days prior to the scheduled meeting. A copy of those comments should be sent to the primary manager of each prospect.

3.4 *Meeting Summary*—Research and PMP staff will record highlights of discussion and decisions made regarding each prospect reviewed. PMP staff will enter this information on the prospect's PMP record and will distribute copies of the meeting summary to all attendees, assigned staff and others not in attendance but determined as appropriate to receive all or portions of the information.

## 4. Management Reports

4.1 *Solicitation Expiration Report (XSER)*—Clearance for solicitation will be for up to a six-month period, at the end of which time the assignment must be renewed and justified. On the report the development officer is asked whether to 1) extend the solicitation for another six (6) months; 2) change the level to cultivation or stewardship; or 3) remove the assignment. If no response is received, the prospect will automatically be moved to cultivation. This report is run monthly for solicitation requests made 6 months prior.

4.2 *Manager's Activity Report (XPMP)*—Bi-monthly reports regarding overall prospect and Development Officer activity will be prepared and distributed to the development officers for their review in order to keep the PMP database clean. If no response is received, the assignment will be removed.

4.3 *Contact Summary Report (MPCS)*—All contacts entered 20 working days after contact will be tracked by IU Foundation and included on the previous month's activity report which will be distributed to development officers and appropriate IUF staff.

**Appendix XII**

# Gift Vehicles Eligible for Matching Endowment Program

## 1. Outright Gifts

All outright gifts that meet the minimum amount of $500,000 or above qualify for the match. An outright gift is one of $500,000 or above that is received all at once or as a pledge paid over five years. The amount to be matched will be the current value of the outright gift. Outright gifts may consist of cash, securities, or real estate. With regard to real estate, the amount matched will be the proceeds from the expected sale of the property.

## 2. Charitable Remainder Trusts

Charitable remainder trusts qualify for the match. However, the payout on the match will be based on the face value of the donor's gift to the Foundation, even though the remainder value may exceed the face value at the time the trust during the match period with $500,000, with an annual payout rate of 5 percent, the annual income will be $25,000 and the match of a gift at this level will be 50 percent of the annual income, or $12,500. This will apply to all charitable remainder trusts which meet the basic criteria, irrespective of trustee.

## 3. Charitable Gift Annuities and Pooled Income Fund

The same criteria apply for charitable gift annuities and the pooled income fund as applied to the charitable remainder trust. That is, because of the irrevocable nature of the gift, they qualify for the match based upon the face value of the gift at the time it is initially received by the Foundation.

## 4. Life Insurance

Life insurance qualifies only if the policy is fully paid-up when given to the Foundation or will be paid-up within a five year period after the date of the gift. The donor must make the Foundation the irrevocable owner and beneficiary of the policy for the matching fund program to apply. The match will be based on the death benefit of the policy and it will apply at the time the policy is received by the Foundation. For example, if a donor makes a gift of a life insurance policy with a $500,000 death benefit with an annual payout rate of 5 percent when the policy matures, the annual income will be $25,000 and the match of a gift at this level will be 50 percent of the annual income, or $12,500. Age guidelines may be considered when deciding whether or not to match life insurance gifts.

## 5. Bequest

Newly established bequest expectancies will qualify as long as they meet the minimum levels, are documented during the matching period and represent a legally binding obligation upon the donor's estate. Age guidelines may be considered when deciding whether or not to match individual bequests.

## 6. Personal Property

Personal property will not qualify for the match primarily due to the fact that personal property held by the Foundation will generate no income, and selling the property may have adverse tax consequences for the donor.

## 7. Remainder Interest in Real Estate

Remainder interest in real estate will qualify for the match when the Foundation receives its remainder interest and completes the sale of the real estate. The match will be based on the amount realized from the sale of the real estate.

## 8. Charitable Lead Trusts

Since charitable lead trusts pay the income they generate directly to the Foundation, they qualify if the income generated by the trust meets the minimum amount required to qualify for the match. For example, a charitable lead trust funded with $2 million in assets with a 5 percent annual payout rate will produce $100,000 in annual income. If this payout is received or pledged during the match period, it qualifies in the same way as an outright gift.

## SAMPLE MONTHLY FINANCIAL REPORT

<u>Confidential</u>

**INDIANA UNIVERSITY
BLOOMINGTON CAMPUS
ENDOWMENT CAMPAIGN**

# Reports

**For Period Ending September 30, 1998**

# INDIANA UNIVERSITY CAMPAIGN PROGRESS REPORT (DOCUMENTED GIFTS, PLEDGES AND EXPECTANCIES).

The Bloomington Campus Endowment Campaign

| Components | Campaign Goal | Thru September 30, 1998 | | Thru August 31, 1998 | | Thru March 31, 1998 | | Thru September 30, 1997 | |
|---|---|---|---|---|---|---|---|---|---|
| | | Total Raised | % of Goal | Total Raised | % of Goal | Total Raised | % of Goal | Total Raised | % of Goal |
| Art Museum | $6,500,000 | $3,589,220 | 55.2% | $3,586,220 | 55.2% | $3,591,221 | 55.2% | $2,589,554 | 39.8% |
| Athletics | $10,000,000 | $13,691,756 | 136.9% | $13,220,981 | 132.2% | $11,100,121 | 111.0% | $9,636,707 | 96.4% |
| Business | $37,000,000 | $31,696,508 | 85.7% | $31,695,543 | 85.7% | $28,934,942 | 78.2% | $28,041,012 | 75.8% |
| COAS | $30,000,000 | $40,225,986 | 134.1% | $39,056,216 | 130.2% | $32,100,323 | 107.0% | $20,633,166 | 68.8% |
| Continuing Studies | $500,000 | $277,449 | 55.5% | $277,474 | 55.5% | $277,274 | 55.5% | $275,749 | 55.1% |
| Education | $6,000,000 | $8,669,385 | 144.5% | $8,667,023 | 144.5% | $6,573,416 | 109.6% | $4,988,170 | 83.1% |
| HPER | $4,000,000 | $6,224,905 | 155.6% | $6,224,780 | 155.6% | $4,732,630 | 118.3% | $3,433,385 | 85.8% |
| Journalism | $4,000,000 | $2,420,039 | 60.5% | $2,319,764 | 58.0% | $2,311,562 | 57.8% | $1,348,114 | 33.7% |
| Law | $13,000,000 | $14,925,261 | 114.8% | $14,910,261 | 114.7% | $13,436,862 | 103.4% | $12,303,314 | 94.6% |
| Library | $4,000,000 | $4,624,840 | 115.6% | $4,621,010 | 115.5% | $4,593,114 | 114.8% | $4,563,289 | 114.1% |
| Library & Information Science | $1,500,000 | $1,021,819 | 68.1% | $1,019,729 | 68.0% | $606,229 | 40.4% | $14,055 | 0.9% |
| Music | $12,000,000 | $17,548,348 | 146.2% | $17,540,034 | 146.2% | $17,417,309 | 145.1% | $16,804,832 | 140.0% |
| Optometry | $3,000,000 | $345,790 | 11.5% | $345,482 | 11.5% | $226,143 | 7.5% | $112,002 | 3.7% |
| Public & Environmental Affairs | $6,000,000 | $2,583,232 | 43.1% | $2,580,232 | 43.0% | $1,560,232 | 26.0% | $1,535,232 | 25.6% |
| Campus-wide Support Not Designated to Above Units | $12,500,000 | $15,569,571 | 124.6% | $15,426,910 | 123.4% | $14,675,132 | 117.4% | $12,876,365 | 103.0% |
| Endowment Total | $150,000,000 | $163,414,109 | 108.9% | $161,491,659 | 107.7% | $142,136,510 | 94.8% | $119,154,946 | 79.4% |
| Ongoing Private Support | $200,000,000 | $138,386,172 | 69.2% | $135,550,132 | 67.8% | $113,991,677 | 57.0% | $95,182,197 | 47.6% |
| Campaign Total | $350,000,000 | $301,800,281 | 86.2% | $297,041,791 | 84.9% | $256,128,187 | 73.2% | $214,337,143 | 61.2% |

# INDIANA UNIVERSITY CAMPUS STATUS REPORT, JULY 1, 1994–SEPTEMBER 30, 1998 (DOCUMENTED GIFTS, PLEDGES AND EXPECTANCIES).

## The Bloomington Campus Endowment Campaign

| Components | Total Campaign Goal | Documented Gifts & Pledges | Documented Expectancies | Total Raised | Percent of Goal Raised |
|---|---|---|---|---|---|
| Art Museum | $6,500,000 | $1,414,012 | $2,175,208 | $3,589,220 | 55.2 percent |
| Athletics | $10,000,000 | $8,208,517 | $5,483,239 | $13,691,756 | 136.9 percent |
| Business | $37,000,000 | $8,356,058 | $23,340,450 | $31,696,508 | 85.7 percent |
| COAS | $30,000,000 | $23,146,590 | $17,079,396 | $40,225,986 | 134.1 percent |
| Continuing Studies | $500,000 | $27,449 | $250,000 | $277,449 | 55.5 percent |
| Education | $6,000,000 | $1,922,719 | $6,746,666 | $8,669,385 | 144.5 percent |
| HPER | $4,000,000 | $1,924,405 | $4,300,500 | $6,224,905 | 155.6 percent |
| Journalism | $4,000,000 | $1,219,343 | $1,200,696 | $2,420,039 | 60.5 percent |
| Law | $13,000,000 | $5,108,441 | $9,816,820 | $14,925,261 | 114.8 percent |
| Library | $4,000,000 | $4,158,174 | $466,666 | $4,624,840 | 115.6 percent |
| Library & Information Science | $1,500,000 | $19,290 | $1,002,529 | $1,021,819 | 68.1 percent |
| Music | $12,000,000 | $7,966,980 | $9,581,368 | $17,548,348 | 146.2 percent |
| Optometry | $3,000,000 | $65,091 | $280,699 | $345,790 | 11.5 percent |
| Public & Environmental Affairs | $6,000,000 | $1,343,080 | $1,240,152 | $2,583,232 | 43.1 percent |
| Campus-wide Support Not Designated to Above Units | $12,500,000 | $10,233,499 | $5,336,072 | $15,569,571 | 124.6 percent |
| Endowment Total | $150,000,000 | $75,113,648 | $88,300,461 | $163,414,109 | 108.9 percent |
| Annual Gifts, Pledges & Expectancies | | $90,739,500 | $4,102,372 | $94,841,872 | 47.4 percent |
| Non-Governmental Grants | | $43,544,300 | | $43,544,300 | 21.8 percent |
| Ongoing Private Support Total | $200,000,000 | $134,283,800 | $4,102,372 | $138,386,172 | 69.2 percent |
| Campaign Total | $350,000,000 | $209,397,448 | $92,402,833 | $301,800,281 | 86.2 percent |

Period of Campaign: July 1, 1994–June 30, 2000

Percent Completed: 69.4 percent

## INDIANA UNIVERSITY CAMPAIGN
## STATUS REPORT, JULY 1, 1994–SEPTEMBER 30, 1998
## (DOCUMENTED GIFTS, PLEDGES AND EXPECTANCIES).

**ONGOING PRIVATE SUPPORT**

| Components | Documented Gifts & Pledges | Documented Expectancies | Total Raised |
|---|---|---|---|
| Art Museum | $904,969 | $0.00 | $904,969 |
| Athletics | $22,939,643 | $120,000 | $23,059,643 |
| Business | $13,961,771 | $840,020 | $14,801,791 |
| COAS | $6,711,817 | $169,500 | $6,881,317 |
| Continuing Studies | $86,273 | $0.00 | $86,273 |
| Education | $1,423,235 | $5,000 | $1,428,235 |
| HPER | $1,152,036 | $50,000 | $1,202,036 |
| Journalism | $767,512 | $100,000 | $867,512 |
| Law | $1,729,292 | $10,000 | $1,739,292 |
| Library | $2,365,518 | $85,000 | $2,450,518 |
| Music | $7,323,581 | $411,252 | $7,734,833 |
| Library & Information Sciences | $145,048 | $0.00 | $145,048 |
| Optometry | $537,203 | $50,000 | $587,203 |
| Public & Environmental Affairs | $235,374 | 0.00 | $235,374 |
| Campus-wide Support Not Designated to Above Units | $30,456,228 | $2,261,600 | $32,717,828 |
| TOTAL ONGOING ANNUAL SUPPORT | $90,739,500 | $4,102,372 | $94,841,872 |

## INDIANA UNIVERSITY CAMPAIGN
## STATUS REPORT, JULY 1, 1994–SEPTEMBER 30, 1998
## (DOCUMENTED GIFTS, PLEDGES AND EXPECTANCIES).

### Campuswide Endowment Support Not Designated to Primary Components

| Components | Documented Gifts & Pledges | Documented Expectancies | Total Raised |
|---|---|---|---|
| Alumni Association | $102,998 | $129,316 | $232,314 |
| Dean of Students | $187,853 | $117,358 | $305,211 |
| Class Campaigns | $2,564,006 | $168,299 | $2,732,305 |
| Indiana Memorial Union | $57,202 | $282,304 | $339,506 |
| IU General | $2,497,889 | $852,636 | $3,350,525 |
| International Programs | $73,759 | $25,000 | $98,759 |
| Office of Student Financial Aid/ Wells Scholars Program | $4,235,546 | $3,551,159 | $7,786,705 |
| Radio & Television | $92,076 | $0.00 | $92,076 |
| Other | $422,170 | $210,000 | $632,170 |
| Campuswide Endowment Support Not Designated to Primary Units | $10,233,499 | $5,336,072 | $15,569,571 |

## INDIANA UNIVERSITY BLOOMINGTON CAMPUS ENDOWMENT CAMPAIGN: GIFTS NEEDED TO RAISE $150 MILLION, JULY 1, 1994–SEPTEMBER 30, 1998.

| Gift Amount | Number of Gifts Needed | Total in Range | Number of Gifts Received to Date | Total Received to Date | Percent of Total Campaign Goal |
|---|---|---|---|---|---|
| $15,000,000+ | 1 | $15,000,000 | 1 | $15,000,000 | 100.0 percent |
| $10,000,000–14,999,999 | 2 | $20,000,000 | 0 | 0 | .0 percent |
| $5,000,000–9,999,999 | 3 | $15,000,000 | 2 | $12,100,000 | 80.7 percent |
| $2,500,000–4,999,999 | 6 | $15,000,000 | 5 | $14,639,354 | 97.6 percent |
| $1,000,000–2,499,999 | 17 | $17,000,000 | 33 | $44,203,212 | 260.0 percent |
| $750,000–999,999 | 20 | $15,000,000 | 13 | $10,626,923 | 70.8 percent |
| $500,000–749,999 | 30 | $15,000,000 | 26 | $13,871,080 | 92.5 percent |
| $250,000–499,999 | 50 | $12,500,000 | 41 | $13,051,585 | 104.4 percent |
| $100,000–249,999 | 100 | $10,000,000 | 144 | $19,684,224 | 196.8 percent |
| $25,000–99,999 | 400 | 10,000,000 | 228 | $10,183,395 | 101.8 percent |
| Under $25,000 | Many | $5,500,000 | Many | $10,054,336 | 182.8 percent |
| Total | | $150,000,000 | | $163,414,109 | 108.9 percent |

# INDIANA UNIVERSITY BLOOMINGTON CAMPUS ENDOWMENT CAMPAIGN:
## DOCUMENTED EXPECTANCIES OF $25,000 OR GREATER, JULY 1, 1994–SEPTEMBER 30, 1998.

| Donor | Amount | Gift Type | Purpose of Gift |
|-------|--------|-----------|-----------------|
|       |        |           |                 |

# INDIANA UNIVERSITY BLOOMINGTON CAMPUS ENDOWMENT CAMPAIGN:
## DOCUMENTED GIFTS AND PLEDGES OF $25,000 OR GREATER, JULY 1, 1994–SEPTEMBER 30, 1998.

| Donor | Account Number | Amount | Account Name |
|-------|----------------|--------|--------------|
|       |                |        |              |

# RESOURCE J

## SAMPLE PUBLIC ANNOUNCEMENT
## EVENT INVITATION AND PROGRAM

### "Dear Invited Guest" Letter

LIBRARY
SQUARE

Dear Invited Guest,

Over five years ago, Vancouver created a dream that demanded strength, courage and dedication. Soon to be realized, this vision stands as a magnificent testament to our enduring civic values. In May of this year, the community will unveil that dream—the new Vancouver Public Library at Library Square.

Ceremony and celebration are traditions important to every society. The opening events for Library Square will be a time for the community to gather, contemplate and applaud an achievement that will forever make us proud. The Main Branch of the Public Library will provide universal access to information and inspire the human spirit to lifelong learning.

"Literazzle: A Family Festival" is a week-long public celebration of the opening of Library Square which will be entirely funded by private donations. To help make this possible, we invite you to purchase tickets to *Literazzi,* the gala evening, on May 24, 1995. By doing so, you will be among the very first citizens to preview Moshe Safdie's great building. Perhaps even more importantly, your support will make the opening festival a *public* success.

Let us describe for you the evening that awaits your pleasure. . . . An affair of sophisticated literary and gastronomic fantasy, *Literazzi* promises to be a "never before" and "never again" evening. Enter the Promenade, a glass-walled atrium of soaring vertical space. Martinis and champagne await, as a twilight melody draws you closer. A profusion of irises and delphinium glow purple and blue in candlelight; cross a bridge to nooks rich and flowing with the finest vintages and epicurean delights presented by Vancouver's most celebrated chefs. Onward still, to delectable desserts—a sweet finale to a cornucopian feast. Distinguished authors, local luminaries and celebrity guests to engage you, entertainment extraordinaire to surprise you—an evening to enchant you.

We hope that you will celebrate with us our community's newest landmark.

Please order your tickets early to avoid disappointment.

Sincerely,

Philip Owen
Mayor
City of Vancouver

Kyle Mitchell
Chair
Board of Trustees
Vancouver Public Library

## Three-by-Five-Inch Card

The Library Capital Campaign Committee would also like you to
know about donation and recognition opportunities at Library Square.
If you wish more information about naming opportunities that will
provide a lasting legacy within the Library, please contact:

### Marilyn Wright
### Capital Campaign Office
### 681-8834

In addition to your purchase of Literazzi tickets, a donation to the
Capital Campaign would be greatly appreciated.

By supporting the Vancouver Public Library you will be investing in
the future of our children, our city and our quality of life.

**Brochure**

Mayor Philip Owen and members of the Vancouver City Council
and Chairman Kyle Mitchell and members of the
Vancouver Public Library Board

request the pleasure of your company at a Gala Evening to celebrate
the Opening of the new Vancouver Public Library
7:00 - 10:00 p.m., Wednesday, May 24, 1995

*LITERAZZI*

Library Square
350 West Georgia Street
Black Tie optional
Tickets $175 per person
Valet Parking available

*A gala evening of grand gourmet and fine vintages—join Vancouver's celebrated
chefs, distinguished authors and entertainers extraordinaire in
Vancouver's new jewel, Library Square.*

WE DO NOT LIVE by words alone, despite the fact that sometimes we have to eat them. *Adlai Stevenson* ▪ The things I want to know are in books; my best friend is the man who'll get me a book I ain't read. *Abraham Lincoln* ▪ A book is the only place in which you can examine a fragile thought without breaking it, or explore an explosive idea without fear it will go off in your face. *Edward P. Morgan* ▪ My education was the liberty I had to read indiscriminately and all the time, with my eyes hanging out. *Dylan Thomas* ▪ In two words: im possible. *Samuel Goldwyn* ▪ In literature as in love, we are astonished at what is chosen by others. *Andre Maurois* ▪ I write at high speed because boredom is bad for my health. I also avoid green vegetables. They are grossly overrated. *Noel Coward* ▪ The best time for planning a book is while you're doing the dishes. *Agatha Christie* ▪ Book love is your pass to the greatest, the purest, and the most perfect pleasure that God has prepared for His creatures. *Anthony Trollope* ▪ Hemingway's re-

Colours fade, temples crumble, empires fall, but wise words endure.

*Edward Thorndike*

I am part of all that I have read.

*John Kieran*

marks are not literature. *Gertrude Stein* • The worst thing about new books is that they keep us from reading the old ones. *Joseph Joubert* • The two most beautiful words in the English language are: "Check enclosed." *Dorothy Parker* • Book— what they make a movie out of for television. *Leonard Louis Levinson* • No passion in the world is equal to the passion to alter someone else's draft. *H.G. Wells* • Reading is to the mind what exercise is to the body • *Sir Richard Steele* • Never judge a cover by its book. *Fran Lebowitz* • Children don't read to find their identity, to free themselves from guilt, to quench the thirst for rebellion or to get rid of alienation. They have no use for psychology. They detest sociology. They still believe in God, the family, angels, devils, witches, goblins, logic, clarity, punctuation and other such obsolete stuff . . . . When a book is boring, they yawn openly. They don't expect their writer to redeem humanity, but leave to adults such childish illusions. *Isaac Bashevis Singer* [*Speech on receiving the Nobel Prize for Literature*].

# Menu

## LITERAZZI

*Prelude:*
7:30 pm – 7:35 pm

*Introductions: Kyle Mitchell*
*Chair, Vancouver Public Library Board*

*Comments: Moshe Safdie*
*Architect, MSA/DAP*

*Toast: Philip Owen*
*Mayor, City of Vancouver*

*... to a gastronomical and entertainment gala on seven levels*

### PROMENADE:

**CinCin**
Applewood Smoked Breast of Quail with Spicy Aioli
Roulade of Lamb Tenderloin and Pesto on Peppered Focaccia
Allergrilled Cured Scallop Ceviche
Tartar of Ahi Tuna and Smoked Yellowfin Tuna
Middle Eastern Tabouleh with Mint and Parsil
Pate of Sun Dried Tomatoes and Goat's Cheese with Onion Crisps

**Mescaluna:**
Southwestern Lambchops
Taquitos with Smoked Chicken Tomato Pesto & Roasted Peppers
Mussels with Sun Dried Tomato Chipotle Cream
Mescalero Marinated Prawns
Chimichangas Crostini, Cornbucula & Carmelized Red Onions

**The Four Seasons:**
House Marinated B.C. Salmon on Peppered Bagel Chips,
topped with Horseradish and Chive Dip
Roasted Bell Pepper and Peppered Goat Cheese Terrine with
Black Olive Crostini
Hummus and Pita Chips
Shrimp and Potato Fritter with Tomato Salsa

### HORS D'OEUVRE SERVICE:

**Major the Gourmet**
Smoked Tuna
Gravlax on a Rye Croute
Shrimp Mousse on a Blini
Crab Cakes
Orange Grilled Prawns

**Culinary Capers:**
Crepe Purses filled with Brie and Papaya Salsa
Moo Shu Pancakes filled with Peking Duck and Scallion
Tortilla Roll Ups filled with Black Bean, Grilled Chicken,
and Roasted Pepper
Risotto Cakes filled with Gorgonzola
Phyllo Triangles with Italian Sausage and Monterey Jack Cheese
Lamb Loin and Tamarind Chutney Wellington
Mini Pizzas with Capicolo and Mozzarella
Quesadilla with grilled Vegetables, Artichoke Hearts,
and Monterey Jack Cheese served with Guacamole

**Bollinger Champagne**
sponsored by MacMillan Bloedel

**Finlandia Martini Bar**

**Select Wine Merchants**
Casillerro del Diablo

**Featherstone & Company Ltd.**
Sebastiani Vendage Chardonnay
Sebastiani Vendage Merlot
Rocca della Macie

**Marquis Wine Cellars**
Swanson Chardonnay
Swanson Merlot

### LEVEL TWO – LIBRARY:

**The Sutton Place**
Library Square: A Sculpture in Chocolate
Assorted Chocolate Desserts

**Portuguese Trade Commission**
Ramos Pinto

**Continental Importers**
Kopke 1977

### LEVEL ONE (Lower) – CHILDREN'S LIBRARY:

**The Pan Pacific Hotel / Aramaa Catering:**
Strawberry and Lemon Tartlets
Sauteed Pears with Vanilla Ice Cream
Playing Card Sugar Cookies

**Murchie's Tea & Coffee**

**Grady Wine Marketing**
CedarCreek 1993 Riesling Ice Wine VQA

**Magnum Consultants**
Bollinger Champagne

### LEVEL ONE (Lower) – MULTI-PURPOSE ROOM:

**Regency Caterers**
Oyster Bar

**Victoria Chinese Restaurant**
Steamed Shrimp Dumpling (Har Gow)
Baked Pork Pie "Huang Que" Style
Two Spring Roll (Egg Roll)
Deep Fried Minced Pork Turnover
Vegetarian Goose (Mock Goose)
Moon Cake
Deep Fried Egg White
Steamed Plain Bun (Man Tou)

**Theodore Allan**
Pyramid Special Bitter
Pyramid Hefeweizen Ale
Pyramid Apricot Ale

**International Cellars**
Heineken Beer

### LEVEL THREE

**The William Tell:**
Swiss Cheese Raclette
Beef Steak Tartare

**The Raintree:**
Cornmeal Crusted Fresh Pacific Salmon served with
Sea Asparagus Tartare
Salad of Fennel and English Cucumber
Cilantro Mint Dressing

**Theodore Allan**
Quail's Gate Pinot Noir
Tailarni Shiraz
Deer Valley Chardonnay

**Termo Agencies**
Kendall Jackson Sauvignon Blanc
Kendall Jackson Chardonnay
Covey Run Merlot

### LEVEL FOUR:

**Quattro on Fourth**
Rotolo Farcito

**Granite Cafe**
Jerk Pork with Mango Chutney

**Clearly Canadian Beverages**

# LITERAZZI

- ENTERTAINMENT -

Bard on the Beach • Christopher Gaze
The Casual Brothers • Duo
The Colorifics • Jazz Quartet
David Johanns & Co • Jazz Trio
Elizabeth Mabee • Mezzo Soprano
The Euphorbics • a Cappella
The Greater Vancouver Historical Festival Performance Society • Dance
Harpist • Zelia's Musical Staff
Mark Hasselbach • Horn
Mortal Coil • Medieval Stilts
Pheasantry Valets
Richard Epp • Piano Accompanist
Siegel Entertainment • Mad Hatter
Sandy Witosky • Tenor
String Quartet • Zelia's Musical Staff

LIBRARY
SQUARE

---

Grady Wine Marketing
CedarCreek 1994 Ehrenfelser VQA
CedarCreek 1993 Pinot Blanc VQA
Wildflower Gamay
Morraen Merlot

**LEVEL FIVE:**

Raku Kushiyaki:
Calamari Salad with Black Bean & Ginger

RainCity Grill:
Lamb Osso Buco

The Vancouver Sushiman:
Assorted Sushi

U.S. Consulate
Assorted American Wines

Sumac Ridge

**LEVEL SIX:**

Regency Caterers:
Oyster Bar
Vegetable and Fruit Display

Okanagan Springs Brewery

Bowen Island Brewery

**LEVEL SEVEN:**

Major the Gourmet:
Mini Crostini Sandwiches
Julienne Smoked Salmon Platter

Joseph E. Seagram & Sons Limited
Scotch Bar

Vintner
Jackson Triggs 1993 Chardonnay
Jackson Triggs 1993 Merlot
Jackson Triggs 1993 Cabernet Sauvignon

# RESOURCE K

## SAMPLE PLEDGE FORMS

### Iowa Endowment 2000: A Covenant with Quality
**Testamentary Provision Statement of Intention**
**(Confidential)**

As an indication of my support of the Major Gifts Campaign for The University of Iowa "Iowa Endowment 2000: A Covenant With Quality," I/we are pleased to certify that I/we have made an estate provision for The University of Iowa Foundation as follows:

___ Outright Bequest
___ Bequest in the Will of the Survivor of Husband and Wife
___ Testamentary Trust
___ Life Insurance Agreement

Description of Type/Value of Estate Provision:

General Description: _____
_____
_____

Life-Income Provisions, if any: _____
_____
_____

Definition of Value of Provision (percentage of estate, description of gift property, specific amount, etc.): _____
_____

With the understanding that values are subject to change, at this time I/we expect the value of my/our future provision to be approximately: $ _____

Our Birth Dates Are: _____  _____
                   Husband    Wife

Description of Purpose of Future Gift:

_____ My/our gift is unrestricted to meet Iowa Endowment 2000 Campaign objectives as the President of The University of Iowa and the Board of Directors of The University of Iowa Foundation shall direct.

_____ I/we have specified that the future gift be used for the following Iowa Endowment 2000 Campaign purpose: _____
_____

Other Descriptive Information: _____
_____

A copy of the above-described testamentary provision relative to The University of Iowa Foundation is enclosed.

It is understood that this statement is not binding upon the Donor or his or her estate as to the value or the receipt of the provision herein described.

Signature of Donor(s) _____ Date _____
                          _____ Date _____

Data Documents 03–425520–01 1F2 1

CARD NO.

A TOTAL GIFT OF:

$ . . . . . . . . . . . . . . . . . . . . .

$ . . . . . . . . . . . . . . . . . . . . .
Payment Herewith:

$ . . . . . . . . . . . . . . . . . . . . .
BALANCE
Campaigner:

"MAKING A WORLD OF DIFFERENCE"

Capital Development Program

The Young Men's Christian Association of Greater St. Louis

FOR THE EXTENSION OF YMCA PROGRAMS AND IN CONSIDERATION OF THE GIFTS OF
OTHERS, I/WE PLEDGE THE SUM OF:

$ . . . . . . . . . . . . . . . . . . . . . . . . . . . . . . . . . . . . . To Be Paid as Follows:

PAYABLE OVER A _____ YEAR PERIOD AS FOLLOWS:

☐ ANNUAL      ☐ SEMI-ANNUAL      ☐ QUARTERLY      ☐ MONTHLY

PAYMENT AMOUNTS                    1ST PAYMENT DUE:

OTHER PAYMENT ARRANGEMENTS:

SIGNED: _____ DATE _____

Data Documents 03–425520–01 1F2 1

CARD NO.

A TOTAL GIFT OF:

$ . . . . . . . . . . . . . . . . . . . . .

$ . . . . . . . . . . . . . . . . . . . . .
Payment Herewith:

$ . . . . . . . . . . . . . . . . . . . . .
BALANCE
Campaigner:

"MAKING A WORLD OF DIFFERENCE"

Capital Development Program

The Young Men's Christian Association of Greater St. Louis

FOR THE EXTENSION OF YMCA PROGRAMS AND IN CONSIDERATION OF THE GIFTS OF
OTHERS, I/WE PLEDGE THE SUM OF:

$ . . . . . . . . . . . . . . . . . . . . . . . . . . . . . . . . . . . . . To Be Paid as Follows:

PAYABLE OVER A _____ YEAR PERIOD AS FOLLOWS:

☐ ANNUAL      ☐ SEMI-ANNUAL      ☐ QUARTERLY      ☐ MONTHLY

PAYMENT AMOUNTS                    1ST PAYMENT DUE:

OTHER PAYMENT ARRANGEMENTS:

SIGNED: _____ DATE _____

CARD NO.

CARD NO.

CARD NO.

Make Checks Payable to:
St. Louis YMCA—Capital Campaign
1528 Locust St., St. Louis, MO 63103
(314) 436–1177

The YMCA of Greater St. Louis Acknowledges with Thanks the
Contribution of

Name

Amount Subscribed $

Amount Paid $

Received By

Date

1. Detach this stub.
2. Do not show to Prospect.
3. Contact only those for whom you hold a Prospect Card.
4. See Prospect Personally.

YMCA Affiliation:

$

Amount suggested
By Appraisal
Committee

Campaigner

Campaigner No.:

| DIV | TM | CPR |
|-----|-----|-----|

Sign, detach and leave this
stub when you select this
Prospect Card.

PART 1

PART 2

PART 3

---

CARD NO.

CARD NO.

CARD NO.

Make Checks Payable to:
St. Louis YMCA—Capital Campaign
1528 Locust St., St. Louis, MO 63103
(314) 436–1177

The YMCA of Greater St. Louis Acknowledges with Thanks the
Contribution of

Name

Amount Subscribed $

Amount Paid $

Received By

Date

1. Detach this stub.
2. Do not show to Prospect.
3. Contact only those for whom you hold a Prospect Card.
4. See Prospect Personally.

YMCA Affiliation:

$

Amount suggested
By Appraisal
Committee

Campaigner

Campaigner No.:

| DIV | TM | CPR |
|-----|-----|-----|

Sign, detach and leave this
stub when you select this
Prospect Card.

PART 1

PART 2

PART 3

# A Pledge to
# The University of Iowa Foundation for
# Iowa Endowment 2000:
# A Covenant with Quality

_____

name(s) (please print clearly)

_____

_____

address

_____

city, state, zip

As an investment in human resources at The University of Iowa
and in consideration of the gifts of others, I (we) hereby subscribe and
agree to pay The University of Iowa Foundation for the Iowa
Endowment 2000 Campaign the sum of:

_____ Dollars ($ _____)

to be paid in either cash, securities or other property
of equivalent value.

_____

signature                                        date

_____

spouse's signature (when joint gift)          date

Total pledge      $ _____

Paid herewith    $ _____

Balance due       $ _____

_____

Balance to Be Paid as Follows:

| Month | Year | Amount |
|-------|------|--------|
| _____ | 19 ___ | $ _____ |
| _____ | 19 ___ | $ _____ |
| _____ | 19 ___ | $ _____ |
| _____ | 19 ___ | $ _____ |
| _____ | 19 ___ | $ _____ |

Payment schedules other than
annual may be arranged.

___ I (we) have made provisions for an
estate/testamentary gift to support
the Iowa Endowment 2000 Campaign.
A description of the deferred gift
arrangement is attached.

Please make checks payable to:
**The University of Iowa Foundation.**
Your gift is tax deductible.

# SAMPLE COMMUNICATIONS MATERIALS CHECKLIST

## COMMUNICATIONS MATERIALS.

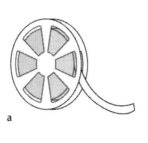

a

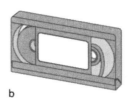

b

c

g

h

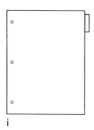

i

j

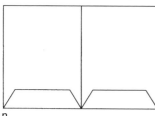

n

a   campaign film
b   videos of film and TV spots
c   podium placard/misc. use
d   alumni center sign
e   campaign volunteers' notebook
f   notebook cover insert
g   notebook back cover insert
h   notebook spine insert
i   notebook  divider
j   notebook  pages stock
k   printed  campaign brochure
l   various brochure inserts
m  folder for meetings
n   same as *m*/also for corp. proposals
o   letterhead
p   letterhead second sheet
q   no. 10 carrier envelope for *o*
r   mailing label
s   pledge form
t   payroll witholding form (campus)
u   campus mail envelope
v   no. 9 postpaid reply envelope
w   pin of the symbol, for volunteers
x   symbol/logo decals for all givers

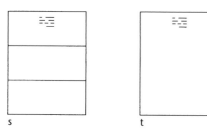

s                    t

# IOWA ENDOWMENT 2000: A COVENANT WITH QUALITY.

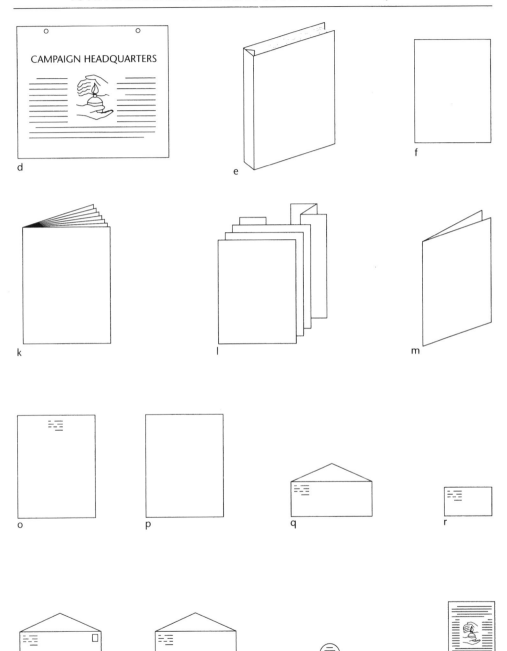

## SAMPLE NEWSLETTERS

# NEWSLETTER

## Second Century Fund aided by gifts of all sizes and types

Every gift and pledge to the Second Century Fund, regardless of amount, brings the University closer to its $25 million fund raising goal and helps ensure a thriving future for Drake during the next 100 years.

Many donors are contributing a variety of gifts to the three-year capital campaign.

Some highlights include:

**Marlyn C. "Mike" Augustine** — A liberal arts graduate of 1944, Mr. Augustine deeded a five-acre parcel of land in Phoenix, Arizona, to Drake as a contribution to the Second Century Fund. Value of the land is estimated at $80,000.

**Jean A. Bandy** — Namesake for a new mineral discovered by her late husband Mark Chance Bandy, Mrs. Bandy Ed'21 Ed'56, an Arizona resident, pledged $10,000 to the Second Century Fund for earth sciences study.

**Bertram Holst** — A liberal arts graduate of 1913, Mr. Holst enjoys a long record of giving to Drake's annual fund. This year, in addition to his annual giving, Mr. Holst made a surprise outright gift of $50,000 to the Second Century Fund in support of the University's capital campaign efforts to assist the College of Liberal Arts.

**Yosh Inadomi** — A former alumni trustee and a 1945 business administration graduate, Mr. Inadomi pledged $25,000 to establish an endowed scholarship in his father's name. The John K. Inadomi Scholarship Fund will be used to assist students studying

business administration.

**Jeffry R. and Sharyn Kopriva Jontz** — The Jontzes pledged $5,000 to Drake's annual scholarship fund as a Second Century Fund contribution. Now a Florida attorney, Mr. Jontz is a 1966 liberal arts graduate; Mrs. Jontz is a 1968 journalism graduate.

**R. Wayne Skidmore** — A life member of the Board of Trustees and a 1933 business graduate, Mr. Skidmore, along with his wife Maxine, have established a named gift in Aliber Hall, the new College of Business Administration building. The seminar room in Aliber Hall will bear the Skidmore name because of their generosity.

The Second Century Fund offers donors a number of methods of giving, including outright gifts of cash, gifts of securities, gifts of real property, gifts of life insurance, planned gifts (which can take many forms) and gifts through a will.

One or a combination of these methods may have a particular appeal in planning a gift. Drake University provides donors with help and advice in planning their gifts.

For more information regarding these or other named or memorial gift opportunities, contact:
Office of Institutional Development, Drake University, 319 Old Main, Des Moines, Iowa 50311, telephone 515/271-3154.

---

**A Gift from the
William Friedman
Memorial Book Fund**

**Established by Gifts
from his family
and friends**

*In memory of William Friedman L'25, longtime trustee and former secretary of the Board of Trustees who died earlier this year, a book fund in the Law Library has been established by gifts from his family and friends as part of the Second Century Fund. Books purchased through the memorial book fund will be affixed with the book plate shown above.*

*Alumni attending a Boca Raton, Fl., reception sponsored by the Second Century Fund campaign included Larry Winker FA'62, Dwight Machesney B'34, his wife Helen LA'36, and Sol Glick L'32.*

*The Boca Raton, Fl., reception also brought together Rob Carney L'75, Larry Witte B'66, his wife Jan Witte Ed'67, Paula (Mrs. Larry) Winker, and Dr. Wilbur C. Miller.*

# Alumni work for Second Century Fund campaign

The Second Century Fund campaign is gaining momentum across the country, with fund raising efforts now actively underway in more than a dozen cities nationwide.

Alumni in many cities are forming local committees to assist with fund raising activities, giving generously of their time and talents to help guarantee a successful campaign.

Local committee efforts are being guided by alumni in the following cities:

**Des Moines area:** L. Donald Easter, chair; Paul Ashby, Virginia Neff Chase; Donald Cook; Robert Frampton; Dorothy Goldberg; William Goodwin, Jr.; David Hawkins; Russell Johnson, Jr.; Kenneth Miller; Dean Mitchell; Rolland Nelson; R. Dale Peddicord; Roscoe Riemenschneider; W. A. Schultz; and William Wimer.

**Newton/Jasper County area:** Murray Nelson, chair; Virginia Bennett; Donald Byers; John Erickson; Harold Forsyth; Ed Hagen; Myrtilla Levin; Delores Matthews; L. D. Norris; Ed Trost; James Tyler; Robert Underwood; and Eleanor Wheeler.

**Cedar Rapids area:** Marion Koontz, chair; Mary Heabel; Kent Johnson; Hyla Lehman; Ken Lemke; Robert Newland; John Sackett; John Siebenmann; Ray Stefani; Ray Stefani II; Mrs. Ray Stefani II; Georgene Stapleton; Rod Teachout; and Larry Zirbel.

**Mason City area:** Diane McNulty, chair; June DeVries; Warren DeVries; Gil Lettow; Kathy Minette; Richard Minette; David Pruess; Don Siefken; and Inez Siefken.

**Dallas/Ft. Worth area:** Larry Katzen, chair; John Bauer; Jayne Buckroyd; Shelly Dawson; Jim Feaster; Dwight W. Heaberlin; Ray Hotchkiss; Jerry Nelson; and Jeannette Oehring.

**Peoria area:** Grant Mathey, chair; Richard Chapman; Marilyn Efinger; Carl Johnson; Peter Johnson; Philip Johnson; Robert Schnarr; and James Yoder.

**Denver area:** Lois Hobson, chair; John R. Coffey; Phil Doty; Robert Harmon; Robert Poulson; and Leo E. Rostermundt.

**Phoenix area:** James D. Bruner, chair; David S. Baker; Donald L. Cross; William Don Carlos; and John Harper.

**San Diego area:** Keith E. McWilliams, chair; Richard T. Cubbage; Robert B. Goode; and Edward Lyon.

**Los Angeles area:** Ronald T. Olsen, chair; Yosh Inadomi; Gerald Knippenberg; Clifford C. Larson; and Stephen T. Pettise.

**Kansas City area:** Patrick Kelly, chair; Don Burger; Lawrence Engel; W. Homer Jennings; Leo Mangels; Russell Reynolds; Michael Rissler; and Elwood Thomas.

**St. Louis area:** James H. Ewoldt, chair; Joann Ewoldt; Norman Handshear; and Robert A. Maddocks.

**San Francisco area:** Dean Showers, chair; George M. Carr; and Richard Marquart.

**Chicago area:** Howard S. Haft.

**Minneapolis/St. Paul area:** Dwight Opperman.

**Rockford area:** Sherwood Anderson.

Alumni interested in joining or forming a local committee helping with Second Century Fund campaign efforts are invited to contact either the chairperson in their area for more information or the Office of Institutional Development, Drake University, 319 Old Main, Des Moines, Iowa 50311, telephone 515/271-3154.

*The Newton/Jasper County area alumni volunteers working on the Second Century Fund campaign include committee chairman Murray Nelson LA'35 L'37, Myrt Levin LA'60, Virginia Bennett FA'65 G'78, Robert Underwood B'39, Edward Hagen B'46 and Edgar Trost B'64.*

# Gift annuities may provide income for life

Ernest K. Henderson of California receives a check from Drake every month and will continue to do so as long as he lives.

How? Through a charitable gift annuity that pays him a guaranteed income for life.

Mr. Henderson, whose only previous acquaintance with Drake was through his neighbor, Duwayne "Bud" Hartzell B'70, had stock in a national company that paid him stock dividends instead of cash dividends. When he decided he would rather have additional income from stock, through his Drake connection he arranged to enter into a gift annuity with Drake funded by his appreciated stock. As a result, Mr. Henderson was entitled to an immediate charitable contribution deduction on his income tax and has since been receiving a monthly check based on the value of his stock and his age at the time of his gift, a rate of return which is established by the Conference on Gift Annuities and currently ranging from 5 to 14 percent based upon the age of the donor.

This is a good way to give highly appreciated stock, according to Bob Clark, director of planned giving at Drake. Since his stock fortunately was highly appreciated, Mr. Henderson would have been required to pay a large capital gains tax if he had sold the stock. By entering into a gift annuity with Drake, he was able to deduct more than half of the stock's appreciated value and

paid much less in capital gains taxes. Plus, he receives his monthly check of a guaranteed amount for life.

Mr. Henderson's case is not at all unusual. To encourage gifts to institutions like Drake, the Federal government provides tax benefits to those who transfer money or securities in exchange for Drake's agreement to pay the donor (and a survivor beneficiary, if desired) a fixed income for life.

The annual income paid depends on the beneficiary's age at the time of the gift and is a guaranteed annual rate of return, remaining constant for life. A large portion of the annual income is tax-free; the tax-free amount also depends on the beneficiary's age at the time of the gift and is determined by official U.S. Treasury tables. Treasury tables also establish the amount of the immediate charitable contribution deduction to which the donor is entitled, and the charitable contribution deduction often completely eliminates the capital gain. There are several other capital gains implications when gift annuities are funded by appreciated property.

Drake has had a charitable gift annuity program for some time, according to Clark, who feels the program could be advantageous for a number of people who might want to help Drake and still retain a life income from their gifts.

"We have plans tailored to fit any amount and any age," he said.

## Law scholarship to honor Lewis

A fund raising effort is being headed by Patrick Kelly L'53 of Kansas City to establish a scholarship fund in honor of Frederick D. Lewis, Jr., professor of law in the Drake Law School from 1949 to 1959 and former executive director of the American Judicature Society.

As part of the Second Century Fund, the Frederick D. Lewis, Jr. Honor Scholarships will help the Drake Law School continue to attract the most gifted students with the potential for outstanding achievement in law and public service and will be awarded on a merit basis.

The Kansas City Area Drake Law Alumni also are involved in fund raising efforts for the Lewis Honor Scholarships.

## Fund reaches 60 percent of goal

Every day brings new gifts and pledges to the Second Century Fund, and as of December 1, the total amount in the Fund was $15,062,689, more than 60 percent of the $25 million goal.

Of the total $9,070,357 were gifts from Drake's Board of Trustees (both personal and company), $1,259,675 from corporations, $2,082,729 from foundations, $501,946 from alumni, $99,392 from others (including parents and friends), and $1,369,815 in 1980-81 annual funds. The total also includes $688,775 in 1981-82 annual funds received as of December 1.

*Larry Katzen B'67 and his wife Susan Ed'68 met with Drake President Wilbur C. Miller at the Dallas/Ft. Worth meeting of alumni volunteers working on the Second Century Fund campaign.*

*Mrs. and Dr. Wilbur C. Miller met with Becky and Bob Taylor B'62 at the Naples, Fl., alumni get-together sponsored by the Second Century Fund campaign.*

# Aliber Hall construction continues on schedule

Construction of Aliber Hall, the new College of Business Administration building and the only major new construction financed through the Second Century Fund, has progressed well in the past few months, with the size and design of the building now clearly evident to passers-by.

Exterior stud walls are being erected, some brick has been put up and the electrical system is about five percent completed, according to construction supervisors. Construction is basically ahead of schedule, according to Richard G. Peebler, dean of the College of Business Administration, who said he was very pleased with the architect and contractors.

All colors, fabrics and carpets for interior decoration have been approved by the buildings and grounds committee of the Board of Trustees and materials are on order, Dean Peebler said.

Contractors plan the building will be completed by mid-summer.

Major funding for the new structure resulted from gifts of $1 million from the Aliber Foundation of Des Moines and $315,000 from the late Robert Aliber and other members of the Aliber family.

*Construction work on Aliber Hall, the new College of Business Administration building financed through the Second Century Fund, is progressing well.*

## Parents establish scholarship fund

For the next three years, gifts and pledges to Drake from the parents of Drake students will be used to establish the Parents Second Century Scholarship Fund as the Parents Association's contribution to the Second Century Fund campaign.

Vince Nelson, director of the parents program, said that the Parents Second Century Scholarship Fund will be included in the $3.5 million set aside for scholarship and fellowship endowment out of the campaign's total $25 million goal.

The Drake Parents Board, which adopted the scholarship fund program at its semi-annual meeting during the Oct. 2-3, 1981 Parents Weekend, set a $250,000 goal for the scholarship fund. The money will be administered by the Financial Aid Office, with scholarships awarded to students based upon academic excellence and financial need.

Parents Board members Bud and Anne Crowl of Council Bluffs, whose son Matt is a sophomore in liberal arts and an Alumni Scholar, are serving as chairpersons of the scholarship campaign.

Solicitation for the Parents Second Century Scholarship Fund will occur through personal visits by Parents Board members, by direct mail and during the annual telethon.

Second Century Fund

DRAKE UNIVERSITY • DES MOINES, IOWA

*Non-Profit Organization*
*U.S. POSTAGE PAID*
*Des Moines, Iowa*
*Permit No. 2217*

VOLUME 2 · NUMBER 3

# UPDATE

THE ENDOWMENT CAMPAIGN
*for* INDIANA UNIVERSITY   SEPTEMBER 1998
BLOOMINGTON

CONTENTS

*Additional $2 Million Investment Could Reap Large Returns*

## TRUSTEES EXPAND ENDOWMENT MATCHING PROGRAM

A $6 million investment that could well bring back $150 million?

It's no dream: Indiana University officials can expect such results, because this particular investment is via the University's innovative Faculty Endowment Income Matching Program.

On May 8, the IU Board of Trustees authorized adding another $2 million to the $4 million already allocated to the successful matching program, which encourages private donors to set up faculty endowments by dedicating University funds to match endowment earnings.

The brainchild of IU president Myles Brand, the program began in 1995 when the trustees agreed to set aside $1 million to match the payout (the spendable income generated by the invested principal) of new endowment gifts of $500,000 or more. The program proved so popular with donors that they added $3 million in 1997. With the latest infusion, a total of $6 million has been set aside for the matching of endowment income. Half of the money comes from the president's budget, and the other half comes from the campuses.

Has it been words jet Brand thinks the numbers speak for themselves. "It's really quite startling," he says. "In its entire 175-year history before the Bloomington Endowment Campaign, the University had received only 31 faculty endowments. I challenged the IU Foundation to increase that number by 100. There was some hard swallowing and a few ashen faces," he chuckles, "but I was optimistic." He convinced the Foundation board of directors and the University trustees that with the matching program as an incentive, donors would give at the high levels needed for endowment support: $500,000 for a professorship, $1 million for a chair. The strategy worked.

As a result of the first $4 million investment, the IU Foundation has already recorded $101 million in gifts. That translates to 105 new faculty endowments. "We've more than tripled our endowed positions in just two years," says Brand.

By that measure, the new $2 million will result in another $40 million in gifts: 50 more endowed positions. "I believe that's a conservative estimate," adds Foundation president Curt Simic. "When this is over, I think we will have leveraged over $150 million."

> ## "we've more than tripled our endowed positions in just two years."
>
> — PRESIDENT MYLES BRAND

The Foundation is so confident, in fact, that it has raised Brand's original challenge—with scarcely a gulp. The goal is now *150* new endowed faculty positions. "That is definitely feasible," says Simic. "Our donors have been remarkably enthusiastic about the idea. That shouldn't surprise us, really. These folks know a good deal when they see one."

As Brand points out, "It's a win-win situation for everyone. The University gets the financial stability and competitiveness the endowments provide, and the donors get the satisfaction of seeing the results of their gifts right away. Suppose a donor

*more on page 2*

"The loyalty and support of Indiana University's donors continues to impress me. They have taken advantage of the matching program at a much faster rate than anyone anticipated. Twice we've had to go back to the trustees to add more funds, just to keep pace with the demand."

— PRESIDENT MYLES BRAND

**endowment (ěn-dou′mənt)** *n.* 1. Money invested for future growth, with only a portion of the return being used today. 2. One of the best vehicles a university can use to keep tuition costs affordable. 3. A good strategy to offset the effects of inflation and reduced state appropriations. 4. An important aid in attracting and retaining today's outstanding faculty, as well as tomorrow's brightest scholars.

MCA Of Greater St. Louis
# CONTRIBUTORS' NEWSLETTER

Corporate Offices • 1528 Locust Street • St. Louis, MO 63103-1897 • 314-436-1177

SAM EDGAR
President

**JULY, 1986**

DICK STOLL
Vice President
Development

## *Thank You . . .*

Your contributions to the YMCA enable children throughout the Metropolitan area to develop and grow in mind, body and spirit. You are indeed a "Partner With Youth" and this newsletter describes only a handful of benefits your generosity makes possible through Y programs.

"Y" pre-school provides important learning experiences for the future while teaching how to share both verbally and socially in a group situation.

Bright lively bundles of energy are entranced with learning new skills in tumbling and beginning gymnastics.

## CAPITAL CAMPAIGN
### "Down the Final Mile"

The "Making A World of Difference" capital campaign of the YMCA of Greater St. Louis is moving strongly through its final stage of solicitation. Gathering $14,000,000 in pledges to date, 78% of the $17.9 million goal, determined campaigners continue their efforts to fund buildings and expand programs for 60,000 - 70,000 more people. Projects made possible by this campaign include:

- West County Y - Construct a new family program and fitness center.
- YMCA of the Ozarks - Build a new lodge and family program center, replace and remodel cabins and develop new program areas.
- North County Y - Complete the Emerson Fitness Center adding a gymnasium, indoor track and expanded locker rooms.
- Downtown Fitness Center - Renovate the existing facility and add a second fitness center east of 9th Street.
- Mid-County Y - Remodel and add additional program space.
- Kirkwood/Webster Y - Construct a gymnasium at the Kirkwood Center and air-condition the Webster Groves Center.
- South Side Y - Improve facilities for expanded latch-key and adult fitness programming.
- Carondelet Y - Enhance building access for senior citizens and revitalize existing facilities.
- Monsanto Y - Add fitness and day-care facilities.
- Northwest County/Westport Y - Establish a cardio-vascular center in the Westport business/residential community.
- Washington University Campus Y - Increase the endowment supporting student services.
- Jefferson County Y - Acquire property and construct facilities to provide day-care and other community based programs.
- St. Charles County/Wentzville Y - Acquire property and construct a program building to serve western St. Charles Co.

*Source:* YMCA of Greater St. Louis, St. Louis, Missouri.

# SAMPLE LETTERHEAD AND ENVELOPES

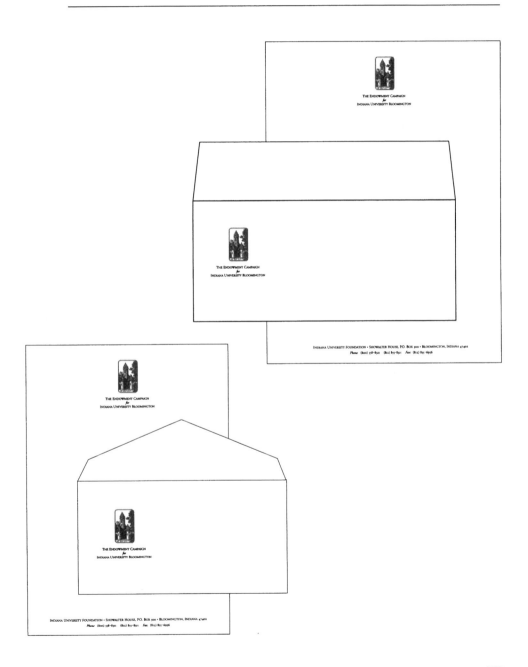

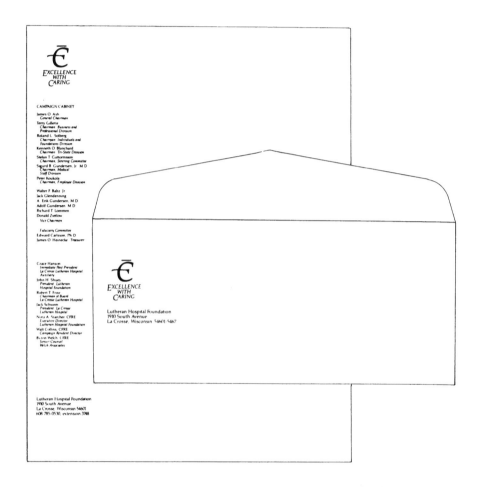

## SAMPLE FINAL REPORT

## Table Of Contents

# Leadership Committee

**Campaign Chair**
Clark G. Quintin
V.P. & General Manager
Western Canada
IBM Canada Ltd.

**Committee Members**
Donald A. Calder
Vice President
Business Planning
B.C. Tel

Robert B. Findlay
President and CEO
MacMillan Bloedel Ltd.

Gerald F. Franciscovich (retired)
Former President
Chevron Canada Ltd.

Robert E. Kadlec
President and CEO
B.C. Gas Inc.

Alex E. Klopfer
President and CEO
Epic Data Inc.

William N. Palm
Senior VP, Information Services
Canadian Airlines International

Michael E. Phelps
President and CEO
Westcoast Energy Inc.

G. Wynne Powell
Vice President
Marketing & Retail Services
Technical Group
London Drugs Limited

J. J. Quinn
President
CIBC Mortgage Corporation

John P. Sheehan
Chief Financial Officer
& Senior V.P.
British Columbia
Hydro and Power Authority

Thomas A. Simons
President
H.A. Simons (International) Ltd.

Brian D. Sung
Regional Comptroller
Canadian Broadcasting
Corporation

Marie Taylor
Chairman
The Laurier Institute

John Watson
President
British Columbia
Institute of Technology

**Chair, School of Health
Sciences Campaign**
Dr. Peter Cooperberg
Professor of Radiology
UBC

**Chair, Campus Centre
Campaign**
Dr. Donald Rix, MD
President
Metro-McNair
Clinical Laboratories Ltd.

**Chair, Public Affairs Committee**
David A. Laundy
VP Public Affairs
Vancouver Stock Exchange

**Chair, Family Campaign**
Jim Mitchell
Director Campus Life/
Recreation & Athletic Services
BCIT

## Campaign Chair's Message

In a world marked by falling trade barriers and new strategic alliances, there remains one constant essential to our global competitiveness and future prosperity—education. Through the High Tech, High Promise: The Drive for BCIT capital campaign, we have added over $13 million in capital to keep BCIT on the leading edge of advanced technology training in Canada. Such investment not only benefits B.C. business and industry but Canadian competitiveness as well. Our "High Tech" investment will undoubtedly yield many dividends through the "High Promise" of BCIT graduates.

While most contributions were directed to the acquisition of equipment and the upgrading of labs, we also established new scholarships and bursaries to help attract talented students to BCIT.

The President's Enterprise Fund was established to help keep BCIT innovative, flexible and technologically advanced through faculty and staff development.

The Campus Centre will create a hub of activity and interaction for the BCIT community and will serve as an enduring legacy of the success of our campaign.

As Chair of the High Tech, High Promise capital campaign, I thank every donor for their contribution. Your confidence in BCIT and support of their efforts are greatly appreciated. I would also like to thank each member of our campaign Leadership Committee, the Public Affairs Committee, the Campus Centre Committee and the BCIT Family Campaign Committee for their time, energy and commitment to raising funds on BCIT's behalf.

Also, my thanks to BCIT faculty and staff who dedicated countless hours in planning for and acquiring needed equipment.

The Drive for BCIT has brought new friends to BCIT and strengthened existing partnerships. As technology continues to advance, so too does the challenge to keep BCIT current. I hope you will all continue to support BCIT generously as "The Drive" continues.

*Clark G. Quintin*
*Vice President and General Manager*
*Western Canada*
*IBM Canada Ltd.*

[The report lists committee members' names here. They have been omitted for the sake of privacy.]

| Public Affairs Committee | Campus Centre Campaign Committee | BCIT Family Campaign Committee | BCIT Development Office |
|---|---|---|---|

## President's Message

Throughout the High Tech, High Promise capital campaign, I have had the opportunity to talk with many of B.C.'s business leaders about their needs for advanced technology and trades training. Their message is clear: they like our job-ready graduates for two key reasons. First, their training is practical and applied, they are comfortable in technology-intensive environments and they quickly become productive employees. Second, our graduates are noted for their ability to work in teams and they have the drive, attitude and ability to succeed. I am committed to ensuring that the excellence in these skills and attributes employers value most will continue to be the hallmark of BCIT graduates.

As a result of the generous investment by our donors through the High Tech, High Promise capital campaign, we have added significantly to the capital resources we urgently require to modernize labs and equipment. Our resources to attract top students and enhance faculty and staff development have also expanded.

Perhaps the most significant accomplishment of the campaign has been the renewal of our partnership with business to meet our province's advanced technology, trades training and applied research needs. Together we can work to enhance the competitive position and future prosperity of British Columbians.

I would especially like to thank the B.C. Government for providing a $5 million fund to match private donations to the campaign. This initiative proved a tremendous asset in attracting private funds to the Institute.

My sincere thanks also to Clark Quintin, for his skillful and dedicated leadership of this campaign and to IBM Canada Ltd. for supporting the philanthropic efforts of their employees and BCIT. Our campaign Leadership Committee and BCIT faculty and staff also deserve our gratitude for their efforts raising funds on BCIT's behalf.

With the completion of this campaign, we will build on our new and existing partnerships to continue fundraising for institute priorities. With your continued support, BCIT will become Canada's leading Institute in advanced technology training, supplying business and industry with the work force and entrepreneurial spirit they need to prosper in our changing society.

*John Watson*
*President*
*BCIT*

## Campaign Achievements

The major challenge of the High Tech, High Promise capital campaign was to update equipment and labs for advanced technology and trades training. Much of our equipment had outlived its usefulness and needed to be replaced in order to continue to produce job-ready graduates. Of the $10 million goal, $7.5 million was earmarked for these purposes. Thanks to the generosity of our donors, with the added incentive of B.C. government matching funds, a total of $11.14 million was raised in gifts-in-kind and cash donations for equipment and labs at BCIT. Throughout the Institute, students and faculty are benefiting from access to current equipment and modern labs.

### HIGH TECH, HIGH PROMISE
### CAPITAL CAMPAIGN FUNDS RAISED

| | | |
|---|---:|---:|
| Gifts of Equipment | $ 4,888,860 | |
| Gifts of Cash | | |
|    Allocated to a program area | $ 379,462 | |
|    Unrestricted | $ 1,100,759 | |
| New Endowed Funds | $ 229,500 | |
| B.C. Government Matching Funds | $ 5,000,000 | |
| **Total Campaign** | **$11,598,581** | **$11,598,581** |

### ADDITIONAL FUNDS RAISED

| | | |
|---|---:|---:|
| Endowed Funds | | |
|    (includes B.C. Government Match) | $ 1,200,161 | |
| Non-endowed Funds | $ 513,457 | |
| **Total** | **$ 1,713,618** | **$ 1,713,618** |
| **Total funds raised throughout** | | |
| **the duration of the campaign** | | **$13,312,199** |

# School of Engineering Technology

From oscilloscopes to Geographic Information Systems software, gifts to the capital campaign have had a wide impact on the School of Engineering Technology. One highlight, in the Electronics Technology department, was the development of a complete state-of-the-art industrial controls systems lab centered around the donation by GE Fanuc Automation Canada Inc. and Gescan Ltd. of Programmable Logic Controllers, automation software and related computer circuit boards. This donation generated matching dollars sufficient to provide 12 new specialized workstations complete with 486 PC computers. The new facility provides students with the opportunity to analyse and program PLC equipment directly from the computer-based workstation.

In the Instrumentation option, Black and Baird Ltd. and Rosemount Instruments Ltd. both donated "smart" instrumentation in the form of flow, pressure, PH and conductivity sensor/transmitters. This equipment provides state-of-the-art equipment for measurement and control systems found in the pulp and paper, mining, petrochemical and other industries.

In the Power Option of Electronics Technology, a substantial donation of control equipment was received from Telemecanique Ltd. This equipment is similar in function to the PLC's given to the Instrumentation Option and provides an essential alternative in technology so that students receive training in various approaches as taken by different manufacturers.

In Telecommunications, the capital program generated the funds necessary for the purchase of highly sophisticated communications analyzers of the type currently used in the mobile radio and cellular communications industry.

The Erdas Inc. donation of the Erdas Software Lab Kit brought a new level of sophistication to the Geographic Information Systems technology. Not only does the software enable students to experience a powerful image processing system, it also links directly to the ARC/Info system providing access to computerized geographic modelling.

The Lynx Geosystems Inc. donation of Microlynx software brought leading mine planning technology to the Mining department. This comprehensive software package, developed partly in collaboration with BCIT Mining staff and students, enables students to experience mine planning as actually practiced in many mines throughout the world.

## School of Business

Updating equipment that no longer met industry standards in the Broadcast Communications program was the major focus of fundraising activity in the School of Business. Thanks to the generosity of Sony of Canada Ltd., we now have five new studio cameras and the back-up support material to replace our existing 20 year old studio cameras. For the first time in years, BCIT has cameras which are fully operational and reliable. Faculty now use current equipment to demonstrate proper procedures to train our students. In addition, the technical quality of student video productions, including a weekly show called "BCIT Magazine," which is broadcast on cable systems throughout the province, has increased dramatically. Now students can direct more energy towards the creative elements of video production. At the recent national Jeffrey Reneau Awards Festival, BCIT won two of seven "Bessies" (out of 68 entries), the only Canadian post-secondary institute to win more than one award.

The matching funds for the Sony of Canada Ltd. donation were further used to update other areas in Broadcast Communications. The Radio program will enter the digital era with new production and on-air facilities and some new practice rooms. Further, Broadcast Journalism will receive a re-vamped newsroom for operation of our campus radio station, CFML.

## Other Schools Benefitting

[Some descriptions have been omitted here for the sake of brevity.]

### School of Trades Training

### School of Health Sciences

## Institute-wide Gifts

Through their generous donation of equipment and services, IBM Canada Ltd. substantially increased the computing capability at BCIT both at institutional and student levels. Of particular benefit to students will be two new advanced microcomputer labs to be located in SW3 2675 and SW3 2625.

# Cash Donations

Unrestricted cash donations are the foundation to a successful fundraising campaign. Through the High Tech, High Promise capital campaign, a total of $2,201,518 (including matching) in cash gifts and pledges was raised for BCIT to direct to areas of greatest need. We would like to extend our sincere thanks to the following donors for their gifts of cash and pledges to the campaign: Unitel Communications, Chevron Canada Ltd., Rogers Cable TV Ltd., Seaspan International Ltd., Royal Bank of Canada, B.C. Gas Inc., CIBC, MacMillan Bloedel Ltd., Canadian Energy Services, Westcoast Energy Inc., Sandwell Inc., Toronto Dominion Bank, Imperial Oil, B.C. Tel, Pacific Foundation of Applied Technology, Weldwood of Canada Ltd., Bank of Montreal, Bank of Nova Scotia, and the Larkspur Foundation.

# New Endowments

### B.C. Hydro Library Renewal Trust

The B.C. Hydro Library Renewal Trust was established to provide funds for new acquisitions by BCIT's permanent library collection in order to ensure quality and accessibility of the library resource to students and faculty.

### President's Enterprise Fund

With a donation from the Hongkong Bank of Canada, the President's Enterprise Fund was established. Designed to foster staff development, the fund will be used to keep BCIT innovative, flexible and advanced, and will enable the BCIT President to pursue creative strategies for promoting advanced technology and entrepreneurship in B.C.

# Scholarship and Bursary Endowments

In addition to contributions to existing endowments, many new endowments were established during this campaign.

### Constructions Specifications Canada

The Constructions Specifications Canada endowment will provide an annual award to a student in the School of Engineering Technology, Building Technology program.

### The George Nelson Muir Memorial Fund

This endowment was established by the Real Estate Board of Greater Vancouver to support students in the Marketing Management program, Real Estate Option.

### The D. Letkeman and D. Utz Memorial Endowment Fund

With matching funds from the B.C. Government, Gulf Canada Resources Limited made a contribution towards this endowment, which provides an annual award to a student in the Surveying and Mapping Technology program.

### Pacific Foundation of Applied Technology, Otto A. Kloss Entrance Awards

The Pacific Foundation of Applied Technology made a substantial contribution towards this existing endowment with B.C. Government matching funds, through the campaign. The endowment provides entrance scholarships for students entering specific entry-level trades training programs and other preemployment programs in the School of Trades Training.

### The BCIT Staff: High Tech, High Promise
### Capital Campaign Bursary and Award

This endowment was established through the fundraising efforts of BCIT faculty and staff in support of BCIT students. By October 30, 1992, the BCIT Family Campaign had raised in excess of $14 thousand towards the High Tech, High Promise capital campaign through a variety of activities and events including the Drive for 500 Lottery, Christmas poinsettia sales, Mother's Day hanging basket sales and Country Hoe Down '92, a barn dance. The endowment will provide bursaries for students with financial need and will recognize students who participate voluntarily in support of their school.

## Donors

Our sincere thanks to the following corporations, groups, and individuals who gave generously to the Capital Campaign from December 1, 1989, to November 30, 1992 (list of donors follows here).

## And the Drive Continues . . .

The High Tech, High Promise Capital Campaign has modernized equipment and labs to meet the training needs of the 1990s. To continue to meet the challenges of rapidly advancing technology, particularly in times of government restraint, BCIT will continue to look to the private sector for leadership and support. Together, we can prepare B.C. for the challenges of a global society.

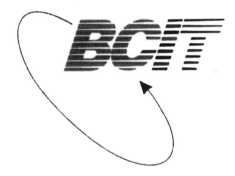

## SAMPLE POST-CAMPAIGN ASSESSMENT

<u>Final Report</u>

VANCOUVER PUBLIC LIBRARY

## "FOR THE LOVE OF LEARNING" LIBRARY SQUARE CAPITAL CAMPAIGN

December 1995

Prepared by:

**Marilyn Wright Fundraising Counsel Inc.**
**Vancouver, British Columbia**

## Table of Contents

## Introduction

The active phase of the Library Square Capital Campaign is now virtually complete. The objective is $12 million and at November 27, 1995, we have documented gifts totalling $8,831,261. Several gifts are expected to be realized before the end of December.

The campaign will have been conducted over a 24-month period: January 1994 through December 1995. This report outlines the activity of the capital campaign, which included the recruitment of strong leadership, the formulation of a strong and convincing case, the identification of viable prospects, and the implementation of a successful plan.

This report gives a campaign chronicle and has appended charts, which show the progress of the campaign as it progressed. (See Appendix I and Appendix II.)

Although this phase of the campaign is winding down, additional gifts are anticipated to be received during the next several months.

The Library will continue to monitor major decisions pending, i.e., 1 Service Club, 11 individual major gift calls, and 1 national company major gift. Receipting of donations for the Library Card Christmas campaign will be ongoing into the new year.

This is a report on professional service and outlines the purpose and strategy used in the campaign. It is impossible to detail and account all incidents and events surrounding the campaign. The specific details are documented in the weekly reports to the leadership of the campaign, which are on file in the Campaign Office.

As the campaign draws to a close, it is vitally important that pledge control for long-term commitments be carefully handled. This process must be fully integrated into the ongoing fundraising endeavours of the Library, directed and in a manner satisfactory to the City's Director of Finance.

In submitting this Final Report for the Library Square Capital Campaign, I want to express my sincere appreciation to the Vancouver Public Library Board, who have assisted the Campaign in this extraordinary financial endeavour, with special thanks to Kyle Mitchell, Madge Aalto, and the senior management of the Library, and Ken Dobell, City Manager, for their leadership and determination to support the fundraising campaign. The entire campaign staff has benefited from this experience and feel privileged to have been a part of this project.

An important element of the campaign was the leadership given by the Campaign Co-Chairs, John and Kip Woodward. Their leadership and dedication were the key factors in making this fundraising effort successful.

Sincere appreciation is extended to all of the campaign committee members for the time and commitment given for the past two years. It is impossible to mention each individual who has contributed to the success of this project. A special thank-you must be given to the Library staff, Friends of the Library, and the 100+ community volunteers who help build "a love of learning" at the new Central Branch.

I am grateful for the confidence placed in my procedures, methods, and systems of fundraising. Please accept my gratitude to all of you, who through your involvement, leadership, and kindness have made the work of counsel successful. Respectfully submitted,
Marilyn Wright Fundraising Counsel Inc.

## Initial Activity

Having outgrown its 1957 home, the Library Board looked to the people of Vancouver to find out what people wanted in a new building. Community input was the foundation of the library planning process and the community spoke on the design of what was to be the new downtown signature building.

A unique partnership with the federal and provincial governments, the City of Vancouver, and private donors was conceived to create a library to serve people across British Columbia.

The Library was responsible for $12 million for equipment and furnishings and the governments would provide the construction cost. It was determined that new sources of income over and above anticipated income would be required to meet the Library's projected needs for furnishings and equipment. The Board decided to launch a major capital campaign.

A key constituent market survey was undertaken in March 1990. A campaign committee was formed with James Cleave as Chair. Early in the campaign the Chair was transferred out of Vancouver and the new campaign co-chairs, Kip and John Woodward, were enlisted in December 1993.

Marilyn Wright was contacted and retained by the City of Vancouver to direct the capital campaign for a period of 18 months, beginning January 1, 1994, and was extended for six months to end December 31, 1995. Support staff were hired and a Library Square Capital Campaign office was established at 1075 West Georgia. Work began immediately on preparation of the database, research on prospects, foundations, and service clubs. At the same time Counsel worked closely with Kip and John Woodward and Kyle Mitchell, Chair of the Library Board, in recruiting the Campaign Leadership Board.

After careful consideration, the following were invited and agreed to become the Leadership Board who would put their energies to actively solicit funds from the private sector to support the new Vancouver Public Library: Graham Bender, Gordon Campbell, Graham Clarke, W.R.P. (Bill) Dalton, Virginia Greene, Michael Horsey, Terry Hui, Robert Hungerford, Lyall Knott, Peter Ladner, Peter Lamb, David Laundy, Gregory McKinstry, Kyle Mitchell, Nancy Self, Ross Smith, and Marie Taylor.

Each member accepted the responsibility for calling on five to ten key prospects and worked with counsel and staff in developing a campaign strategy for each one. Most members made more than ten calls.

## The Campaign Plan

It should be noted that when this campaign began there was no history of organized giving by the private sector to the Vancouver Public Library. A decision was made early in the planning of the campaign to help the public take ownership of their new Library. At the same time a program of educating and involving the internal Library family about the long-term benefits of a capital campaign to the Library system was undertaken. Both external and internal support early in the campaign needed to be backed up by a broad-based public relations program.

The scheduling of campaign activity by phases put a strong focus on target objectives, which helped not only to elevate donor sights but also developed momentum by creating a campaign atmosphere.

Campaign leadership was effective throughout the appeal because of their belief in the following recommended concepts:

- Recruitment and solicitation was conducted on a personal face to face basis.
- Larger gifts were solicited early in the program to develop momentum.
- Long-term commitments were encouraged.
- Recognition opportunities were available for consideration.
- A gift made to the VPL through the British Columbia Library Foundation was available.
- Planned gifts were sought.
- Donors were asked for specific gifts or gift plans.

# Gifts

Essential to the campaign plan was a strong emphasis on receiving Major Gifts from corporations, financial institutions, service clubs, individuals, foundations, etc. It was hoped that there would be several gifts in the $2–3 million range. This has not as yet been realized.

The Vancouver Foundation's lead gift of $1,000,000 and the Hong Kong Festival '92 Gala Dinner gift of $200,000 that was matched by the Hongkong Bank were both made during Jim Cleave's time.

The plan was to announce the campaign to the public with a significant amount of the money in hand. At the same time we wanted to build the awareness of the campaign through a media programme. Pacific Press joined with the Library campaign as a media partner and agreed to place recognition display ads in the Vancouver Sun and to support all the events leading up to and including the opening of the Library. The campaign kicked off January 24, 1995, with the announcement of $4,676,000 raised.

To encourage gifts, tours were conducted with prospects almost daily during the construction phase of the building and continued well after the Library was opened. These tours were conducted by the Leadership Board, Campaign Staff, and members of City Council, and I would be remiss if I did not recognize the tremendous effort and support put forth by Shelagh Flaherty of the Library Staff, who always made time to conduct tours.

From January 1995 through to the opening, the Campaign Office Staff became integrally involved with the events around the opening of the Library. Much time and energy was spent in ensuring that the campaign and opening would both be successful and that all activities would be positive for the donors.

Partnerships were formed with Concord Pacific and Fletcher Challenge. This is a new concept for the Vancouver Public Library and with thoughtful and careful planning shows promise as a source of revenue to future endeavours.

"Great Libraries of the World," a contest supported by the Vancouver Sun and Vancouver Bank branches, was held in conjunction with the opening of the new Library. This popular contest introduced the commemorative Library card.

A mailing to 10,000 Business in Vancouver Subscribers was sent in May 1995.

The Ismaili Community chose to support Library Square with the proceeds of their annual Walk. Six months of intensive planning went into this event, which was chaired by Councillor Lynne Kennedy and Alnoor Samji. A committee of 20 comprised of Ismaili members, Friends of the Library, Library staff, and campaign staff worked together to ensure a most successful event on October 1, 1995 (see Appendix III).

Recognition ads have appeared in the Vancouver Sun throughout the campaign thanking donors who have made gifts of $50,000 or more for their contribution to Library Square. The placement of these ads in the newspaper was part of the Pacific Press gift (see the Ronald McDonald Children's Charities ad).

The Chinese Community Support the Library Week was held October 28–November 5, 1995. This very dedicated, hardworking committee chaired by Bill Yuen and Vice Chairs Councillor Maggie Ip and John Cheng were assisted by Honourary Chairs Maria Ko and Stella Wong. They brought together 18 people who planned a week of cultural events at Library Square. To date the total raised from this event is $520,000.

## Money Raised

*To date, money raised by category:*

Individuals—13 gifts totalling $3,435,000, ranging from $25,000 to $1,000,000.

Corporations—43 gifts totalling $2,021,600 ranging from $5,000 to $200,000.

Foundations—8 gifts totalling $1,405,000 ranging from $5,000 to $1,000,000.

Service Clubs—4 gifts totalling $268,500.

*Community phase generated gifts totalling $646,161*

- Banks Financial Program (Gift-a-lopes in Banks)
- Commemorative Library Cards
- Downtown Rotary Bike-a-thon
- Ismaili Walk for the Vancouver Public Library
- Chinese Community Support the Library Week
- Wine and Dine British Columbia (not received, not included in total)
- The Vancouver Bank (anticipate proceeds next year)

Gifts-in-kind total $330,000.
Included in the total raised is $1,850,000 in Planned Gifts (Insurance Based)
Total raised to date: $8,831,61.
Of note: The Forest Industry gave over $1,000,000 and the Financial Institutions gave $620,000.

It is encouraging for future fundraising endeavours that the campaign has attracted cash donations and in-kind gifts to the Library that are not included in the campaign total because it is for programs and books.

## Recommendations

At the end of any major campaign, there are a number of items that must be dealt with after the departure of counsel. The transition plan is in place and two of the campaign staff will be staying on for two months to help ensure the smooth conversion to a full development program. The Library will be reporting to Council on a continuing development program.

There are outstanding calls that show real potential and there must be continued cultivation and contact with the prospects to realize this possibility.

Communication with the cash donors and pledgors is critical for the next five years. Every effort should be made to keep the donors informed on activities at the Library and any special event that is held should offer these special friends an invitation. In fact opportunities to invite major donors into the Library should be encouraged—keeping those who supported the campaign close will benefit everyone. It is very important to keep current with pledge reminders. As much as possible the practice of a forty-eight-hour maximum receipt turnaround for gifts should be supported.

A complete listing of every donation to the capital campaign is on confidential record in the Development Office. A chronological history of the campaign has been kept by the campaign office and will be presented to the Library Board at the completion of the active phase of the campaign.

## Appendix I

### DECEMBER 1995 GIFT LEVEL ANALYSIS.

| Dollar Amount | Number of Gifts | Dollar Value |
|---|---|---|
| 1,000,000 | 2 | 2,000,000 |
| 500,000 | 2 | 500,000 |
| 425,000 | 1 | 425,000 |
| 300,000 | 1 | 300,000 |
| 250,000 | 2 | 500,000 |
| 200,000 | 4 | 800,000 |
| 150,000 | 1 | 150,000 |
| 120000 | 5 | 600,000 |
| 100,000 | 9 | 900,000 |
| 60,000 | 1 | 60,000 |
| 50,000 | 6 | 300,000 |
| 40,000 | 1 | 40,000 |
| 30,000 | 2 | 60,000 |
| 27,500 | 1 | 27,500 |
| 25,000 | 5 | 125,000 |
| 20,000 | 2 | 40,000 |
| 15,000 | 6 | 90,000 |
| 10,200 | 1 | 10,200 |
| 10,000 | 10 | 100,000 |
| 6,900 | 1 | 6,900 |
| 5,000 | 5 | 25,000 |
| 4,500 | 1 | 4,500 |
| Under 4,500 | Many | 636,161 |
| In-kind | Many | 330,000 |
| | | $8,831,261 |

# Appendix II

## VANCOUVER PUBLIC LIBRARY CAPITAL CAMPAIGN CUMULATIVE DONATIONS
## (JANUARY 1994–NOVEMBER 27, 1995).

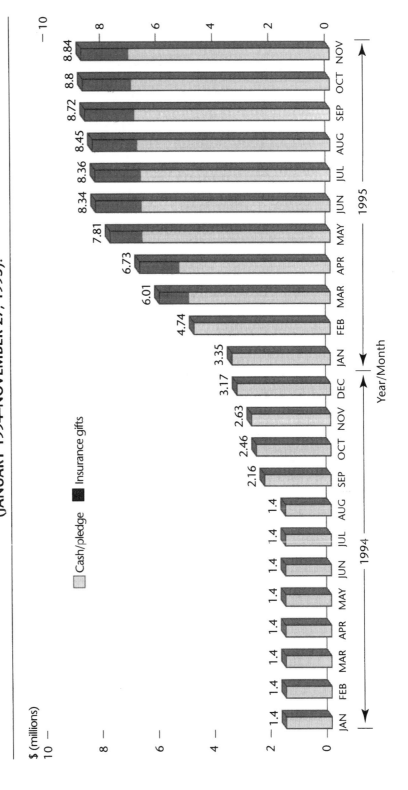

**Appendix III**

# FOR THE
# LOVE OF LEARNING...

*Your opportunity to support Library Square*

Library Square is an immense resource for us all – students, children and explorers of all stripes. Vancouverites have proven themselves to be voracious readers – 5,000 people visit the Central Library each day. Each hour, 450 business people call for research assistance.

## SMALL BUSINESS

### RECOGNITION
### Gifts of $5,000 to $9,999

- Naming of shelving (compact and open stacks)
- Listing in *Business in Vancouver*

### Gifts of $1,000 to $4,999

- Naming of furnishings
- Listing in *Business in Vancouver*

Additional naming opportunities are available for contributions over $10,000. For more details on how to support this remarkable project, please contact the Library Square Capital Campaign Office at (604) 681-8834.

## LITERAZZI

A gala fund raiser in support of Library Square and the Open House Family Weekend, *Literazzi* welcomes guests to a magical evening within the seven dramatic floors of Library Square.

Join prominent British Columbian and Canadian authors, special celebrity guests and award-winning chefs for a taste of the city's finest wines, gourmet cuisine and best entertainment. *Literazzi* promises to be a once-in-a-lifetime event you won't want to miss.

Tickets are $175 – call 257-3818 soon to order.

**LIBRARY SQUARE**

The goal of the capital campaign is to raise $12 million to furnish and equip Library Square.

*Thanks to the Sounding Board for making this advertisement possible.*

## Appendix III, cont'd.

# Bank of Montreal

## knows books
### are our best investment.

On behalf of the citizens of Vancouver and the Library Square Campaign Leadership Board, John and Kip Woodward, co-chairs, acknowledge the generous contribution Bank of Montreal has made to Library Square.

With their major support, Bank of Montreal has demonstrated their commitment to creating one of the country's finest libraries. Their gift makes it possible to purchase the technology, equipment and furnishings needed for Library Square to ensure universal access to information and education.

We wish to express our sincere thanks to the Bank of Montreal. You are playing an essential role in building a legacy of learning for generations to come.

 **Bank of Montreal**

*Library Square thanks the Vancouver Sun for making this advertisement possible.*

**LIBRARY SQUARE**
*For the Love of Learning.*

"**PJS**"
PJS Docket No:
Item: 5101.Donor Ad – Page 1
Size: 6.5"x7"
Client: LIBRARY SQUARE
Revised: 16 March 1995
Karacters No: 2656.5101

Appendix III, cont'd.

# Ismaili Walk for The Vancouver Public Library

Mark your calendar and join in the fun! Bring the whole family!

**Sunday, October 1**

**The Walk kicks off at the Plaza of Nations at 10 a.m.**

Walk, stroll or run the 5 km route which takes you through The Vancouver Public Library.

After the Walk join in the fun, food and festivities of the Family Fair at the Plaza of Nations

**All proceeds to the Vancouver Public Library in support of a Children's Exploration Gallery**

Pick up a pledge sheet at your nearest Library Branch. For more information call 331-3895.

**The Ismaili Walk for The Vancouver Public Library**
*Co-chairs Lynne Kennedy and Alnoor Samji*
*Advertising space donated by The Vancouver Board of Trade*

## Appendix III, cont'd.

# Ronald McDonald Children's Charities wants each child to know the joy of reading.

On behalf of Vancouver and the Library Square Campaign Leadership Board, John and Kip Woodward, co-chairs, acknowledge the generous contribution Ronald McDonald Children's Charities has made to Library Square.

Ronald McDonald Children's Charities of Canada is dedicated to improving the quality of life for children. Their gift makes it possible to purchase information technology and reading equipment for special needs children at Library Square, ensuring universal access to learning and education.

Thank you Ronald McDonald Children's Charities — you are building a legacy of learning for generations to come.

*Library Square thanks the Vancouver Sun for making this advertisement possible.*

# REFERENCES

American Association of Fund-Raising Counsel. *AAFRC Book on Fund-Raising Consulting 1998.* New York: American Association of Fund-Raising Counsel, 1998.

American Association of Fund-Raising Counsel Trust for Philanthropy. *Giving USA, 1986.* New York: American Association of Fund-Raising Counsel Trust for Philanthropy, 1986.

American Association of Fund-Raising Counsel Trust for Philanthropy. *Giving USA, 1997.* New York: American Association of Fund-Raising Counsel Trust for Philanthropy, 1997.

American Association of Fund-Raising Counsel Trust for Philanthropy. *Giving USA, 1998.* New York: American Association of Fund-Raising Counsel Trust for Philanthropy, 1998.

Anderson, G. M. "At Home on the Gift Range." *CASE Currents,* May 1986, pp. 42–44.

"Annual Survey of State Laws Regulating Charitable Solicitations as of January 1, 1998." *Giving USA Update,* 1998, *1,* pp. 1–7.

Arenson, K. W. "$100 Million Donation to Cornell for Medicine." *New York Times,* May 1, 1998, p. A27.

Association of Healthcare Philanthropy. *AHP Fellow Accreditation Program Information and Application.* Falls Church, Va.: Association of Healthcare Philanthropy, 1998.

A. T. Kearney, Inc. *Indiana University Foundation: Building a Long-Term Strategic Plan.* Chicago: A. T. Kearney, Inc., 1997.

Barth, S. "Finding the Needle in the Haystack: Use Computer Screening and Database Analysts to Discover the Hidden Major-Gift Prospects Among Your Alumni." *CASE Currents,* June 1998, pp. 32–36.

Baxter, F. R. "Prospect Management." Unpublished paper, University of California– Berkeley, 1987.

Billian, J. M. "Prospect Research, Evaluation, Cultivation, and Solicitation." Presentation made at the annual CASE conference, Nashville, Tenn., Mar. 1985.

"The Billion Dollar Club." *NonProfit Times*, Oct. 1998, p. 25.

Broce, T. E. *Fund Raising*. Norman: University of Oklahoma Press, 1979.

Bryson, J. M. *Strategic Planning for Public and Nonprofit Organizations: A Guide for Strengthening and Sustaining Organizational Achievement*. (Rev. ed.) San Francisco: Jossey-Bass, 1995.

Builta, J. *The Campaign Manuals*. Vol. 1: *The Campaign*. Cleveland, Ohio: Third Sector Press, 1984a.

Builta, J. *The Campaign Manuals*. Vol. 2: *Steps and Procedures*. Cleveland, Ohio: Third Sector Press, 1984b.

"Campaign Update." *Chronicle of Philanthropy*, May 7, 1998, p. 26.

"Campaign Update." *Chronicle of Philanthropy*, June 18, 1998, p. 40.

"Campaign Update." *Chronicle of Philanthropy*, Aug. 13, 1998, p. 28.

Campbell, D. A., Jr. "The Capital Campaign: Soliciting the Lead Gift(s)." Presentation made at the annual CASE District VI conference, St. Louis, Mo., Jan. 1985.

Capek, M.E.S. *Women and Philanthropy: Old Stereotypes, New Challenges*. Princeton, N.J.: Princeton University Press, 1997.

Chewning, P. B. "The Attitudes of Alumni Non-Donors, Donors, and Consecutive Donors Toward Drake University." Unpublished doctoral dissertation, Drake University, 1984.

Conrad, D. L. *How to Solicit Big Gifts*. San Francisco: Public Management Institute, 1978.

Council for Advancement and Support of Education. *CASE Campaign Standards: Management and Reporting Standards for Educational Fund-Raising Campaigns*. Washington, D.C.: Council for Advancement and Support of Education, 1996a.

Council for Advancement and Support of Education. *CASE Management Reporting Standards*. Washington, D.C.: Council for Advancement and Support of Education, 1996b.

"Drake University Receives $50 Million Gift from Dwight Opperman and Launches $190 Million Campaign." Press release, Drake University, Nov. 1, 1997.

Dunlop, D. R. "Suggestions for Working with Volunteers." Presentation made at CASE Summer Institute in Educational Fund Raising, Dartmouth College, July 1981.

Evans, G. A. "Relationship of Capital Campaign to Annual Fund and Deferred Giving Program." Presentation made at the annual CASE conference, Detroit, Mich., Aug. 1978.

Evans, G. A. "Decisions About the Big Three." *CASE Currents*, Mar. 1979, pp. 34–37.

"Exploring Women and Philanthropy: Interview with Gwinn Scott." *Counsel*, Summer 1998, pp. 1–2.

"Fact-File: Capital Campaigns to Raise $100 Million or More." *Chronicle of Higher Education*, Sept. 2, 1987, p. A76.

"Fund-Raising Campaigns of 142 U.S. Colleges and Universities, 1994–95." *Chronicle of Higher Education*, Dec. 20, 1996, p. A29.

Gallup Organization. *Patterns of Charitable Giving by Individuals II*. Report commissioned by he 501(c)(3) Group, Independent Sector, and the National Society of Fund Raising Executives. Washington, D.C.: Independent Sector, 1982.

Gallup Organization. *An Analysis of Charitable Contributions by Upper-Income Households for 1986 and 1987*. Report commissioned by the American Association of Fund-Raising Counsel Trust for Philanthropy. New York: American Association of Fund-Raising Counsel Trust for Philanthropy, 1987.

Gibson, E. B. "The Role of Professional Counsel." Discussion notes from presentation made at the annual CASE conference, Philadelphia, Mar. 1983.

Hale, E. E. Remarks made at the annual CASE conference on capital fundraising, Atlanta, Apr. 1980.

Hartsook, R. F. "Predictions for 1997." *Fund Raising Management,* Jan. 1997, p. 48.

INDEPENDENT SECTOR. *Giving and Volunteering in the United States, 1994.* Washington, D.C.: INDEPENDENT SECTOR, 1994.

INDEPENDENT SECTOR. *Giving and Volunteering in the United States, 1996.* Washington, D.C.: INDEPENDENT SECTOR, 1996.

Indiana University Center on Philanthropy. *The Philanthropy Giving Index (PGI).* Indianapolis: Indiana University Center on Philanthropy, 1998.

John Grenzebach and Associates, Inc. *Campaign Evaluation Questionnaire.* Chicago: John Grenzebach and Associates, Inc., 1986.

Kughn, J. C., Jr. "Using Volunteers Effectively." Presentation made at the annual CASE conference, Nashville, Tenn., Mar. 1982.

Legon, R. D. *The Board's Role in Fund Raising.* Washington, D.C.: Association of Governing Boards of Colleges and Universities, 1997.

Livingston, H. J., Jr. "The Role of Trustees in a Capital Campaign." *Bulletin on Public Relations and Development for Colleges and Universities,* Mar. 1984, pp. 1–4.

Lord, J. G. *The Raising of Money.* (3rd ed.) Cleveland: Third Sector Press, 1996.

Miller, A., and Nayyar, S. "The New Hands-On Philanthropy: Women Are Going the Distance to Make Their Money Count." *Working Woman,* July–Aug. 1998, pp. 52–57.

Milton, J. "The Ship of the Commonwealth Is Always Under Sail." London: Livewell Chapman at the Crown in Popes-Head Alley, 1660.

National Society of Fund Raising Executives. *Membership Survey Profile.* Alexandria, Va.: National Society of Fund Raising Executives, 1995.

National Society of Fund Raising Executives. *Certified Fund Raising Executive (CFRE) Candidate Handbook.* Alexandria, Va.: CFRE Professional Certification Board, National Society of Fund Raising Executives, 1998.

Panas, J. *Mega Gifts.* Chicago: Pluribus Press, 1984.

"Pat Lewis on Fund Raising in the 1990s." *Nonprofit Management Strategies,* June 1994, pp. 8–9.

Pendel, M. H. *What Is a Case Statement?* Arlington, Va.: Thompson and Pendel Associates, 1981.

Perkins, D. R. "Public Relations Support for the Capital Campaign." Presentation made at the annual CASE conference, Nashville, Tenn., Apr. 1985.

Pickett, W. L. "What Determines Fundraising Effectiveness?" *CASE Currents,* Sept. 1984, pp. 45–48.

Picton, R. R. "Effective Follow Through." Presentation made at the annual CASE conference, Nashville, Tenn., Mar. 1982.

Price, A. P., and File, K. M. *The Seven Faces of Philanthropy: A New Approach to Cultivating Major Donors.* San Francisco: Jossey-Bass, 1994.

Rose, S. J. *The American Profile Poster: Who Owns What, Who Makes How Much, Who Works Where, and Who Lives with Whom.* New York: Pantheon Books, 1986.

Schervish, P. G., and Havens, J. J. "Wherewithal and Beneficence: Charitable Giving by Income and Wealth." In W. Ilchman and C. Hamilton (eds.), *Cultures of Giving, Part Two: How Heritage, Gender, Wealth, and Values Influence Philanthropy.* New Directions for Philanthropic Fundraising, no. 8. San Francisco: Jossey-Bass, 1995.

Seymour, H. J. *Designs for Fund Raising.* New York: McGraw-Hill, 1966.

Smith, D. H. "The Rest of the Nonprofit Sector: Grassroots Associations as the Dark Matter Providing 'Flat Earth' Maps of the Sector." *Nonprofit and Voluntary Sector Quarterly,* June 1997, pp. 117–118.

Smith, J. P. "Rethinking the Traditional Capital Campaign." In F. C. Pray (ed.), *Handbook for Educational Fund Raising: A Guide to Successful Principles and Practices for Colleges, Universities, and Schools.* San Francisco: Jossey-Bass, 1981.

Stuhr, R. L. *Gonser Gerber Tinker Stuhr on Development.* Chicago: Gonser Gerber Tinker Stuhr, 1977.

Thiede, J. A. "Establishing a Marketing Department at the Indiana University Foundation." Unpublished report, Indiana University Foundation, 1998.

Thompson, D. M., and others. *Typical Outline for the Case Statement.* Arlington, Va.: Frantzreb, Pray, Ferner, and Thompson, 1978.

United Auto Workers. "Focus On: The Distribution of Wealth." [http://uaw.org/publications/jobs_pay/1097/stat1097_03.html]. Fall 1997.

Warwick, M. *Technology and the Future of Fundraising.* Berkeley, Calif.: Strathmore Press, 1994.

White, A. H. *The Charitable Behavior of Americans.* Washington, D.C.: Independent Sector, 1986.

Whittaker, F. M. "Prospect Research, Evaluation, Cultivation, and Solicitation." Outline of presentation at the annual CASE conference, Philadelphia, Mar. 1983.

# INDEX